EVIDENCE

AUSTRALIA
LBC INFORMATION SERVICES
SYDNEY

CANADA AND USA
CARSWELL
TORONTO

NEW ZEALAND
BROOKER'S
AUCKLAND

SINGAPORE AND MALAYSIA
SWEET & MAXWELL ASIA
SINGAPORE AND KUALA LUMPUR

GREENS CONCISE SCOTS LAW

EVIDENCE

THIRD EDITION

By

FIONA E. RAITT, LL.B.
*Solicitor, Senior Lecturer in Law, Department of Law,
University of Dundee*

EDINBURGH
W. GREEN/Sweet & Maxwell
2001

First published 1988 David Field
Second edition 1996 David Field & Fiona Raitt

Published in 2001 by W. Green & Son Limited
21 Alva Street
Edinburgh EH2 4PS

Typeset by J. P. Price
Chilcompton, Somerset

Printed in Great Britain by
Creative Print and Design (Wales), Ebbw Vale

Reprinted 2002

No natural forests were destroyed to make this product;
only farmed timber was used and replanted.

A CIP catalogue record for this book is available from the British
Library.

ISBN 0414 013 360

PREFACE

It is only five years since the last edition of this text but there have been a number of significant legislative changes since then, not least the Scotland Act 1998 and the Human Rights Act 1998. While the former has altered the political and constitutional landscape, the latter has already disturbed and challenged several established principles and practices of Scots common law, such as the right not to incriminate oneself, the fairness test in admissibility of evidence and the concept of a trial within a trial. Reference to European Convention rights has, almost overnight, become an essential component in every lawyer's repertoire and I have tried to highlight this where appropriate in the text.

Separate from new legislation, though in some cases because of it, there have been several major cases that have changed the law, often over-ruling familiar authorities, chief of which must be *Brown v. Stott* the first Scottish criminal case to be taken to appeal before the Judicial Committee of the Privy Council. There are also many reported cases now on key evidential provisions of the Criminal Procedure (Scotland) Act that have arisen since the last edition.

Looking ahead, the Scottish Executive has already demonstrated a commitment to change in various areas of the criminal and civil justice system and as this book goes to press there are proposals under active consideration in regard to the conduct of sexual offence trials that will almost certainly lead to further legislation.

I was given invaluable assistance with the preparation of this third edition. Special thanks are due to my colleague Colin Reid who clarified some of the more obscure parts of the Scotland Act and to Lynn Mannion and Margaret Barron-Linton who carried out a lot of the leg-work involved in identifying, collecting and organising the material for the rewrite, thereby making my life considerably easier. As ever, any errors are my responsibility. Finally, my thanks to my commissioning editors, Karen Taylor and her successor, Jill Barrington both of whom have always exhibited considerable patience and support in the face of shifting deadlines.

Fiona E. Raitt
May 2001

CONTENTS

TABLE OF CASES

ix

TABLE OF STATUTES

TABLE OF STATUTORY INSTRUMENTS

CHAPTER 1

RELEVANCE, ADMISSIBILITY, WEIGHT AND SUFFICIENCY OF EVIDENCE

INTRODUCTION

The law of evidence is concerned with how facts are proved in **1.01** court. It is intimately connected to the law of procedure, but whereas the latter is largely a product of statute, the former mainly derives from principle and precedent. One of the foremost modern evidence scholars, William Twining, has defined the law as, "a series of disparate exceptions to a single principle of freedom of proof".[1] This chapter sets out the key features underpinning the principle of freedom of proof. Much of the rest of this book examines these "disparate exceptions" referred to by Twining. Throughout the text an underlying theme must be that, ultimately, evidence is about telling a story, an account of people's experiences, a narrative of events.

The law of evidence in Scotland today remains firmly rooted in common law but there is an increasing statutory influence, where procedural provisions frequently modify and shape the development of the rules of evidence. This area of law has a great many rules—the disparate exceptions referred to by Twining. One of the main reasons for having rules is to control what facts can be presented to a court. It would not be practicable for a court of law to consider every item of evidence that might conceivably have a bearing on the issues before it. Rules have therefore evolved to govern what facts will be admitted before the court. These rules are designed to promote justice during the course of the trial of an action, be it civil or criminal. These rules, when considered in aggregation, constitute a large proportion of what we call the law of evidence, a loosely compiled, confusing and occasionally contradictory set of principles that do not always form a harmonious pattern.

---

[1] W. Twining, *Rethinking Evidence: Exploratory Essays*, p. 178.

Without the law of evidence, all items of information, no matter how remote or however unreliable, unfair or misleading, would be put before the court. This could make the court process tiresome and time-consuming and in an action involving laypersons, whether in a jury or a district court, or forming the majority in a tribunal, there would be much potential for confusion and conjecture. For these and other reasons, items of evidence that are undoubtedly relevant in the broad sense, will often be excluded on the grounds that they are "inadmissible", and a study of the law of evidence is largely a study of those reasons.

We may therefore begin with the deceptively simple statement that in a court of law, "all admissible evidence must first of all be relevant, but not all relevant items of evidence will be admissible".

RELEVANCE GENERALLY

1.02 Since no item of information may even be considered as potential evidence in a case until it is relevant to that case, it is necessary first to establish what is meant by "relevance". The concept of relevance is not a fixed one, for it can only be expressed in general terms as a relationship that exists between two facts. Fact A is relevant to fact B when, instinct combined with collective human experience, tells us that the two tend to exist together. They are logically connected. When one of those two facts requires to be established in proof, then the existence of the other fact, which is logically connected with it, is potentially an item of evidence. Walker and Walker define relevance thus: evidence is relevant if it is in some way "logically connected with those matters in dispute . . .".[2] A more recent definition was provided by Lord Osborne: "the ultimate test [of relevance] is whether the material in question has a reasonably direct bearing on the subject under investigation."[3] The following illustrations may assist.

Where an accused person is found to be in possession of recently stolen property, in criminative circumstances, that fact is an admissible item of evidence in that person's subsequent trial for almost any crime of dishonesty relating to that property.[4] Why? Because it is part of human experience that persons who are found to be in possession of property shortly after its theft, and who cannot give an innocent explanation of such possession, tend to

---

[2] Walker and Walker, *The Law of Evidence in Scotland*, para. 1.3.1, quoted in *Inland Revenue Commissioners v. Stenhouse's Trustees*, 1993 S.L.T. 248.
[3] *Strathmore Group Ltd v. Credit Lyonnais*, 1994 S.L.T. 1023 at 1031H.
[4] For an example of this principle in action, see *Cassidy v. McLeod*, 1981 S.C.C.R. 270: see also Gordon, "The Burden of Proof on the Accused", 1968 S.L.T. (News) 29 and 37 at 40.

have been involved in some way in its dishonest appropriation, usually as thieves or as resetters. Fact A (the possession of recently stolen property in criminative circumstances) is so logically related to fact B (the guilt of the person in possession) that it cannot be ignored, and is therefore relevant to the case. In this example, the logical link between the two facts is so strong that it creates a presumption of guilt against the person in possession, which must then be rebutted by some innocent explanation.[5]

Similarly, in assessing the guilt or innocence of a person charged with a crime, the relevant facts include: (i) that the person was seen running away from the *locus* shortly after the commission of the crime[6]; (ii) that a statement was made by that person admitting their guilt to police officers[7]; or (iii) that an attempt was made by that person to bribe a prosecution witness.[8] In these two examples, the facts offered as evidence are relevant (*i.e.* logically related to) the central issue in the case, namely the guilt or innocence of the accused. Of equal relevance, of course, to the same central issue will be items of defence evidence, such as the fact that the accused was 100 miles away from the *locus* at the time,[9] that the accused has never been in trouble before,[10] and that the accused gives evidence on oath denying any knowledge of the crime. Whether or not all or any of these items of evidence will be regarded as *admissible* is, however, a separate consideration.

The two examples given have been from criminal cases, but the basic requirement of all items of evidence—that they be relevant— is equally applicable to civil actions. For example, in an action for damages arising from the negligent driving of a motor vehicle, it is relevant to know how the vehicle was being driven shortly before, and shortly after, the collision that gave rise to the action.[11] Or, when it is alleged that a local highway authority ignored the known state of a road, in breach of its statutory duty, it is relevant to cite examples of other accidents on the same stretch of road in the weeks prior to the accident in question.[12] In each of these examples, the item of evidence is relevant because of its logical link

---

[5] This presumption is dealt with more fully in Chap. 3, but certainly predates Alison, *Principles of the Criminal Law of Scotland*, p. 320.

[6] *Teper v. R.* [1952] A.C. 480.

[7] For which see Chap. 13.

[8] Which might well constitute a separate offence in itself; see Gordon, *Criminal Law* (2nd ed.), p. 1070.

[9] An alibi defence, which would require special notice to be given to the prosecution.

[10] Character evidence is generally admissible in favour of the accused; see *Slater v. H.M. Advocate*, 1928 J.C. 94 at 105, and Chap. 13.

[11] Lord President Cooper in *Bark v. Scott*, 1954 S.C. 72 at 76.

[12] *W. Alexander & Sons v. Dundee Corporation*, 1950 S.C. 123.

with a fact in issue, *i.e.* respectively, the care being taken by the driver at the time of the accident, and the state of knowledge of the local authority concerning the condition of the road. The resulting inference is that one fact is probably accompanied by the other. As with criminal cases, the logical connection between the two facts is sometimes so strong in civil actions that it gives rise to a presumption which the party against whom the first fact is proved is then obliged to counter with other evidence.[13]

It is dangerous to generalise about relevance: it is the ultimate in moving targets and depends very much on the facts and circumstances in any given case. In broad terms, facts which a party wishes to adduce as evidence must have a logical link with an issue raised by the case in hand. There are, however, different categories of facts, of varying significance. The next section considers these.

Relevant Facts

1.03 In every criminal trial or civil proof there are facts in dispute between the parties that will have to be considered by the court, and proven or disproven in order to determine the case. These facts must themselves be relevant to the eventual outcome of the case. The facts in issue are traditionally referred to as the *facta probanda*, or "those matters in dispute between the parties".[14] While in each case there is only one ultimate issue to be determined (whether or not the accused is convicted, or whether the pursuer succeeds in a civil action), the process of arriving at that determination comprises various facts in issue which together make up the case. The facts in issue are also known as the "essential facts" or "crucial facts". It is possible for a party to lose on one or more of the essential facts, *i.e.* fail to establish them in his or her favour by means of admissible evidence, and yet still succeed on the ultimate issue. Equally, but unusually, a party could prove every one of the points raised as facts in issue and still lose the case. This might occur, for example, when an accused offers no evidence in contradiction of the prosecution case, but is acquitted following a successful submission of "no case to answer".[15] The court in such a situation has found the totality of the prosecution

---

[13] A clear example of this process is the so-called "presumption against donation *inter vivos*"; see *Grant's Trs v. McDonald*, 1939 S.C. 448. The presumption rests upon the simple knowledge that people do not normally give away their property free of charge.

[14] Walker and Walker, *loc. cit.* n. 2.

[15] See s.97 (solemn proceedings) and s.160 (summary proceedings) of the Criminal Procedure (Scotland) Act 1995.

case insufficient to prove the accused's guilt beyond reasonable doubt.

Using the example of the criminal accused quoted above, the essential facts would include the fact that the accused was identified running away from the *locus* shortly after the commission of the crime, the fact that a guilty confession was made to police officers, the fact of the alibi and the fact of the denial of any knowledge of the incident. As listed, these facts are of course contradictory, since two form part of the prosecution case while the other two are urged by the defence. Once they have been disentangled and assessed, the court will be in a position to give a ruling on the ultimate issue: the innocence or guilt of the accused. Exactly the same process operates in a civil action, the ultimate issue being whether or not the pursuer succeeds in his or her claim.

Often a court is asked to consider facts that are not facts in issue, but instead are facts that have some bearing on the probability or improbability of the facts in issue.[16] Such facts comprise circumstantial evidence and are known as *facta probationis*. For example, it would be extremely important for a court hearing testimony from an eye-witness to a robbery to know that the witness was short sighted since that could affect the reliability of the witness, and may result in the testimony being ignored. The fact that a witness has such impairment is circumstantial evidence, in that it has no immediate bearing on the ultimate issue, but it may be highly relevant to a fact in issue, *i.e.* the accurate identification of the accused.

Another illustration of the distinction between the facts in issue and circumstantial evidence can be drawn from a reparation action. In a case of alleged medical negligence of a surgeon, the facts in issue—the essential facts—include the fact of the injury, the existence of a duty of care, the fact of a breach of that duty and the existence of a causal link between the injury and the breach of the duty. The fact that the surgeon has previously been found negligent in two similar cases is not in itself an essential fact, but it certainly has a bearing on the probability or improbability of the facts in issue, and is thus circumstantial evidence.

The question of relevancy is complex. Once an item of evidence is regarded as relevant it then has to pass the test of admissibility, *i.e.* not be excluded on one of the many grounds upon which relevant evidence can be withheld from the court.

---

[16] Walker and Walker, n. 2. *N.B.* that when the fact sought to be proved is insufficiently relevant to a primary issue to justify its tendency to confuse matters, it will be rejected as an inadmissible "collateral" issue, for which see Chap. 13. See also *Swan v. Bowie*, 1948 S.C. 46 at 51.

ADMISSIBILITY

1.04 The fact that an item of evidence is relevant does not guarantee that the court will admit it as evidence, let alone that it will attach any great weight to it. As already noted, the Anglo-American adversarial system does not permit "free proof" whereby all relevant evidence is placed before the court. Instead, most of the rules of evidence are described as "exclusionary" in that they prevent evidence being considered by the court on the ground that it is not admissible. Examples of these exclusionary rules are discussed briefly below, but a simple example illustrates the point. The fingerprints of an accused person found at the scene of a murder may be highly relevant and apparently incriminating, but the evidence in relation to these fingerprints will not be admissible if it turns out they have been "planted" by the police. The "planting" of incriminatory evidence is unlawful, and thus, quite properly, inadmissible. The decision as to the admissibility of any item of evidence lies with the judge.

There are various reasons why certain items of evidence, although relevant, are unacceptable in a court of law. This may be because they are unreliable or because they are potentially misleading, and on occasion simply because the public interest requires that the information in question should remain undisclosed. Separately, in many cases the actual fact that the party wishes to establish by evidence is perfectly acceptable, but the objection is to the form in which it is sought to produce this evidence. These various considerations have a common objective— the desire to ensure that every issue before a court is considered fairly and accurately.

(1) Unreliability

1.05 Considering first the objection that an item of proposed evidence could be unreliable, the following major exclusionary rules apply.

(a) Hearsay[17]

1.06 It may well be highly relevant to know what a particular witness saw or heard, but in criminal cases (and until 1989 in civil cases) such information must come from A and not someone else, B, to whom A recounted the experience. For this reason the hearsay rule generally prohibits the evidence of A being given by B. The exceptions to this rule arise when there is some additional factor which makes B's evidence of what A experienced more reliable than it would otherwise have been.

---

[17] Dealt with in Chap. 8.

(b) Opinion[18]

Unless the witness is an expert on the matter in hand, all that the **1.07** court requires from him or her is an accurate statement of *fact*, namely what was seen, heard, etc. It does not require—and will not accept—the witness's *opinion* of how these facts should be interpreted, since interpretation of facts is for the court. Thus, the witness may say "The car was travelling fast", but not "The car was exceeding the speed limit".

(c) Involuntary confession[19]

A confession which is involuntary, although arguably still **1.08** relevant, is likely to be less reliable than one freely volunteered, and its relevance may be far outweighed by its prejudicial effect on the accused during the trial. It will therefore normally be excluded.

(2) Tendency to mislead

Among the items of evidence normally rejected on the grounds **1.09** that they are potentially misleading are the following.

(a) The previous misdeeds of the accused[20]

As a general rule, a criminal court is only concerned to establish, **1.10** whether on the occasion libelled, the accused committed the offence(s) libelled. It is not concerned with what may or may not have been done by the accused on a previous occasion. While it would often be relevant to know that the person now charged with an offence has several previous convictions for the same offence, it is regarded as misleading and unjustifiably prejudicial to the accused to raise the issue. The exceptions which exist to this rule arise when another factor exists which makes the relevance of the accused's previous misdeeds so compelling that it outweighs the prejudicial effect of that evidence. For example, when the accused claims to be of good character and to have no such previous convictions then the true position can be made known to the court.

---

[18] Dealt with in Chap. 16.
[19] Dealt with in Chap. 14.
[20] For which see Chap. 13.

(b) Unsworn precognitions

1.11   The contents of an unsworn precognition given on an earlier occasion cannot be put to a witness giving testimony in court. Precognitions are excluded because the court is required to consider only what the witness is now saying on oath, and not what he or she is alleged to have said earlier to the precognoscer. Such evidence would inevitably carry less weight and to allow it would be to undermine the value our legal system places on sworn oral testimony.

(3) Public policy

1.12   There are also other items of evidence, which although no doubt relevant, are denied to the court on general grounds of public policy. Each exclusion proceeds upon its own rationale, and among those more commonly encountered in practice are the following.

(a) Confidentiality[21]

1.13   A witness can be relieved of the duty of answering a particular question or series of questions on the ground of confidentiality. The law recognises certain categories of relationship, such as that between a legal adviser and a client, as being confidential and therefore privileged. Whether or not the privilege of confidentiality exists, or applies to a particular situation, is a matter of public policy.[22]

(b) Public interest immunity[23]

1.14   From time to time a Government department or agency will claim that disclosure in court of certain information is contrary to the public interest. When successful this results in certain often highly relevant, or even conclusive evidence, being denied to the court. In 1992 this issue became the focus of much public concern following the collapse of the highly publicised Matrix Churchill trial. In those proceedings, various businessmen narrowly escaped conviction and likely imprisonment, when certain government documents essential to their defence were withheld on the ground of public interest. A wide ranging public enquiry was set up under Lord Justice Scott which considered, *inter alia*, the way in which this privilege should operate in the future.[24]

---

[21] Dealt with in Chap. 12.
[22] *e.g.* it applies between solicitor and client, but not between doctor and patient.
[23] Dealt with in Chap. 12.
[24] The Scott Report was published in February 1996, and is dealt with further in Chap. 12.

This is not an exhaustive list of examples of relevant evidence being deemed inadmissible, but they are among the most important. They illustrate that there are many areas of the law in this field in which evidence, which would otherwise be deemed relevant, is excluded from a court.

WEIGHT AND SUFFICIENCY OF EVIDENCE

The "weight" of an item of evidence is simply the degree of reliance that the court places upon it. Weight must be distinguished from admissibility of evidence. The latter is a matter of law for the judge, while the former is a question of fact and is a matter for "the tribunal of fact".[25] There is no pre-assessment of weight and no legal rules governing it. The tribunal of fact has to assess the evidence for itself, using what one judge[26] described as "rules of common sense". In so doing it has a wide discretion, though in a jury trial guidance will often be given from the bench in the summing-up. **1.15**

Separate from the question of the weight to be attached to any individual item of evidence, there is always a question as to whether a party has adduced *sufficient* evidence for the case to succeed. Sufficiency of evidence is a matter of law and often a matter of inference.[27] There are many situations in which, as a matter of law, a party's evidence must reach a certain minimum standard of persuasion before it will succeed. It is traditional to refer to such standards of persuasion as being a "sufficiency" of evidence to support a finding by a court.[28] It is possible in certain situations for a party to produce sufficient evidence in law to prove the case, but the other party still succeeds because their evidence is more convincing. It is also possible for a party to produce the only evidence in a case, and still find that this evidence is *insufficient* in law to justify a decision in their favour. This is what happens in criminal cases when a judge rules that there is "no case to answer",[29] or where a trial judge refuses to allow a particular point to go to the jury because insufficient evidence has been led to justify it. For example, if, on an indictment libelling "assault to

---

[25] *i.e.* the judge, sheriff or magistrate when there is no jury, and the jury when there is. In the case of a tribunal, it will be a majority decision by the members of that tribunal.

[26] Lord Blackburn in *Lord Advocate v. Lord Blantyre* (1879) 6 R. (H.L.) 72 at 85.

[27] See, for example, *Donaghy v. Normand*, 1992 S.L.T. 666.

[28] Walker and Walker, n. 2, para. 5.1.1. See, for example, *White v. Mackinnon*, 1987 G.W.D. 4–110. For a discussion and application of sufficiency, see *F. v. Kennedy*, 1988 S.L.T. 404.

[29] See *Lockhart v. Crockett*, 1987 S.L.T. 551 and *Wallace v. McLeod*, 1986 S.C.C.R. 678.

severe injury and to the danger of life", the prosecution failed to adduce sufficient evidence to establish that the victim's life was actually in danger, then normally the prosecution, at the suggestion of the judge, would delete reference in the indictment to "danger of life" before the judge's charge to the jury.

In determining the legal question of sufficiency, more than one principle may be involved. It may be, for example, that there is no conviction in a criminal case because there is a lack of corroboration.[30] Or it may be that a vital ingredient of a party's case in a reparation action, such as failure to take reasonable care, has not been established. Or it may be that taking a party's case as a whole, insufficient acceptable evidence has been proven to permit a decision to be made in their favour. This final possibility introduces the concept of the burden of proof, which takes up the next chapter.

---

[30] Corroboration is dealt with in Chap. 7.

CHAPTER 2

BURDENS OF PROOF

INTRODUCTION

A burden of proof may be defined as the onus to prove. It is the **2.01**
obligation that rests upon the party who seeks to have a particular
issue decided in their favour, to adduce sufficient evidence to
support their argument. This preliminary definition is deliberately
wide because it is required to cover more than one burden of
proof. There are, in Scots law, two well defined and distinct
burdens of proof,[1] namely:

(1) the *persuasive burden*: the burden of satisfying a court to
the appropriate standard of proof on a particular issue;
and
(2) the *evidential burden*: the burden of adducing enough
evidence on a particular issue to warrant the court at
least considering it.

Each of these burdens exists in respect of every issue in a case, is
fixed by law, and never shifts from whichever party it is allocated to
at the commencement of the hearing. They are, however, very
different in their purpose and function, and must be considered
separately.

THE PERSUASIVE BURDEN

If A is asking a court to make a particular finding of fact (*e.g.* that **2.02**
B owes her money) then she must produce some evidence to that
effect or she will fail in her action. To this extent, therefore, A
carries a burden of proof on that issue. At the same time, if it is B's
contention that he did indeed at one time owe A money, but has

---

[1] See Macphail, *Evidence*, Chap. 22.01. The terminology employed is that used by
him.

since repaid it, then B bears a burden of proof on the separate issue of repayment.

However, B is under no obligation to begin discharging this burden (*i.e.* to begin leading evidence to show that the debt has been repaid) until A has proved to the satisfaction of the court that the money is still due. The two burdens are clearly connected, and occupy sequential positions in the development of the overall court action.

On each and *every issue* in a case, there is a persuasive burden of proof which attaches to one or other of the parties. If no evidence at all is led on that issue, or if the evidence leaves the matter finely balanced, then the party relying on that issue as part of their case will lose, at least on that issue. A legal action, be it civil or criminal, is in effect a series of related issues and therefore in the course of the trial of any action with more than one issue, the persuasive burdens of proof are distributed among the parties in accordance with the issues raised.

The actual distribution of these burdens in a case, as between the parties, is always a matter of law, since it is the substantive law that determines what each party must prove in order to succeed in any given case. Thus in the debt example above, if A wishes to secure decree for the repayment of money due to her, it is incumbent upon her to produce evidence of the existence of the debt. However, even if she does so, she will not obtain decree if the court is satisfied that the money has been repaid, hence the obligation placed upon B to prove repayment once the existence of the debt has been established.

In reality, of course, judgment will be given on the totality of the evidence produced, and it is not usually possible to identify, in the course of the hearing, a moment at which A sits back having discharged her burden and waits for B to set about discharging his. But in the process of coming to a decision, the judge will require to analyse the evidence in this way.[2]

In a criminal case, it is now well established that it is for the prosecution to prove the guilt of an accused person, and only rarely does the law place upon the accused the obligation to produce exculpatory evidence.[3] On this basis, the burdens of proof on each issue in a criminal case are fairly rigidly distributed, with a high proportion of them resting with the Crown.

In England, these persuasive burdens, allocated as they are by the operation of law, are described as "legal burdens".[4] However,

---

[2] See, *e.g.* the analytical approach taken by Lord Denning in *Brown v. Rolls Royce*, 1960 S.C. (H.L.) 22 at 27.

[3] Two such exceptions arise in relation to the defences of insanity and diminished responsibility. These are discussed below.

[4] See Cross and Tapper, *Evidence*, p. 108.

this description has not found favour in Scotland,[5] where the name given to the main burden of proof on each issue is the "persuasive" burden.[6]

When a party bears the persuasive burden on an issue, the court must be satisfied on that issue to the required degree or "standard" of proof, or the party will lose on that issue. Whether or not the entire case is then lost depends upon how crucial that issue is to the overall case. As Walker and Walker put it,[7] "if on any issue of fact no evidence is led, or the evidence leaves the matter in doubt, the party upon whom the burden of proof rests has not discharged it, and accordingly fails on that issue."

A party may fail to discharge the persuasive burden on an issue without any evidence at all having been led in replication by the other party (to counter the evidence already led). This may be, for example, because the evidence is "insufficient" in law, or because it fails to come up to the requisite standard. Alternatively, the party with the persuasive burden may find that the court prefers the evidence of the other party. Or the other party's evidence may have created sufficient doubt on the matter to prevent the party with the persuasive burden from discharging it to the required standard.

THE EVIDENTIAL BURDEN

As was indicated above, the evidential burden may be defined as **2.03** the burden of adducing sufficient evidence on a particular issue to allow the court to begin considering it as a live issue. In the example quoted earlier, for instance, A cannot expect the court even to begin considering the possibility that B owes her money unless and until she produces *some* credible evidence of the existence of the debt. Without at least this, her case would have no foundation. Once she *has* produced some such evidence, and the court is prepared to consider the possibility that a debt exists, she will hope to go on to reinforce the point with further evidence.

The same item of evidence may of course achieve both objectives at once, but often a stage can exist in connection with any issue at which the court has accepted that some evidence exists, but is looking for more before it will regard the persuasive burden as having been discharged.

---

[5] The existence of more than one burden of proof has only been acknowledged relatively recently in Scotland: see Gordon, "The Burden of Proof on the Accused", 1968 S.L.T. (News) 29.

[6] See Renton and Brown, *Criminal Procedure*, para. 24–01, and Macphail, n. 1, Chap. 22.03. See also Gordon, *loc. cit.*

[7] *Law of Evidence in Scotland*, para. 2.1.1; see also *Brown v. Rolls Royce*, n. 2 above.

The most appropriate description for this second major burden is the "evidential" burden,[8] and it may be more formally defined as the burden of adducing sufficient evidence on an issue to warrant its consideration by a court.

The evidential burden is, like the persuasive burden, fixed by law upon a particular party, and the general rule is that the party bearing the persuasive burden on any given issue also bears the evidential burden. This is both logical and just, since one would expect the party who is required to convince the court on a particular issue to have to set the ball rolling, as it were, with some evidence pointing in that direction. However, historically confusion has arisen by the position of an accused in a criminal trial who raises a specific defence.[9]

As will be seen later, in a criminal trial it is for the accused to discharge the evidential burden on any specific defence which is offered to a charge. Thereafter, with the exception of the defences of insanity and diminished responsibility, it is for the Crown to discharge the persuasive burden on that *same* issue. Thus, where an accused puts forward a defence of alibi, the evidential and persuasive burdens are divided between the defence and the prosecution. The accused must produce *some* credible evidence to suggest the existence of an alibi (the evidential burden), but it remains for the Crown to prove their version of the facts beyond reasonable doubt (the persuasive burden).[10] That, in effect, may mean proving that the alibi is false.

The failure to distinguish carefully between the persuasive and the evidential burdens in cases in which they rest with different parties has led to several successful appeals in criminal cases. Unfortunately, these cases have not resulted in a clear distinction being laid down for future reference, doubtless because the circumstances giving rise to appeal are so varied, but the distinction between the two burdens has been implicit in each appeal judgment.

For example, in *Campbell v. Mackenzie*,[11] the accused in a drink-driving case sought to explain away the analyst's certificate showing

---

[8] A description in general use in England: see Cross and Tapper, *loc. cit.* Although the existence of this second burden has been recognised in Scotland, and is implicit in several recent criminal appeal judgments (see *Earnshaw* at n. 11) the use of the term "evidential burden" seems still to be confined to academic works. See Gordon, "The Burden of Proof on the Accused", 1968 S.L.T. (News) 29, and Macphail, *loc. cit.*

[9] A specific defence is any defence other than a general denial of guilt, and not necessarily a "special" defence, for which see below.

[10] See *Lambie v. H.M. Advocate*, 1973 J.C. 53. Note that this evidence need not necessarily come from the accused or the defence witnesses, but may come from the prosecution evidence: see *Ritchie v. Pirie*, at n. 12.

[11] 1982 S.L.T. 250; see also *Earnshaw v. H.M. Advocate*, 1982 J.C. 11, 1982 S.L.T. 179 and *McGregor v. Jessop*, 1988 J.C. 98.

his blood/alcohol level to be higher than that permitted by law at the time of the taking of the sample. He claimed that he had consumed enough alcohol between the time of his driving and the taking of the sample to account for the excess reading. The sheriff ruled that since it was the accused who was raising the "defence" of post-accident drinking, it was for him to prove it on a balance of probabilities—the appropriate standard of proof for an accused who bears the persuasive burden on an issue. On appeal, although the conviction was upheld on other grounds, it was clearly stated that in such cases, once the accused has raised the issue (*i.e.* discharged the evidential burden) it is for the Crown to disprove it beyond reasonable doubt (*i.e.* to discharge the persuasive burden).

In an earlier case on the same point,[12] Lord Justice-Clerk Wheatley had made it clear that the sort of evidence required to raise such a defence, which the Crown then have to disprove beyond reasonable doubt, can come from any source, and not necessarily the accused. In his words:

"The onus of proving the case beyond reasonable doubt rests with the prosecution, and remains on the prosecution throughout, and whether that has been done depends upon all the evidence before the court, whether adduced by the prosecution or by the defence, and on the view which the court takes of it."[13]

In short, the persuasive burden of convincing the court on the issue of a defence raised by an accused (other than insanity or diminished responsibility) rests with the Crown, but not until some evidence has been adduced which might suggest such a defence. Since this evidence is, however, hardly likely to come from the prosecution witnesses,[14] it is incumbent upon the accused to provide the evidence. In this respect the accused bears the evidential burden—and *only* the evidential burden—on the issue of a specific defence. The Crown bears the responsibility for discharging the persuasive burden beyond reasonable doubt and in the process of doing so would need to negate the issues raised by the accused.

The evidential burden is therefore simply the burden of ensuring that enough evidence is before the court to allow it to consider the issue at all. Such evidence will normally come from the party bearing the evidential burden, but it need not, even in a criminal case.

---

[12] *Ritchie v. Pirie*, 1972 J.C. 7; see also *Tudhope v. Miller*, 1978 J.C. 26.
[13] *ibid.*, at 17.
[14] Although if it did, it would have precisely the same effect, *per Ritchie,* n. 12.

THE TACTICAL BURDEN

2.04 As has been seen, the two major burdens—the persuasive and evidential burdens—may be said to apply to each and every issue in a case, and to be fixed as a matter of law. In particular, they do not shift from one party to another in the course of hearing the evidence on a particular issue. The party who bears the persuasive burden on an issue at the outset will still bear it at the close of the evidence. The party who bears the evidential burden on that same issue (usually, as noted earlier, the party bearing the persuasive burden) will have discharged it once that issue is being actively considered by the court.

However, most cases consist of more than one issue,[15] and the persuasive burdens on these issues may well be allocated between the parties in a sequential pattern. Taking the original example of a simple debt action by A against B, it will be recalled that B's obligation to begin proving that the debt was in fact repaid did not arise until A had adduced some evidence of the existence of the debt. It may well be, for reasons stated earlier, that this evidence may not of itself win the case for A, or indeed even prove to the appropriate standard of proof that the debt ever existed.[16] However, once A has discharged the evidential burden on the issue of the existence of the debt, B would need to counter with evidence that the debt is in fact discharged by repayment.

The procedure adopted in the Scottish courts does not reveal this process very clearly. Each party leads their respective witnesses in turn, and each in turn is open to cross-examination, until at the end of the hearing the court is left with a mixture of conflicting testimonies that it then has to assess. Neither an impartial observer, nor indeed the lawyers on either side, could identify the moment at which B in the example given would need to begin leading evidence of his own.[17] Nevertheless the court, when assessing the evidence as a whole, very often requires to establish whether or not issue X has been established before being obliged to go on to consider issue Y.

---

[15] For example, in a criminal case, in which it is well established that the prosecution must prove the accused's guilt beyond reasonable doubt, it is incumbent upon the Crown to prove both the *actus reus* and *mens rea*. Most forms of *actus reus* involve more than one issue (*e.g.* the accused's presence at the locus, his actions, his subsequent possession of incriminating items, etc.). In civil cases the persuasive burden is normally only relevant when the court is unable to make up its mind on an issue: *Thomas v. Thomas*, 1947 S.C. (H.L.) 45.

[16] *i.e.* A may fail to discharge the persuasive burden on that issue.

[17] The possibility of a plea of "no case to answer" in both solemn and summary criminal proceedings under ss. 97 and 160 of the Criminal Procedure (Scotland) Act 1995 for solemn and summary proceedings respectively, has, however, made it possible for the defence lawyers in criminal cases to ascertain whether or not the Crown has discharged the evidential burdens on the crucial issues, thus requiring the accused to lead evidence in his or her own defence.

For this reason, it is sometimes asserted that once A has established a particular issue, the burden of proof "shifts" to B. This statement is misleading, not least because it fails to indicate *which* burden, and it suggests that a burden, which is fixed by law, can transfer to another party. If it is accepted that each issue carries its own persuasive and evidential burdens that are fixed from the outset, then neither of these may be said to "shift".

And yet, clearly, something significant happens once A discharges either of the burdens on an issue and requires B to lead evidence in replication. It places what might be termed a "tactical" obligation on B to begin leading some evidence of his own, or run the risk that the court will be persuaded by the unchallenged evidence it has heard. As Lord Justice-Clerk Grant put it in *McIlhargey v. Herron*[18] explaining a principle equally applicable to a civil action:

> "I am not . . . suggesting that any fact in a criminal prosecution can be established merely by failure to cross examine, and there are many cases where wise defending counsel asks as few questions in cross as possible. On the other hand, the silent defender does take a risk, and, if he fails to challenge evidence given by witnesses for the Crown by cross-examination or, in addition, by leading substantive evidence in support of his challenge, he cannot complain if the Court not merely accepts that unchallenged evidence but also, in the light of all the circumstances, draws from it the most unfavourable and adverse inferences to the defence that it is capable of supporting."[19]

In many cases, all that B requires to do once A appears to have **2.05** discharged the evidential burden on an issue, is to cross-examine so as to challenge, contradict or weaken that evidence, *i.e.* to take action so as to prevent A from discharging the persuasive burden on the *same* issue. On other occasions, however, B's only course of action is to introduce another issue entirely (on which B will normally bear both the evidential and persuasive burdens) which will neutralise the issue which A has raised. Once A has discharged the persuasive burden on an issue, this is the *only* course of action that B can take.

Thus, in the example quoted, once A has produced evidence of the existence of the debt, B has no interest in denying that the debt

---

[18] 1972 S.C. 38.
[19] *ibid.* at 42; see also *O'Donnell v. Murdoch Mackenzie & Co.*, 1967 S.C. (H.L.) 63, in which the opinion was given that when a defender in a civil case calls no evidence, only the most favourable inferences should be drawn from the pursuer's evidence. This principle was also followed in *Davidson v. Duncan*, 1981 S.C. 83.

existed. He is more interested in proving that it has been repaid. He therefore leaves the first issue alone, and begins leading evidence of the repayment, which A in her turn must counter if she wishes to win the case. What is being observed in such a situation is a succession of *different* issues (which may not, of course, be presented to the court in quite such a tidy sequence). When one issue is succeeded by another on which a different party bears the burdens, it is indeed tempting to speak of a "shifting" of the burden of proof. And if one is referring simply to what one might call the "tactical burden",[20] then undeniably something is shifting between one party and another. This is in the sense that "if the trial were to stop at any particular time the jury would be entitled, and indeed likely, to find for one side, and . . . if the other side wish to avoid such a finding it behoves them to produce counter evidence".[21]

Put in such a way, the concept of a "shifting" of a burden is harmless enough. Unfortunately, until fairly recently Scots law recognised only one burden of proof, namely the persuasive burden, and there is a danger that any reference to a shifting of "the" burden of proof will be taken, incorrectly, to mean a shift in the persuasive burden.[22]

For example, in *Tallis v. H.M. Advocate*[23] the trial sheriff directed the jury in the following terms:

> "the situation may arise, ladies and gentlemen, that the Crown puts forward such a strong case that it is only if you are satisfied with the explanation given by the accused, that you would be entitled to acquit him and again that may very well be the situation here you feel, but again it is a matter for you to make up your minds about, ladies and gentlemen."[24]

On appeal, it was said of this charge that it was a "serious misdirection in law", in that it was a "plain indication to the jury that in certain circumstances the onus of proof shifts to the accused and unless he can discharge it by an explanation which satisfies the jury, *i.e.* of his innocence, then conviction must follow."[24a]

---

[20] A term recognised under English law; see Cross and Tapper, *Evidence*, p. 113, where it is also described as a provisional burden. See also its use by Gordon, "The Burden of Proof on the Accused", 1968 S.L.T. (News) 29 at 37.

[21] Gordon, *ibid.*

[22] See Macphail, n. 1, Chap. 22.03 who acknowledges this problem and does not use the term.

[23] 1982 S.C.C.R. 91. See similarly, *McDonald v. H.M. Advocate*, 1990 J.C. 40 where a conviction was quashed after a sheriff suggested in his charge to the jury that, in relation to the doctrine of recent possession, it was for the accused to prove his or her innocence. As to the need for precision in explaining the burden of proof to a jury, see *Craddock v. H.M. Advocate*, 1994 S.L.T. 454.

[24] *Tallis,* above at p. 99.

[24a] *Tallis, ibid.*

As we will see later, the only common law circumstances in **2.06** which any persuasive burden (which was the "onus" referred to in *Tallis*) rests with the accused, arise when the defence of either insanity or diminished responsibility is raised by the accused. On all other issues in a criminal trial, the persuasive burdens rest and remain with the Crown. At common law, at no stage, and in no circumstances does the persuasive burden ever shift to the accused. Thus, if at the end of the day the court has any reasonable doubt, that doubt must work in favour of the accused and lead to an acquittal because the Crown have failed to discharge the persuasive burden. This was the fatal error which the sheriff made in *Tallis*, in assuming that the force of the Crown evidence could in some way transfer the persuasive burden to the accused, so that it was suddenly for him to prove his innocence.

At the same time, it should be noted that any accused who remains silent in the face of cogent Crown evidence enhances the chances of conviction, because "the silent defender does take a risk".[25] What shifts, once the Crown have produced a strong case against an accused, is of course the *tactical* burden of explaining it away. An accused who fails to rise to the challenge, has failed to prevent the Crown from discharging the persuasive burden. This is because "there are certain cases in which . . . the proved facts may raise a presumption of guilt, and in which, in the absence of some explanation by the person accused—where the person accused is the one person who can know the real truth—a jury may be entitled to draw an inference of guilt".[26]

In the case from which this excerpt from the charge to the jury is taken, the accused was convicted of a fraudulent attempt to pose as the husband of a deceased lady whose estate was to be distributed. The accused claimed that he had married her some years earlier in a form of ceremony witnessed by certain named persons. Since he failed to call any of these persons as witnesses, and he chose not to give evidence himself, it was hardly surprising that the Crown succeeded in discharging the persuasive burden. In this case Lord Justice-Clerk Aitchison said (in relation to the standard of proof):

---

[25] *McIlhargey*, above at p. 42; see also *O'Donnell v. Murdoch Mackenzie & Co.*, 1967 S.C. (H.L.) 63.

[26] Lord Justice-Clerk Aitchison in *H.M. Advocate v. Hardy*, 1938 J.C. 144, this passage was approved in *Mochan v. Herron*, 1972 S.L.T. 218, in which the sheriff, in his stated case to the High Court, added at p. 219: "If the appellant had an innocent explanation he was fully entitled to exercise his right to remain silent about it, in which case, however, I could see no objection to the court drawing its own conclusion from such evidence as was before it, which is what I did." The conviction was upheld.

"If an explanation had been given, it might have thrown doubt upon the Crown case—it might have satisfied you, or it might have made you think that it was unsafe to find the case established . . ."[27]

As will be seen in Chapter 3, a party to a case (even a criminal case) may not have to lead any further evidence on an issue because of the operation of a presumption. All that this means is that the presumption takes the place of any further evidence which might have been required to be led, and places a tactical burden on the other party to counter the effect of that presumption with evidence of their own. For example, as was seen in Chapter 1, an accused who is found in possession of recently stolen property in "criminative" circumstances, and is charged with theft has, in most cases, a good deal of explaining to do in order to avoid a conviction. But this does not mean that the traditional burden that rests upon the Crown to prove the guilt of the accused beyond reasonable doubt has suddenly transformed itself into a burden on the accused to prove his or her innocence. It simply means that if the accused does not come up with some convincing explanation of apparently incriminating circumstances, the prosecution will have had their work done for them by the presumption.[28] The burden of proof has not shifted—it is simply about to be discharged, unless the accused produces some credible evidence to explain legitimate possession of stolen goods.

2.07   In distinguishing between the persuasive and tactical burdens, and in arguing that the persuasive burden on an issue never shifts from one party to another, the examples have so far been taken from criminal law, because it is in this context that the greatest danger lies in confusing the two. But the problem can also arise under civil law, where a failure to allocate correctly a persuasive burden at the end of the evidence (*i.e.* by mistakenly believing that it has somehow shifted to the other party) can clearly result in injustice.

In *Brown v. Rolls Royce*[29] the pursuer had worked for the defenders as a machine-oiler, during the course of which he had contracted industrial dermatitis. He claimed damages for negligence, based on the fact that the defenders, his employers, had not provided him with the same barrier cream that other employers supplied in similar circumstances. The defenders admitted this fact, but claimed in replication that they had been persuaded by medical advice that the barrier cream in question was not effective. They further claimed that the provision of good washing facilities, which they had made available, was an effective precaution against dermatitis.

---

[27] *H.M. Advocate v. Hardy* above, at p. 147.
[28] In the present example, of guilt, arising from the circumstances of possession.
[29] 1960 S.C. (H.L.) 22.

The defenders lost their case at first instance and appealed to the Court of Session. They won by a majority ruling after a dissension among their Lordships as to where "the burden of proof" rested. The pursuer then appealed to the House of Lords, who upheld the Court of Session judgment, but Lord Denning had much to say about their approach to the question of the burden of proof, namely that:

> "This difference of opinion shows how important it is to distinguish between a *legal* burden[30] properly so called, which is imposed by the law itself, and a *provisional* burden[31] which is raised by the state of the evidence. The legal burden in this case was imposed by law on the Pursuer. In order to succeed, he had to prove that the Defenders were negligent, and that their negligence caused the disease . . . In order to discharge the burden of proving negligence, the pursuer proved that 'barrier cream was commonly supplied by employers to men doing such work as the pursuer was doing.' This was a cogent piece of evidence and raised no doubt a 'presumption' or a *'prima facie'* case, in this sense, that if nothing more appeared, the Court might well infer that the defenders were negligent, and in that sense it put a burden on the defender to answer it. But this was only a provisional burden which was raised by the state of the evidence as it then stood. The defender might answer it by argument, as indeed they did . . . In this way, a provisional burden may shift from one party to the other as the case proceeds or may remain suspended between them. But it has no compelling force. At the end of the day the Court has to ask itself—not whether the provisional burden is discharged—but whether the legal burden has been discharged, that is to say: Has the pursuer proved that the defenders were negligent?"[32]

The effect of the tactical burden in civil cases is well illustrated by the facts of *Inglis v. L.M.S.*,[33] a case in which the parents of a young boy sued a railway company for negligence in causing his death. It was proved for the pursuers that the boy had fallen through the door of a moving train, and that there had been no interference with the door handle by either the boy or any other of the passengers in the carriage. In awarding damages to the pursuers, the court found that once the facts were proved, the onus transferred to the defenders in the sense that it was for them to   **2.08**

---

[30] *i.e.* The term in English law for the persuasive burden.
[31] *i.e.* The term in English law for the tactical burden.
[32] *ibid.* at 27.
[33] 1941 S.C. 408, in which the burden was never referred to as such.

absolve themselves of the inference that the door had been insecurely fastened when it left the station.[34] The suggestion was that the railway company had been negligent, a fact already *prima facie* proved by the pursuers' evidence, and confirmed by the defenders' silence on the matter.

It was always for the pursuers to discharge the persuasive burden, but their evidence had passed a tactical burden to the defenders, which they had then failed to discharge. By remaining silent, the defenders had allowed the pursuers' interpretation of events to seem the more probable, so that the latter were able to discharge the persuasive burden on a balance of probabilities, the standard applicable in a civil case. If, at the end of the evidence, the defenders' version of the facts had seemed more probable, or the pursuers' evidence had been insufficient to tip the scales of probability, then the pursuers would have lost.

The reference, therefore, to the "shifting" of a burden during the course of a civil proof or a criminal trial, is not to either the persuasive or evidential burdens, which are fixed by law on the parties to whom they are allocated. Instead, the reference is to the tactical burden which arises when one party has adduced sufficient evidence to make it at least a possibility that the court will find in their favour on the case as a whole unless the other party produces some contradictory evidence of their own.

THE INCIDENCE OF THE BURDENS OF PROOF IN CIVIL CASES

2.09 The "incidence" of the burdens of proof is the term used to describe the way in which the two major burdens—persuasive and evidential—are allocated between the parties to the case. Bearing in mind that each case will normally consist of more than one issue, and that the burdens of proof fall to be allocated on each and every issue, the following rules apply in civil cases.

The general rule with respect to both the persuasive and evidential burdens of proof is this. The burdens rest with the party who will lose on that issue if no other evidence is led,[35] or if at the end of the day there is an equal balance in the persuasiveness of the evidence led by both parties on that issue.[36] This is another way of saying that the party who raises an issue must prove it. As we saw in the earlier debt example, A, who asserts that B owes her

---

[34] *ibid.* Lord Moncrieff at 563.
[35] Dickson, *Evidence*, para. 25.
[36] Although the point may sometimes be confused by requirements of court practice and procedure, *e.g.* the question of which party should lead evidence first. See below and Maxwell, *The Practice of the Court of Session*, p. 264, and Macphail, *Sheriff Court Practice*, paras 8.55–8.56.

money, must produce the necessary evidence of this, and therefore the persuasive and evidential burdens on this issue rest with her.

To this extent, therefore, it ought to be possible in a civil action to examine the closed record, identify the remaining live issues, and allocate the burdens of proof according to which party is making which assertion. However, it is not always as simple as this. Sometimes a party appears to be asserting a negative (*e.g.* that the defender has failed to honour a contract, or that the pursuer failed to take reasonable care for her own safety) and it can seem that a party is being asked to prove a negative. However, if it is "the substance and not the grammar",[37] which is considered such averments are positive and not negative.

For example, in order to show that the pursuer in a negligence action failed to take reasonable care for her own safety (the essence of a defence of "contributory negligence") the defender will require to produce positive evidence of the pursuer's behaviour. This might be a failure to follow safety procedures, or a failure to look both ways at a road crossing. For this reason, an averment, whether phrased in the positive or the negative, will normally impose the burdens of proof on the party making it.

The general rule is that in the absence of any specific interlocutor before proof, it is for the pursuer to lead. This reflects the fact that in most cases the pursuer must discharge the burdens of proof on at least some of her averments before the defender is required to prove anything. Thus, in the original example, A had to prove the existence of the debt before B was required to prove that it had in fact been repaid. There will though be occasions when the court rules that the defender should lead. This could occur, for example, if the defender has raised an issue on the record, which, if proved, would end the case without the need to hear evidence from the pursuer. In such a case the burdens of proof remain where the averments have placed them—it is simply the case that the court has altered the order in which the parties set about discharging them.

Another problem surrounds the operation of presumptions.[38] **2.10** These have the effect of relieving a party of the need to prove anything further once the facts upon which a presumption is based have been established. If the facts upon which the presumption is based are admitted on the record, it is for the party against whom that presumption operates to lead evidence immediately so as to counter its effect. This may well create the impression that the burden of proof has somehow shifted to that party. However, for reasons explained above, this is not the case. It is simply that the

---

[37] Dickson, n. 35.
[38] Dealt with in Chap. 3.

party making use of the presumption has employed it in the discharge of the burdens. This places a tactical burden upon the other party to lead evidence in replication. Exactly the same process arises when, in the absence of any presumption, the opponent simply admits certain facts on the record, thus relieving the asserting party of the burden of proving them. Also, where two presumptions conflict, it will be the party who seeks to overcome the stronger of the two presumptions who will be required to bear the burdens of proof.[39]

The position may also be complicated by the operation of a statute, which may, for defined and limited purposes, allocate the burdens of proof. For example, section 30(2) of the Bills of Exchange Act 1882[40] states that once it is proved that the acceptance, issue or subsequent negotiation of a bill is affected by fraud, duress, force and fear or illegality, then the burden of proof is upon the "holder" to show that, subsequent to the incident complained of, value in good faith has been given for the bill. This is in contrast to the normal position, under which the holder is presumed to be the "holder in due course" (*i.e.* to have taken the bill in good faith and for value) until the contrary is proved.[41]

Similarly, a statute may provide that a court must be "satisfied" that a particular event happened, or that a particular state of affairs exists, or alternatively that such an issue must "appear to the court" to be so. In such a case the burdens of proof fall upon the party who is relying on, or asserting, the point.

For example, in *Kerrigan v. Nelson*[42] the court was considering the effect of a section in the Rent and Mortgage Interest Restrictions (Amendment) Act 1933[43] which entitled a court to grant an ejectment order against a domestic tenant where it could be shown that the landlord reasonably required the premises for his own occupation. The section contained a proviso which prevented the court from issuing such an order where the court was satisfied that greater hardship would be created by granting the order than by refusing it. It was held that the "onus of proof" (*i.e.* the persuasive burden) on the issue of greater hardship rested with the tenant.

---

[39] See *Penman v. White*, 1957 S.C. 338, a case involving the presumption against donation.

[40] One of several sections in this Act which reallocate the persuasive burden, see also ss.13, 21(2) and (3), 32(5), 63(3) and 65(4).

[41] See generally, Gloag and Henderson, *Introduction to the Law of Scotland*, para. 23.18.

[42] 1946 S.C. 388; for other examples of the same process see *McLaughlin v. Caledonia Stevedoring Co.*, 1938 S.C. (H.L.) 31, *Moore v. Harland & Wolff*, 1937 S.C. 707 and *McCallum v. Arthur*, 1955 S.C. 188.

[43] A similar rule to which may now be found in the Rent (Scotland) Act 1984, s.11(3) and Sched. 2, Pts I and III.

Finally, there is the problem posed by statutory sections that create a right, or establish some other position, but subject to some proviso, excuse, exemption or qualification. As will emerge below, the position in criminal cases would appear to be that it is for the person relying on such a proviso, etc., to prove that it applies to them. The position is not authoritatively settled under civil law, partly because of conflicting early dicta,[44] but in the most recent House of Lords authority on the point, it seems to have been taken for granted that the principle applies equally in civil cases.

In *Nimmo v. Alexander Cowan & Sons*[45] the pursuer, a papermill worker, was seeking damages in respect of an accident sustained at work. The House of Lords had to consider the effect of section 29(1) of the Factories Act 1961, which requires that every place at which any person has to work shall be kept safe "so far as is reasonably practicable". It was held that once the pursuer had shown that they were not safe in general terms, the effect of the words quoted was to create a qualification which it was for the defenders to bring themselves within. Thus, the defenders had to aver, and subsequently to prove, that the premises were safe, in terms of section 29(1). In the course of what was in fact a dissenting judgment on other grounds, Lord Wilberforce referred to "the orthodox principle (common to both the criminal and the civil law) that exceptions etc. are to be set up by those who rely on them".[46]

The general rule, operating in the vast majority of cases, is that **2.11** the party bearing the persuasive burden on an issue also bears the evidential burden on that same issue. This is logical since the party who will lose an issue if no evidence is led is the one who should begin leading it. However, in certain exceptional cases, what are essentially practical considerations may dictate that the two burdens be separated. This situation arises in those cases in which a fact which requires proof one way or the other lies exclusively (or, to use the accepted legal term, "peculiarly") within the knowledge of one of the parties. In such a case, although it will require very little evidence to enable a party without the knowledge to place a burden on the party with such knowledge, the former still bears the initial burden of leading evidence.

In *McClure, Naismith, Brodie and Macfarlane v. Stewart*[47] a solicitor was asked by a client to secure a loan on a patent he was

---

[44] Notably those in *Coul v. Ayr County Council*, 1909 S.C. 422 at 424, and *Brydon v. Railway Executive*, 1957 S.C. 282 at 290.

[45] 1967 S.C. (H.L.) 79.

[46] *ibid.* at 109. See also Macphail, n. 1, Chap. 22.28, in which he calls for clarification on the point for the purposes of the civil law. The Scottish Law Commission, Memo. No. 46, para. V.13, rejected this proposal, recommending that each statute should be interpreted according to its own wording.

[47] (1887) 15 R. (H.L.) 1.

taking out. The solicitor had another client who was persuaded to lend £5,000 on the patent, which was then found to be invalid because it had been anticipated. The creditor client sued the solicitor concerned, alleging that the solicitor had known of the invalidity of the patent, but had failed to communicate that fact to him in time.

It was held that where one party (in this case the creditor) is obliged to make a negative averment (*i.e.* the failure to communicate with him), the proof or otherwise of which lies peculiarly within the knowledge of the other party (*i.e.* the solicitor), then that other party, who is asserting the affirmative, must prove it. But he is not obliged to do this unless and until the party asserting the negative has at least produced some evidence (in this case that he had received no communication from the solicitor). This is another way of saying that the persuasive burden on the issue (in this case the issue of communication) rests with the person with the knowledge of the facts, but he is not obliged to begin discharging it until the party without the knowledge has discharged the evidential burden.[48]

THE INCIDENCE OF THE BURDENS OF PROOF IN CRIMINAL CASES

General rule

2.12   The general rule concerning the incidence of the burdens of proof in a criminal case was succinctly and authoritatively stated by Lord Justice-Clerk Thomson in *Mackenzie v. H.M. Advocate*[49] as being that: "The presumption of innocence is a fundamental tenet of our criminal procedure. It follows that the burden of proof rests on the Crown to displace this presumption." This is essentially another way of saying that the Crown bear both the persuasive and evidential burdens on every issue in a case which tends to prove the guilt of the accused of the crime(s) libelled in the complaint or indictment.

With one exception, at common law, these burdens remain with the Crown throughout the trial, and never shift to the accused.[50] At

---

[48] See also *Cruickshank v. Smith*, 1949 J.C. 134 at 151–152. The significance of these cases is not, of course, that the pursuer is asserting a negative, but that the facts are almost exclusively within the knowledge of the defender. See also *Burns v. Royal Hotel (St Andrews) Ltd.*, 1958 S.C. 354.

[49] 1959 J.C. 32 at pp. 36–37.

[50] See, *e.g.* Lord Justice-General Normand's judgment in *Lennie v. H.M. Advocate*, 1946 J.C. 79 at 80. See also *Owens v. H.M. Advocate*, 1946 J.C. 119, and Renton and Brown, n. 6, para. 24–01. *N.B.* also *Tallis v. H.M. Advocate*, n. 23.

the conclusion of the trial any "reasonable doubt" which remains in the minds of the jury or sheriff must be exercised in favour of the accused. However, the position is confused by the existence of various exceptions to the general rule. There are a number of categories which to a greater or lesser extent place a burden on the accused. The sole common law exception when both the persuasive and evidential burdens shift to the accused is the special defence of insanity (and that includes the lesser defence of diminished responsibility). There is a wider range of exceptions which involve the shifting of just the evidential burden to the accused, including other special defences, and certain statutory provisions.

Insanity and diminished responsibility

Insanity and diminished responsibility are known in criminal law **2.13** as special defences. It has been established at least since the days of Hume[51] that when an accused person seeks to assert that he was insane at the time of the offence,[52] the persuasive burden of proof is upon that accused. So also is the evidential burden, though there may be sufficient evidence of the accused's insanity from other sources to discharge this burden.

The clearest modern statement of the law on this point is that of Lord Justice-Clerk Thomson in *H.M. Advocate v. Mitchell*,[53] who directed a jury in the following terms:

> "There is a special defence in this case, and the special defence is that at the time of the act charged the accused was insane and not responsible for his actions, and you have got to consider then . . . whether this defence is made out . . . on this issue the burden of proof is on the defence, because in our law there is a presumption that a man is sane."[54]

There remains, however, the problem situation (albeit a fairly rare one) in which the sanity of an accused is questioned by the Crown. This could happen, for example, if the accused has raised a defence of diminished responsibility, and the Crown wish to counter it by asserting that in fact the accused should be committed to a mental hospital.[55] There is no clear and authoritative ruling on this point,

---

[51] I, 43.

[52] The same rule would seem to apply to insanity in bar of trial, which is a procedural matter outwith the scope of this book; see Renton and Brown, n. 6, para. 26–05.

[53] 1951 J.C. 53 at 53–54; see also *Lambie v. H.M. Advocate*, 1973 J.C. 53 at 58.

[54] Insanity is only described as a "special" defence, because it attracts special procedures.

[55] For which procedure see Renton and Brown, *loc. cit.*

but dicta and commentary suggest that the persuasive burden of proving insanity in such a case will rest with the Crown.[56]

Despite the historical and procedural differences between insanity and diminished responsibility,[57] the latter has always been regarded as a form of "partial insanity"[58] and it makes sense that the evidential implications of a plea of diminished responsibility should be the same as those for insanity. Thus in *Carraher v. H.M. Advocate*[59] Lord Russell directed the jury that: "If the Crown have established here that the accused did this thing, it is not for the Crown to go further and show that the accused was fully responsible for what he did; it is for the accused to make good his defence of partial irresponsibility . . ."

In other words, the persuasive burden on the issue of diminished responsibility is upon the accused, as also is the evidential burden. This is in the sense that it will normally be for the accused to raise enough of a suggestion that he was not fully responsible for his actions to warrant the judge leaving that possibility for the jury's consideration.

Special defences

2.14   The special rules applicable to insanity defences have already been examined. The remaining "special defences", as they are called, are alibi, self-defence and incrimination (otherwise known as impeachment).[60] None of these defences impose a persuasive burden on the accused, although they do impose an evidential burden on the accused. These defences are described as special only because their use invokes a particular procedure. This was explained in *Lambie v. H.M. Advocate*[61] where Lord Justice-General Emslie stated: "The only purpose of the special defence is to give fair notice to the Crown and once such notice has been given the only issue for a jury is to decide upon the whole evidence

---

[56] See Macphail, n. 1, Chap. 22.06, quoting *H.M. Advocate v. Harrison* (1968) 32 J.C.L. 119, and The Scottish Law Commission, Memo 46. para. V.03. For a discussion of the standard and onus of proof in a plea of insanity in bar of trial see *Jessop v. Robertson,* 1989 S.C.C.R. 600.

[57] For which see Gordon, *Criminal Law,* (3rd ed.) Chaps 10 and 11.

[58] And was described as such in *H.M. Advocate v. Braithwaite,* 1945 J.C. 55. Alison, *Practice of the Criminal Law in Scotland,* described a person suffering from diminished responsibility as being "partially deranged" (II, 652).

[59] 1946 J.C. 108 at 113. This passage was adopted in *Braithwaite,* above. The categories of special defences are probably now closed, Renton and Brown, n. 6, and *Sorley v. H.M. Advocate,* 1992 S.L.T. 867.

[60] See Renton and Brown, n. 6, para. 14–26. Since *H.M. Advocate v. Cunningham,* 1963 J.C. 80 it is assumed that somnambulism is no longer (if it ever was) a special defence, and as such belongs in the category of "specific" defences referred to below. Similarly, automatism is not a special defence: *Ross v. H.M. Advocate,* 1991 S.L.T. 564.

[61] 1973 J.C. 53 at 58–59.

before them, whether the Crown has established the accused's guilt beyond reasonable doubt."

A number of cases have created confusion regarding the burden carried by the accused, but the position was settled in *Lambie*. This case involved a classic example of a potentially fatal misdirection to a jury on the subject of the special defence. The defence in question was incrimination, and although the trial judge made it clear to the jury that the Crown were required to prove the accused's guilt, he withdrew the special defence from them on the ground that it was not supported by corroborated evidence.[62] This was an error as in this situation there was no persuasive burden on the accused, and no requirement to produce corroboration of his defence.

The misunderstanding regarding the burden carried by an accused who relies on a special defence stemmed from dicta in various earlier cases involving special defences, in particular, *Lennie v. H.M. Advocate*,[63] *Owens v. H.M. Advocate*[64] and *H.M. Advocate v. Cunningham*.[65] These cases treated the special defence (a) as a defence in itself, which it was for the accused to prove; and (b) as a possible source of "reasonable doubt" which might lead to an acquittal. Whatever historical reasons there may have been for such a distinction,[66] at the end of the day the accused requires only to raise a reasonable doubt to secure an acquittal. It is therefore misleading to direct a jury, as in *Lambie* in terms which suggest that the accused must bear the persuasive burden of proof on a special defence.

Reviewing some of the earlier cases Lord Justice-General Emslie concluded in *Lambie* that "references in *Lennie* and *Owens* to there being an onus upon the defence were unsound". The correct position was instead:

> "When a special defence is pleaded, whether it be of alibi, self-defence or incrimination, the jury should be so charged in the appropriate language, and all that requires to be said of the special defence, where any evidence in support of it has been given, either in course [sic] of the Crown case or by the accused himself or by any witnesses led by the defence, is that if that evidence, whether from one or more witnesses, is believed, or creates in the minds of the jury reasonable doubt

---

[62] In the event in *Lambie* the appeal court held that taken as a whole the charge to the jury narrowly avoided amounting to a misdirection. The appeal was sustained on a different ground.

[63] 1946 J.C. 79.

[64] 1946 J.C. 119.

[65] 1963 J.C. 80.

[66] These are examined by Gordon in "The Burden of Proof on the Accused", 1968 S.L.T. (News) 29.

as to the guilt of the accused . . . the Crown case must fail and that they must acquit."[67]

2.15 Although the appeal court in *Lambie* did not refer to the evidential and persuasive burdens as such, it is clear from subsequent opinions that the special defence has no special evidential implications.[68] Instead, as with all "specific" defences raised by an accused (*i.e.* defences which are something more than a flat denial of guilt), the evidential burden rests with him or her. Once that burden has been discharged, it is for the prosecution to disprove the defence raised, *i.e.* to discharge the persuasive burden on that issue. Thus, to quote Renton and Brown:

"There is no duty on the prosecution to refute any specific defence until it is raised in evidence by the accused or arises out of the evidence led for the Crown, but once a specific defence, whether or not technically 'special', has been raised, it is for the prosecution to exclude it beyond reasonable doubt. The only burden laid on the defence is what is sometimes called the 'evidential burden', the onus of raising the issue. The 'persuasive burden' remains on the Crown."[69]

The correct way for a trial judge to approach any specific defence raised by an accused is that laid down by Lord Justice-General Cooper in *Crawford v. H.M. Advocate*[70] who ruled, in the context of a plea of self-defence, that:

"[It] is the duty of the presiding Judge to consider the whole evidence bearing on self-defence and to make up his own mind whether any of it is relevant to infer self-defence as known to the law of Scotland. If he considers that there is no evidence from which the requisite conclusion could reasonably be drawn, it is the duty of the presiding Judge to direct

---

[67] *Lambie v. H.M. Advocate*, n.61, at p. 59.

[68] See for example, *Dunn v. H.M. Advocate*, 1987 S.L.T. 295 and *Harrison v. H.M. Advocate*, 1993 S.C.C.R. 1087.

[69] n.6, para. 24–01. Macphail, n. 1, Chap. 22.08, took the implication of *Lambie* to be that, in the case of the special defences other than insanity and diminished responsibility, "the persuasive burden of proof remains on the Crown and the only duty on the defence is to discharge the evidential burden of raising the issue in such a way that it has to be left to the jury". Another effect of *Lambie* became apparent in *McAvoy v. H.M. Advocate*, 1982 J.C. 117 and *Fraser v. H.M. Advocate*, 1982 S.C.C.R. 458 in which it was held that, with the exception of the defence of insanity, there is no need for any direction to be given to a jury on any requirement for a corroborated case to support such a defence. *Lambie* was also followed in *Mullen v. H.M. Advocate*, 1978 S.L.T. (Notes) 33 and *Donnelly v. H.M. Advocate*, 1977 S.L.T. 147.

[70] 1950 J.C. 67 at 69. See also the direction given to trial judges in *Dunn v. H.M. Advocate*, 1987 S.L.T. 295.

the jury that it is not open to them to consider the special defence. If, on the other hand, there is some evidence, although it may be slight, or even evidence about which two reasonable views might be held, then he must leave the special defence to the jury subject to such directions as he may think proper."

The case of *Gilmour v. H.M. Advocate*[71] illustrates the importance of an accurate charge to the jury, particularly in regard to a special defence and the function of corroboration and reasonable doubt. The accused had raised special defences of alibi and incrimination. The sheriff directed the jury that "there is no special burden on the accused to prove his special defence—corroboration is not necessary . . . " The appeal court described this charge to the jury as "quite unsatisfactory" and "defective" because of the failure to explain to the jury that, "if what is raised by the special defence leaves them with any reasonable doubt, the accused must be given the benefit of that doubt".[72]

Statutory provisions

In contrast to the common law, where there is only one **2.16** exception to the general rule regarding the persuasive burden, a large number of statutory exceptions exist. Perhaps the most obvious are those[73] which require the accused to show that they had some lawful justification or excuse for what they did, or which require them to prove that they had no knowledge of some vital fact essential to the commission of the offence.[74] A frequently used defence arises under sections 4(3) and 5(2) of the Road Traffic Act 1988 whereby an accused may escape conviction for being in charge of, or driving, a motor vehicle under the influence of drink or drugs if he "proves" that at the material time there was no likelihood of his driving while he remained in such a condition.

The difficulty in such cases is that of establishing exactly what burden the accused bears: is it persuasive or evidential? There appears to be no rule of universal application to these various, unrelated statutory impositions. However, despite the absence of a general rule, the courts when interpreting such statutory provisions appear to conclude that their effect is to impose a persuasive

---

[71] 1989 S.L.T. 881.
[72] at p. 882F.
[73] Such as the Prevention of Crime Act 1953, s.1(1), which makes it an offence to carry an offensive weapon in a public place without lawful authority or reasonable excuse, the proof whereof shall lie on him (*i.e.* the accused).
[74] *e.g.* Misuse of Drugs Act 1971, s.28(2). See also Licensing (Scotland) Act 1976, s.126.

burden on the accused.[75] This is probably due to the relatively recent emergence of the evidential burden in Scots law, but Macphail has criticised it as a general practice, and suggested that all burdens falling upon an accused should be evidential only.[76] With the advent of the Human Rights Act 1998 it is most likely that challenges will be taken to any provisions that appear to undermine the presumption of innocence by imposing a persuasive burden on the accused.

It has been suggested in some English cases that statutory provisions that reverse the onus of proof, at least where the onus appears to place a persuasive burden on the accused, conflict with Article 6(2) of the European Convention of Human Rights. This was argued in the Privy Council decision in *Att.-Gen. (Hong Kong) v. Lee Kwong-kut*[77] when the impact of human rights jurisprudence in the U.K. had yet to be felt. Also, in *R. v. DPP, ex p. Kebilene*,[78] the House of Lords had to determine what kind of onus section 16A(3) of the Prevention of Terrorism (Temporary Provisions) Act 1989 placed upon an accused. The section relates to possession of articles for commission of terrorist offences. It provides that: "It is a defence for a person charged with an offence under this section to prove that at the time of the alleged offence [the articles in question] were not in his possession . . . " Relying on the European Court decision in *Salabiaku v. France* (A/141-A)[79] the Lords held that it was not necessarily a reversal of the presumption of innocence to place an onus of proof, whether evidential or persuasive, on an accused. The issue was whether there was a reasonable balance between the public interest and an individual's rights.

At least one respected commentator has criticised *Kebilene* and called for urgent legislation to amend the effects of those statutes that impose a persuasive burden on an accused, arguing that such

---

[75] See, *e.g. Neish v. Stevenson*, 1969 S.L.T. 229 for the imposition of such a burden on the accused in a drink/driving case involving a defence of "no likelihood of driving", in terms of s.1(2) of the Road Safety Act 1967. And *King v. Lees*, 1993 S.L.T. 1184, which held there was a persuasive burden on the accused to prove his statutory defence, though the court said the evidence led need not be corroborated. See also *Grieve v. Macleod*, 1967 J.C. 32, in which the accused in a complaint under s.1 of the Prevention of Crime Act 1953 lost his appeal because the court was not satisfied that it was "reasonable" for an Edinburgh taxi driver to protect himself from customers with a length of rubber hose. The persuasive burden was clearly regarded as being his. For a critical discussion of these issues see, Sheldon, "Hip Flasks and Burdens", 1993 S.L.T. (News) 33.

[76] See Macphail, *Evidence*, Chaps 22.19 and 22.23.

[77] [1993] 3 All E.R. 933.

[78] [1999] 4 All E.R. 801.

[79] (1991) 13 E.H.R.R. 379 at 388.

provisions (sometimes described as reverse onus clauses) infringe Article 6(2) of the Convention.[80]

An example of a general statutory provision that has created confusion and uncertainty in the area of reverse onus clauses in Scotland is paragraph 16 of Schedule 3 to the Criminal Procedure (Scotland) Act 1995,[81] which provides:

> "Where, in relation to an offence created by or under an enactment any exception, exemption, proviso, excuse or qualification, is expressed to have effect whether by the same or any other enactment, the exception, exemption, proviso, excuse or qualification need not be specified or negatived in the indictment or complaint, and the prosecution is not required to prove it but the accused may do so."

This provision was encountered in *Earnshaw v. H.M. Advocate*,[82] in the context of the defence of "reasonable excuse" for failure to provide a blood or urine sample in a drink/driving case.[83] Its predecessor in summary cases was section 16(d) of the Summary Jurisdiction (Scotland) Act 1954, which was also considered in *Nimmo v. Alexander Cowan & Sons* (for which see 2.10 above), an action for personal injuries sustained as the result of an alleged breach of statutory duty under the Factories Act 1961. In that case the opinion was given that where it applied its effect was to require the person claiming such an excuse to "prove the facts by which they contend that they are excused".[84]

In the case of *Gatland v. Metropolitan Police Commission*[85] it was held that an accused in such a situation bears the persuasive burden, and there seems little doubt that this is also the position under Scots law. In practice, the greatest difficulty encountered in connection with paragraph 16 of Schedule 3 of the 1995 Act would seem to be that of establishing when it applies.[86]

Facts peculiarly within the knowledge of the accused

It was noted, when dealing with the incidence of the burdens of **2.17** proof in civil cases, that when certain facts are "peculiarly within the knowledge of" one of the parties, the court takes the view that

---

[80] See, for example, J.C. Smith, Commentary in [2000] Crim. L.R. 480–481 and the discussion in P. Lewis, "The Human Rights Act 1998: Shifting the Burden" [2000] Crim. L.R. 667.

[81] See Renton and Brown, n. 6, para. 8–57.

[82] See n. 11 above.

[83] But the court did not consider the application of s.66 in depth as the Crown conceded they had the persuasive burden of proof. See also *Kennedy v. Clark*, 1970 J.C. 55.

[84] 1967 S.C. (H.L.) 79 at 114. This point is considered further below.

[85] [1968] 2 Q.B. 279, an English case based on the equivalent of para. 16 of Sched. 3 to the 1995 Act.

[86] See Renton and Brown, *loc. cit.*

the party with that knowledge bears the persuasive burden on that issue. The onus on the other party is at least to generate sufficient evidence to make it a live issue, *i.e.* must discharge the evidential burden.[87] The objection to applying such a rule to a criminal case is that the person with the knowledge is the accused, and to require the accused to prove his or her own innocence in the face of merely *prima facie* evidence from the Crown conflicts with the presumption of innocence.

Reference in older texts,[88] to "the onus" which rests upon an accused who has all the facts upon an issue peculiarly within his own knowledge, stem from the period before the recognition of more than one burden of proof. The preferred view today is that "the onus" on an accused is merely an evidential burden that arises when certain inferences of guilt must be drawn from adverse circumstances.[88a]

In *Mochan v. Herron*,[89] the accused remained silent in the face of cogent prosecution evidence. The effect was to leave the Crown evidence unchallenged. The terms of the sheriff's stated case (on which he was upheld by the appeal court) made it clear that he regarded it as one of those cases in which the evidence for the Crown placed a tactical burden[90] on the accused, which he had failed to discharge. Significantly, one of the cases he founded on as supporting his ruling was *H.M. Advocate v. Hardy*,[91] another case where the accused said nothing in his own defence, and clearly failed to discharge the tactical burden placed on him by the Crown evidence.

In *Cruikshank v. Smith*,[92] the accused was charged with a statutory offence involving illegal fishing. The breach was one in which the statute required it to be shown whether or not the accused had a legal right to be fishing where he was. It was held that "the burden of proof" on the issue rested with the Crown, but that they need only produce *prima facie* evidence of illegal fishing for the onus to pass to the accused to show that he was fishing lawfully. The failure to acknowledge the existence of two burdens, one evidential and the other persuasive, has contributed to some ambiguity in the interpretation of the burden resting on the accused in such situations.

---

[87] See, for example, *McClure, Naismith, Brodie and Macfarlane v. Stewart*, at n. 47 above.

[88] Notably by Dickson, n. 35, para. 32, and Walker and Walker, para. 83(c) (first edition). See also *Irving v. Jessop*, 1988 S.L.T. 53.

[88a] See Walker and Walker, n. 7, para. 2.12.3.

[89] 1972 S.L.T. 218; see also *Donaghy v. Normand*, 1992 S.L.T. 666.

[90] Note that the term "tactical burden" was not used as such.

[91] 1938 J.C. 144, also considered below.

[92] 1949 J.C. 134.

One interpretation, arguably the approach adopted in *Mochan v. Herron*, given the court's endorsement there of a passage in the first edition of Walker and Walker, is that the accused bears the persuasive burden whenever the facts are peculiarly within his knowledge, and the Crown merely have the evidential burden of producing a *prima facie* case against him. The alternative, and modern view, is that both the evidential and persuasive burdens in such cases rest throughout with the Crown, but that once they have discharged the evidential burden, the tactical burden takes over and the accused is expected to produce some evidence to raise the reasonable doubt.[93]

Macphail has argued[94] that it would be erroneous to rely on any general rule that places a persuasive burden on an accused whenever exculpatory facts are peculiarly within his or her knowledge. In effect the rule would apply in every case, on the basis that only the accused really knows whether or not he or she is guilty. His view was endorsed by Sheriff Kermack in *McNeill v. Ritchie*,[95] who observed: "I interpret the effect in Scots law of a fact being peculiarly within the knowledge of the accused as requiring him to produce evidence of that fact and not as requiring him to substantiate it by full legal proof."

The doctrine of possession of recently stolen goods

Reference was made in Chapter 1 to the so-called presumption **2.18** of guilt which arises when an accused person is proved to have been found in possession of recently stolen property in "criminative" circumstances. Its relevance in the present context is that this presumption is popularly believed to shift the persuasive burden from the Crown to the accused once the qualifying facts are proved.

Gordon regards it merely as a cogent item of circumstantial evidence, and puts forward a strong argument that it is historically unsound to regard the presumption as placing a persuasive burden on an accused found in such circumstances.[96] The fact remains that this is the effect which the doctrine is regarded as having. In the

---

[93] *Stair Memorial Encyclopedia,* para. 755, and Walker and Walker, *loc. cit.*

[94] Macphail, n. 76, Chap. 22.15.

[95] 1967 S.L.T. (Sh. Ct) 68. See now *Irving v. Jessop*, 1988 S.L.T. 53, which supports the view that the Crown need only produce a *prima facie* case. For a recent case outlining the difficulties facing the Crown in such circumstances, see *R. v. Gibson* [2000] Crim. L.R. 479.

[96] Gordon, "The Burden of Proof on the Accused", 1968 S.L.T. (News) 29 at pp. 40–43, in which he describes this doctrine as: "The clearest example of the tendency to discuss a tactical burden of proof in terms which suggest that it is a persuasive burden." See too Macphail, n. 76, Chap. 22.13.

leading case of *Fox v. Patterson*[97] it was stated by Lord Justice-General Cooper[98] that, provided three conditions were met—possession of stolen goods; a short interval between theft and discovery; and other criminative circumstances beyond the bare fact of possession—the full effect of the rule was "in shifting the onus from the prosecution to the accused, and raising a presumption of guilt which the accused must redargue or fail".

This dictum has been criticised by Gordon who declared Lord Cooper's attempt to define the conditions when the onus shifts as "misleading and tautologous".[99] However, the "onus" in question is not the full persuasive burden, but an evidential or perhaps tactical burden which an accused person bears in the face of the cogent evidence required in order to establish the presumption. There is no doubt that the accused found in possession of property shortly after it was stolen, in circumstances suggestive of guilt, has in popular parlance, "a lot of explaining to do", in order to argue away a formidable body of circumstantial evidence. If this is not done then a conviction is neither unpredictable nor unreasonable, and in many cases it will make little practical difference whether the conviction arises from a failure to discharge an evidential burden or a failure to discharge a tactical burden.

The preferred position must be that where the facts suggest an accused person has custody of recently stolen goods, those facts give rise to an inference of guilt that may be sufficiently strong to permit the Crown to discharge their persuasive burden of proving guilt beyond reasonable doubt. To prevent this occurring, the accused has to put forward some explanation such as to persuade a jury that a reasonable doubt exists. Gordon's analysis of the confusion in this area is that, "all that is needed is a rule that guilt can be proved by circumstantial evidence".[1]

These two areas, cases in which facts are said to be peculiarly within the knowledge of the accused, and cases arising from possession of recently stolen property, require clarification. Macphail, in his Research Memorandum to the Scottish Law Commission,[2] recommended that the burden placed upon the accused be regarded as an evidential burden only. An alternative approach might be to leave both the persuasive and evidential burdens in

---

[97] 1948 J.C. 104, followed in many subsequent cases, including *Simpson v. H.M. Advocate*, 1952 J.C. 1; *Brannan v. H.M. Advocate*, 1954 J.C. 87; *McSorley v. H.M. Advocate*, 1975 S.L.T. (Notes) 43, and *Cassidy v. McLeod*, 1981 S.C.C.R. 270.

[98] *Fox v. Patterson*, above, at p. 108. The same assertion was made in *Cameron v. H.M. Advocate*, 1959 J.C. 59 at 63, and *Cryans v. Nixon*, 1955 J.C. 1 at 6.

[99] n. 96, at p. 42.

[1] Gordon, n. 96, at p. 43.

[2] n. 76, Chap. 22.13 and 22.16. His recommendation *quoad* recently stolen property was endorsed by the Scottish Law Commission (Memo. No. 46, para. V.07).

both cases with the Crown, and allow the tactical burden to take its course. This would preserve the presumption of innocence, but allow the court to react accordingly to a failure on the part of the accused to give an explanation when one is naturally called for.

Summary

It may be helpful to summarise this complex section into several general statements concerning the incidence of the burdens of proof in criminal cases.

(a) Persuasive burden

The general rule in criminal cases is that the persuasive burden **2.19** on all issues rests with the Crown throughout the trial. The only situations in which a persuasive burden on an issue will be borne by the accused are:

(1) when he or she raises the defences of insanity and diminished responsibility;

(2) when a statute imposes upon him or her a burden of proof which may be interpreted as being a persuasive one.

(b) Evidential burden

The general rule in criminal cases is that the evidential burden **2.20** on all issues rests with the Crown throughout the trial. The only situations in which an evidential burden on an issue will be borne by the accused are:

(1) when a specific defence is raised (*i.e.* a defence other than a general denial of guilt). In all other cases, once the accused has discharged the evidential burden, the Crown must go on to prove the accused's guilt (*i.e.* to discharge the persuasive burden on the defence raised by the accused). *N.B.* that the term "specific defence" is wider than the term "special defence", which is special only in a procedural sense; and in the cases of insanity and diminished responsibility the accused also bears the persuasive burden;

(2) when a statute imposes upon an accused a burden which may be interpreted as being only evidential in nature;

(3) when facts are peculiarly within the accused's knowledge, or when it is proved that the accused was in possession of recently stolen property in criminative circumstances.

Arguably the burden borne by an accused in such cases is evidential alone or perhaps only a tactical one.

THE STANDARDS OF PROOF ON THE PERSUASIVE BURDEN

2.21 The phrase "standard of proof" is used to describe the amount and quality of evidence required to discharge a burden of proof. There are basically two such standards in use in connection with the persuasive burden of proof, namely proof "beyond reasonable doubt" in a criminal case, and proof "on the balance of probabilities" in a civil action.

The general rule

2.22 When referring to "the standard of proof", commentators, textbook writers and judges are normally alluding to the persuasive burdens. It has been said that: "It is now clear that there are only two standards of proof known to the law of Scotland; proof beyond reasonable doubt, and proof upon the balance of the probabilities on the evidence".[3]

In a criminal case, therefore, it is traditional for juries to be directed by the trial judge that the prosecution must establish the guilt of the accused beyond reasonable doubt, since this is the standard of proof required whenever the Crown bear the persuasive burden.

The concept of beyond reasonable doubt cannot be rigidly defined. But it is understood as meaning the sort of doubt which a reasonable person would entertain, something more than a fanciful possibility,[4] and "more than a merely speculative or academic doubt".[5] As an English Lord Chief Justice put it, in a case in 1949: "Once a judge begins to use the words 'reasonable doubt' and to try to explain what is a reasonable doubt and what is not, he is much more likely to confuse the jury than if he tells them in plain language 'It is the duty of the prosecution to satisfy you of the prisoner's guilt'."[6]

The standard of proof applicable to persuasive burdens in civil cases generally creates less confusion, and judges only rarely have

---

[3] Macphail, n. 76, Chap. 22.29, quoting *inter alia Brown v. Brown*, 1972 S.C. 123 and *Lamb v. Lord Advocate*, 1976 S.C. 110.

[4] See Lord Justice-Clerk Cooper in *Irving v. Minister of Pensions*, 1945 S.C. 21 at 29, something more than "a strained or fanciful acceptance of remote possibilities". See also *H.M. Advocate v. McGinlay*, 1983 S.L.T. 562 and *Tudhope v. Craig*, 1985 S.C.C.R. 214.

[5] Lord Justice-Clerk Thomson in *McKenzie v. H.M. Advocate*, 1959 J.C. 32 at 37.

[6] *R. v. Kritz* [1949] 1 K.B. 82 at 90. Lord Justice-Clerk Thomson, in *McKenzie v. H.M. Advocate*, n. 5, warned that "it is desirable to adhere so far as possible to the traditional formula and to avoid experiments in reformulation".

to explain the concept of balance of probabilities to a jury. In civil cases it is simply that in order to win on a particular issue, the party bearing the persuasive burden must persuade the court that their version of the facts is more probable than that of their opponent's.[7] As Macphail has explained: "What is being weighed in the 'balance' is not quantities of evidence but the probabilities arising from the acceptable evidence and all the circumstances of the case".[8]

The foregoing covers the general position, but there are some specific situations that need special consideration. These are now examined.

The accused in a criminal case

As was seen earlier, there are situations in which an accused **2.23** person bears a persuasive burden on a particular issue, and the question arises as to the standard of proof which must be employed in order to discharge it.

Dealing first with the common law situation (*i.e.* the defences of insanity and diminished responsibility), the standard of proof was clearly settled so far as insanity is concerned in *H.M. Advocate v. Mitchell*,[9] when Lord Justice-Clerk Thomson directed a jury that:

> "the burden of proof is on the defence, because in our law there is a presumption that a man is sane. But you must keep clearly in mind that the burden in the case of an accused person is not so heavy a burden as the burden which is laid on the Crown . . . the Crown has to prove its case beyond reasonable doubt . . . Where, however, the burden of proof is on the accused, it is enough if he brings evidence which satisfies you of the probability of what he is called upon to establish . . . *it is a question of the balance of probabilities.*"

In those situations where a statute places a persuasive burden upon an accused, the appropriate standard of proof is also on a balance of probabilities. For example, in *Robertson v. Watson*,[10] a prosecution under Sale of Milk Regulations, milk found to have been adulterated was presumed to have been adulterated by the accused

---

[7] Provided there is a sufficient case in law.

[8] n. 76, at Chap. 22.30. See also Lord Jamieson in *Hendry v. Clan Line Steamers*, 1949 S.C. 320 at 328.

[9] 1951 J.C. 53 at 54 (emphasis added). The same standard was established for the defence of diminished responsibility in *Carraher v. H.M. Advocate*, 1946 J.C. 108 at 113, and *H.M. Advocate v. Braithwaite*, 1945 J.C. 55, in which Lord Justice-Clerk Cooper at p. 58 directed the jury that: "If you think the balance of probability to be in favour of that defence, you must sustain it."

[10] 1949 J.C. 73.

unless and until he proved otherwise. Lord Justice-General Cooper considered the appropriate standard of proof required for the accused to discharge the persuasive burden thus placed upon him[11]:

> "I adopt, as an accurate statement of Scots law of general validity the rule laid down in *R. v. Carr-Briant*[12] that, when (as in this instance) some matter is presumed against an accused person unless and until the contrary is proved, the burden of proof on the accused is less than that required at the hands of the prosecutor in proving the case beyond reasonable doubt, and that this burden may be discharged by evidence satisfying the jury or the Court of the probability of that which the accused is called upon to establish."

Certainly it is difficult to see why an accused should be required to produce evidence of a higher standard on an issue such as this than would be required on, for example, the issue of sanity. Moreover, for the reasons discussed above, any suggestions of a standard of proof higher than on a balance of probabilities, would run counter to the Human Rights Act 1998. In any case, it is arguable that the principle expounded in *Robertson v. Watson* is of general applicability to any situation in which some fact is presumed against an accused unless the contrary is proved. This is how *R. v. Carr-Briant* has been interpreted in the English courts. In *Farrell v. Moir*[13] it was held that an accused who bore the persuasive burden of showing "special reason" why he should not be disqualified for drunken driving need only discharge it on a balance of probabilities.[14]

In those cases where an accused bears an evidential burden on an issue, either because he or she is peculiarly in possession of the necessary facts or because they have been found in possession of recently stolen property in criminative circumstances, they need only raise a reasonable doubt on the evidence.

Special cases

2.24   Over the years, problems have arisen in determining the appropriate standard of proof in civil actions that either have characteristics of criminal activity, or have consequences that have criminal sanctions. Should it be beyond reasonable doubt or on the balance of probabilities? There is a steady trend of case law where it has

---

[11] *ibid.*, p. 88.
[12] [1943] K.B. 607, which is still the leading authority on the same point in England.
[13] 1974 S.L.T. (Sh. Ct) 89.
[14] For an analysis of the confusion created in this area see David Sheldon, "Hip Flasks and Burdens", 1993 S.L.T. (News) 33.

been argued that a higher standard of proof should be required than a mere balance of probabilities. It has been suggested that some third, intermediate, standard should apply. Each case must be examined separately.

(a) Divorce and judicial separation

Prior to 1976, a party seeking a decree of divorce or separation **2.25** on any one of the grounds of adultery, sodomy or bestiality on the part of the alleged guilty spouse was required to prove the allegation beyond reasonable doubt.[15] However, the Divorce (Scotland) Act 1976, ss.1(6) and 4(1), reduced the applicable standard on the ground of adultery to one on a balance of probabilities. This brought adultery into line with the standard of proof of all the other grounds of divorce or separation, including unreasonable behaviour. In cases of unreasonable behaviour it is frequently averred that the defender behaved in a manner which would constitute a crime, such as breach of the peace or assault. However, for the purposes of the civil action the standard of proof is on a balance of probabilities.[16]

(b) Declarator of death

Under the Presumption of Death (Scotland) Act 1977, a court **2.26** may grant a declarator that a person is dead when that person has not been known to be alive for a period of at least seven years. This provision is dealt with more fully in Chapter 3, but section 2(1) of the Act specifically states that the appropriate standard of proof is on a balance of probabilities. This overrules the previous leading authority of *McGeachy v. Standard Life Assurance Co.*,[17] in which it was agreed by the parties that the standard of proof on the persuasive burden borne by the pursuer was proof beyond reasonable doubt.

(c) Breach of interdict and other contempts of court

An action for an alleged breach of interdict raises an interesting **2.27** problem, since the possible sanctions following upon proof of such a breach include criminal penalties.[18] The concurrence of the Lord

---

[15] An example of such a case being *Burnett v. Burnett*, 1955 S.C. 183; see also *Brown v. Brown*, n. 3.

[16] See, *Hastie v. Hastie*, 1985 S.L.T. 146, in which it was held, on a balance of probabilities, that a false allegation of, *inter alia*, an incestuous relationship contributed to the irretrievable breakdown of a marriage.

[17] 1972 S.C. 145.

[18] See Scott Robinson, *The Law of Interdict*, Chap. 16.

Advocate is required before such an action may be raised since it is possible criminal proceedings may arise out of the act complained of as a breach of interdict and these would pre-empt any civil action. Despite the possibility of criminal sanctions, proceedings for breach of interdict are civil proceedings within the meaning of section 1(1) of the Civil Evidence (Scotland) Act 1988 and corroboration is unnecessary.[19] But since the proceedings have criminal implications the question arises as to what is the appropriate standard of proof. In *Gribben v. Gribben*,[20] it was held that where a wife raised an action alleging a breach by her husband of an interim interdict to prevent him from molesting her, she was required to prove the breach beyond reasonable doubt.

Breach of interdict is a breach of a court order and as such is a contempt of court. It is thought that proof beyond reasonable doubt is also the appropriate standard of proof for all cases of alleged contempt of court, of which breach of interdict is only one example. This is because it is punishable as a crime, by admonition, censure, fine or imprisonment.[21]

A helpful dictum in this connection is that issued in *Morrow v. Neil*,[22] a rare action of lawburrows[23] brought by a widow in a tenement flat who was apprehensive of further assaults by her neighbours. Sheriff Macphail held that the question of the standard of proof fell to him to determine because it had never been raised before. He acknowledged that since the case of *Brown v. Brown*[24] he had only two standards of proof to choose from, and that in an action for contravention of lawburrows, which bears a similarity to an action for breach of interdict and requires the concurrence of the procurator fiscal, the appropriate standard would probably be proof beyond reasonable doubt.

---

[19] *Byrne v. Ross*, 1993 S.L.T. 307.

[20] 1976 S.L.T. 266, following *Eutectic Welding Alloys Ltd. v. Whitting*, 1969 S.L.T. (Notes) 79.

[21] See Macphail, n. 76, Chap. 22.37, and *H.M. Advocate v. Airs*, 1975 J.C. 64, in which all contempts of court were judged to be essentially the same in nature. The Scottish Law Commission opted also for proof beyond reasonable doubt in such cases (Memo. 46, para. V.18). *Gribben* was followed in *Inland Revenue v. Ruffle*, 1979 S.C. 371, *quoad* a tax penalty.

[22] 1975 S.L.T. (Sh. Ct) 65.

[23] Essentially a civil action brought by someone fearing harm to either themselves or their family. The defender is required to find caution for good behaviour, with the threat of imprisonment unless he or she does so. The circumstances of any breach may also be made the subject of criminal charges: see Stair Memorial Encyclopaedia, *The Laws of Scotland*, Vol. 13, paras 901–926.

[24] 1972 S.C. 123, dealt with more fully below.

(d) Fatal accident inquiries

Whatever doubts may have existed before, it is now settled by **2.28** statute that the appropriate rules of evidence, including standard of proof, for a fatal accident inquiry are "as nearly as possible those applicable to an ordinary civil cause".[25]

(e) Legitimacy

There is, as will be seen in Chapter 3, a statutory presumption of **2.29** legitimacy arising either from the marriage of the parents, or from the fact that the husband has acknowledged paternity. This arises under section 5 of the Law Reform (Parent and Child) (Scotland) Act 1986, and that same section provides that the presumption may be rebutted by evidence on a balance of probabilities. This therefore resolves the problems created by the older case authorities[26] to the effect that the appropriate burden of proof was beyond reasonable doubt.

(f) Children's Hearings

Children's hearings were set up by the Social Work (Scotland) **2.30** Act 1968, but their regulation is now contained in the Children (Scotland) Act 1995, which largely re-enacted with some modification the provisions of the earlier statute. Their principal function is to determine whether a child is in need of compulsory measures of care under any of the eleven grounds mentioned in section 52(2) of the 1995 Act. Compulsory measures of care may be deemed appropriate because of the child's offending behaviour, or because the child is at risk from external factors and requires protection. Children's hearings generate frequent applications to the sheriff court for proof of the grounds of referral. The grounds have to be clearly established, and the standard of proof to be applied is the civil standard of a balance of probabilities, except in a case of a referral under section 52(2)(g) of the Act where the criminal standard of proof of beyond reasonable doubt applies. The justification for the lower standard of proof for the remaining ten grounds is the primacy of the protection of the child. In Lord Justice-Clerk Ross's view, "it is still a justification even if the person concerned is ultimately acquitted of the offence in the criminal courts".[27]

---

[25] *i.e.* proof on a balance of probabilities: Fatal Accidents and Sudden Deaths Inquiry (Scotland) Act 1976, s.4(7).

[26] *e.g. Imre v. Mitchell*, 1958 S.C. 439 at 462; *Brown v. Brown*, n. 3 at 125, *S. v. S.*, 1977 S.L.T. (Notes) 65 and *Docherty v. McGlynn (No. 2)*, 1985 S.L.T. 237. In *A. v. G.*, 1984 S.L.T. (Sh. Ct) 65, it was held that the appropriate standard of proof of paternity in an affiliation action is also on a balance of probabilities.

[27] *Harris v. F*, 1991 S.L.T. 242 at 246C.

(g) Allegations of crime in a civil action

2.31   The possibility of a third or intermediate standard of proof raises
its head from time to time, despite strong authorities to the
contrary. For various reasons, one of the parties to a civil action
may set out to prove facts that will indicate that the other party has
committed a crime. Were that same crime to be libelled against the
party in a criminal court, the prosecution would be required to
prove those facts beyond reasonable doubt. The question then
arises whether or not a party in a civil action should be required to
prove these allegations of criminal behaviour to the same standard.

The position has shifted considerably since 1964 when, taking
the general tenor of the authorities as they then stood, Walker and
Walker in their first edition,[28] acknowledged that the question had
not been authoritatively considered very often, but that the criminal standard (*i.e.* proof beyond reasonable doubt) had been said to
apply.[29] Since then the point has been considered in a number of
cases. In *Buick v. Jaglar*,[30] the defender in an action for repayment
admitted a course of embezzlement from the pursuer, but disputed
the amount to be repaid. Sheriff Wilkinson distinguished between
cases in which the guilty party admitted the criminal conduct
(which is therefore no longer a live issue anyway) and those in
which such conduct is "altogether disputed". He concluded that:
"if a higher standard of proof applies in Scotland it is clear that
that standard is restricted in its application and it does not apply to
all civil allegations of crime".[31] Sheriff Wilkinson also noted that
English law only required proof on a balance of probabilities.[32]
Many technical crimes such as breaches of the Road Traffic Acts
and Factories Acts have been held to have been committed, for the
purposes of civil action, on a balance of probabilities.[33]

There have been numerous other cases where an intermediate
standard has been suggested, particularly where the proceedings
are considered "quasi-criminal". For example, cases involving
malpractice in returns to the Inland Revenue,[34] and cases

---

[28] *Law of Evidence in Scotland,* 1964, para. 85. See now the second edition, 2000
para. 4.3.1.

[29] By Lord Neaves in *Arnott v. Burt* (1872) 11 M. 62 at 74.

[30] 1973 S.L.T. (Sh. Ct) 6. See also *Sloan v. Triplett,* 1985 S.L.T. 294 at 297 and
Wilson v. Price, 1989 S.L.T. 484, where the same opinion was expressed in the
Outer House.

[31] *ibid.,* p. 7.

[32] By virtue of *Hornal v. Neuburger Products* [1957] 1 Q.B. 247. See also *R. v. Hants
C.C., ex p. Ellerton* [1985] 1 W.L.R. 749.

[33] See, *e.g. Nimmo v. Alexander Cowan & Sons,* 1967 S.C. (H.L.) 79, considered
earlier, in which Lord Reid at p. 97 said of the pursuer's burden of proving a
breach of s.29(1) of the Factories Act 1961 that: "It is true that the standard of
proof is lower in a civil case, so that the Pursuer only has to show that it is
probable that an offence was committed."

[34] *Inland Revenue v. Ruffle,* n. 21, and *Irving v. Minister of Pensions,* n. 4.

concerning alleged assault. In *Guest v. Annan*[35] a conviction for excessive chastisement of a child—in effect an assault—was quashed because the sheriff had used the words, "on balance . . . I convict". The language was suggestive of the application, incorrectly, of the civil standard in a criminal case.[36] Similarly, in *Sereshky v. Sereshky*,[37] an action for reduction of a deed for forgery, Lord Weir said that the standard of proof was less than that required in a criminal case but, "must be proved to a very high degree of probability having regard to the criminal implications involved". And in *Lennon v. Co-operative Insurance Society*[38] Lord Kincraig held, in a case involving an insurance claim following a fire in a boarding house in which there was an allegation that the insured started the fire, that since the insurance company was alleging facts which amounted to an accusation of wilful fire-raising on the part of the insured, there was a "much higher onus" on the company, which could only be discharged on a balance of probabilities.

In his recommendations to the Scottish Law Commission,[39] **2.32** Sheriff Macphail confirmed the frequency with which, as a matter of practice, allegations of statutory crimes are accepted on a balance of probabilities in actions for damages for personal injuries. He cited the authority of *King v. Patterson*,[40] in which it was held that it was for the defender to show "on a balance of probabilities, that the conviction was wrong and that the presumption of negligence has been rebutted".[41] His recommendation was that it should be clarified that in all cases in which a crime is alleged in the course of a civil action, the standard of proof is on a balance of probabilities. He addressed the issue of the gravity of certain behaviour sometimes justifying a higher standard of proof by asserting that: "The nature of the offence with which the court was concerned would cause variations in the *amount* of evidence required to tilt the balance of probability, but would not alter the standard of proof."[42]

---

[35] 1988 S.C.C.R. 275.

[36] See also *Ward v. Chief Constable of Strathclyde*, 1991 S.L.T. 292, an action of damages for injuries allegedly sustained when mounted police cantered into a crowd. The appropriate standard was held to be on a balance of probabilities, but it was observed that it would be difficult for a pursuer to overcome evidential hurdles and demonstrate want of probable cause and malice on the part of the police.

[37] 1988 S.L.T. 426 at 427E.

[38] 1986 S.L.T. 98.

[39] n. 76, Chap. 22.33.

[40] 1971 S.L.T. (Notes) 40, considered more fully in Chap. 3.

[41] *ibid.*, p. 40.

[42] n. 1, Chap. 22.34 (emphasis added). See the opinion of Lord Cowie in *Ashcroft's C.B. v. Stewart*, (O.H.) 1988 S.L.T 163. The Scottish Law Commission (Memo. 46, para. V.16) accepted his basic proposal, but see *Lennon v. Co-operative Insurance Society*, n. 38.

It has sometimes been suggested that there are special types of cases which require the application of a standard of proof different from the standard of proof beyond reasonable doubt or proof on a balance of probabilities. Thus, in *Anderson v. Lambie,*[43] a civil action for reduction of a probative deed was said by Lord Reid to place "a heavy onus" on the pursuer. In that case, the House of Lords held that the pursuer "has proved his case beyond reasonable doubt".[44] Lord Keith said that the onus was one which would leave "no fair and reasonable doubt upon the mind".[45] This terminology is suggestive of the appropriate standard in criminal cases and is confusing in the context of civil cases, especially where no criminal conduct is alleged. However, these terms can be explained as emphasising the amount of evidence and degree of persuasion required of a pursuer in such an action.

The debate continued in *Rehman v. Ahmad*[46] an action brought under section 8(1) of the Law Reform (Miscellaneous Provisions) (Scotland) Act 1985, which provides for an application to the court to rectify the terms of an agreement under certain limited circumstances. The statute makes no specific provision regarding the applicable standard of proof, but must be read in the general context that the courts will not lightly look behind the terms of any written document to determine the parties intentions. Lord Penrose noted that those earlier cases that considered the possibility of an intermediate standard all involved allegations of criminal conduct in civil cases where no person was exposed to criminal penalties. He declined to apply an intermediate standard saying: "It is clear that the reason for adopting the intermediate position was in each case the nature of the allegations, and the present case raises no issues of that kind."[47]

The ambiguity over an intermediate standard has now been authoritatively settled in the five bench decision in *Mullan v. Anderson.*[48] In this case a widow whose husband had been murdered raised an action for damages against the man who had been acquitted of the murder. In her pleadings she alleged that the defender had indeed murdered her husband. The question arose as to what was the appropriate standard of proof. The appeal court reviewed many of the earlier cases and affirmed that there was a "well established principle that in civil cases the standard of proof required of a pursuer is that he prove his case on a balance of probabilities".[49]

---

[43] 1954 S.C. (H.L.) 43.
[44] at p. 63.
[45] at p. 69.
[46] 1993 S.L.T. 741
[47] at p. 745J.
[48] 1993 S.L.T. 835.
[49] at p. 842D.

THE STANDARDS OF PROOF ON THE EVIDENTIAL BURDEN

There is virtually no direct authority on the standard of proof **2.33** required to discharge the evidential burden. This is no doubt due partly to the failure of the courts formally to note its existence as a separate burden of proof, and partly to the fact that since it is not a matter on which a court normally requires formally to direct itself, or on which a judge has to advise a jury, there is little opportunity in practice for formulae to be laid down for future adoption.

In criminal cases, as we have seen earlier, on most issues the Crown bear both the persuasive and evidential burdens. It was also noted above that the standard of proof required in order to discharge the persuasive burden is proof beyond reasonable doubt. As a result, the standard of proof necessary to discharge the evidential burden on the same issue could, in theory, be any standard lower than proof beyond reasonable doubt.

What the Crown are seeking to do when attempting to discharge the evidential burden on an issue, is to produce sufficient evidence to justify the court considering that issue. To avoid a conviction the accused then needs to raise sufficient doubt over that evidence to create a "reasonable doubt" in the minds of those deciding the issue. If a reasonable doubt is raised it will prevent the Crown discharging the persuasive burden. Before that stage is reached though the Crown must produce enough evidence to make the issue a "live" one.

The court will be more likely to accept as true an item of evidence from the prosecution that the accused has not bothered to refute, since "the silent defender does take a risk".[50] This risk may be so serious as to allow a single unchallenged item of evidence from the prosecution to discharge not only the evidential burden but also the persuasive burden on that issue. As a result, in such cases the standard of proof required to discharge the evidential burden may be no more than *prima facie* evidence.

Thus in *Tudhope v. Miller*,[51] Lord Justice-Clerk Wheatley, when considering the evidential implications of an analyst's certificate under section 6(1) of the Road Traffic Act 1972[52] observed as follows:

---

[50] Lord Justice-Clerk Grant in *McIlhargey v. Herron*, n. 18 above.

[51] 1978 J.C. 26 at 27. See also *Mochan v. Herron*, n. 26 above, in which the High Court upheld the sheriff's ruling that when the Crown produce simply a *prima facie* case arising from possession of recently stolen property in criminative circumstances, this will be sufficient to discharge even the ultimate burden (*i.e.* the burden of proving the accused's guilt) if the accused offers no innocent explanation. In a rare commentary on the standard of proof required of the Crown when discharging an evidential burden, the Judicial Committee of the Privy Council, in *Jayasena v. R.* [1970] A.C. 618 at 624, said that the evidence required is "such evidence as, if believed, and if left uncontradicted and unexplained, could be accepted by the jury as proof".

[52] Now s.5 of the Road Traffic Act 1988.

> "the position is that the Crown had established a *prima facie* case under reference to the appropriate certificate, and there had been a failure to adduce evidence before the court of a sufficiently definite and conclusive nature to invalidate the evidential value of that certificate. That being so, there was but one course for the Sheriff to follow, and that was to find the respondent guilty."

In effect the Crown had provided *prima facie* evidence of the accused's guilt, which was enough to discharge the evidential burden. This evidence, having been left unchallenged by the accused, had been sufficient to discharge the persuasive burden also.

On the other hand, it may be that vigorous cross-examination by the defence of a witness called by the Crown to give the evidence that is intended to discharge the evidential burden, will result in the sheriff or judge doubting the acceptability of that evidence. The court may ultimately rule that the evidence cannot be considered or that it should be withdrawn from the jury. To this extent, therefore, the quality of evidence required to discharge the evidential burden may vary according to the strength with which it is contested. In order to overcome a strong defence challenge the prosecution may require evidence that tilts the balance of probabilities simply in order to discharge the evidential burden.

It will also be recalled that when an accused bears the persuasive burden on an issue, then only evidence on a balance of probabilities is required in order to discharge that burden.[53] It follows from this that something less than evidence on a balance of probabilities will be sufficient to warrant the issue which is raised being considered by the court (*i.e.* for the accused to discharge the evidential burden).

In *Crawford v. H.M. Advocate*[54] Lord Justice-General Cooper, in speaking of the duty of a trial judge when directing a trial jury on the issue of self-defence, said that while such an issue must be withdrawn from them if there is *no* evidence to support it:

> "If, on the other hand, there is some evidence, although it may be slight, or even evidence about which two reasonable views might be held, then he must leave the special defence to the jury subject to such directions as he may think proper."

2.34 This means that where an accused bears both the evidential and persuasive burdens on any issue, that issue must be left to the jury once the accused has adduced what amounts to only *prima facie*

---

[53] See, in particular, *H.M. Advocate v. Mitchell*, 1951 J.C. 53.
[54] 1950 J.C. 67 at 69, referred to at n. 70 above.

evidence,[55] and thereby discharged the evidential burden. This is equally applicable where the accused bears the evidential burden, but the persuasive burden rests with the Crown once the accused has discharged it. At the end of the day a "reasonable doubt" is enough for an acquittal, and Lord Justice-General Cooper's reference to "some evidence, although it may be slight", may well amount to a reasonable doubt and be sufficient to discharge the evidential burden.

In civil cases, as was seen above, the appropriate standard of proof to discharge the persuasive burden is normally proof on a balance of probabilities. It follows that the standard required to discharge the evidential burden on the same issue (which will normally be borne by the same party who bears the persuasive burden) will be something less than this.

In *Inglis v. L.M.S.*[56] the parents of a boy killed when he fell from the doorway of a moving train were held to have passed a tactical burden to the defenders once it was shown that no one, including the boy, had interfered with the door handle. It was held that this was *prima facie* evidence of negligence on the part of the defenders, in the face of which, the ensuing silence on the part of the defenders served to discharge the persuasive burden. Had the defenders countered with some evidence of their own, the court would undoubtedly have considered all the evidence in its totality. This suggests that by producing a *prima facie* case, the pursuers had discharged the evidential burden, and that this is the appropriate standard of proof for the discharge of an evidential burden in civil cases.

Similarly, in *Brown v. Rolls Royce,*[57] a case involving the contracting of industrial dermatitis, the House of Lords held that once the pursuer had raised what amounted to a *prima facie* case, then "if nothing more appeared, the Court might well infer that the defenders were negligent".[58] Again, the court was referring to the effect of a tactical burden, but was making the point in passing that a *prima facie* case is enough, in a civil action, to call for a reply. In short, a *prima facie* case will discharge the evidential burden.

It could therefore be argued that, with one exception, the standard of proof required to discharge an evidential burden on any given issue is always one level lower than the standard required to discharge the persuasive burden on the same issue. Thus, where the persuasive burden must be discharged beyond reasonable doubt then the standard required to discharge the evidential

---

[55] Assuming, of course, that it is not totally discredited in cross-examination by the Crown.
[56] 1941 S.C. 551, referred to above.
[57] 1960 S.C. (H.L.) 22, considered more fully above.
[58] *ibid.*, p. 27.

burden, when it rests with the Crown, may be as high as a balance of probabilities, unless the accused chooses to remain silent on the matter, and thus invoke the operation of a tactical burden. Where the persuasive burden requires only evidence on a balance of probabilities for its discharge, then the evidential burden on the same issue may be discharged by evidence which is really only *prima facie* in nature.

The one exception arises in those criminal cases in which the persuasive burden rests with the Crown, but the evidential burden falls on the accused. Although the evidence required to discharge the persuasive burden is proof beyond reasonable doubt, the evidential burden may be discharged by the accused by means of *prima facie* evidence only.

THE STANDARDS OF PROOF ON TACTICAL BURDENS

2.35 A tactical burden is essentially a floating burden. It needs to be discharged only when the other party has adduced evidence that calls for a reply. There is no fixed standard of proof for the discharge of a tactical burden. It is instead a matter of adducing more persuasive evidence than that adduced by the other party.

Chapter 3

PRESUMPTIONS

Introduction

Normally, a party seeking to establish the existence of a fact must **3.01** prove that fact by evidence. However, in some circumstances a party may bear a burden of proof on a particular issue, but there may be no need to lead all or any direct evidence in discharge of that burden. There are four main situations when this arises:

(i) when a presumption operates in favour of a party;
(ii) when the matter is "judicially noted";
(iii) when a matter between the parties is said to be *"res judicata"*;
(iv) when the point is formally admitted by the other party at the outset.

Judicial notice, facts which are *res judicata* and formal admissions form the subject of the next three chapters. This chapter concentrates on presumptions.

Presumptions Defined

A presumption has been defined as "an inference as to the **3.02** existence of one fact, drawn from the existence of another fact".[1] Thus, a party may offer to the court certain facts from which the court is invited to conclude that other facts must also exist. For example, the fact that an accused person charged with a crime of dishonesty is found, in "criminative" circumstances, in possession of recently stolen property, is sufficient evidence to bring into operation a presumption that he or she is guilty of a crime of dishonesty in respect of that property. Fact A (the possession, etc.)

---

[1] Dickson, *Evidence*, para. 109. See too Cross & Tapper, *Evidence*, p. 122.

51

gives rise to a suggestion that Fact B (the guilt of the accused) is established. The rationale for a presumption is that if a certain set of facts prevails, then ordinary human experience permits certain conclusions to be inferred from those facts without the need for formal proof.

In practice presumptions are found in a wide variety of contexts, and may arise either under statute or as the result of common law. In many cases their rationale is founded upon practical convenience, public policy or long usage, and in some cases they fail to reflect modern attitudes and practices. They are also so numerous that it is impossible to refer to them all in this chapter, and reference should be made to standard reference works on the substantive law for a full list.

Presumptions fall into three general categories, according to their effect on the evidence, if any, which falls to be heard once the particular presumption has been invoked. This chapter aims to distinguish between these three categories by reference to some of the principal examples from each.

The three categories are as follows:

(1) Irrebuttable presumptions of law
(2) Rebuttable presumptions of law
(3) Rebuttable presumptions of fact

In distinguishing the three categories of presumption from each other, two important considerations arise. The first is whether the presumption has a legal or a factual basis. The second is whether or not it is "rebuttable", *i.e.* can evidence be led to negative its operation. In practice the latter is more important. Each type of presumption is now examined more closely to consider the various ways in which a presumption may be rebutted.

IRREBUTTABLE PRESUMPTIONS OF LAW

GENERAL PRINCIPLE

3.03 An irrebuttable presumption of law is a fixed principle of law that cannot be "rebutted", or argued away by means of evidence to the contrary. On some occasions they amount to legal fictions, but once the basic facts which give rise to the presumption are proved, the presumed fact is thereby automatically also proved. They are said to be "irrebuttable" because no evidence, however strong, can contradict them, and they are presumptions of "law" because they can only arise from an authoritative law-making source, namely statute or common law.

It might be accurate to describe "irrebuttable presumptions of law" as "irrevocable conclusions of law", since this is in effect what they are. For a variety of reasons often connected with considerations of public policy, proof of certain facts leads to certain conclusions being drawn. These conclusions drive from the proof of certain basic facts, which brook no argument, however powerful the potential rebutting evidence. Strictly speaking, such presumptions have no place in the law of evidence, since they arise as points of substantive law and are not even arguable. But they can affect the outcome of a trial. In extreme cases they prevent any trial of an action taking place, because the party against whom such a presumption operates knows in advance that there is no prospect of persuading the court, by means of evidence, to take a different view from that prescribed by law. For example, because the age of criminal responsibility is eight years, a procurator fiscal faced with a birth certificate showing an accused child to be only seven years of age, cannot take any criminal proceedings against that child. In short, where an irrebuttable presumption of law applies, a court faced with Fact A, must, as a matter of law, reach Conclusion B. Some of the more common examples of this process are now considered.

EXAMPLES OF IRREBUTTABLE PRESUMPTIONS OF LAW

(1) Nonage as a bar to criminal trial

By virtue of section 41 of the Criminal Procedure (Scotland) Act **3.04** 1995, "it shall be conclusively presumed that no child under the age of eight years can be guilty of any offence". This "conclusive presumption", is based upon the principle that a child under eight is deemed incapable of forming the necessary *mens rea* for the commission of a crime. The effect is, of course, that no charge may be brought.

(2) Lack of sexual consent by a girl under 12

At common law, since at least the days of Hume,[2] a girl aged **3.05** under 12 has been regarded as being incapable of giving the necessary "consent" to intercourse which would reduce a charge of rape to one of a less serious sexual offence. The origin of this rule has been said to be a "legal presumption" that a girl so young cannot give effective consent in a matter so serious.[3] The offence with which an accused is charged in such a case is described by Gordon as one of "constructive rape".[4]

---

[2] Who seems to have regarded effective consent as being commensurate with the onset of puberty in a girl: see Hume, I, 303.
[3] See, *e.g. Chas Sweenie* (1858) 3 Irv. 109 at 138 and 147.
[4] *Criminal Law*, para. 33–14.

The Sexual Offences (Scotland) Act 1976 has various statutory provisions that reflect the reality of sexually active teenagers. Section 3 of the Act provides an alternative charge of sexual intercourse with a girl under 13 years, while section 15 of the Act allows the jury in a rape trial involving a girl under 13 to convict the accused of the section 3 alternative.

(3) Capacity in the law of contract

3.06   Since September 25, 1991 when the Age of Legal Capacity (Scotland) Act 1991 came into force, a child aged 16 years and over is deemed to have legal capacity. The Act is not retrospective. Prior to it a boy under 14 and a girl under 12[5] were deemed incapable of giving the consent necessary for the formation of a legally binding contract, and any contracts by a pupil had to be entered into through the medium of his or her tutor. The presumption of the pre-1991 position was reflected in the fact that any purported contract by a pupil would be regarded as a nullity.[6]

(4) Previous convictions in a defamation action

3.07   For the purposes of any defamation action in which the question whether the pursuer did or did not commit a criminal offence is relevant to an issue arising in the action, proof of a conviction of that offence is regarded as conclusive evidence of the commission of the offence. This is in terms of section 12 of the Law Reform (Miscellaneous Provisions) (Scotland) Act 1968 and is dealt with further below.

(5) Prescription

3.08   Prescription is a process whereby legal rights may be both created and extinguished by the passage of time. Such creation and extinction is achieved by the application of a conclusive legal presumption once the qualifying facts have been established. The modern law is contained in the Prescription and Limitation (Scotland) Act 1973, which deals with both "positive" and "negative" prescriptions.[7]

The effect of the positive prescription is to establish conclusively a party's right to an "interest in land". This can arise where such a right is either founded upon a recorded title accompanied by 10 years' continuous possession; or upon 20 years of such possession either in certain special cases, or where there is no foundation writ

---

[5] The ages again reflecting the legal view of the age of puberty: see Stair I, iv, 35.
[6] *McGibbon v. McGibbon* (1852) 14 D. 605.
[7] For a detailed discussion see Gloag and Henderson, *Introduction to the Law of Scotland*, Chap. 15.

which the party claiming title would ordinarily be required to register. Once the party has established these facts, and there is no evidence of any "judicial interruption" of the qualifying period of possession (*e.g.* by court action), then the effect of section 1 of the 1973 Act is to exclude "all inquiry into the previous titles and rights to the lands".[8] In short, a 10-year "prescriptive" title is valid against the whole world, and provides a good example of an irrebuttable presumption of law.[9]

The negative prescription serves to extinguish certain obligations after they have been enforceable for five, ten or twenty years,[10] and have been neither claimed by the creditor nor acknowledged by the debtor. On proof of these facts, the court has no alternative but to declare the obligation extinguished, since it is conclusively deemed to be so by statute.

CONCLUSION

Every irrebuttable presumption of law, once invoked, has the effect **3.09** of excluding further argument on the subject. Only a limited number of examples have been discussed here and numerous additional examples may be encountered under statute.[11] However, as with all presumptions, the basic facts must be established first, so that in many cases a party must appear before a court in order to establish the facts necessary for the operation of the presumption in their favour. Needless to say, if the other party is unable to refute the facts, then the point will be settled in favour of the first party.

---

[8] See Gloag and Henderson, n. 7, Chap. 15.11. So final is the effect of this presumption that it forms the basis of the modern conveyancing practice of seeking only a 10 year prescriptive process of titles when confirming that the seller has title to the subjects of the disposition.

[9] The presumption being that the title is valid. It would seem to proceed upon what Lord Chancellor Halsbury, in *Clippens Oil Co. Ltd. v. Edinburgh and District Water Trs*, 1903 6 F. (H.L.) 7, referred to at p. 8 as: "that principle of presumption in favour of long-continued use or possession, from which the presumption arises that such use or possession was lawful in its origin".

[10] ss. 6, 22A and 7 respectively of the 1973 Act as amended—the appropriate period depends upon the nature of the obligation.

[11] *e.g.* Companies Act 1985, s.13(7) of which makes a certificate of incorporation "conclusive" evidence of (i) the existence of the company from the date thereof, and (ii) compliance with all the statutory formalities of incorporation: see Gloag and Henderson, n. 7, Chap. 51.7. For a further example, see the Bills of Exchange Act 1882, s.38, which gives the holder in due course a title to a bill of exchange which is free from any defect in the title of prior parties to it: see Gloag and Henderson, n. 7, para. 23.18.

REBUTTABLE PRESUMPTIONS OF LAW

GENERAL PRINCIPLE

3.10 Like the first category, rebuttable presumptions of law are the creation of law, in the sense that they have been laid down for future reference for the courts to follow. This category of presumption, which is also known as a presumption *"juris tantum"*,[12] is just as much the creation of law as the type considered in the previous section. However, unlike the first category, a rebuttable presumption may be countered by evidence which shows that in the particular case it is unsafe to arrive at Conclusion B purely on the basis of Fact A. They are therefore said to be "rebuttable". However, unless some rebutting evidence is produced, the conclusion almost certainly will be drawn. The effect of a presumption *juris tantum* is therefore to place a burden of disproof[13] on the party against whom it operates.

Like their irrebuttable counterparts, presumptions *juris tantum* come from any valid legal source. They may even arise through commercial custom, such as the presumption arising from *apocha trium annorum*, and have on occasions developed from what were, for many years previously, mere presumptions of fact. All that is required to convert a presumption of fact into a presumption of law is that it be adopted in the *ratio* of a judgment, and thereby laid down for future courts to follow. Most of the best-known presumptions *juris tantum* are in practice judge-made, as the succeeding examples show. However, presumptions may also be created by statute. An established example of such a statutory presumption is that found in section 13 of the Bills of Exchange Act 1882, under which a bill of exchange, and any acceptances and endorsements thereon, are presumed, until the contrary is proved, to have been executed on the dates which they bear.[14]

Use may be made of statutory presumptions *juris tantum* to resolve uncertainty in many areas of law. For example, the Family Law (Scotland) Act 1985 contains two such presumptions which are designed to settle arguments over the division of moveable

---

[12] Walker and Walker, *Law of Evidence in Scotland*, para. 3.1.1.

[13] Which may be persuasive, evidential or tactical, depending upon the circumstances: see Chap. 2.

[14] This is a statutory example of the principle known for short as *omnia praesumuntur*, and is examined more fully below.

property upon the break-up of a marriage. Section 25 states that in the case of "household goods obtained in prospect of or during the marriage other than by gift or succession from a third party, it shall be presumed, unless the contrary is proved,[15] that each has a right to an equal share in the goods in question".[16]

Section 26 attempts to do the same for what used to be called the "wife's *praepositura*",[17] by enacting that in the case of "money derived from any allowance made by either party for their joint household expenses or for similar purposes, or . . . any property acquired out of such money, the money or property shall, in the absence of any agreement between them to the contrary, be treated as belonging to each party in equal shares".[18]

Statutory presumptions can also be created to achieve law reform. Thus, one proposal currently under consideration by the Scottish Executive is to extend the general terms of sections 25 and 26 of the Family Law Act 1985 to cohabitees.[19]

The next section looks in more detail at some of common examples of presumptions *juris tantum*.

(1) *Omnia Praesumuntur Rite Et Solemniter Acta Esse*

This phrase, usually referred to by its shortened name *omnia* **3.11** *praesumuntur*, means simply that there is a general presumption that where an act is performed in accordance with normal procedure, it is an act lawfully and properly done. In the words of Lord Chancellor Halsbury in *Bain v. Assets Co.*,[20] "every intendment should be made in favour of what has been done as being lawfully and properly done". This case illustrates the essentially practical considerations that lie behind the presumption. It concerned a bank that had been liquidated 20 years earlier under court supervision. It was alleged that one of the contributories to the

---

[15] A clear indication that the presumption is rebuttable, and that it imposes a persuasive burden on the other party.

[16] The section goes on, interestingly, to exclude as rebutting evidence the fact that while the parties were married and cohabiting, the goods in question were purchased from a third party (*e.g.* a shop) by either party alone or by both in unequal shares. Any alternative legal view would, of course, circumvent s.26.

[17] Repealing and replacing a somewhat similar provision under the Married Women's Property Act 1964; the new provision envisages a situation in which the wife makes an allowance to the husband, and both Acts replaced a previous common law ruling that money given to a wife for household expenditure remained the property of the husband in so far as it was not spent.

[18] Other examples of modern presumptions *juris tantum* are provided by ss.10 and 11 of the Law Reform (Miscellaneous Provisions) (Scotland) Act 1968, considered in Chap. 5; and s.280(9) of the Criminal Procedure (Scotland) Act 1995, considered in Chap. 7.

[19] See the Scottish Executive White Paper, *Parents and Children*, September 2000.

[20] (1905) 7 F. (H.L.) 104 at 106.

liquidation had not made a full disclosure of his assets. It was therefore argued that his discharge of liabilities to the bank ought to be set aside. The court, mindful of the passage of time that had elapsed since the discharge, held that the essential validity of the discharge proceeded from a lawful process that had not subsequently been challenged, and could not therefore be questioned without clear proof that it had been falsely obtained. The burden of proof was on the party seeking to set the discharge aside to show that there had not been a full disclosure at the time, and since he had failed to do so, he lost the action and the discharge stood.[21] In short, the discharge was presumed to be valid until the contrary was proved.

The time factor has also been regarded as important in other cases, such as *Sutherland v. Barbour*.[22] In this case the proprietor of a tenement comprising, *inter alia*, a shop and a house, sought a building warrant to extend his property to the street line. It was argued against him that to do so would violate the terms of a feu charter under which the land had originally been conveyed with a burden to erect a building in accordance with the title deed plan. At the date of the hearing, the plan was lost. The court held, in the absence of the plan, that since the building had been erected many years before, it must be presumed that its finished state complied with the plan, and that therefore any further building would violate the plan. It was said to be for the applicant to produce the plan in order to show that he would not be violating it, and since he had failed to do so, he lost the application.[23]

In all cases involving the presumption *omnia praesumuntur*, the use of a valid process is taken to be evidence of the validity of the action taken under that process. Thus, where a person purports without challenge to act in an official capacity, he is presumed to have been duly appointed.[24] Similarly, a decree duly recorded in old judicial records will be presumed to have been validly and properly pronounced.[25]

In *Hamilton v. Fyfe*,[26] H was convicted under a local authority closure order of keeping his shop open for longer than permitted under the order. Under the Shop Hours Act 1904, the order had the effect of a statute once it was confirmed by the then Secretary for Scotland. H argued that the order was invalid because certain

---

[21] Clearly in this case the challenging party bore the persuasive burden.

[22] (1887) 15 R. 62.

[23] Again the persuasive burden appears to have been imposed on the party against whom the presumption operated.

[24] As in *Marr v. Procurator Fiscal of Midlothian* (1881) 8 R.(J.) 21, in which the presence on the bench of an interim sheriff substitute was taken to be evidence of his appointment.

[25] *Duke of Athole v. Lord Advocate* (1880) 7 R. 583 at 589.

[26] 1907 S.C. (J.) 79.

procedures required by law prior to the making of the order had not been complied with, but the court refused to investigate this on the grounds that any earlier irregularity had been "entirely superseded" by the official confirmation. As no one had objected prior to the confirmation, the order was held to have been made *solemniter*.

The doctrine of *omnia praesumuntur* applies even to regular business or office practices, which may be used to set up a presumption that they were followed on a particular occasion simply because they are normally followed.[27] The doctrine also lies behind the principle that a "probative" writ, which appears to be in accordance with required form, is presumed to have been validly executed. This aspect of the law of evidence is now largely regulated by the provisions of the Requirements of Writing (Scotland) Act 1995.

Finally, the principle applies in cases of disputed marriage, whereby the essential validity of the marriage may be presumed from the performance of the formalities of a wedding ceremony leading to the issue of an authorised certificate.[28] The whole rationale of the principle *omnia praesumuntur* is summarised in the words of Lord Simons in *Morris v. Kanssen*,[29] who pointed out that: "The wheels of business will not go smoothly round unless it is assumed that that is in order which appears to be in order."

(2) Presumption against donation

The presumption against donation proceeds from the generally **3.12** accepted observation that people do not as a rule give away their money or possessions to strangers. Therefore, when it is claimed by A that B gave her something as a gift, the courts tend to be sceptical and to look for some other explanation for the transfer of the property. Since at least the days of Stair[30] there has been a legal presumption against the transfer of moveable property by free gift. In relation to donation *inter vivos*, McBryde states that "there is a strong presumption against outright donation. By contrast there is less of a presumption against the revocable gift constituted by *donatio mortis causa*."[31]

The presumption against donation *inter vivos*, may only be rebutted by clear evidence of (a) actual delivery by the donor to the alleged donee, and (b) intention on the part of the donor to gift the property in question. However, "it may be that, if necessary,

[27] *Edinburgh District Council v. MacDonald*, 1979 S.L.T. (Sh. Ct) 58.
[28] *Burke v. Burke*, 1983 S.L.T. 331.
[29] [1946] A.C. 459 at 475.
[30] I, viii, 2, who described it even then as "a rule in law . . . whatsoever is done, if it can receive any other construction than donation, it is construed accordingly".
[31] *The Law of Contract in Scotland*, 1987, p. 18.

comparatively weak evidence in support of one of these requisites may be eked out by comparatively strong evidence in support of the other".[32] In addition, it would seem to be incumbent on the party seeking to rely on the presumption to indicate to the court what the *real* nature of the transaction is alleged to have been. This is because: "Donation, undoubtedly, is not to be presumed; but, on the other hand, it is not to be rejected, unless some other tangible solution consistent with the whole facts of the case can be suggested; and the want of any such alternative amounts to real proof in its favour."[33]

Many of the cases that illustrate this presumption involve a variety of additional factors that complicate the issue.[34] However, a few relatively clear examples indicate the sort of circumstances in which the presumption might still be invoked. In *Grant's Trustees v. MacDonald*,[35] the court was required to examine the motivations behind a grant of money by Miss Grant, an elderly lady who lived alone and was bedridden. She had an estate of some £6,000, of which £2,000 had been placed on deposit receipt. Miss Grant had endorsed the £2,000 over to a neighbour, with the words: "I give this money in deposit receipt for £2,000 to Mrs MacDonald for anything she has had to get for me, and to do with as I have instructed her." Before Miss Grant's death, Mrs MacDonald made no attempt to have the money transferred to herself, but upon Miss Grant's death she claimed it as a gift to herself by the deceased. The court had before it no tangible evidence of any other motivation on the part of the deceased than to provide for her own requirements before death, and to leave her neighbour the balance of the money for herself. It held that the presumption had been overcome by lack of evidence of any other arrangement that was fully consistent with the facts. The neighbour was therefore held to be entitled to the money.

In *Strang v. Ross Harper & Murphy and Macdonald*,[36] a mandate was executed by the pursuer's mother, Mrs S, in respect of one-half of the sale proceeds of her house. The mandate declared that one-half of the proceeds should pass to her daughter, Mrs M, "to be held by her in an account in her sole name". Mrs S then died and

---

[32] *MacPherson's Exrx v. Mackay*, 1932 S.C. 505 at 514.
[33] Lord Jeffrey in *British Linen Co. v. Martin* (1849) 11 D. 1004 at 1011, an interesting example of the rebuttal of a presumption by negative evidence.
[34] Which may often be found entangled with other presumptions, such as that whereby services performed by A or B are presumed to have been intended to be paid for by B (see *e.g. Turnbull v. Brien*, 1908 S.C. 313—board and lodging) and that under which a loan of money attracts interest (*Smellie's Exrx v. Smellie*, 1933 S.C. 725).
[35] 1939 S.C. 448, or *Macaulay v. Milliken*, 1967 S.L.T. (Notes) 30, an action of debt where the alleged debtor claimed donation.
[36] 1987 S.C.L.R. 10.

the mandate was challenged by the pursuer who argued that the mandate did not amount to a gift and was not effective and instead the proceeds should form part of the testate estate. Upholding the pursuer's argument, the court agreed that there had been no effective transfer of funds. The crucial element of *animus donandi* was absent when the mandate was executed, there was no completed assignation in favour of Mrs M and the mandate was, in any event, revoked by the death of Mrs S.

The presumption against donation has no application to heritable property, in respect of which infeftment or physical possession under habile title are conclusive.[37]

(3) *Apocha trium annorum*

This term means "discharges for three years". According to old **3.13** authority, when a particular debt or obligation is to be repaid on a termly basis, then the possession by the debtor of receipts for payment for three consecutive terms raises a presumption that all prior instalments due have in fact been paid.[38] The principle rests upon the assumption that no creditor would allow a debtor to honour three consecutive recent debts without either demanding payment of an earlier debt or in fact "ascribing" payment to that earlier debt.[39] The presumption will not apply unless and until there are three separate receipts—one single document containing a receipt for three previous payments will not suffice, at least not according to the older authorities.[40]

Few of the leading cases are less than 100 years old and it is uncertain how far this presumption has survived into the age of computerised banking, standing orders, direct debits and electronic credit control. In one of the most recent of these cases, *Cameron v. Panton's Trustees*,[41] a widow due an annuity from her late husband's estate, was opposed in her application to court by the trustees for the estate who said the payments had been made. The court found for the widow, based on her oral evidence that she had not understood the effect of one document she had signed, coupled with the lack of probative force of another document containing five receipts which was rejected by the court as evidence of a formal discharge because it was not properly stamped.

---

[37] For which see Chap. 3 above and the presumption created by prescription.
[38] Stair (I, xviii, 2), but limited by the Institutional writers to annual or biannual payments.
[39] For which process see Gloag and Henderson, n. 7, para. 14.7.
[40] Dickson, *Evidence*, para. 177.
[41] *Cameron v. Panton's Trs* (1891) 18 R. 728.

(4) Presumptions arising from possession or destruction of documents

3.14   Over the years there has been a rich harvest of presumptions relating to possession of both property and the titles to property, and their destruction. Possession of heritable property is, as has been seen, now largely a matter of recorded title and prescription, while possession of moveable property gives rise to a factual presumption of ownership which is dealt with below. This section, therefore, concentrates on the remaining legal presumptions that surround the possession and destruction of documents that constitute evidence of title to property.

One long established presumption[42] relates to delivery of title deeds. When a deed granted by A to B is found to be in the possession of B, it is presumed to have been duly delivered, thus grounding a claim for an effective transfer of property.[43] Except in circumstances where the document in question is alleged to be held in trust by the grantee for the grantor, the presumption may be rebutted by any form of evidence acceptable to the court,[44] and the evidence required will obviously vary according to the circumstances.

In *Semple v. Kyle*[45] the court was faced with evidence of delivery by K to S of a cheque drawn by K and payable to S, a classic case for the application of the presumption. It was argued for S that he was therefore entitled to the value of the cheque as the holder in due course. The court held the presumption to have been rebutted by oral testimony from K that he had only delivered the cheque on condition that he received a separate cheque from a named third party to cover the amount in question. This was held to be effective against any indorsee who was not a holder in due course, which S clearly was not.

The presumption is based on the belief that a grantor would not voluntarily place such a document outwith their control unless they intended to make an effective delivery of it to the grantee.[46] The evidence that is normally heard in rebuttal will be of some condition attached to the delivery (*e.g.* that the alleged grantee was in fact only intended to be a custodier) which demonstrates that the grantor did not intend to lose control over it. Alternatively, of course, it may be evidence of fraud on the part of the alleged grantee.

---

[42] Referred to by Stair, I, vii, 14 and Erskine III, ii, 43.

[43] See Gloag and Henderson, n. 7, para. 37.9 for discussion of impact of presumption; and *Grant's Trs v. MacDonald*, 1939 S.C. 448.

[44] Or, to use the formal term, *prout de jure*.

[45] (1902) 4 F. 421.

[46] Which in many cases is tantamount to an effective delivery of the rights evidenced in the document. See Gloag and Henderson, *loc. cit.*

The same underlying principle—that the grantee is the only person who, by their actions, can retain or demit control of their own document—gives rise to a second presumption. This is where a document, which is known to have been made by a person and to have been in their custody, is not discovered after their death, and it is then presumed that they destroyed it with the intention of revoking it. The same is true of an undelivered deed which is found after a person's death, but in a mutilated condition. An obvious type of document to fall into this category is a will. In an action to prove the tenor of the will to show that it is still valid and effective, the terms of the original will can be proved by other means. Such means could include the continued existence of a draft.

In *Clyde v. Clyde*,[47] a testator made a will in favour of his nephew, and deposited it with his solicitors. Twelve years later it was returned to him at his request, and seven years after that he died. There was no trace of the will among his papers, but his nephew—who was also his business partner—gave evidence that the two parties had remained on good terms, and that the deceased had never evinced any intention of altering or revoking his will. It was held[48] that these facts were not sufficient to rebut the presumption that the testator had destroyed the will *animo revocandi, i.e.* with the intention to revoke it, and that he had therefore died intestate.

In assessing how much evidence must be adduced to rebut the presumption, much will depend upon the nature and purpose of the document. In particular, where the document is normally one which would be destroyed after its purpose has been served (*e.g.* a bill of exchange, cautionary obligation or revoked will), then: "the presumption is that such destruction or cancellation took place in the exercise of his power of revocation, and that presumption can be obviated only by very clear evidence to the contrary."[49]

One of the most transient types of document is an obligation of debt such as an IOU or a bond of caution, and there is yet a third presumption attached to this type of document. It is to the effect that if the document of obligation is found in the hands of the debtor, cautioner or other obligant, it is presumed that the debt or obligation which it evidenced is discharged. It is based upon a similar consideration to the two previous presumptions considered in this section, namely that the creditor has control, and would not

---

[47] 1958 S.C. 343.
[48] Relying on *Bonthrone v. Ireland* (1883) 10 R. 779, a case in which the presumption was confirmed as a "legal" (*i.e.* persuasive) one, but in which it was not required anyway because the court accepted the corroborated evidence of the deceased's daughter (who stood to gain the entire estate on an intestacy) that she had, before her father's death, destroyed the will on his instructions.
[49] Lord Guthrie in *Clyde v. Clyde*, n. 47 above at p. 345. See, too, the arguments presented in *Lauder v. Briggs*, 1999 S.C. 453.

otherwise have relinquished possession of the document which evidenced the debt or obligation.

It is obviously for the creditor seeking to enforce the document of which he or she has lost possession to explain how this came about. This must be done in terms which are fully consistent with the facts and which are sufficiently convincing to override the strong suggestion that the debt or obligation was discharged.[50]

The presumption has in fact been extended further, and now applies to all situations in which a creditor in a written obligation cannot produce the document of debt, whether it is in the hands of the debtor/obligant or not. It is for the creditor to overcome the presumption that the debt or obligation evidenced by the document has been discharged.[51]

(5) Age of child-bearing in a woman

3.15   The Court of Session, in *G.'s Trs v. G.*,[52] laid down the rebuttable presumption that, in any case where no interests are affected other than a possible unborn child, a woman of 53 years or older is incapable of child-bearing.[53] This is an example of a presumption that would be more easily rebutted today given recent advances in reproductive technology. The facilities now exist to permit women to bear children at a much later stage than was once assumed.

(6) Presumption of continuance

3.16   There is a general common law presumption[54] that conditions which are proved to have existed at one time may be presumed to have continued in existence. There are a variety of applications of this general presumption, of which two specific applications of the general rule are now considered in detail. They are the presumption of continued life and the presumed continuance of a person's domicile of origin.

(a) Presumption of continued life

3.17   At common law, there is a general presumption that human life extends for a period of between 80 and 100 years, and that, in the absence of specific indications to the contrary, a person may not be

[50] *Henry v. Miller* (1884) 11 R. 713 at 716 suggested that proof would not be restricted to writ or oath if an allegation of fraud was made. The Requirements of Writing (Scotland) Act 1995 now renders that point irrelevant as proof would not be restricted anyway.
[51] *Walker v. Nisbet*, 1915 S.C. 639 at 641.
[52] 1936 S.C. 837.
[53] For an example of a similar presumption of a man's ability, to father a child see *Munro's Trustees v. Monson*, 1965 S.C. 85.
[54] Noted by Dickson, *Evidence*, para. 114(5) and Walker and Walker, *Law of Evidence in Scotland*, para. 3.5.1.

presumed dead until he or she has reached at least the lower of these two ages. To this general rule there are now two statutory exceptions. Under the Succession (Scotland) Act 1964, where a person dies in a "common calamity"; and, under the Presumption of Death (Scotland) Act 1977 where a person disappears for at least seven years. These are dealt with below as a separate presumption of death. However, since there could be circumstances in which neither statutory provision will apply, *e.g.* if a person has not been missing for seven years, and the case is not one involving succession the common law rule may still have relevance.

One of the clearest statements of the common law rule may be found in *Secretary of State v. Sutherland*.[55] Mrs S's right to a pension depended upon the validity of her marriage to S, a point which was in turn dependent upon whether or not a previous husband was still alive. If he were still alive, he would have been 72 at the date of the hearing, but evidence was given that he had deserted Mrs S 44 years previously, and had not been heard of for the past 40 years. Mrs S had heard a rumour to the effect that he had died many years before, but she had not bothered to investigate. The underlying legal principle was neatly summarised by Lord Moncrieff,[56] who ruled that:

> "[While] in a case in which there are no special features our common law assumes life will continue up to the age of eighty years[57] or even longer, it is always a jury question in each particular case whether or not the presumption of continuance of life has been displaced. The considerations which influence a finding for or against that presumption have long been well established; either there must be direct proof of something amounting to a proper *casus amissiones*, or there must at least be facts and circumstances indicating such a break in the continuing relations of the absentee as would have been wholly out of character with his conduct had he been in life."

In the present case there was no reason why Mrs S would have seen her first husband, and indeed, in the words of Lord Normand, they "had every motive for avoiding one another". The wife therefore failed to discharge the onus of proof placed upon her of proving that he was dead, and therefore failed in her claim for pension rights as the widow of the second "husband". It was also

---

[55] 1944 S.C. 79.
[56] at pp. 85–86.
[57] The period suggested by the Institutional writers; Lord President Normand at p. 84 referred to "a period of between eighty and a hundred years."

held that the presumption of death after seven years' absence, which could be invoked under the Divorce (Scotland) Act 1938,[58] in no way diminished her burden of proof, since it was relevant only on a direct application for declarator of death and dissolution of marriage.

An illustration of the sort of circumstances in which the common law presumption may be rebutted, is afforded by *Greig v. Merchant Company of Edinburgh*.[59] G brought an action against the trustees of a fund for declarator that she was entitled to a widow's annuity because her husband must be presumed dead. In 1893 he had begun drinking heavily, his business had collapsed and he had been sequestrated. The parties had been judicially separated in 1896, and he had then left Scotland to lead a somewhat unsettled life. Until 1900 he had made spasmodic appearances in Scotland, always in reduced circumstances, in poor health and in a drunken condition. He had last been seen in 1901, after which nothing more had been heard of him despite extensive inquiries. By the date of the original action, in 1918, he would have been 61. The court granted declarator to the effect that the husband was presumed to have died as at December 31, 1910,[60] on the grounds that "the reasonable result from all the evidence is that he did not survive 1910."[61]

These cases must, of course, be considered now in the light of subsequent statutory changes explained below.

(b) Presumption of continued domicile of origin

3.18   There is a well-established common law rule[62] that a person's domicile of origin (*i.e.* the domicile acquired at birth) is presumed to continue as their domicile for legal purposes until they are shown to have acquired another domicile not only by residence (*facto*) but also by intentionally abandoning that domicile of origin (*animo*). The (persuasive) burden of proof rests with the party seeking to rebut the presumption and rely upon the new domicile.

One of the best illustrations of the presumption in use is *Liverpool Royal Infirmary v. Ramsay*.[63] B had died in Liverpool, leaving a will which was valid under Scots law but not English. It therefore fell to be decided which jurisdiction applied. This in turn raised the question of his domicile at the date of his death. He had been born in Glasgow and had spent the first 45 years of his life

---

[58] And is now subsumed under the 1977 Act.
[59] 1921 S.C. (H.L.) 83.
[60] An unusually specific choice of date, which contrasts with the normal practice under statute in such circumstances: see 1977 Act discussed below.
[61] Lord Justice-Clerk Scott-Dickson at p. 84.
[62] Noted by Dickson, n. 1, para. 27.
[63] 1930 S.C. (H.L.) 83.

there, but had moved to Liverpool to be nearer to his family. He remained in Liverpool for 37 years until his death at the age of 82, even after the last remaining member of his family had died. However, there was evidence to suggest that his continued residence in Liverpool was largely the product of lethargy.

Referring to the presumption of continued domicile of origin, Lord MacMillan[64] said that: "The acquisition of a domicile of choice is a legal inference which is drawn from the concurrence of evidence of the physical fact of residence with evidence of the mental fact of intention that such residence shall be permanent." Lord Thankerton[65] put it in more practical terms by ruling that "the appellant undertakes the burden of proving that [B] acquired an English domicile *animo et facto*; his long residence establishes the *factum*, but there remains the question of the *animus*. It seems clear on the authorities that mere length of residence by itself is insufficient evidence from which to infer the *animus*, but the quality of the residence may afford the necessary inference."

It was held that, on the facts, that B's prolonged absence in England did not rebut the presumption that his domicile was still Scotland, because there was insufficient evidence of the abandonment of the domicile *animo*.

A disputed will is one obvious context in which the question of domicile can arise. It can also be used by the living as a defence against litigation, to underpin the argument that the court has no jurisdiction over the defender.[66]

(7) Presumption of death

As was explained above, the presumption of death is entirely **3.19** statutory, the common law preferring a presumption of continued life at least until a person has reached the age of 80. There are, however, occasions upon which the common law presumption is either inconvenient or inequitable or both, and Parliament has intervened to provide a practical alternative. These occasions are identifiable under two main statutory provisions.

(a) Succession (Scotland) Act 1964, s. 31

At common law, when two persons died in what is referred to as **3.20** a "common calamity",[67] there was no presumption as to which of them died first. If, for example, father and son died in a house fire

---

[64] at p. 89.
[65] at p. 88.
[66] *McLelland v. McLelland*, 1942 S.C 502. See also *Labacianskas v. Labacianskas*, 1949 S.C. 280 for a case in which the presumption was invoked in regard to a statutory presumption of death.
[67] *i.e.* circumstances, not necessarily the same incident, in which two people are found to be dead such that it is impossible to tell which, if either, died first.

or an air crash, there would be no presumption that the son had survived the father, so as to regulate the problems of succession which might thereby arise. Some of the older authorities reveal that such a rule could clearly defeat the testamentary intentions of the parties. For example, in *Drummond's Judicial Factor v. H.M. Advocate*,[68] a man, his wife and two children were killed when their house was completely destroyed by enemy bombing. There was no evidence to show if any of the victims had lived longer than the others, and at the time of the tragedy the husband was 41 and his wife 39. Both died intestate,[69] the wife leaving in her estate some 250 war savings certificates, and legal argument ensued as to whether these fell into the husband's estate or to the Crown as *ultimus haeres*.

In finding in favour of the Crown, the court held that there was no presumption under Scots common law as to survivorship among those killed in a common calamity. Survivorship was held to be solely one of fact. In order to prove survivorship, some factual evidence was required.[70]

It was to prevent the potentially harsh operation of the common law that section 31 of the 1964 Act was enacted for the limited purpose of regulating succession. Under the section, where two persons have died in circumstances indicating that they died simultaneously, or rendering it uncertain which of them (if either) survived the other, then there is a presumption that they died in order of seniority, that is, that the younger survived the elder. To this rule there are two exceptions, so that in either of these exceptional cases the old common law rule will prevail, and no survivorship will be presumed.

The first exception is where the two persons in question are husband and wife. There is then a statutory presumption that neither survived the other.[71] This means in practice that neither of the two inherits the estate of the other, and cannot thereby pass on that estate, together with his or her own estate, to persons who may not be within the immediate family. Were the facts of *Drummond's Judicial Factor v. H.M. Advocate* to arise again, therefore, the result would be the same notwithstanding the 1964 Act.

The second exception is where the older person (*i.e.* the one presumed to have died first) has left a testamentary provision in

---

[68] 1944 S.C. (H.L.) 298.

[69] Although in the circumstances, the case would probably not have been decided differently had they left wills bequeathing their estates to members of their immediate family. Since the court was not prepared to presume survivorship by anyone in the absence of evidence, the children could not possibly inherit, whether the parents died testate or not, because not even the children could be presumed to have survived either parent.

[70] *Ross v. Martin*, 1955 S.C. (H.L.) 56.

[71] *per* s. 31(1).

favour of the younger (*i.e.* the presumed survivor), whom failing to some third party, and that younger person has died intestate. In such a case, for the purposes of that testamentary provision only, there is a presumption that the older person survived the younger, so as to prevent the older person's testamentary wishes being thwarted by the legacy passing into the younger person's intestacy. By virtue of this exceptional presumption, the legacy will pass to the third party as if the younger person had died first.

It will have been noted that the presumption only applies where two people die in circumstances that render it "uncertain" which of them survived the other. If there is evidence that one of them survived the other, then section 31 does not apply at all, not even the exceptions to it. If, for example, in the case of husband and wife it can be shown by evidence that one seems to have survived the other, then the court is not bound by the statutory presumption that neither survived the other.

This point emerged clearly in *Lamb v. Lord Advocate*,[72] a case in which a sister was claiming under the intestacy of a lady who died in a house fire along with her husband. The husband had been bedridden at the time of the fire, and his wife had rushed out into the street to summon assistance. As she did so, there was an explosion in the house which turned it into an inferno. The wife rushed back into the house in a vain attempt to reach her husband, but died in the attempt. The husband was 69 and the wife 66.

The sister argued that there was evidence to show that the husband must have died first, and that therefore his wife must have inherited his estate under his will, albeit for a brief period only. When the wife died, it was further argued, her estate contained the estate left to her by the husband, and the sister was entitled to this. On behalf of the Lord Advocate, it was argued that since it was uncertain which died first, section 31(1) applied. The husband died without heirs (having no other family) and therefore his estate fell to the Crown as *ultimus haeres*. The position was explained by Lord Wheatley thus[73]:

> "Section 31 was introduced to clarify the position, by way of legal presumptions, when a pursuer had failed to prove survivance. But if a pursuer can establish survivance, the section does not begin to apply. There is then no uncertainty . . . the question is one for determination by proof and not by presumption. There is nothing . . . which I can find to suggest that the answer to the question would be determined otherwise than by the normal standard in civil proceedings in Scotland, namely on a balance of probabilities on all the evidence."

---

[72] 1976 S.L.T. 151.
[73] at p. 153.

It was held that the pursuer had established, on a balance of probabilities, that the husband had died first, and that the sister was therefore entitled to claim from the wife's estate. This latter remark regarding standard of proof, made *obiter*, confirms that when a section 31 presumption applies, it requires evidence on a balance of probabilities to rebut it.

(b) Presumption of Death (Scotland) Act 1977

3.21   By virtue of section 1 of this Act, any person "having an interest"[74] may apply to the court for a declarator that a person who is missing is in fact dead. This may be for any legal purpose, and not just the limited one of divorce. The pursuer must produce either evidence which points to the conclusion that the missing person has died, or evidence to the effect that he or she "has not been known to be alive for a period of at least seven years."

In either case, the court need only be persuaded on a balance of probabilities,[75] and may thereafter grant declarator. Where the court is satisfied that the missing person died, the declarator must include a finding as to the date and time of death. Where this is uncertain, it may simply find that he died at the end of the period of time during which he must be presumed to have died. Where the court is satisfied merely that the missing person has not been known to be alive for a minimum of seven years, the declarator must simply state that the missing person died at the end of the day occurring seven years after the date on which he was last known to be alive.

At the same time, the court is empowered to determine the domicile of the missing person as at the time of his death, determine any question relating to any interest in property raised by his death, and appoint a judicial factor on the estate of the "deceased".[76] Once the appeal period has expired, the decree is, in terms of section 3, "conclusive" of the matters contained in it, and is "effective against any person[77] and for all purposes including the dissolution of a marriage to which the missing person is a party and the acquisition of rights to or in property belonging to any person". Even if the person in question is subsequently found to have been alive at the date specified in the decree as being the date of death, in terms of section 3(3), the marriage stays dissolved by virtue of the decree. Section 13 of the Act also provides a defence to a bigamy charge where the accused can show that at no time during the period of seven years ending with the date of the second

---

[74] Which can include the Lord Advocate, for the public interest, *per* s.17.
[75] *ibid.*, s.2.
[76] *ibid.*, s.2. See *Labacianskas v. Labacianskas*, 1949 S.C. 280.
[77] *i.e.* it is a judgment *in rem*.

marriage had he "any reason to believe that his spouse was alive". This is, of course, in the absence of any decree *per* section 2. The decree may be varied or recalled at any time by any person having an interest.[78]

(8) Presumption of legitimacy

Prior to 1986, the common law recognised three different **3.22** presumptions, each of which sought to uphold the legitimacy of a child born to a married woman, but each of which related to a different set of facts. These in turn depended upon the chronological relationship between the conception, the birth and the marriage of the mother to the putative father.

Section 5 of the Law Reform (Parent and Child) (Scotland) Act 1986, largely replaced these common law presumptions with a statutory one which provides that:

> "(1) A man shall be presumed to be the father of a child—
> > (a) if he was married to the mother of the child at any time in the period beginning with the conception and ending with the birth of the child;
> > (b) where paragraph (*a*) does not apply, if both he and the mother of the child have acknowledged that he is the father and he has been registered as such in any register kept under section 13 . . . or section 44 . . . of the Registration of Births, Deaths and Marriages (Scotland) Act 1965 or in any corresponding register kept under statutory authority in any part of the United Kingdom other than Scotland."

Subsection (4) provides that: "Any presumption under this section may be rebutted on a balance of probabilities", with the result that all the old case law[79] which established the burden of proof as being that beyond reasonable doubt is now redundant. Even when the husband denies that he is the father of the child, it will be presumed that he is (once the facts come within section 5(1)(a)), until it is proved otherwise on a balance of probabilities.[80]

---

[78] This is the effect of s.4, and may be necessary, *e.g.* when the missing person turns up, or fresh evidence is available which makes it more likely that he is still alive, or varies the date at which he may be presumed to have died. However, a dissolved marriage cannot be revived, and a variation or recall made more than five years after the original cannot affect property rights: *ibid.*, s.5.

[79] See Chap. 2, para. 2.29.

[80] Such evidence may take the form of blood tests which can be used to provide a genetic fingerprint through DNA techniques. See s.6 and Chap. 9.

The only situation in which there is now no presumption of legitimacy, either at common law or under the 1986 Act, is that in which the husband marries the mother of the child after its birth and fails to comply with the provisions of section 5(1)(b). The law on this point remains as it was laid down in *Brooks' Executrix v. James*.[81] The court in this case found itself in the difficult position of having to examine events which occurred almost 100 years previously. A woman (A) married a man (M) at a time when she already had an illegitimate child (W) aged three, and was seven months pregnant with another child (J) which was duly born after her marriage to M. No one disputed the legitimacy of J, which could presumably have been proved by means of the then common law presumption that arose when a man married a pregnant woman.[82] The parties admitted that J was M's child, thus legitimating J *per subsequens matrimonium*. But it was argued successfully that the presumption could not apply to the child (W) who was already born at the date of the marriage. As Lord Reid put it[83]:

> "There is undoubtedly a presumption that a child born during marriage is the child of the husband. But there can be no presumption that, if a man marries a woman who has an illegitimate child, that child is his child . . . Suppose a man marries a woman who has an illegitimate child of twelve, it would be absurd to presume that the child is his: that would have to be proved on a balance of probability."

There is, therefore, no presumption of legitimacy in such a case, and the court must instead look for positive evidence of legitimacy, because the burden of proof is now on the party seeking to prove that a child born outside the marriage is in fact the child of the subsequent husband. In reaching the conclusion that W was indeed the legitimate son of M, the court made use of another presumption, namely that of "common reputation".[84] This was on the basis that:

> "Where, owing to the passage of time or for other good reasons, there is no other evidence at all, then common reputation ought to be regarded as *prima facie* evidence displacing the onus of proof . . . all the information we have points to (W) having been (M)'s son, and there is nothing pointing the other way."[85]

---

[81] 1971 S.C. (H.L.) 77.

[82] *i.e.* the child was legitimated by virtue of the subsequent marriage.

[83] *ibid.*, at 81.

[84] Which has a similar underlying rationale to marriage by "cohabitation and repute", the only form of irregular marriage still recognised by law.

[85] Lord Reid, *ibid.*, at 81. The onus of proof in this instance appears to have been only on a balance of probabilities.

The presumption created by section 5(1)(b) is a totally new one, which had no forerunner at common law, under which an entry in the appropriate register was only one adminicle of evidence. The new presumption based on a register entry does not apply if the presumption created by section 5(1)(a) does, so that if Mrs A has a child while she is married to A, but it is registered in the name of B, A will still be presumed to be the father of that child. However, the register entry would perhaps serve to rebut that presumption on a balance of probabilities, particularly if A did not assert paternity.

It is possible that all presumptions in the area of legitimacy will shortly be swept away as part of the proposals for family law reform under consideration by the Scottish Executive. It is proposed that the law should be amended to do away with the concept of legitimacy, so that no person shall in future be regarded as illegitimate.[86] There would thus no longer be any need for presumptions of legitimacy, a move that is consistent with contemporary attitudes.

REBUTTABLE PRESUMPTIONS OF FACT

INTRODUCTION

The final category is rebuttable presumptions of fact. These arise **3.23** not from the operation of some established legal principle, but from the facts of particular cases derived from common human experience. In regard to a rebuttable presumption of fact, Fact A usually means Fact B, but because this is not invariably the case the court will listen to rebutting evidence. There is only one major distinction between a rebuttable presumption of fact and an item of circumstantial evidence, and this is considered below.

Because rebuttable presumptions of fact arise, not from any established principle of law, but from facts specific to a particular case, they are difficult to classify and do not make particularly reliable precedents. They are distinguishable from the single items of circumstantial evidence of which they are composed only by the fact that, as presumptions, they impose a burden of proof (and not necessarily a persuasive burden) on the party against whom they operate. This party then needs to produce some evidence in rebuttal, or the issue will almost certainly go against him or her. In the case of a single item of circumstantial evidence, on the other hand, there is no guarantee that the court will rely upon it, even if it goes unchallenged.

---

[86] The Scottish Executive White Paper, *Parents and Children*, 2000.

The main distinction between a rebuttable presumption of law and an equivalent one of *fact* is that the former is usually invoked by the production of relatively few facts which are required by law, and which are well identified in advance; whereas the latter may require a whole battery of facts of an imprecise nature before the court will be persuaded that a presumption has come into operation.

For example, as was seen earlier, the legitimacy of a person may be presumed by the relatively simple process of adducing evidence that she was born during the continuance of her parents' marriage. The point is universally recognised, and it is a simple question of whether or not the establishing facts can be proved. Once they are, then the presumption must be invoked, although it may of course be rebutted.

By comparison, a party seeking to advance their case to the point at which a presumption of fact comes into play does not know precisely which facts will have this effect, or how many different types of fact may require to be established. This is because presumptions of fact only come into operation after a certain stage has been reached on the amassed facts, at which the obvious inference from them cannot be ignored.

This process is more than simply the combined effect of various items of circumstantial evidence all pointing in the same direction. Unlike circumstantial items taken singly, the facts that together invoke the presumption of fact, also impose a burden of proof on the party against whom they operate. From that point onwards, that party will almost certainly lose on that issue if there is no rebuttal.[87] It is the aggregation of a mass of facts, virtually all of them circumstantial to the main issue, which leads to the operation of a presumption of fact.

The process of isolating and defining presumptions of fact is not assisted by two particularly common misuses of the word "presumption", namely in references to "the presumption of innocence" and "the presumption of sanity". It is commonplace for juries to be advised at the outset of a judge's charge to them that there is "a presumption of innocence" which operates in favour of the accused. This is simply another way of explaining that the persuasive burden of proving guilt rests with the prosecution. There are no basic facts that require to be proved before an accused person may be said to begin the trial with a "clean sheet". Rather, it is for the prosecution to prove the accused's guilt if they can.

By the same token, when reference is made to a "presumption of sanity", this merely reflects the requirement of law that an accused

---

[87] For examples of the process in action, see *Pickup v. Thames Insurance Co.* (1878) 3 Q.B.D. 594, especially at 599, and *Klein v. Lindsay*, 1911 S.C. (H.L.) 9.

person who wishes the court to believe that he or she was insane at the time of the commission of the offence has the persuasive burden of proof to demonstrate this. In *H.M. Advocate v. Mitchell*,[88] Lord Justice-Clerk Thomson advised the jury that on the issue of insanity, "the burden of proof is on the defence, because in our law there is a presumption that a man is sane".

This chapter is not concerned with the normal operation of the pre-ordained burdens of proof, but with the inferences to be drawn from facts adduced during the trial. This can be illustrated by examining some of the more common situations that arise in the course of a criminal trial or civil proof.

THE PRESUMPTION ARISING FROM POSSESSION OF MOVEABLE PROPERTY

It has already been seen how possession of heritable property for **3.24** the requisite period of time, together with a recorded title, forms the basis of a positive prescription which operates as an irrebuttable presumption of law. Since moveable property is not normally subject to registration of title, there cannot be the same documentary evidence of ownership as there is in the case of heritable property. Therefore, the mere fact of possession is regarded as some evidence of ownership, but is more easily rebutted.

There is accordingly a common law presumption that the person in possession of moveable property is the rightful owner.[89] The party seeking to assert "true ownership" and against whom the presumption operates, must show, "not only that the moveables once belonged to [him] but that his possession terminated in such a way that the subsequent possessor could not have acquired a right of property in them".[90]

It is clearly not enough for the party seeking to rebut the presumption to show that he or she once owned the property. Evidence must be led to eliminate any possibility that the present possessor could have acquired lawful title to it in the interim. This may be done in a variety of ways. For example, by showing that the goods were stolen from the pursuer, or proving that the present possessor is merely a custodier in the course of a business and has no right of lien over the property.[91]

---

[88] 1951 J.C. 53.

[89] Lord President Cooper in *George Hopkinson Ltd. v. Napier & Sons*, 1953 S.C. 139. See also Stair, II, i, 42, Erskine, II, i, 24 and Dickson, n. 1.

[90] Dickson on *Evidence*, para. 150, quoted with approval in *Prangnell O'Neil v. Lady Skiffington*, 1984 S.L.T. 282.

[91] Lord Cockburn in *Anderson v. Buchanan* (1848) 11 D. 270, who observed (at p. 284) that the presumption was one "liable to be rebutted, and perhaps liable to be rebutted easily."

It is very common today for a person to be in legitimate possession of goods which he or she does not own. This can arise in connection with hire purchase, auction sales and contracts involving repair or storage. As Gloag and Henderson point out,[92] "the mere fact that the true owner has allowed another to be in possession of his property will not preclude him from asserting his right as against those who purport to have acquired the property or rights over it from the possessor".

The separation of ownership from possession has become very marked in recent years, and the modern context in which the presumption arising from possession of moveable property must be judged is illustrated in the case of *George Hopkinson v. Napier & Sons*.[93] H, a Glasgow furnishing store, sold furniture to a married couple under a hire-purchase agreement. The furniture was delivered to their home, but a few months later another finance company (N) obtained decree against the couple for a different debt entirely. N sought to poind the items on hire-purchase from H, on the basis of the so-called "doctrine of reputed ownership".[94] It was held that in the absence of some personal bar operating against the true owner, the fact of possession merely established a factual presumption of ownership which was capable of being rebutted, as it was in this case. Lord President Cooper[95] warned that:

> "I do not think that it is an overstatement of the position today to say that any creditor preparing to poind the furniture in an average working-class dwelling is put on his inquiry as to whether the furniture is the property of the debtor or is only held by him upon some limited title of possession."

The class assumptions in this dictum can be discarded given the widespread use and availability of credit today, but the point remains that the mere location of goods in a house does not infer ownership on the part of the householder.

An illustration of the presumption in operation is apparent in the ruling in *Prangnell-O'Neill v. Lady Skiffington*.[96] In this case, the pursuer had lived with the defender from 1968 until 1979, with only

---

[92] *Introduction to the Law of Scotland*, para. 37.3. Note, however, the general exception to this rule (*per* Factors (Scotland) Act 1890) which gives "ostensible authority" for sale, pledge or other disposition, to a "mercantile factor".

[93] 1953 S.C. 139.

[94] A variant of the presumption now under consideration, whereby if A allows B to possess her property as apparent owner, she cannot assert her true ownership as against a third party who has relied on that apparent ownership when extending credit to B.

[95] at p. 147.

[96] 1984 S.L.T. 282.

one gap of some 18 months. He left following a deterioration in their relationship. The defender refused to allow him back into her home, although she handed over to him a number of items of moveable property that she admitted were his. The pursuer then raised an action against the defender for the return of various other items of moveable property which he claimed were his but of which she maintained possession.

It appears not to have been disputed that the items in question had at one time been the property of the pursuer. It was equally not in dispute that by the time of the raising of the action, the *de facto* possession of those items rested with the defender. Even counsel for the pursuer conceded that, in the words of Lord Hunter,[97] "the defender starts with a presumption in her favour of ownership of the articles still in dispute, that presumption, which is one of fact, being based on her possession of the said articles as at the date when the present action was raised".

The court therefore required the pursuer to show that (a) he had once been the owner of the disputed items; and (b) he had parted with possession of them in such a way that the defender could not now assert ownership. In fact, although prepared to accept that he had proved (a), the court was firmly of the opinion that he had not proved (b), because he could not even show that he had retained possession of the items in question until the parties had finally separated. On this point, the court accepted the finding of fact from the court below that the pursuer's evidence was no more persuasive than that of the defender, and that therefore, the matter being finely balanced, the defender won by virtue of the presumption.[98]

PRESUMPTION OF GUILT FROM POSSESSION OF RECENTLY STOLEN PROPERTY

It was noted in both preceding chapters that when a person is **3.25** found, in "criminative circumstances", in possession of recently stolen property, this is sometimes said to give rise to a "presumption of guilt". This presumption operates against that person on any charge of dishonesty relating to that property. However, what is really meant by this is that the prosecution have produced "a state of facts from which it is reasonable to infer guilt".[99] The presumption is therefore at best a factual one, which, at least, casts a tactical burden upon the accused who runs a considerable

---

[97] at p. 284.
[98] Clearly the court was of the opinion that the presumption imposed a persuasive burden of proof on the pursuer: see Chap. 2.
[99] Renton and Brown, *Criminal Procedure*, para. 24–02.

risk of conviction unless rebutting evidence is produced.[1] Given this reservation, we now examine those factors which bring the presumption into play.

The underlying rationale for the presumption was observed by Alison to be that[2]:

> "Possession of the stolen property recently after the theft is the circumstance of all others which most strongly militates against a panel[3]; and, unless explained by him in some way consistent with his innocence, almost always leads with sensible juries to conviction."

In the light of cases decided since the days of Alison,[4] it is unwise to take his words too literally, but they illustrate the important principle that in such circumstances "the silent defender does take a risk".[5]

The leading case is generally accepted as being that of *Fox v. Patterson*.[6] F was a scrap metal dealer charged with reset of scrap metal bought in the course of his business from a man who could not subsequently be traced. F had obtained a receipt from the man, and had thereafter resold the metal with no attempt to conceal what he was doing. He sold it for a fair price, had it weighed on a public weigh-bridge, and upon discovering that it was stolen, made an offer of repayment to his customer. At his trial F was convicted of reset, and appealed. Lord Justice-General Cooper[7] said of the presumption that had led to his conviction:

> "When applied with due regard to its limitations, the result of recent possession of stolen goods is salutary and sensible: but, if its limitations are not observed, the cardinal presumption of innocence may easily be transferred into a rash assumption of guilt."

3.26 He reiterated that mere recent possession was not enough. In addition to that, the court required some "other criminative circumstances", and he said of these constituent factors: "Even when they concur, the weight of the resulting presumption, and the evidence required to elide it, will vary from case to case."[8] In the

---

[1] See Chap. 2, and Gordon, "The Burden of Proof on the Accused", 1968 S.L.T. (News) 29 at 40.

[2] *Principles of the Criminal Law of Scotland*, p. 320.

[3] A now somewhat outmoded term for the accused in a solemn trial.

[4] Notably *Wightman and Collins v. H.M. Advocate*, 1959 J.C. 44.

[5] Lord Justice-Clerk Grant in *McIlhargey v. Herron*, 1972 I.C. 38 at 42, referred to more fully in Chap. 2. See also *McHugh v. H.M. Advocate*, 1978 J.C. 12.

[6] 1948 J.C. 104.

[7] at p. 107.

[8] at p. 108.

present case the appeal court held there was not even sufficient evidence of possession on the part of the accused shortly after the theft, let alone any evidence that he had attempted to conceal his actions. There therefore could not have been any "criminative circumstances" such as to invoke the presumption, and the conviction was set aside.

It seems from the authorities that the three constituent factors of the presumption (*i.e.* possession, brevity of time since the theft, and criminative circumstances) may be used to complement each other. Thus, strong evidence of recent possession may compensate for relatively weak additional evidence of criminative circumstances, and vice versa. As Lord Justice-Clerk Thomson put it in *Cryans v. Nixon*[9]:

> "The necessity for the presence of other criminative circumstances arises because the degree and character of possession may vary greatly, and the fact of possession may be so bare as not by itself to be incriminating. Of course, the fact of possession may be in the circumstances so suspicious that very little in the way of incriminating circumstance may be enough . . . Very different circumstances may rule according to whether a stolen article is found in an accused's pocket or in his back garden."

This case illustrates the principle well, since the stolen property had been found hidden in premises occupied by the accused, but to which others had free access. The accused, when questioned by the police, had simply stated that he knew nothing about it. Given the fact that the only evidence against him at that stage was bare possession, then the presumption could not be invoked.[10]

The necessary criminative circumstances may come from all manner of sources. In *Cameron v. H.M. Advocate*,[11] for example, the criminative circumstance that secured the accused's conviction was the fact that he ordered his wife to throw the stolen property out of the window only seconds before the police knocked on his door. In *Cassidy v. McLeod*,[12] on the other hand, it came from a persuasive series of circumstantial items of evidence.

---

[9] 1955 J.C. 1 at 5. *N.B.* that the necessary possession must occur in a personal capacity, and not, *e.g.* as an employee: *Simpson v. H.M. Advocate*, 1952 J.C. 1. In *MacLennan v. Mackenzie*, 1987 J.C. 99, possession two and a half months after the theft was held not to be "recent".

[10] Nor may the accused's silence when cautioned and charged, or thereafter, be said to constitute criminative circumstances: see *Wightman and Collins v. H.M. Advocate*, n. 4 above. A failure to answer preliminary police questions, or a false explanation, may however be sufficient—see *Cryans v. Nixon*, n. 9 above, at 6.

[11] 1959 J.C. 59.

[12] 1981 S.C.C.R. 270.

The presumption may be invoked in respect of any offence involving theft, including aggravated theft,[13] and whether the accused is charged as actor or art and part.[14] It will also support a conviction for reset.[15]

PRESUMPTION OF NEGLIGENCE: *RES IPSA LOQUITUR*

3.27 In an action arising from the alleged negligence of the defender, the courts can, in some circumstances, infer negligence on the part of the defender from the facts adduced in proof by the pursuer. The practical outcome is that if a defender does not produce evidence to show that despite appearances they were not negligent, they will almost certainly have decree pronounced against them. This could be regarded as imposing a provisional burden of proof on the defender,[16] or the imposition of a tactical burden of disproof on the defender.[17]

It is extremely difficult to generalise about presumptions of fact, and the parameters of a "presumption of negligence" doctrine are almost impossible to define. It can be seen as merely the operation of a natural principle which ensures that when one party produces a cogent case which *prima facie* points the finger of blame at the other, then that other party needs to adduce evidence to dispel the presumption created. A few examples will illustrate how widely the principle operates.

In *Inglis v. L.M.S.*[18] a railway company was found liable for the death of a young boy after offering no evidence to counter the suggestion of negligence on their part. The presumption of negligence had been raised when the boy was proved to have fallen through the carriage door of a moving train, the handle of which had not been interfered with in any way by anyone in the carriage, including the boy. Likewise, in *Gunn v. McAdam & Son*[19] a railway company was held liable for the negligence of its employees who had removed a block from under the wheel of a bogie that had been standing on an incline. The bogie careered down the incline and collided with a trolley whose operator was killed—a clear indication of negligence that was never rebutted by defence evidence.

---

[13] *Christie v. H.M. Advocate*, 1939 J.C. 72; *Cameron v. H.M. Advocate*, above.

[14] *Christie, loc. cit.*

[15] *Christie* and *Cameron, loc. cit.*

[16] The description given to the process by Walker and Walker, *Law of Evidence in Scotland*, para. 2.6.1.

[17] The more likely effect of such evidence: see Chap. 2, esp. *Brown v. Rolls Royce*, 1960 (S.C.) (H.L.) 79.

[18] 1941 S.C. 551.

[19] 1949 S.C. 31. Lord President Cooper said of the facts of this case at p. 38 that they were "clamorously calling for some explanation from [the defenders]."

Another illustration of this presumption can be seen in *Fleming v. C. & W. West.*[20] The proprietors and occupiers of a house sued an electrical contractor for damages in respect of a fire that caused severe damage in the roof area. The fire broke out within 30 minutes of the defenders' workmen having completed the installation of an electric immersion heater in the water storage tank located in the roof area. Before leaving, the workmen had declared the heater to be in satisfactory working order, and the technical evidence showed that the fire had begun in the roof area.

The court repelled the defenders' plea to the relevancy of the pursuers' averments of negligence. Lord Stewart said of the facts of the case that: "the pursuers here have averred enough to raise a *prima facie* presumption of negligence on the part of the defenders' servants and thus to entitle them to a proof of their averments, even though they have not specified in detail the cause of the fire."[21] Although the inference might well be "displaced for any number of reasons", said Lord Stewart, there was enough of a relevant case to allow the parties a proof.

There have been many other examples of the process in action over the years,[22] and each one may be taken as laying down a precedent only for future cases whose facts correspond. In fact, there would probably be no need to consider the concept of a "presumption of negligence"[23] at all were it not for one variant of it that has emerged in the past 100 years. This is the so-called doctrine of *res ipsa loquitur*. The development of this "doctrine" or principle has attracted much criticism.[24]

The doctrine emerged with the judgment of Erle C.J. in *Scott v. London and St Katherine Docks Co.*,[25] who, in dealing with a case in which a barrel had fallen from the window of a warehouse owned and operated by the defenders, offered this observation:

"There must be reasonable evidence of negligence. But where the thing is shown to be under the management of the

---

[20] 1976 S.L.T. (Notes) 36.

[21] at p. 37.

[22] *e.g. Craig v. Glasgow Corporation*, 1919 S.C. (H.L.) 1 (pedestrian knocked down when vehicle had enough time to slow down or stop) and *Moffat v. Park* (1877) 5 R. 13 (damage from a water pipe which was 30 years old and had been repaired six times in the previous 12 months).

[23] Which, after all, is only a collection of unrelated cases in which the proved facts militated strongly against the defender, and which has no apparent general principle behind it.

[24] See, for example, P.S. Atiyah, *"Res Ipsa Loquitor* in England and Australia" (1972) *Modern Law Review*, 344. For recent misapplications of the principle, see *Fryer v. Pearson and Another* [2000] T.L.R. 260 and *Dewar v. Winton*, 1999 S.C.L.R. 1014.

[25] (1865) 3 H. & C. 596 at 601. His definition of *res ipsa loquitur* was adopted into Scots law in *Milliken v. Glasgow Corpn*, 1918 S.C. 857 at 867.

defender and his servants, and the accident is such as in the
ordinary course of things does not happen if those who have
the management use proper care, it affords reasonable
evidence, in the absence of explanation by the defendants,
that the accident arose from want of care."

Taken at face value, and limited to cases in which, "a thing tells its
own story",[26] it is no more than a particular application of the
general principle already noted. This is that the facts may point the
finger so strongly at the defenders that the court will inevitably
look to them for an explanation of what happened which is at least
consistent with a lack of negligence on their part. Unfortunately,
the doctrine appears to have developed as something else, and to
have been used as authority for the statement that once something
that is involved in an accident is shown to have been under the
control of the defender, it is for the defender to show that all
reasonable care was taken. This inverts the normal operation of the
burdens of proof.

3.28   In more recent years the doctrine has been relegated to its
rightful place in the general approach to a negligence action. This
is best expressed in the words of Lord Moncrieff in *O'Hara v.
Central S.M.T. Co.*[27]:

"The characteristic of such cases is, or in my opinion ought to
be, that the action or conduct which is charged as negligent
has not been open to observation by witnesses, and so must
be spoken to by according a voice to the subsequent event
itself."

An example of such a situation is afforded by the leading modern
authority on *res ipsa loquitur, Devine v. Colvilles Ltd.*[28] In this case,
a workman at Ravenscraig steelworks was injured after leaping 15
feet from a platform on which he had been working. He did so
because of a violent explosion nearby which placed him in a state
of fear and alarm for his own safety. The cause of the explosion
was unexplained, but was known to have resulted from a fire in a
hose conveying oxygen to a converter. The oxygen came from a
plant operated by British Oxygen, and the defenders maintained
that in the circumstances they could not be held to blame.
However, further evidence established that responsibility for filter-
ing impurities from the oxygen stream lay with the defenders, who
could not prove that their filters were working properly. Even after
accepting the opinion of the court below (the Court of Session)

---

[26] The literal translation from the Latin.
[27] 1941 S.C. 363 at 388.
[28] 1969 S.L.T. 154.

that "the maxim [of *res ipsa loquitur*] is of limited ambit",[29] the House of Lords nevertheless had no doubt that this was a situation in which it applied. In the words of Lord Guest[30]:

> "The res which is said to speak for itself was the explosion. I must say that, without evidence to the contrary, I should have thought it self evident that an explosion of such violence that causes fear of imminent danger to the workers does not occur in the ordinary course of things in a steel works if those who have the management use proper care . . . [The appellants] are absolved if they can give a reasonable explanation of the accident and show this explanation was consistent with no lack of care on their part."

The court held that on the facts the defenders had failed to do so, because they had failed to show that the filters for which they were responsible had been working properly. In so doing they affirmed the view of the Lord Justice-Clerk in the court below[31]:

> "I accept their explanation of how the explosion happened, but I am unable to see how that explanation rebuts the presumption of negligence raised against them. It explains how the explosion probably occurred, but on exculpation, even at the best for the reclaimers, it is silent. The res has the last word as well as the first."

It would seem, therefore, that *res ipsa loquitur* will only normally operate where (a) there is no direct evidence of how an accident happened; and (b) the fact that the cause of the accident was something within the exclusive management and control of the defender. This becomes the starting point for the court. If the defender can rebut the inevitable inference of mismanagement that arises from such facts, all well and good, but if not, then indeed "the res has the last word". The presumption will not, however, apply when there is some direct evidence of what happened,[32] or where the offending item was not in the exclusive management or control of the defender.[33]

---

[29] Lord Guest at p. 154.
[30] at pp. 154–155.
[31] Reported at p. 155, and adopted by their Lordships in the House of Lords.
[32] See, *e.g. O'Hara v. Central S.M.T.*, n. 27.
[33] *McLeod v. Glasgow Corpn*, 1971 S.L.T. (Notes) 64; *Murray v. Edinburgh D.C.*, 1981 S.L.T. 253; *Carrigan v. Mavisbank Rigging Co.*, 1983 S.L.T. 316.

CHAPTER 4

JUDICIAL KNOWLEDGE

INTRODUCTION

4.01 "When a court takes judicial notice of a fact, as it may in civil and criminal cases alike, it declares that it will find that the fact exists, or direct the jury to do so, although the existence of the fact has not been established by evidence".[1]

Judicial notice is permissible whenever the points in issue "are matters which can be immediately ascertained from sources of indisputable accuracy, or which are so notorious as to be indisputable".[2] Examples of "notorious" matters are facts such as the streets of Edinburgh are busy during the rush hour, or that New Year's Day falls on January 1. In such cases the judge simply takes note of these facts when assessing evidence of which they are part, without even formally noting that this is what has been done. In practice, therefore, many facts are judicially noted by the courts without any formal record being made of the process in action. On some occasions a judge will take the time to acknowledge on the record what is being done. In others he or she is obliged to refer to some recognised work of authority on the subject because, although the point at issue is beyond dispute, it is not within the immediate knowledge of the judge.

The process and the legal consequences are the same in both cases—the fact judicially noted need not be argued in evidence but must be taken as proved. In general, judicial knowledge falls into two categories, one involving judicial notice without inquiry, and the other with judicial notice after inquiry.

JUDICIAL NOTICE WITHOUT INQUIRY

4.02 As already noted, a fact that may be judicially noted without inquiry is one that is "notorious", or well known to everyone. It is just as much a product of everyday human experience of life as the

---

[1] Cross and Tapper, *Evidence,* p. 67. This definition is an equally valid description of the process under Scots law. *N.B.* the terminology, also used under Scots law, whereby a fact that is within "judicial knowledge" is "judicially noted".

[2] Walker and Walker, *Law of Evidence in Scotland,* para. 11.6.1.

type of factors that give rise to a factual presumption or to circumstantial evidence. However, with judicial notice the observed fact is in most cases incontrovertible and it will be pointless for the party against whom it operates to attempt to argue it away.

There are many possible illustrations of the sorts of facts that the courts will judicially note without inquiry. For example, courts have shown themselves willing to take notice of the consequences of basic laws of mechanics that result in skids, collisions and physical injuries.[3] Only where it is alleged that something unusual occurred, or that "freak" conditions prevailed, will the parties request that the court consider the testimony of expert witnesses.[4]

In *Ballard v. North British Ry. Co.*,[5] for example, the court was considering a claim for damages arising from the fact that while on a steep incline, leading on to the quayside at Tayport, a railway wagon broke loose from a defective coupling, raced down the incline and crashed on to the deck of a ship. Although it was proved that the defect in the coupling was a latent one,[6] the court nevertheless found the defenders liable because they had placed too much strain on it, by first of all approaching the incline too fast and then braking too hard. As Viscount Haldane put it, in explaining how the court had come to this conclusion: "Of the character of such an operation, it is said that Judges must take notice of their own knowledge as men experienced in the affairs of life."

Carruthers v. Macgregor[7] provides an example of the way in which judges make use of their experience "in the affairs of life" without necessarily acknowledging that they have done so. The case concerned a claim in respect of an allegedly faulty building, where the issue was whether cracks which had appeared in the walls of a house were caused by poor quality concrete flooring or the use of unseasoned timber in the roof. Lord Blackburn observed,[8] without the benefit of expert evidence:

---

[3] Notably in run-of-the-mill cases arising from accidents involving motor vehicles. For example, a judge would be expected to accept without further need for proof the fact that, in icy conditions, a motorist should travel at a lower speed than normal.

[4] See Chap. 16. However such witnesses frequently base their own opinions on works of reference which then become part of their testimony as items of "received knowledge" on the subject—see, *e.g. Davie v. Magistrates of Edinburgh*, 1953 S.C. 34.

[5] 1923 S.C. (H.L.) 43, a case in which *res ipsa loquitur* was applied; see Chap. 3.

[6] And therefore not necessarily the responsibility of the defenders.

[7] 1927 S.C. 816.

[8] at p. 819.

"The walls being rigid, it is of course obvious that any
shrinkage of the roof beams and rafters, by drawing the top
of the walls inwards, might produce the same effects as would
be produced by an expansion of the concrete floor forcing the
base of the walls outwards."

It is regarded as one of the functions of a judge to know the
ordinary meanings of words, wherever they appear in contracts,
defamatory statements, confessions or other documents. It is only
when it is alleged that a word is being used in an unusual, or
technical context, that expert evidence will be admissible to assist
the court. One manifestation of this principle is the "parole
evidence rule" under the law of contract, which generally denies to
the parties the opportunity of contradicting apparently clear wording in a written contract.[9]

In practice the courts make use of everyday knowledge in an
impressive variety of contexts. Thus, in *Kelly v. Glasgow Corporation*,[10] the Court of Session, more than doubled the award of
damages given by the Lord Ordinary in respect of the death of a
mother of five knocked down by a Glasgow bus. The appeal court
reminded judges at first instance of their duty always to keep in
mind the falling value of money. Another civil case, *Taylor v.
Glasgow Corporation*,[11] illustrated the judicial knowledge of the
habits of children, and the fact that special precautions must be
taken to protect them from dangers which would be obvious to
adults. In *Taylor* a successful claim for compensation was made
against the operators of Glasgow Botanic Gardens by the father of
a seven-year-old boy who died from the effects of eating poisoned
berries. In *Manson v. H.M. Advocate*,[12] a criminal court took
judicial notice of the fact that witnesses in criminal trials are often
subject to intimidation.

The extent to which a matter is presumed to be within judicial
knowledge will vary according to the circumstances of the case.
Thus, in *McLelland v. Greater Glasgow Health Board*[13] Lord
MacFadyen observed that he regarded it as within his judicial
knowledge that the state makes financial provision for the maintenance of adults with disabilities. In *Doyle v. Ruxton*,[14] a case
involving alleged trafficking in alcoholic liquor without a licence,
the appeal court upheld the decision of the sheriff to rely on his
judicial knowledge that the brands of the liquor in question,

---

[9] See *Inglis v. Buttery* (1878) 5 R. (H.L.) 87 at 90, and also *Tancred, Arrol & Co. v.
Steel Co. of Scotland* (1887) 15 R. 215; affd. (1890) 17 R. (H.L.) 31.
[10] 1949 S.C. 496; 1951 S.C. (H.L.) 15.
[11] 1922 S.C. (H.L.) 1.
[12] 1951 J.C. 49 at 52.
[13] 1999 S.C. 305.
[14] 1999 S.L.T. 487.

including McEwan's Export, Guinness, and Carlsberg Special Brew, were of sufficient alcoholic strength that they would require a licence. The appellant had tried to argue that expert evidence should have been led as to the nature of the contents of the bottles and cans. In dismissing the appeal the court noted that "we found the argument that judicial knowledge did not extend to these matters somewhat unattractive and unrealistic"[15] given the wide-spread media advertising of such products. The inference from the decision is clearly that where information is widely available to the public, it can be assumed to be within judicial knowledge.

JUDICIAL NOTICE AFTER INQUIRY: GENERAL

When a matter is noted *after* judicial inquiry, it is one in which a judge has referred to some other source for verification of what is argued to be within judicial knowledge. Certain information may be incontrovertible, but not committed to memory. Thus, while an undoubted function of any occupant of the bench is to "know" Scots law on any matter which may be placed before the court, it is not unreasonable for there to be a requirement to consult author-itative books on the subject, or to peruse case reports or statutes. **4.03**

Similarly, in some cases it is necessary for a judge to consult a reference book or other learned tome before judicially noting that the matter in hand is beyond argument. When judicial notice is taken after inquiry, then the court is merely refreshing its memory on some point which it is taken to "know" anyway, and merely requires reminding of. It is a different matter if the subject is the province of a specialist, and is contested, since then the more appropriate course is to hear expert testimony and receive it as oral evidence.[16] Nor may the judge simply read a textbook and judicially note its findings.[17]

Given, then, that there is a dividing line between being reminded of the obvious, and taking unchallenged expert opinion as if it were fact, which books may the courts use in order to assist them in the pursuit of judicial knowledge? It is now well established that they may employ a dictionary, as in *Inland Revenue Commrs v. Russell*,[18] in which by reference to the *Oxford Dictionary* the Court of Session satisfied itself that a person could be the "stepchild" of another for the purposes of the Finance Acts, even though that person's natural parents were still alive. No doubt other unimpeachable sources of pure reference may also be employed without any great

---

[15] at 490 F–G.
[16] See Chap. 16.
[17] *Davie v. Magistrates of Edinburgh*, n. 4 above.
[18] 1955 S.C. 237. See also *Edinburgh Corporation v. Lord Advocate*, 1923 S.C. 112.

danger, for example Ordnance Survey maps for measurements of distance, and marine charts for ocean depths. However, although a text may be commonly regarded as a reference book, that does not necessarily raise its contents to the status of being within judicial knowledge. For example, the courts have held that the fact that there is a Highway Code is within judicial knowledge, but the stopping distances given in it are not and cannot be referred to without leading evidence.[19]

Further problems arise when what is employed is in itself a disputable work, on whose contents there can be more than one opinion. An example of this type of work is the medical or scientific textbook, which, while it may be the summation of all contemporary wisdom when it is first published, rapidly becomes overtaken by new research.[20] Such areas ought perhaps to be reserved for expert testimony, where textbooks and other academic research can be used as a secondary source and "spoken to" by the witness.

Occasions remain though when judges consider it appropriate to form their own opinions. An example of this was seen in the consideration of the normal, or likely, period of human gestation. In *Preston-Jones v. Preston-Jones,*[21] Lord Normand observed: "If the only period to be considered were the period of gestation, I have myself no doubt that ordinary men and women would unhesitatingly say that a 360-days gestation is beyond the limits of what is possible, and a court of law would so decide without evidence. So far at least judicial knowledge may be allowed to reach."

As we will see, the appeal courts have on occasions stepped in to prevent the judges from becoming instant experts on matters which ought not to be left to judicial knowledge. For the only matters which should be judicially noted, even after inquiry, are undisputed items of common knowledge. Care should therefore be taken before assuming that any standard work of reference may be employed in place of an expert witness.

With this *caveat*, some of the items that are most frequently judicially noted after inquiry are now considered.

---

[19] *Cavin v. Kinnaird*, 1994 S.L.T. 111. See also Macphail, *Evidence*, Chap. 11.35A.

[20] For example, great strides were made in the field of blood grouping in the years after the Second World War, during which period nuclear physics also emerged as a separate science. Yet textbooks on either subject published prior to 1945 would today be greatly out of date.

[21] [1951] A.C. 391 at 406. But see *Williamson v. McLelland*, 1913 S.C. 678, in which the court ignored the expert medical evidence in order to rule that a child born to a woman only 306 days after intercourse with the pursuer could not be his.

ACTS OF PARLIAMENT

It has been accepted for many years that the provisions of Acts of **4.04**
Parliament need not be proved in court, but may be judicially
noted.[22] The point is now succinctly established by the Interpretation Act 1978, section 3 of which states: "Every Act is a public Act
to be judicially noticed as such, unless the contrary is expressly
provided by the Act."[23] Section 3 is stated[24] to apply to all Acts
passed subsequent to January 1, 1979, and to all Acts passed after
1850. In practice, judicial notice is also taken of public Acts passed
by the United Kingdom Parliament from 1707 to 1850, and of
public Acts of the Scottish Parliament prior to 1707.[25] Only when
the actual contents of a statute are in dispute[26] will the court call
for authentication, in the form of a copy bearing to be printed by
the Queen's Printer or under the authority of H.M. Stationery
Office.[27]

STATUTORY INSTRUMENTS

There is some uncertainty about whether statutory instruments[28] **4.05**
are within judicial knowledge, and therefore not requiring to be
proved in court. The authority for such an assumption is challenge-
able,[29] and the authorities discussed by Walker and Walker[30]
underline the lack of clarity.

---

[22] As is required anyway of any Scots judge, all of whom are required to have
judicial knowledge of the entire law of Scotland, from whatever source. By virtue
of the decision in *Pepper v. Hart*, 1993 A.C. 593 the courts are permitted to
examine Hansard for the relevant debates where the construction of a statute is
ambiguous or obscure or the literal meaning would lead to an absurdity.
[23] This in turn is derived from the Interpretation Act 1889, s.9 and s.21(1) of the
1978 Act defines "Act" so that it "includes a local and personal or private Act".
"Subordinate legislation" means Orders in Council, orders, rules, regulations,
schemes, warrants, byelaws and other instruments made or to be made under any
Act.
[24] *ibid.*, s.22(1) and Sched. 2.
[25] Walker and Walker, n. 2, para. 19.2.1, relying on the authority of *McMillan v.
McConnell*, 1917 J.C. 43 and *Herkes v. Dickie*, 1958 J.C. 51, considered more fully
below.
[26] *e.g.* where it is alleged that the copy produced contains a misprint.
[27] Walker and Walker, n. 2.
[28] Which term has since 1948 included Orders in Council (Statutory Instruments
Act 1946, s.1(1)) and Acts of Sederunt and Adjournal (*ibid.*, s.1(2)). Acts of
Sederunt and Adjournal passed prior to that date also appear to have had
statutory effect, first under the Act 1540, c. 10, and then under the Rules
Publication Act 1893, s.4.
[29] See Macphail, *Evidence*, Chap. 11.02, who argued that there was a need for a
U.K. statute to put the point beyond doubt.
[30] n. 2, para. 19.8.1.

In *MacMillan v. McConnell*,[31] a publican was prosecuted for liquor offences under (1) the Defence of the Realm Regulations 1915, and (2) an Order of the Central Control Board (Liquor Traffic) for Scotland West Central Area. Neither of these two subordinate instruments was produced by the fiscal, and the sheriff felt himself unable to convict. It was held by the High Court that a conviction should have been entered, since the production of the relevant legislation was unnecessary because under the wartime legislation which had produced both the Regulations and the Order, they were to be regarded as equivalent to statutes. The key passage appears at page 47, where it was held that: "The law, indeed, is presumed to be known to everyone. A statute or order having the force of statute is not produced to prove what the law is, but merely to refresh the memory of the Judge or lieges."[32]

There are, however, stronger authorities for the current practice of regarding a statutory instrument as being the equivalent of an Act of Parliament. For example, in *Sharp v. Leith*[33] the accused had been convicted of the illegal movement of cattle, contrary to the Foot and Mouth Disease Order 1892, and local authority regulations which were made under the Order and given the status of statutory instruments by that Order. In rejecting an appeal based on the ground that neither the Order nor the regulations had been produced in court, Lord McLaren ruled[34]:

> "When an Act of Parliament authorises the making of Regulations, it points out the manner in which proof of such regulations is to be given, but where there is no dispute as to the existence and substance of the order or regulations,[35] it is, in my opinion, quite unnecessary, and would be quite out of place to adduce such proof. I agree that . . . if any mistake has been made in setting out the terms of the Regulations, or doubt as to the power of the Board to impose them, we should be quite willing to hear argument on these points, but it is a different proposition altogether to say that an Order having the force of an Act of Parliament[36] must be produced as a matter of evidence under a complaint charging a person with having contravened it."

---

[31] 1917 J.C. 43.

[32] Quoting the authority of Dickson, *Evidence*, para. 1105.

[33] (1892) 20 R. (J.) 12.

[34] at pp. 15–16.

[35] Where there is, then in practice it is customary to call for a Stationery Office copy: see Documentary Evidence Act 1868, s.2 and 1882, s.2 and Macphail, n. 29.

[36] Which again seems to be begging the important question of whether or not a statutory instrument does have the force or status of an Act of Parliament if the "enabling Act" does not give it such force or status.

A firmer authority is *Hutchison v. Stevenson*,[37] which concerned a conviction under the Sale of Food and Drugs Act 1875 of an offence of selling milk which did not comply in quality with regulations issued under that Act for quality control purposes. The accused appealed on the ground that the regulations themselves had not been adduced in evidence as a production. In the process of quashing the appeal on the totally unconnected ground that the correct sampling procedure had not been followed, Lord McLaren stated[38] that:

> "The production of the regulations seems to me like the production of an Act of Parliament in order to satisfy the Judge as to the existence of the law on the particular point. The regulations are not part of the proof of the contravention of the law, and therefore they are not documents necessary for the proof of the prosecutor's case."

As will have been noticed from these leading authorities, the most **4.06** likely context in which it may be argued that an item of delegated legislation such as a statutory instrument should be produced in court is in the course of a summary prosecution. The position is clear in relation to statutory instruments that are relied upon in a summary prosecution. Section 154(2) of the Criminal Procedure (Scotland) Act 1995, states that:

> "Any order by any of the departments of state or government or any local authority or public body made under powers conferred by any statute, or a print or copy of any such order, shall when produced in a summary prosecution be received in evidence of the due making, confirmation and existence of such order without being sworn to by any witness and without any further or any other proof."

There is a proviso that allows any such order to be challenged on the grounds that it was made *ultra vires* of the authority that made it, or "on any other competent ground". This is a comprehensive provision that affirms those common law authorities which held statutory instruments to be of equivalent status to an Act of Parliament.[39] As Renton and Brown observe[40]:

> "Orders etc. which do have statutory status form part of the general law of the land and need not be produced. All

---

[37] (1902) 4 F. (J.) 69.
[38] at p. 72.
[39] See the cases referred to at ns. 33 and 37 above.
[40] *Criminal Procedure*, para. 24–121.

statutory instruments fall into this class. In other cases it is a question for the court whether the particular order or regulation does have statutory force."

While the position in relation to summary criminal cases may be clear, it remains unclear whether judicial notice may be taken of statutory instruments in civil cases, or in solemn criminal cases.[41] For this reason, Macphail[42] recommended that, "it may be desirable to enact in a United Kingdom statute a provision to the effect that judicial notice shall be taken of all statutory instruments, and that in case of doubt as to their terms they may be established by reference to a Stationery Office copy".

There have been a number of cases concerning the status of the breathalysing equipment used by the police in cases where drivers are alleged to have been driving with excess alcohol.[43] In *Valentine v. McPhail*[44] the appeal court held that it was within judicial knowledge to know that the Camic device was a breathalyser of a type approved by the Breath Analysis Devices Approval (Scotland) Order 1983. It was not therefore necessary to produce the Order as evidence to prove the Camic was an approved device.[45]

The position regarding the legal status of local authority byelaws is distinct and separate. Such byelaws are another form of delegated legislation, but they do not normally arise directly "under powers conferred by any statute".[46] When they do not acquire statutory status by virtue of an enabling Act they must be produced in court as an item of evidence, and are not, for example covered by section 154 of the 1995 Act.[47]

The leading authority is that of *Herkes v. Dickie*,[48] a case in which a burgh licensing court made byelaws which required all public houses in their area to close at 1 p.m. on New Year's Day. A licensee was convicted of a contravention of these byelaws, but appealed on the ground that the byelaw in question had not been produced in court. Even counsel for the prosecutor had to concede that they should have been, and Lord Cameron[49] gave his opinion that:

---

[41] Since s.154(2) of the 1995 Act applies only in summary cases. In practice it is rare for a case involving the breach of a statutory instrument to be placed on indictment, and in many cases the enabling statute under which it was made provides for summary prosecution only.

[42] n. 2 above.

[43] *McIlhargey v. Herron*, 1972 J.C. 38

[44] 1986 J.C. 131.

[45] This case overruled the decision of *Knox v. Lockhart*, 1985 S.L.T. 248. For a discussion of the problems implicit in the judgment, see Sheriff Gordon's commentary on the case at 1986 S.C.C.R. 326.

[46] See 1995 Act, s.154(2).

[47] See Renton and Brown, *Criminal Procedure*, para. 24–121.

[48] 1958 J.C. 51. See also *Johnston v. MacGillivray*, 1993 S.L.T. 120.

[49] *ibid.*, at 58–59. See also Lord Patrick at 55.

"While it can never be suggested that a public general statute requires to be produced or proved in criminal proceedings, it has never, so far as I know, been argued that there is any such general presumption in favour of bye-laws of limited personal and local application made by a local authority . . . In my opinion, the extent to which such local orders or bye laws prove themselves is a question to be decided in each case in light of the statutory provisions which authorise the making of such orders or bye-laws and lay down the method by which their existence and validity is to be established in any legal proceedings."

Scots Law

We have already considered the extent to which judges, sheriffs **4.07** and stipendiary magistrates are expected to be aware of the effect of statutory law in so far as it forms part of the law of Scotland. It would seem that the same is true of any order having statutory effect. Such matters are deemed to be within judicial knowledge, and therefore require no proof.[50] This statement has never been challenged in the Scots courts, and both statutes and judicial precedents are quoted daily in the courts without need for proof. The practice of quoting at length from statutes and case reports is officially simply a process whereby the court's memory is refreshed. It is the duty of all those who appear in the courts to bring to the courts' attention *all* the relevant law on the matter in hand, whether it is favourable to their case or not. The judgment of the House of Lords in *Glebe Sugar Refining Corporation v. Greenock Harbour Trustees*[51] reinforced this duty:

"It is not, of course, in cases of complication possible for their Lordships to be aware of all the authorities, statutory or otherwise which may be relevant to the issues which in the particular case require decision. Their Lordships are there-fore very much in the hands of counsel, and those who instruct counsel, in these matters, and this House expects, and indeed insists, that authorities which bear one way or the other upon matters under debate shall be brought to the attention of their Lordships by those who are aware of these authorities. This observation is quite irrespective of whether

---

[50] Walker and Walker, n. 2, at para. 11.7.2: "Scots law, including Scottish judicial decisions in the House of Lords and the lower courts, and the practice and procedure of the Scottish courts, are within judicial knowledge, and evidence regarding these matters is excluded." See also Macphail, *Evidence*, Chap. 2.02.
[51] 1921 S.C. (H.L.) 72 *per* the Lord Chancellor, Lord Birkenhead at 73–74.

or not the particular authority assists the party which is so aware of it."

Therefore, whenever a matter may be said to be one of Scots law, the Scots courts are taken to be aware of it without need for proof, simply a need for the refreshment of judicial memory. The extent to which a point of law is within judicial knowledge is therefore coterminous with the extent to which the point comes under Scots law.[52] Clearly this will be true of any statute that covers Scotland, and any decision reached by a Scots court, and this latter category will include even the House of Lords, as the supreme court of appeal for all civil cases from Scotland.[53]

FOREIGN LAW

4.08 Judges of the Scottish courts are expected to take judicial notice of all Scots law, from whatever source. This will occasionally encompass the judgments of the House of Lords, on points not only of Scots law but also points from other jurisdictions that are the same as Scots law. Since the passing of the Scotland Act 1998 there is now a final right of appeal from the High Court of Justiciary in Edinburgh to the Judicial Committee of the Privy Council whose decisions are binding in all legal proceedings other than those before the Judicial Committee itself.

Since the coming into force of the Human Rights Act 1998, Scottish courts have had to take account of the judgments of the European Court of Human Rights on matters relating to the interpretation of the European Convention on Human Rights. From the implementation in 1999 of the devolution arrangements under the Scotland Act 1998, acts of the Scottish Executive and legislation from the Scottish Parliament have been subject to legal challenge on the basis that they are incompatible with Convention rights. From October 2, 2000 the Human Rights Act has had wider application and all public authorities, including the courts themselves, are bound to give effect to the Convention rights embodied in the Act, whether the legal context involves legislation emanating from Westminster or Holyrood, or the common law.

---

[52] The extent to which, in the case of judicial precedent, the court will be bound by it will of course depend upon the relative positions of the two courts (*i.e.* the trial court and the court which laid down the precedent) in the hierarchy of Scots courts.

[53] For the precise status of the House of Lords in this context, see *Trs of Orr-Ewing v. Orr-Ewing* (1884) 11 R. 600, in which it was also established that the Scots courts must defer to rulings of the House in English or Irish cases in which the point of law involved is analogous to the law of Scotland. The same is believed to be true of rulings of the Judicial Committee of a similar nature.

These principles do not generally oblige the Scots courts to note judicially any point of "foreign" law. Foreign law is regarded in the Scots courts as a question of *fact* to be proved like any other. There is, however, a rebuttable presumption of law[54] to the effect that foreign law[55] is the same as Scots law on any given point. The burden of proving that the foreign law is in fact different rests upon the party relying on that assertion.[56] The same party must also prove what that law is, and must do so by means of evidence.[57] A variety of methods may be used,[58] but the important point in the present context is that foreign law may not, as a general rule, be judicially noted.

In *Duffes v. Duffes*[59] the Court of Session refused to declare incompetent a divorce petition against the defender on the alleged grounds, (a) that he was domiciled in the American state of Ohio; and (b) that he had obtained a divorce decree against the pursuer in the Ohio courts in 1970 that was valid in Scotland. In the course of granting a proof, Lord Emslie felt himself obliged to follow "the rule that questions of foreign law are, in the Court of Session, questions of fact, which must be focused in averment . . . It may be that there is such a rule of reciprocity as the defender maintains, but I cannot notice it judicially in procedure roll where it is not admitted by the parties".[60]

To this general rule there are two broad categories of exception. First of all, as has already been noted, the House of Lords in civil cases is the highest Scottish court, and it may judicially note the laws of all the jurisdictions which also send appeals to it. For example, it would be perfectly competent when hearing a Scottish appeal for the House of Lords to note judicially and incorporate in its judgment a point of English law that did not conflict with Scots law.

---

[54] For the general nature of such presumptions, see Chap. 3.

[55] Which term encompasses the law of any jurisdiction outwith Scotland and includes English law (see *Trs of Orr-Ewing v. Orr-Ewing* n. 53 above).

[56] Anton, *Private International Law*, p. 773; see also *Bonnor v. Balfour Kilpatrick Ltd.*, 1974 S.C. 223 and *Emerald Stainless Steel Ltd. v. South Side Distribution Ltd.*, 1982 S.C. 61.

[57] Anton, n. 56, at p. 774: "The rule that foreign law must be proved by evidence is always applicable in the Scottish courts." Since any point of law discovered is for the purposes of that case a fact, it may not be founded on as a precedent for any future action: see *Killen v. Killen*, 1981 S.L.T. (Sh. Ct) 77. Where the court merely wishes to make use of a foreign jurisdiction's law and practice to aid in the construction of a contract governed by the provisions of a European directive, proof of that foreign law by expert evidence is not necessary: see *Roy v. M. R. Pearlman Ltd.*, 1999 S.C. 459.

[58] *e.g.* remit of consent to a foreign lawyer, the hearing of expert testimony, or a stated case to a Dominions court.

[59] 1971 S.L.T. (Notes) 83.

[60] at p. 84.

This process may be observed in operation in reverse in *Elliot v. Joicey*,[61] an action raised in the English courts over a will made by a woman domiciled in Scotland. It was held by the House of Lords that in the circumstances her will fell to be interpreted under Scots law, but that:

> "No doubt in the courts below[62] the law of Scotland is a matter of fact and must be vouched there by evidence or admission. But in your Lordships' House the law of Scotland is a matter not of fact but of law, for this House is the *commune forum* of both England and Scotland, and your Lordships have judicial knowledge of the laws of both countries."[63]

Secondly, there is a group of situations in which, by virtue of various statutory requirements, Scottish courts are obliged to take judicial notice of foreign law, mainly English. Thus, in *Commrs for the Special Purposes of the Income Tax v. Pemsel*,[64] it was held that when dealing with income tax cases, the Scottish courts are obliged to apply the English law of charities. The same duty is also imposed upon them in any other context in which the English charity laws are stated by statute to apply to Scottish cases.[65] Moreover, and also for the sake of uniformity, when sitting in their capacity as judges in the Courts-Martial Appeal Court, Scottish judges are required to adopt the criminal law and procedure of England, as well as its laws of evidence, since these are the basis of courts-martial hearings.[66] Finally, under the Maintenance Orders (Reciprocal Enforcement) Act 1972, and for various connected purposes,[67] certain requirements are placed upon the Scottish courts. They are required to note the law operating in any country from which a maintenance case originates if it has a reciprocation agreement with Scotland, and they must make a decision in conformity with the law of that country.[68]

---

[61] 1935 S.C. (H.L.) 57.

[62] *i.e.* the English courts below the House of Lords.

[63] Lord MacMillan, at p. 68.

[64] [1891] A.C. 531.

[65] An example is the Consumer Credit Act 1974, s.189, which requires the definition of "charity" to be as it is under the Income Tax Acts. In *Scottish Burial Reform Society v. Glasgow Corporation*, 1967 S.C. (H.L.) 116, when dealing with a claim for rate exemption under the 1962 Act, Lord Reid observed (at p. 122) of the effect of s. 4: "It is well settled that that means that we have to apply the English law of charities."

[66] See Courts-Martial (Appeals) Act 1968, s.2(1)(b) which provides for the appointment of Scottish judges to sit in such appeals. And, see *Hendry*, 1955 S.L.T. (Notes) 66.

[67] *e.g. per* s.7 for the confirmation of a provisional maintenance order, and *per* s.9 for the revocation of a registered maintenance order.

[68] *Killen v. Killen*, n. 57.

EC LAW

In addition to taking judicial notice of Acts of the United Kingdom **4.09**
Parliament, and Scots law from whatever source, the Scottish
courts must also now take notice of legislation emanating from the
EC. Thus, by virtue of the European Communities Act 1972,
s.2(1):

> "All such rights, powers, liabilities, obligations and restric-
> tions from time to time created or arising by or under the
> Treaties, and all such remedies and procedures from time to
> time provided for by or under the Treaties, as in accordance
> with the Treaties are without further enactment to be given
> legal effect or used in the United Kingdom shall be recog-
> nised and available in law, and be enforced, allowed and
> followed accordingly."

Section 3 goes on to require all Scottish courts to treat questions of
Community law as questions of law, and not questions of fact
which require to be proved as items of foreign law (see above). The
same section requires such courts to take judicial notice of:

> "the Treaties, of the Official Journal of the Communities and
> of any decision of, or expression of opinion by, the European
> Court on any such question as aforesaid: and the Official
> Journal shall be admissible as evidence of any instrument or
> other act thereby communicated of any of the Communities
> or of any Community institution."[69]

Under section 2(1) of the Civil Jurisdiction and Judgments Act
1982, judicial notice must be taken of the EC Convention which
gave rise to the 1982 Act, which has the force of law in Scotland. A
similar provision is laid down for decisions of the European Court
on conventions, *per* section 3(2).

HISTORY AND CURRENT AFFAIRS

It can be competent for the courts to take judicial notice of matters **4.10**
of historical fact or contemporary custom. In some cases[70] the
courts are able to do so without reference to standard works, and
without the need for any sort of inquiry, but certain cases demand

---

[69] *ibid.*, subs. (2). Even those instruments not published in the Official Journal may
be proved, per subss. (3), (4) and (5), by production of a certified true copy.
[70] *e.g.* when noting the identity of the current U.K. Prime Minister, or the existence
of a national stoppage such as the 1984 miners' strike.

some preliminary research. In *Read v. Bishop of Lincoln*[71] the House of Lords had to consider whether or not the mixing of communion wine with water was a practice at variance with the law of the Church. It was held that when the judge's own historical knowledge on such matters proved inadequate, reference might be made to historical reference works, since "where it is important to ascertain ancient facts of a public nature the law does permit historical works to be referred to".[72]

In *Renoufs Trs v. Haining*,[73] the question in issue was the validity of a clause in a will which provided for payment of the salaries of two "native missionaries" to preach "the Gospel of Jesus Christ my Lord among the heathen". It was alleged that the clause fell for lack of specification, since it did not identify any particular branch of the Church from which such missionaries might be chosen. Lord Guthrie, in holding that it was not too vague in its purpose, combined history with current affairs in the course of his finding that: "Judicial knowledge involves acquaintance not only with ancient history but with present day conditions."[74]

In *MacCormick v. Lord Advocate*[75] the Court of Session found itself in the unique situation of being petitioned by two members of the Scottish Covenant Association, to interdict Her Majesty's Government from describing the present Queen as "Elizabeth II". It was argued for the pursuers that this royal title allegedly contravened an article of the Treaty of Union of 1707, and was inconsistent with both historical fact and political reality. Lord President Cooper began by judicially noting the fact that the Queen had used this title when taking the statutory oath in relation to the rights and privileges of the Church of Scotland, and that so far as he was concerned that was enough to settle the issue. He stated she had been confirmed in that title, and it was now too late for challenge. He based his judicial knowledge on his examination of the appropriate entry in the Books of Sederunt after the signed oath had been presented to the Court of Session.[76]

ECONOMIC AND BUSINESS AFFAIRS

4.11 Judicial knowledge can also be applied in the world of business and commerce, in which the Scots courts have never found difficulty in displaying a lively awareness of economic reality. Many of the most

---

[71] [1892] A.C. 644.

[72] Lord Halsbury, at p. 653.

[73] 1919 S.C. 497.

[74] at pp. 510–511.

[75] 1953 S.C. 396.

[76] Lord Russell, at p. 415, also took judicial notice of the fact that at every Coronation since 1707, the incoming monarch had been proclaimed in his or her royal styles and title, and this practice had never been challenged. His Lordship did not therefore feel that the present court was in any position to raise a challenge.

common examples[77] pass unnoticed and unrecorded in court proceedings, and only rarely will a case report contain a record of the court having consulted some indisputable source of reference before coming to a conclusion.

In *Naismith v. Assessor for Renfrewshire*[78] the rateable values of all properties in Renfrewshire were increased by a flat rate of 20 per cent, regardless of individual circumstances. In an appeal against this policy, the Court of Session held that the failure of the assessor to lead evidence in justification of the increase in the particular case was fatal to his defence of the appeal. Lord Hunter stated that although the court could take into account various known facts such as the increase in the value of houses since the 1914–18 war and the general rise in living costs, it could not apply it on a flat-rate basis to all cases, as it was conceivable that some properties had actually gone down in value. Lord Hunter observed, in relation to legislation dated from 1919 which allowed landlords to increase the "standard rents" for properties, that:

> "It is a matter of general knowledge that the increases made lawful by the latter Act are within the increases which the operation of economic causes consequent upon the war would in the ordinary case have justified landlords in exacting."[79]

The introduction of new business methods can also become a matter of judicial knowledge. In *Muirhead & Turnbull v. Dickson*,[80] the Court of Session was called upon to decide whether the payment of instalments of 15 shillings per week in respect of a piano arose under a contract of hire or a contract of hire purchase. The Lord President, referring to the relatively recently-emerged form of business finance known as hire-purchase, said of it[81]: "It is a form of contract which has become common enough in modern times, and it was judicially inquired into and noticed in the case of *Helby v. Matthews*."[82] A few years later, when examining the repayment provisions of a hire-purchase contract in *Taylor v. Wylie & Lochhead*,[83] the Lord President said: "It is quite evident that, according to the ordinary business view, the instalments will be so

---

[77] *e.g.* allowances for inflation, knowledge of contemporary industrial trends and awareness of underlying economic conditions such as unemployment.

[78] 1921 S.C. 615.

[79] at p. 264.

[80] (1905) 7 F. 686.

[81] at p. 691.

[82] [1895] A.C. 471, a House of Lords case in which the term "hire purchase" seems not to have actually been used. The term was, however, employed in *Lee v. Butler* [1893] 2 Q.B. 318, a case noted in *Helby v. Mathews*.

[83] 1912 S.C. 978 at 983.

calculated as to provide for interest on so much of the principal as is not paid. All that, I think, may be taken to be common judicial knowledge of this class of agreement."

It was observed in the *Lord Advocate's Reference No. 1 of 1992*[84] that it could not be said to fall within judicial knowledge that the Halifax Building Society was a building society within the meaning of the Building Societies Act 1986.

LIMITATIONS ON THE USE OF JUDICIAL KNOWLEDGE

4.12 There are limitations to the use and application of judicial knowledge. Judges should not make use of their own personal experience of a particular matter where direct evidence is available which might have a bearing on the subject. Judicial notice is only supposed to be taken of matters that are beyond dispute, and not those that are in issue between the parties.

The danger of invoking personal knowledge was highlighted in *Gibb v. Edinburgh and District Tramways*.[85] In this case the pursuer was seeking damages for injuries sustained when her dress was caught on an unguarded section of a tramcar which lay beneath the tramcar and between the front and back wheels. She averred in her pleadings that it should have been guarded. On appeal, after noting his own surprise that a tramcar might be so designed as the present one was averred to be, the Lord President in a sense corrected himself, by adding[86]:

> "I do not think one is entitled to use what, of course, one cannot help having—one's knowledge of the construction of ordinary tramway cars, and then making oneself into a jury to pronounce a judgment one way or the other upon whether a certain thing is an ordinary and reasonable precaution, the absence of which means fault and negligence . . . I think it can only be done by the tribunal that is to try the facts of the case."

Even when one is the "tribunal of fact" in a case,[87] it is still not the function of judicial knowledge (which merely notes the existence of a matter beyond dispute) to usurp the function of evidence on a contested matter. In *Dyer v. Wilsons and Clyde Coal Co. Ltd.*[88] an arbitrator sat to hear a claim by a workman who, despite injuries,

---

[84] 1992 S.L.T. 1010.
[85] 1912 S.C. 580.
[86] at p. 583.
[87] *i.e.* the jury, or the judge in a non-jury trial.
[88] 1915 S.C. 199.

had been declared fit for light duties. The workman argued that he should in fact receive a full disablement allowance because there was no such work to be had in the district. He cited in evidence the considerable efforts he had made to obtain it. The arbitrator, without hearing this evidence in full, found against the workman on the basis that from his own personal knowledge, there was such work available in the area. In overturning this finding on the grounds of a fundamental flaw in procedure, Lord Skerrington[89] summed up the view of the Court of Session as follows: "The arbitrator . . . pronounced a decision upon the merits based not on evidence but on his own local knowledge. I do not say that such local knowledge could not be used as an element in the proof: but the arbitrator used his local knowledge as the sole evidence in the case."

Reference has already been made to the case of *Herkes v. Dickie*,[90] in which it was held that local byelaws could not be judicially noted unless they had statutory force, or were otherwise provable without the giving of evidence. The byelaws in question (which it was held could not be judicially noted) had been made by the local burgh licensing court. The magistrate who sat in judgment over the case, who was a member of that licensing court, had been prepared to note the existence of the byelaws and their content from the fact that he had helped to draft them. Lord Patrick, in rejecting such an approach, reminded the court that "if any matter requires to be proved in a criminal prosecution, the want of proof of the matter cannot be mended by the private knowledge of the Judge".[91]

On occasions, judges seeking to make use of personal knowledge **4.13** have gone so far as to supplant or supplement expert testimony. In *Kennedy and Others v. Smith*[92] it was held that a judge might not form his own unaided opinion of the likely effect of one and a half pints of lager on a man who was not a regular drinker and who had had an empty stomach at the time. Likewise, in *Davie v. Magistrates of Edinburgh*[93] an expert witness, giving evidence on the effect of shock waves in blasting operations, made reference to a section of a pamphlet that he claimed supported his view. The Lord Ordinary rejected the expert testimony, and in doing so adopted other parts of the same pamphlet to which the expert had not referred. In disapproving this course of action, the Court of Session ruled[94] that "the Court cannot . . . rely upon such works for the purpose of displacing or criticising the witness's testimony".

---

[89] at p. 204. See also the Lord President at p. 203.
[90] 1958 J.C. 51.
[91] at p. 55.
[92] 1976 S.L.T. 110.
[93] 1953 S.C. 34.
[94] at p. 41.

Criticism has also been levelled at judges who have sought to turn themselves into witnesses by examining productions or scenes of incidents for themselves and forming their own conclusions. While a court may take a "view" of something in order more easily to understand the evidence which they are about to hear, it is not competent for this to occur independently of such evidence. Otherwise, in effect the court is simply substituting its own view, regardless of what the witnesses have to say.[95]

Finally, a matter which may be judicially noted without difficulty in a particular locality, or at a particular time, may require further inquiry, or even expert testimony, in a different locality or only a few years later. In *Oliver v. Hislop*,[96] for example, the accused was charged with an offence under a local statute which made it an offence to be caught salmon fishing by means of a "cleek". No evidence was led as to what a "cleek" was, and whether or not such a definition corresponded with the article which had been found in the accused's possession, and the sheriff felt himself unable to note judicially what a "cleek" was. On appeal, Lord Justice-Clerk Cooper held that[97]:

"I do not consider that a Border sheriff, through whose territory the Tweed flows, requires, or ought to require, to be instructed by expert or other evidence as to the meaning of the terms which have been employed in the statutory regulation of the river for a period of close on ninety years."

Similarly, in that case, the fact that knowledge can change over time was acknowledged by Lord Sorn,[98] who ruled that:

"It seems to me that the learned Sheriff-substitute was too diffident in refraining from using what I really think must have been within his own knowledge. The word 'cleek' has a dictionary meaning and it is also used in section 16 of the Act in a way which shows that in the locality and in this river it bears the meaning of what today would be more usually referred to as a gaff."

So, judicial knowledge is a variable and had these cases been heard in a city court, those involved would be forgiven if they wished to hear evidence on the precise nature of a cleek or a gaff.

---

[95] See *e.g. Hattie v. Leitch* (1889) 16 R. 1128 and *McCann v. Adair*, 1951 J.C. 127.
[96] 1946 J.C. 20.
[97] at p. 24.
[98] at p. 27.

CHAPTER 5

RES JUDICATA

INTRODUCTION

The rule of evidence known as *res judicata* prevents a matter that **5.01** has already been adjudicated, being adjudicated on a subsequent occasion. The rule was summarised by Dickson[1] thus: "When a matter has been the subject of judicial determination by a competent tribunal, the determination excludes any subsequent action in regard to the same matter between the same parties on the same grounds." It operates as a procedural bar to any further court action on the matter, and "is based upon considerations of public policy, equity and common sense, which will not tolerate that the same issue should be litigated repeatedly between the same parties on substantially the same basis".[2]

The rule is most frequently encountered in civil cases, although it is applicable in criminal cases also, as a plea in bar of retrial for the same offence. There is also a limited form of *res judicata* applicable between civil and criminal cases. The rule is one that has considerable overlap with the law of procedure and specialist texts on that subject will provide a more detailed study.[3] The remainder of this chapter considers these three contexts.

GENERAL RULE IN CIVIL CASES

The conditions to be satisfied before a plea of *res judicata* will be **5.02** accepted in a civil action were summarised in *Esso Petroleum Co. v. Law*[4] as follows: "There must have been an antecedent judicial

---

[1] Dickson, *Evidence* (3rd ed.), para. 385.
[2] Lord President Cooper in *Grahame v. Secretary of State for Scotland*, 1951 S.C. 368 at 387.
[3] For example, Maxwell, *Practice of the Court of Session*, Macphail, *Sheriff Court Practice*, and Maclaren, *Court of Session Practice*.
[4] 1956 S.C. 33, *per* Lord Carmont at 38; see also Maxwell, n. 3, at p. 196.

decree of a competent tribunal, pronounced *in foro contentioso* between the same parties (or their authors) relative to the same subject-matter and proceeding on the same grounds."

There are therefore five separate elements, all of which are considered below:

    (i)   an antecedent decree pronounced *in foro contentioso*;
   (ii)   a competent antecedent tribunal;
  (iii)   the same subject matter;
  (iv)   the same grounds of action; and
   (v)   the same parties.

ANTECEDENT DECREE *IN FORO CONTENTIOSO*

5.03 A decree *"in foro"* is: any decree pronounced in a cause after defences have been lodged. It includes every kind of decree—interlocutory, interim and final—other than a decree of dismissal[5] or a decree in absence.[6] A decree in absence is one in which there has been no appearance for the defender, or where, despite an initial appearance, defences are never lodged. Such a case is not regarded as a "defended" one.[7] It does not constitute a decree *in foro* and it cannot constitute the basis of a later plea of *res judicata*.[8] If there are no defences lodged, and no appearance entered by the defender, no plea of *res judicata* may be based on any resulting decree.

However, once the defender has entered an appearance *and* lodged defences, any resulting decree (including one granted by default) will be regarded as *in foro*, and a suitable base for a subsequent plea of *res judicata*.[9] A decree of absolvitor, for whatever reason granted, will also be sufficient to support the plea.[10]

---

[5] *Duke of Sutherland v. Reed*, (1890) 18 R. 252. The recent case of *Waydale Ltd v. DHL Holdings (UK) Ltd*, 2000 S.C. 172 reviewed the authorities in regard to the effect of a decree of dismissal and affirmed the rule that such a decree left it open to a party to bring a fresh action whereas a decree of *absolvitor* did not.

[6] Maxwell, n. 3 at p. 617. It was observed in *Gibson & Simpson v. Pearson*, 1992 S.L.T. 894 that a decree in absence might found a plea of *res judicata* if personal bar operated. For the purposes of the sheriff court, a decree *in foro* has been defined by Dobie (Sheriff Court Practice, p. 249) as: "A decree granted after both parties have been heard, and where both have been represented in the course of the process", a definition adopted in *McPhee v. Heatherwick*, 1977 S.L.T. (Sh. Ct) 46 at 47, for which see also below.

[7] *Esso Petroleum v. Law*, n. 4.

[8] *Lockyer v. Ferriman* (1876) 3 R. 882 *per* Lord Gifford at 911–912.

[9] *Forrest v. Dunlop* (1875) 3 R. 15. See also Maxwell, n. 3.

[10] Maxwell, n. 3. See *Hynds v. Hynds*, 1966 S.C 201, *per* Lord Cameron at 202 and *Waydale Ltd v. DHL Holdings (UK) Ltd* n. 5 above at p. 183.

A decree *in foro* may be set aside where it is obtained by fraud or collusion between the parties. In such a case it will cease to be a decree *in foro*.[11]

COMPETENT ANTECEDENT TRIBUNAL

Before a plea of *res judicata* will be upheld, it must be shown that **5.04** the decree *in foro* that is founded upon was issued by a "competent tribunal". This will normally be a court of law, and in Scottish civil cases the only available courts are the sheriff court,[12] the Court of Session and the House of Lords.

A decree-arbitral issued by an arbiter is binding upon the parties both in point of law and in point of fact. The position was explained in *Farrans v. Roxburgh County Council*[13] to be that once a decree-arbitral has been given, it follows that: "that decision is as good as a decree of court of a type which founds *res judicata*".

A ruling by a "tribunal" in the narrow sense of the word[14] may be sufficient to found a plea of *res judicata* in the mainstream civil courts. Generally, tribunals have exclusive jurisdiction over the matters remitted to them, subject to an appeal on a point of law only. For example, an appeal from a decision of an industrial tribunal lies first to an employment appeal tribunal and then to the Court of Session,[15] while appeals in cases relating to social security go via a commissioner to the Court of Session.[16] The legislation that establishes such tribunals normally provides that a case which comes before a tribunal cannot be raised elsewhere. Because of this privative jurisdiction granted to tribunals, it is unlikely that a case litigated before a tribunal could competently arise in the same form elsewhere, so that the question of whether a ruling by a tribunal would be *res judicata* in, say, the sheriff court is unlikely to arise in practice.

In *Turner v. London Transport Executive*[17] it was observed that since an industrial tribunal deals with statutory cases of unfair dismissal, while the traditional courts handle common law claims of wrongful dismissal, a wrongful dismissal claim would not be barred by the previous hearing of an unfair dismissal action by a tribunal arising from the same dismissal.

---

[11] See *Lockyer v. Ferriman*, n. 8, at p. 911.
[12] *Murray v. Seath*, 1939 S.L.T. 348 at 352 confirmed the competency of the plea of *res judicata* in the Court of Session when founding upon a sheriff court decree.
[13] 1969 S.L.T. 35, *per* Lord Stott at 36.
[14] *i.e.* a judicial body such as an industrial or a social security tribunal, which exist outside the traditional court structure.
[15] See Employment Protection (Consolidation) Act 1978, ss. 135 and 136.
[16] See Social Security Administration Act 1992, s.24(4)(b).
[17] [1977] I.C.R. 952.

Finally there is the problem posed by foreign decrees,[18] and the unsettled question of whether, once a case has been the subject of an equivalent decree *in foro* issued by a foreign court, the matter may be raised afresh in a Scottish court, always assuming that the latter has jurisdiction.[19] A foreign decree may found a plea of *res judicata* in the Scottish courts. There are various statutes under which foreign decrees may be enforced by Scottish courts.[20] The effect of such statutory provisions is that in cases in which they apply, the party against whom the judgment operates will normally be unable to contest the obligation thus created, but will be bound by the original judgment, and the practical outcome is the same as a plea of *res judicata* by the enforcing party.[21]

Same Subject-Matter

5.05 For the operation of the rule of *res judicata*, the matter to be litigated in the present case must have been litigated between the same parties on a previous occasion. In *Hynds v. Hynds*[22] a wife raised a divorce action in the Court of Session on the grounds of her husband's cruelty. She had earlier raised an action for separation and aliment in the sheriff court, based on the same grounds, and a joint minute between the parties in that case had led to the husband being assoilzied of consent. It was held that since the decree in the first action, had it been granted, would have kept the marriage intact, whereas the present action was raised with the intention of having the marriage dissolved, the two actions were not the same, and *res judicata* could not therefore apply. As Lord Cameron put it[23]:

---

[18] *i.e.* decrees issued by any court outwith Scotland.

[19] *Law of Evidence in Scotland,* para. 11.5.1 and see Anton with Beaumont, *Private International Law,* pp 234–237.

[20] See, *e.g.* the provisions of the Foreign Judgments (Reciprocal Enforcement) Act 1933.

[21] *N.B.* that s.10 of the Presumption of Death (Scotland) Act 1977, which makes provision for the recognition in Scotland of a declaration by a foreign court that a person domiciled or habitually resident in that country is dead, only states that such a declaration shall be "sufficient evidence of the facts so declared". The presumption is clearly rebuttable, and there can be no question of it being *res judicata* of any action in Scotland relating to the same death (*e.g.* in respect of Scottish property).

[22] n. 10 above and also *Rorie v. Rorie,* 1967 S.L.T. 75, in which *Hynds* was followed in an even clearer case in which the earlier sheriff court action had been for adherence and aliment, rather than separation and aliment.

[23] *ibid.* at pp. 203–204.

"I do not think that it alters the position that the point to be decided in evidence[24] may be the same, *i.e.* has the defender been guilty of cruelty in law towards his wife . . . a difference in the matter to be litigated, even if the *media concludendi* are identical, is sufficient to differentiate the subject-matter of the proceedings between the parties and to prevent them being regarded as identical . . . Having regard to the differences in the nature of the rights which are in dispute in the two actions . . . and the marked differences in the remedies sought and their effect if granted, I think there is no identity of subject-matter between the two actions here."

A similar case is *Ryan v. McBurnie*,[25] in which an earlier action between the driver of a car and the operators of a bus, arising from a collision between the two vehicles, had led to the award of damages to the car driver. A passenger in the bus then raised an action for damages against the car driver, who pleaded *res judicata* on the general ground that the matter in issue (*i.e.* the liability for the accident) had already been litigated. It was held that the two actions were different, since the first dealt with the injuries of the car driver (and the duty of care of the bus driver to him) while the second dealt with the injuries of the passenger (and the duties of care of both drivers to her).[26]

It could be thought that the "subject-matter" of a case was confined to the narrow legal remedy sought by the pursuer. But there is authority for a broader approach to the problem, and to ask simply: "What did the previous case decide?" The start of this process may be detected as early as *Glasgow and South Western Ry. v. Boyd and Forrest*,[27] an action for the reduction of a document. Lord Shaw rejected the suggestion that a pursuer might systematically exhaust all available legal remedies one by one in separate cases, by ruling that:

"I am not prepared . . . to assent to the proposition for instance, that an action of reduction, grounded on fraud, and failing, can be competently succeeded by another action of reduction with reference to the same document and founded on the same facts, but the ground of action being, not fraud, but, say, force and fear, or error arising from innocent misrepresentation."

---

[24] *i.e.* the *medium concludendi.*
[25] 1940 S.C. 173.
[26] See also *Mitchell's Trs v. Aspin*, 1971 S.L.T. 29, in which it was held that the issues created by the liferent of a share in an estate enjoyed by one daughter of the testator were not the same issues as arose in the case of another liferent enjoyed by another daughter.
[27] 1918 S.C. (H.L.) 14 at 30. See also Lord Kinnear in *Edinburgh and District Water Trs v. Clippens Oil Co.* (1899) 1 F. 899 at 909.

5.06 In *Grahame v. Secretary of State for Scotland*,[28] Lord President Cooper referred to:

> "a tendency which can be detected in earlier Scottish cases to concentrate too narrowly upon the precise terms of the conclusions of a summons which was corrected in the third *Boyd and Forrest* appeal, in which we were directed to look at the essence and reality of the matter rather than the technical form, and simply to inquire—What was litigated and what was decided?"

A narrower approach of the test of "what was litigated and what was decided?" was also applied in *Bacon v. Blair*.[29] This case arose from a collision between two cars. An earlier court had found that the driver of one car, A, had been 25 per cent contributorily negligent during the course of his action for damages against the driver of the second car, B. In a second action brought by C, who was the owner of the car driven by B, it had been held that A was fully liable for C's costs. The present (third) action was then brought by A against B for relief against the damages awarded against him in the second action. B argued that the entire issue of liability for the accident was now *res judicata*. However, the court held that the subject-matter of the present action had not been litigated because:

> "There is no identity of subject matter between the present action and the earlier action between the same parties, since no claim was made in the earlier action for loss which the pursuer had to pay to [C] in respect of damage to his car . . ."

Certainly, in cases involving a multiplicity of claims arising from one incident, the courts do not always seem prepared to take a broad approach and to conclude that the first action must be taken to have resolved, for all time, the question of who was to blame. Instead, the various duties of care owed by the parties to each other will be treated as separate issues. Thus in *Anderson v. Wilson*[30] the Court of Session preferred to rely on the authority of *Ryan v. McBurnie*,[31] and said of it that it was:

> "adverse to the general proposition that, where there is a multiplicity of potential claims arising out of the one motor accident, the decision on apportionment of liability reached

---

[28] 1951 S.C. 368 at 387.
[29] 1972 S.L.T. (Sh. Ct) 11.
[30] 1972 S.C. 147.
[31] 1940 S.C. 173.

in relation to one claim constitutes *res judicata* as regards the other claims".[32]

In reference to the apparently broad test laid down in *Grahame*,[33] Lord Keith[34] said: "I do not regard Lord Cooper's observations as an invitation to decide questions of *res judicata* on a broad equitable basis or otherwise than in accordance with established principles."

Part of the reason for the confusion between these two lines of authority can be attributed to the requirement that before *res judicata* will succeed as a plea, the *media concludendi* of both cases must be the same, and this additional factor is now considered.

SAME *MEDIA CONCLUDENDI*

The *media concludendi* of a case may be defined as "the grounds of **5.07** action in fact and law",[35] or "the points to be decided in evidence".[36] As such they represent the narrow factual issues raised by a case. They may be distinguished from the "subject matter" of a case, in that while the latter deals with the overall legal relationship between two or more parties (*e.g.* whether A is entitled to a divorce from B, whether C is liable to pay damages to D and so on), the *media concludendi* are the facts in issue in each case. Thus, as was seen in *Hynds v. Hynds*,[37] the question of whether or not a husband has been "cruel" to his wife is a *medium concludendi* (being both a question of fact and a conclusion in law), but one which may arise in two cases with a different subject matter (*e.g.* separation and divorce).

It is essential that the *media concludendi* is the same for the operation of *res judicata*. An earlier case will only be *res judicata* of a second case when both the subject matter and the *media concludendi* are the same. If the subject matter is different, then even though the *media concludendi* are the same, the earlier case is not *res judicata* of the second. By the same token, even if the subject matter of both cases is the same the earlier case will not support a successful plea of *res judicata* if the *media concludendi* are different. This latter point was emphasised by Lord Kinnear in *North British Ry. Co. v. Lanarkshire and Dunbartonshire Ry. Co.*,[38] who said:

---

32 *ibid.* at 151.
33 *ibid.* n. 28.
34 *ibid.* at 150.
35 Maxwell, n. 3 at p. 197. See also Lord Shaw in *Glasgow and South Western Ry. Co. v. Boyd and Forrest*, n. 27 at 28, who defined them as "the reality and substance of the thing disputed between the parties".
36 *Hynds v. Hynds*, n. 10, *per* Lord Cameron at 203.
37 *ibid.*
38 (1897) 24 R. 564 at 572. See also *Boyd and Forrest*, n. 27 above *per* Lord Shaw at 31.

"I take it to be clear that in order to support a plea of *res
judicata* it is necessary to show not only that the parties and
the subject-matter in two suits are identical, but also that the
two suits present one and the same ground of claim, so that
the specific point raised in the second has been as directly
raised in the pleadings and concluded by the judgment in the
first."

In *Malcolm Muir Ltd. v. Jamieson*[39] a money lending contract for
the sum of £60 provided for the repayment of the capital sum plus
interest of approximately £30. A clause in the contract provided
that in the event of default, the debtor was to repay the whole sum
plus interest calculated from the date of default. An earlier action
under the default clause was held to be incompetent since the
clause was unenforceable due to the rate of interest charged
thereunder being higher than that permitted by law. The creditors
therefore raised a second action for the principal sum plus 12
instalments of interest at the permissible statutory rate of interest,
but the debtor pleaded that the first action was *res judicata* of the
second. The plea was rejected on the grounds that the first case
had dealt with the pursuer's right to charge a higher interest rate,
while the present dealt only with the lawful interest in terms of the
contract. The *media concludendi* were therefore different.

In *Matuszczyk v. National Coal Board*,[40] on the other hand, it was
held that common law negligence and breach of statutory duty
leading to common law liability to an employee involved the same
media concludendi.

However, a line of authority beginning with *Glasgow and South
Western Ry. v. Boyd and Forrest*[41] has complicated matters by
apparently authorising the application of *res judicata* to those cases
in which the *media concludendi* of the second case *could* have been
raised by the pursuer in the previous action, but were not. The case
itself was a complex one involving a contract for the construction of
a section of railway line which turned out to be more expensive for
the contractors than had originally been anticipated because of a
misleading geological survey by the railway's own engineer. The
present case was the third in a series, all based on the same facts,
and in a previous action, the House of Lords absolved the railway
company on a claim by the contractors that the contract was not
binding upon them because of fraud by the railway company, and
essential error. The present case was raised by the contractors in an
attempt to secure extra payment under an arbitration clause in the
contract. It was held that the present action was *res judicata*

---

[39] 1947 S.C. 314. See also *Edinburgh Water Trustees v. Clippens Oil Co.*, n. 27 above.
[40] 1955 S.C. 418.
[41] n. 27 above.

because it was an issue which could easily have been included by the contractors in their pleadings in the previous action.

The effect of this ruling would seem to be that a pursuer, in raising an action for the first time, must take care to include in it every issue of law which can reasonably be associated with it, otherwise a later court may uphold a plea of *res judicata*, not on *media concludendi* which were raised, but on ones which might have been raised.

The same principle was clearly under consideration in *Bacon v.* **5.08** *Blair*,[42] when it was suggested that the owner of a car, who had in an earlier action sued the driver of a second car, could have included in his claim for damages a sum to represent the amount which a later court found him liable to pay to the owner of the second car. The application of the general principle was rejected by the sheriff, who ruled that:

> "I do not think it enough for the defender to say that the pursuer 'could have' included the loss which he has incurred to the owner of the other car in his original claim for damages against the driver of the other car or that he knew from correspondence of [that] claim."[43]

The reason for this was that:

> "without the gift of second sight he was not to know with certainty that (contrary to his own contention) he would be found partly to blame for the accident. It is, moreover, hard to see how he would have quantified his liability for expenses in the court of first instance and in an uncertain number of courts of appeal."

The ruling of Lord Shaw in *Boyd and Forrest* to the effect that multiple claims on the same issue were not possible where the new reasons were legal, but were possible when they were factual, was another way of referring to the principle of *res noviter*,[44] which operates in such a way as to cancel out the effect of a plea of *res judicata*.

The extent of this principle was described by Lord Blackburn in *Phosphate Sewage Co. v. Molleson*,[45] as "nearly equivalent to saying

---

[42] n. 29 above. See too, *Short's Trustee v. Chung*, 1999 S.C. 471 for circumstances where it was argued (unsuccessfully) that the remedy sought in the previous action had effectively anticipated the remedy now being sought, and that a plea of *res judicata* was justified.

[43] at p. 13.

[44] In effect, "new facts."

[45] (1879) 6 R. (H.L.) 113 at 121.

that you were taken by surprise, and have since discovered material evidence". This was a case where the pursuers sought to reopen a case in the Scottish courts (having lost an earlier one there) and having secured in the interim a favourable decree in the English courts. Lord Chancellor Cairns[46] rejected the action, on the grounds that the first Court of Session ruling was *res judicata* of the present action because:

> "it is perfectly clear, upon the statement of the present appellants themselves, that this fact was within their knowledge before their proof was led in the former action, and they were just as free to have had the record opened and to have had it stated as if it had come to their knowledge before the record was closed".

5.09   Finally, it should be noted that the operation of *res judicata* is sometimes obscured by the effect of another procedural bar known as "competent and omitted". This plea prevents a pursuer from putting forward, as a new *medium concludendi*, a ground of action which could have been pled (but was not) in an earlier case between the same parties in which the pursuer was the defender. The operation of "competent and omitted", and its rationale, were summarised by Lord Milligan in *Rorie v. Rorie*[47] as follows:

> "The plea of 'competent and omitted' is designed to deal with a situation where a defender who has been unsuccessful in an action seeks to have the decision in that action reversed on the ground that he had not put forward in the first action all the defences which he might have done. The purpose of the doctrine is to avoid endless litigation."

The way in which it does so is to set up a procedural bar against a party who seeks to reopen the case on the narrow technical ground that, because the issue had not been raised by him or her in the previous action, *res judicata* cannot apply. Any *medium concludendi* which is deemed to have been competent and omitted in the previous action will be given no consideration in assessing whether or not the first action is *res judicata* of the second.[48]

To summarise this complex topic, the following general statements may be made:

---

[46] at p. 117.
[47] 1967 S.L.T 75 at 78. See also article by P. Beaumont, "Competent and Omitted", 1985 S.L.T. (News) 345.
[48] For a case in which a plea of "competent and omitted" was upheld, see *Glasgow Shipowners v. Clyde Navigation Trs* (1885) 12 R. 695. For a more recent case in which it was repelled, see *Cantors Properties (Scotland) Ltd. v. Swears & Wells Ltd*, 1978 S.C. 310.

(i) A successful plea of *res judicata* requires that the *media concludendi* of the previous case and the present one be identical.

(ii) The *media concludendi* may be identified as the legal and factual issues in a case which lead to a legal conclusion.

(iii) The principle may extend to cover all the *media concludendi* which the pursuer could have raised in the previous case, whether or not this was done.

(iv) The *media concludendi* will not be regarded as identical if the present claim introduces new facts (*res noviter*) which were not available to the pursuer in the previous action.

(v) The *media concludendi* will not be regarded as different if the allegedly new issue raised is one which was "competent and omitted" in an earlier action between the parties in which the present pursuer was the defender.[49]

SAME PARTIES

A prerequisite of a successful plea of *res judicata* is that the action **5.10** now brought should have been litigated before by the same parties in their same capacities. If, for example, a previous action was by A against B, then it will be *res judicata* of any subsequent action by A against B, or B against A. However, it will not operate so as to prevent a subsequent action by A against C, or B against D, unless the new party is in some way *legally* associated with the former one.

For example, where one of the parties to a previous action is the agent of a party to the present action, and acting in that capacity at the time, the principal cannot reopen the action, since he or she was represented earlier. If, on the other hand, the agent was acting in a personal capacity in the first action, its outcome will not be binding upon the principal, who was not represented in it. The same would be true where the intending party in the second action has the same "interest" to protect as a party in the earlier action.

This principle was applied in *Glasgow Shipowners v. Clyde Navigation Trustees*[50] so as to prevent a shipowners' association from reopening an issue concerning the extension of certain piers with the trustees of navigation on the Clyde. In an earlier action between the trustees and a riparian owner, the interests of the shipowners had been represented by the trustees themselves. The

---

[49] It will not apparently operate where the present pursuer was also the pursuer in the earlier action—*Edinburgh Water Trs* n. 27 above.

[50] n. 48. See also *Macfie v. Scottish Rights of Way Society* (1884) 11 R. 1094, where it was held that an earlier action for declarator of a public right of way raised by a member of the public was *res judicata* as regards other members of the public.

present action was said[51] to have been rendered *"res judicata* in a litigation in which the proper interests of navigation were duly represented".

In *Allen v. McCombie's Trs*,[52] one of two beneficiaries under a trust deed raised an action against the trustees in the estate for the restoration of trust funds allegedly lost by improper investment. It was held that intimation of the action should be given to the other beneficiary, because the outcome of the action would be *res judicata* against her also. One beneficiary was taken to represent the interest(s) of the other(s).

The principle that a previous judgment is *res judicata* of a second action by the same parties concerning the same subject matter and *media concludendi,* is extended to cover all potential future litigants to the same issue whenever the original decree was one *"in rem"*. This has been defined as meaning: "A judgment of a court of competent jurisdiction determining the status of a person or thing, or the disposition of a thing (as distinct from a particular interest in it of a party to the litigation)".[53] Its effect is that it is "conclusive evidence for and against all persons whether parties, privies or strangers, of the matters actually decided".[54]

Examples of judgments *in rem* are decrees of divorce or nullity of marriage,[55] declarators of legitimacy and death, and the award of confirmation on the estate of a deceased. A decree for the reduction of a deed or contract operates as a judgment *in rem,* rendering the deed void so far as concerns not only the parties to it, but also anyone else having an interest in the subject-matter.

Where, however, a particular previous finding was not *in rem,* and the parties to the present case are not the same as those in the previous case, the doctrine of *res judicata* will not be extended so as to debar a party from reopening an issue which has not previously been litigated, and by which that party is not bound. This rule can be seen in operation in road traffic accidents that sometimes give rise to multiple claims. Where there has been a decree in an earlier court establishing the proportions of liability for the accident, that finding will not be *res judicata* in another case arising from that accident that involves different parties.

The leading case here is *Anderson v. Wilson*,[56] which arose out of a collision between a minibus and a car. In an earlier action in the sheriff court, brought by a passenger in the minibus, the court had found both drivers to blame, and had apportioned liability between

---

[51] *per* Lord Shand at p. 701.
[52] 1909 S.C. 710.
[53] Halsbury's *Laws of England* (Hailsham, ed.), Vol. 13, p. 405.
[54] *Lazarus-Barlow v. Regent Estates Co. Ltd.* [1949] 2 K.B. 465 at 475.
[55] See, *e.g. Administrator of Austrian Property v. Von Lorang,* 1926 S.C. 598 at 622, 1927 S.C. (H.L.) 80; and *Murray v. Murray,* 1956 S.C. 376.
[56] 1972 S.C. 147.

the employer of the bus driver and the judicial factor on the estate of the car driver. In a subsequent action in the Court of Session five other passengers in the minibus sued both drivers for damages. The court accepted that the original action was not *res judicata* as between the new pursuers and the defenders, but it was argued that at least the question of the liability of the two drivers *inter se* had been settled for all time. Counsel for the employer of the bus driver urged the court to regard "the true issue to be simply what person or persons were to blame for the accident, and, if more than one person were to blame, in what proportions they were to blame".[57] Counsel urged adoption of the approach suggested by Lord President Cooper in *Grahame v. Secretary of State for Scotland*[58] and to ask simply, of the first case: "What was litigated and what was decided?"

Lord Keith, however, was not prepared to follow this line of reasoning because he felt that it "would involve some departure from, or at least significant extension of, the principles which have hitherto governed *res judicata* in the law of Scotland".[59] Nor did he regard "Lord Cooper's observations as an invitation to decide questions of *res judicata* on a broad equitable basis or otherwise than in accordance with established principles".[60] He therefore approved for jury trial all the issues raised by the present action, including the proportions of liability for the accident.

It would seem therefore, under Scots law as presently formulated, that provided that the true identity of one of the parties to a subsequent case is different from those in an earlier case, no finding of fact from that earlier case will be *res judicata*.[61] This creates an obvious risk "that in comparatively simple cases different courts will reach different decisions on the same issues of fact and the same evidence".[62]

However, this does not mean that a finding in a previous civil **5.11** case between different parties will always be without any legal significance. In two particular instances, both created by section 11 of the Law Reform (Miscellaneous Provisions) (Scotland) Act 1968, findings in earlier civil proceedings give rise to presumptions in subsequent civil cases. The material part of section 11 states as follows:

"In any civil proceedings—

> (a) the fact that a person has been found guilty of adultery in any matrimonial proceedings, and

---

[57] at p. 150.
[58] n. 2 above.
[59] at p. 153.
[60] at p. 150.
[61] Unless, of course, the previous finding was *in rem*.
[62] Macphail, *Evidence*, Chap. 11.28.

(b) the fact that a person has been found to be the
father of a child in affiliation proceedings in any
court in the United Kingdom,

shall ... be admissible in evidence for the purpose of
proving, where to do so is relevant to any issue in those civil
proceedings, that he committed the adultery to which the
finding relates or, as the case may be, is (or was) the father of
that child, whether or not he offered any defence to the
allegation of adultery or paternity and whether or not he is a
party to the civil proceedings; but no finding other than a
subsisting one shall be admissible in evidence by virtue of this
section."[63]

Subsection (2) goes on to make the finding in each case probative
"unless the contrary is proved", which clearly places a persuasive
burden on the party seeking to disprove the point, who may not of
course be the party to whom the finding relates. The subsection
also renders admissible in the subsequent proceedings, as evidence
of "the facts on which the finding was based, the contents of any
document which was before the court, or which contains any
pronouncement of the court" in the earlier proceedings. The
definition of "matrimonial proceedings" for the purpose of
section 11 is extended so as to cover proceedings in the English,
Welsh or Northern Irish courts, so that both presumptions apply to
any competent United Kingdom findings.

Leaving aside the implications of the section so far as concerns
the law on presumptions,[64] the section does create a situation in
which a finding from an earlier hearing will have evidential effect
in a subsequent case in which the parties are different. If, for
example, A is found to be the father of X in affiliation proceedings
brought by X's mother, B, then when A dies, X may use the finding
against other claimants on A's estate.

Another potential use of the section is in a case in which A has
been found guilty of adultery with Mrs B in an action for divorce
raised by B. That finding may then be relied upon in an action for
divorce by Mrs A against A, based on the *same* act of adultery.
Prior to section 11, a finding by a court that B had committed
adultery with A was not regarded, in subsequent proceedings, as
evidence that A had committed adultery with B.[65]

Section 11 may also be applied where the parties in the present
case are the same as in the previous case. This could arise, for
example, where a wife wishes to rely upon a decree of judicial

---

[63] *ibid*., subs. (1).
[64] These are dealt with more fully in Chap. 3.
[65] See Clive, *Husband and Wife*, p. 505. But see *Andrews v. Andrews,* 1971 S.L.T. 44.

separation on the grounds of her husband's adultery as evidence in pursuance of a subsequent divorce action.[66]

RES JUDICATA IN CRIMINAL CASES

As a general rule, the two parties in a criminal case will always be **5.12** the Crown and the accused, and the *media concludendi, i.e.* the guilt or innocence of the accused, are always the same. As a result, in practice the application of *res judicata* in a criminal case is limited to the question of whether, when a previous trial of A is followed by another trial, the "subject-matter" is the same and has been fully litigated. If so, then *res judicata* will apply; if not, then it will not. When *res judicata* does apply, the accused is said to have "tholed his assize".[67]

(1) Matter fully litigated

It was noted, when examining the application of the principles of **5.13** *res judicata* to civil cases, that a when a civil action was dismissed it was not regarded as having created a decree *in foro* sufficient to form the basis of a later plea of *res judicata*. The same principle applies in criminal cases, at least where the matter is being raised subsequently in the High Court, on the ground that "the justiciary court could not be held bound by the decision of an inferior judge".[68] The position is different where the issue claimed to be *res judicata* is raised in the same court. In *Longmuir v. Baxter*[69] it was held that the prosecution could not proceed, before the sheriff, on a libel which the sheriff-substitute had earlier rejected as irrelevant.

In a criminal case, the equivalent of a decree in foro in a civil case, is a finding of guilt, a formal admission of guilt, or a finding of not guilty or not proven.[70] The same result is achieved by a

---

[66] Which is not *res judicata* because the subject-matter is different in the two cases: see *Hynds v. Hynds* n.10 above; and s.3(1) of the Divorce (Scotland) Act 1976, which has the same effect for other grounds of separation/divorce.

[67] See generally Renton and Brown, *Criminal Procedure*, para. 9–08—9–31/1.

[68] *George Fleming* (1866) 5 Irv. 289 at 292.

[69] (1858) 3 Irv. 287, which was followed in *McNab*, Petitioner; *H.M. Advocate v. McNab*, 1994 S.C.C.R. 633.

[70] *N.B.* that in all cases the court must be one of "competent Jurisdiction"—*i.e.* it must be a district court, a sheriff court or the High Court, and must be acting within its jurisdiction. But it would also seem that the accused can plead tholed assize when he has been tried by an English court in a case in which a crime could also have been charged in Scotland (*e.g.* a fraud by an English based company advertising in Scotland); see Renton and Brown, n. 67.

desertion *simpliciter*,[71] which, whether it comes from a Crown motion or from the court *ex proprio motu*, has the effect of terminating the Crown criminal process in respect of those particular charges for all time.[72]

When an accused pleads not guilty and proceeds to trial, *res judicata* will not apply[73] unless and until "the trial, properly conducted, has concluded in a determination of the issue of guilt or innocence".[74] When an accused pleads guilty before the trial has commenced,[75] a different rule apparently applies, and the accused has not tholed his assize until he has been sentenced.[76] In fact, it may now be the case that the principles of *res judicata* do not apply until that sentence has actually been recorded, following the ruling in the High Court in *Tudhope v. Campbell*.[77]

(2) Subject-matter the same

5.14   The remaining question concerning the applicability of a plea of *res judicata* to a criminal trial is whether or not the subject matter of the proposed new trial is the same as that for which the accused has already stood trial. Macdonald[78] states that before the plea of tholed assize will be upheld, the previous trial "must have been for the same crime, depending upon the same evidence, and not for what is truly another crime."

Lord Justice-Clerk Grant in *H.M. Advocate v. Cairns*[79] interpreted this as meaning: "It is identity of the charges and not of the

---

[71] *N.B.* not a desertion *pro loco et tempore*, which is a desertion of the diet but not of the right of the prosecutor to reraise the charge(s) against the accused; see Renton and Brown, n. 67, para. 10–15 and *Herron v. McCrimmon*. 1969 S.L.T. (Sh. Ct) 37 at 39. However, formal intimation of abandonment has the same effect as a Crown desertion *simpliciter*; see Renton and Brown, n. 67, paras 9–32 to 9–34; *Thom v. H.M. Advocate*, 1976 J.C. 48; *H. v. Sweeney*, 1983 S.L.T. 48; and *Lockhart v. Deighan*, 1985 S.L.T. 549.

[72] See Renton and Brown, n. 67, paras 9–08—9–13/1.

[73] *i.e.* the accused will not be regarded as having "tholed his assize".

[74] *i.e.* a verdict of guilty has been pronounced: Lord Justice-General Emslie in *Dunlop v. H.M. Advocate*, 1974 J.C. 59 at 67. He need not apparently be sentenced. See *Milne v. Guild*, 1986 S.L.T. 431, which is authority for this view at least in relation to summary cases.

[75] *i.e.* before the jury is sworn in, or before the first witness is called in a summary case; see Renton and Brown, n. 67, para. 18–67 (solemn cases) and Criminal Procedure (Scotland) Act 1995, s.152 (summary cases). This will also include a plea of guilty at a specially convened diet under s.76 of the Criminal Procedure (Scotland) Act 1995.

[76] Renton and Brown, n. 67, para. 9–27; see *Herron v. McCrimmon*, n. 71 above at p. 39.

[77] 1979 J.C. 37 at 41.

[78] *Criminal Law of Scotland* (5th ed.), p. 272. Lord Justice-General McNeill in *Fraser* (1852) 1 Irv. 66 at 73 gave as his test whether or not the present charge was one that the accused was "in jeopardy of" at the previous trial.

[79] 1967 J.C. 37 at 41. For a recent application of this same principle see *H.M. Advocate v. M.*, 1986 S.C.C.R. 624.

evidence that is the crucial factor." In that case, C had on an earlier occasion stood trial on a charge of murder by stabbing M, and following his own sworn testimony, in which he denied the stabbing, the charge was found not proven. The Crown then served an indictment for perjury upon him, libelling that he had falsely denied the stabbing at the earlier trial. The defence objected to the new indictment on the ground that C had already stood trial (tholed his assize) on the question of the stabbing. It was held that the new indictment was competent and that *res judicata* was not applicable, because the two charges (*i.e.* murder and perjury) were wholly different in nature, and the two crimes were allegedly committed on different dates and at different places.

It is also well established that the same facts may give rise to different charges in different trials where events have occurred which alter the nature of the crime. For example, when a trial for assault is followed by the death of the victim, an accused may be re-indicted for murder or culpable homicide.[80] However, unless there has been some material change of circumstance that gives rise to a charge which was not available to the prosecution at the earlier trial, they cannot bring a second charge after the completed trial for the first, "for the same facts, under a new denomination of the crime".[81] For example, having failed to secure a conviction for robbery against D, the prosecution cannot recharge him with separate charges of assault and theft arising from the same alleged incident. On the other hand, where an indictment is dismissed as irrelevant for lack of specification a fresh indictment libelling the same offences may be competent, and not *res judicata*, provided there is a material difference in the way the charges are expressed.[82]

In terms of section 118 (solemn proceedings) and section 185 (summary proceedings) of the Criminal Procedure (Scotland) Act 1995, the High Court may, on appeal, dispose of the case by setting aside the verdict of the trial court and granting authority to the Crown to bring a new prosecution.[83] In both cases the effect of the statutory provision is that a plea of tholed assize will not be available to the defence. In summary cases, however, no sentence

---

[80] See, *e.g.* Macdonald, n. 78. See also, *Stewart* (1866) 5 Irv. 310 and *O'Connor* (1882) 5 Couper 206.

[81] Hume, II, 466. See *H.M. Advocate v. M.*, n. 79 above, in which the material difference between the first indictment and the second was said to be a narrower "latitude" of time, and a different wording of the charges. A plea of tholed assize was rejected.

[82] *H.M. Advocate v. M.*, n. 79, where the Lord Justice-Clerk said at p. 630 that the test for *res judicata* is "whether the second libel is identical with the previous libel at the instance of the same prosecutor and charges the accused with precisely the same crime."

[83] See *Mackenzie v. H.M. Advocate*, 1982 S.C.C.R. 499.

may be passed on conviction in the retrial which could not have been passed on conviction in the earlier proceedings. Sections 119(6) and 185(6) provide, respectively, that where a new prosecution proceeds under these sections either party can lead evidence which it was competent to lead in the earlier proceedings.[84]

(3) Private prosecutions

5.15   A plea of *res judicata* does not operate so as to prevent a private prosecution in those cases in which the Crown have simply thrown in their hand by means of a desertion *simpliciter*, or given formal intimation of abandonment. This is because such an action operates as a personal bar only against the Crown, and no one else.[85]

Although private prosecutions are extremely rare they are competent. The most recent successful example was the highly publicised case of *H. v. Sweeney*,[86] in which three youths were indicted by the Lord Advocate in the High Court on charges of rape and assault. Subsequently, relying on the advice of a psychiatrist who stated that the alleged victim would be unable to withstand the rigours of a trial for several months, the Lord Advocate sent a letter to each accused informing them that no further proceedings were to be taken against them.

The victim subsequently applied to the High Court with a bill for "criminal letters" which would allow her to raise a private prosecution on the same charges. The case was almost unique in the sense that not since 1829 had an application for leave to prosecute privately been made in a case in which the Crown had formally abandoned charges against an accused.[87] The case therefore raised directly the question of the effect of a Crown abandonment on subsequent private proceedings. In granting the bill, and therefore allowing the private prosecution to proceed, Lord Justice-General Emslie ruled[88] that "the only effect of desertion of a diet *simpliciter* on the prosecutor's motion is to disable that prosecutor from taking fresh proceedings against the accused upon the same charge or charges." Lord Cameron added[89] that "the abandonment of the prosecution by the Crown in no way excluded the right of a private prosecutor to seek at the hands of this court the issue of criminal letters in her own name".

---

[84] See *Diamond v. H.M. Advocate*, 1999 J.C. 244 for the limits of the operation of s.119(6) and (7).

[85] Where desertion *simpliciter* is by the court *ex proprio motu*, it binds all future parties.

[86] n. 71 above.

[87] In all other such cases, the Crown had simply declined to proceed at all.

[88] at p. 55. Earlier his Lordship impliedly equated desertion *simpliciter* with the formal abandonment which had occurred in this case, and the two may therefore be taken as having the same effect so far as concerns a subsequent right of private prosecution.

[89] at p. 52.

Another application for a private prosecution occurred in 1995 in the case of *C. v. Forsyth*.[90] It was unsuccessful and highlighted the very substantial obstacles facing a complainer in such circumstances.

RES JUDICATA: CIVIL AND CRIMINAL CASES *INTER SE*

On the face of it, it is unlikely that *res judicata* could operate **5.16** between civil and criminal cases since the parties to each action are normally different, and, to a lesser extent, the same issues will not arise in the same "cause of action". For these reasons, the older authorities[91] recognised a general rule that the doctrine could not apply between civil and criminal cases. The older cases also follow the same theme, allowing in civil actions what were in substance retrials of issues which had already been considered in criminal cases. Thus, in *Wood v. North British Ry. Co.*,[92] a cab operator who had already been convicted of a breach of the peace by resisting his removal from the forecourt of Edinburgh Waverley Station was allowed to raise an action for damages for assault and illegal arrest against the police officer responsible for his removal. In that case a defence averment of *res judicata* was specifically rejected.

In *Wilson v. Bennett*,[93] W, who had earlier been convicted of an assault on a police officer, raised a civil action against the same officer in respect of an alleged assault upon him immediately before the incident which had led to his conviction. The two issues were clearly not the same anyway, but in rejecting the defence plea that the whole incident was now *res judicata* by virtue of the earlier conviction, Lord Traynor[94] gave a more general opinion that "a conviction or judgment in a criminal court is not a *res judicata* effectual to bar an action or claim in a civil action arising, or alleged to arise, out of the same circumstances".

Notwithstanding this general rule, there are circumstances in which an earlier conviction before a criminal court may have evidential relevance in a later civil action. These circumstances fall into two broad categories. First, where the earlier action does, as an exception to the general rule, operate so as to resolve the matter for all time. Second, where the earlier action creates a presumption of guilt.

---

[90] 1995 S.L.T. 905.
[91] *e.g.* Hume, 1171, 479 and Dickson, *Evidence*, para. 3.5.
[92] (1899) 1 F. 562. See also *Faculty of Procurators of Glasgow v. Colquhoun* (1900) 2 F. 1192.
[93] (1904) 6 F. 269.
[94] at p. 271.

(1) Finding of guilt *res judicata* of later civil action

5.17   The main exceptions to the general rule are statutory, but even at common law there is some authority for regarding a previous finding of guilt as being *res judicata* of a particular issue where it is re-raised in a later civil action between the same parties. Since it is rare for a private individual to be a party to a criminal case, such cases will clearly not arise often, but where they do, all the necessary ingredients are present for a successful plea of *res judicata*.

In *Young v. Mitchell*,[95] a servant had earlier brought a criminal complaint of illegal dismissal against his former employer under the Master and Servant Act of 1867, and the charge had been found not proven. The servant then raised a civil action based on precisely the same facts. In holding that the criminal case was *res judicata* of any subsequent civil action, the Lord President stated[96]: "I think that a judgment in a criminal complaint may be *res judicata* in a civil action, provided the parties are the same, the ground of action the same, and the remedy sought the same."[97]

The general principle is just as applicable to a case in which a common law crime is prosecuted privately by the victim[98] in a case in which the Crown have declined to proceed.[99] If, having obtained a conviction for, say, assault, the victim then raises a civil action for damages in compensation for the same assault, there is no reason why the conviction may not be regarded as *res judicata* of the question of whether or not the assault occurred, unless one takes the narrow view that the "remedy" sought is not the same. Bearing in mind that in the criminal action the issue has been resolved between the parties beyond reasonable doubt, whereas in the civil action the pursuer need only prove the same point on a balance of probabilities, such a narrow view is unreasonable.

(2) Presumption of guilt from previous conviction

5.18   The Law Reform (Miscellaneous Provisions) Act 1968 provides for two situations in which a conviction in previous criminal proceedings will create a presumption of guilt in later civil proceedings. The first situation is created by section 12, which states that:

> "In an action for defamation in which the question whether a person did or did not commit a criminal offence is relevant to

---

[95] (1874) 1 R. 1011. See also *Kennedy v. Wise* (1890) 17 R. 1036.
[96] at p. 1013.
[97] The classic formulation of the prerequisites of *res judicata*—see above.
[98] Which Walker and Walker, n. 19, para. 11.53 regarded as "rare", and limited to cases in which "the proceedings in the criminal court were of a quasi-civil character and the parties in both proceedings were the same."
[99] A possibility that is now stronger following *H. v. Sweeney*, n. 71 above.

an issue arising in the action, proof that, at the time when that issue falls to be determined, that person stands convicted of that offence shall be conclusive evidence that he committed that offence; and his conviction thereof shall be admissible in evidence accordingly."

The obvious use for this provision arises when, say, a newspaper publishes an item describing someone as "a convicted thief", or even simply "a thief", and the person concerned challenges the writer to prove that he actually committed the offence. This is what happened in several well-publicised cases involving English offenders,[1] and the Law Reform Committee, in its 15th Report,[2] recommended a corresponding change in the law, which in Scotland found expression in section 12.

The effect of section 12 is that a conviction is regarded in later defamation proceedings[3] as conclusive of guilt of the offence to which it relates, and subsection (2) provides that once the conviction itself has been proved:

"the contents of any document which is admissible as evidence of the conviction, and the contents of the complaint, information, indictment or charge-sheet on which that person was convicted, shall, without prejudice to the reception of any other admissible evidence for the purpose of identifying the facts which constituted that offence, be admissible in evidence for the purpose of identifying those facts."

The conviction may be by any court in the United Kingdom, or any court-martial.[4]

There is a very good practical reason for authorising the production of documents such as copy complaints, namely that it is not always obvious from the bare record of a conviction what exactly the accused did. For example, an extract conviction for a breach of the peace encompasses a wide range of criminal behaviour. Where a newspaper article refers to a person as being a "Peeping Tom"[5] the journalist may find it difficult to make use of section 12 as a defence to a defamation action if armed only with an extract conviction showing that the pursuer committed a breach of the peace, with no further specification.

---

[1] See, *e.g. Hinds v. Sparks* [1964] Crim.L.R. 717 and *Goody v. Odhams Press* [1967] 1 Q.B. 333.

[2] Another recommendation of the committee, that acquittal of an offence should also be regarded as conclusive evidence of innocence, was rejected.

[3] But no other type of action, *e.g.* damages for unlawful arrest.

[4] *ibid.*, subs (3). *N.B.* that certified copies are allowed under subs. (2) by virtue of subs. (4).

[5] A species of breach of the peace identified in *Raffaelli v. Heatly*, 1949 J.C. 101.

An example of the problem in practice is the English case of *Levene v. Roxhan*,[6] in which a newspaper article alleged that L, by means of a bogus bomb-scare telephone call, had caused a four hour shutdown of Victoria Station. The court in the subsequent libel action refused to consider an extract conviction that stated merely that L had been convicted of maliciously abstracting electricity belonging to the Postmaster-General.

Another potential barrier to the effective use of section 12 may be the difficulty of proving that the extract conviction relates to the person who is now the pursuer in the defamation action. This is a problem frequently encountered in criminal cases in which it is essential to the present charge to prove that the accused has a previous conviction.[7]

5.19 The second situation is created by section 10 of the 1968 Act which was intended to obviate the need in civil proceedings of proving the conduct which led to a criminal conviction. Section 10(1) of the 1968 Act states:

> "In any civil proceedings the fact that a person has been convicted of an offence by or before any court in the United Kingdom or by a court-martial there or elsewhere shall . . . be admissible in evidence for the purpose of proving, where to do so is relevant to any issue in those proceedings, that he committed that offence, whether he was so convicted upon a plea of guilty or otherwise and whether or not he is a party to the civil proceedings; but no conviction other than a subsisting one shall be admissible in evidence by virtue of this section."

Subsection (2)(a) goes on to state that where the person in question is proved to have been convicted of an offence then "he shall be taken to have committed that offence unless the contrary is proved". The section therefore creates a rebuttable, not conclusive, presumption of guilt. It places a persuasive burden on the person concerned of proving that, despite the conviction, he or she was in fact innocent. Although not settled, it is likely that the standard of proof borne by a person in these circumstances is on a balance of probabilities.[8] As with section 12, documents such as complaints,

---

[6] [1970] 1 W.L.R. 1322.

[7] *e.g.* on a charge of driving while disqualified; see *Herron v. Nelson*, 1976 S.L.T. (Sh. Ct) 42.

[8] See Chap. 2 and *King v. Patterson*, 1971 S.L.T. (Notes) 40. See also Macphail, *Evidence*, Chap. 11.08, and the English cases quoted there.

indictments and charge-sheets are admissible to show the real nature of the offence,[9] and extracts may be used.

Frequent use is made of s.10 in civil cases such as actions for damages arising from a road accident in which the defender has been convicted of a motoring offence arising from the same accident. Similarly in a divorce action, a wife pursuer may seek to prove the criminal behaviour towards her of her husband by reference to relevant convictions. Once again, however, the pursuer may face difficulties in identifying the precise nature of the offence, and showing that the person named in the conviction is the defender.[10] The pursuer still requires to link the present defender with the previous accused, and to demonstrate that the two incidents are the same. In some cases it may be easier to prove *de novo* that the defender committed the act(s) in question.

---

[9] *e.g.* in the case of an "assault", that it was in fact an assault by a man upon his wife, which may be an essential factor in a separation or divorce action. This provision may be even more important when the convicted person is not a party to the present proceedings.

[10] See, *e.g. Caldwell v. Wright*, 1970 S.C. 24. and *Andrews v. Andrews*, n. 65 above.

CHAPTER 6

JUDICIAL ADMISSIONS

INTRODUCTION

6.01 A matter that has been judicially admitted is one that is regarded as proved just as if a witness had given unchallenged evidence on the point. According to Walker and Walker, in relation to civil evidence[1]:

> "judicial admissions are in themselves, and without anything more, conclusive against the party making them, for the purposes of the action in which they are made".

The reason behind the rule is that there is little point requiring a party to lead evidence on a particular issue if the other party is prepared to admit it. Judicial admissions cannot be used for any other purpose, and they must be taken subject to any explanations or qualifications that accompany them, but their effect is to relieve the other party of the need to lead any evidence on the fact or facts admitted.

This is another aspect of the law of evidence that encroaches into the law of procedure, and the civil law position will be considered separately from that of the criminal law.

JUDICIAL ADMISSIONS IN CIVIL CASES

6.02 In the course of a civil action, there are basically three procedures in which a fact or set of facts may be judicially admitted formally by one of the parties, and usually without any objection from the other. These arise (i) in the closed record adjusted between the parties; (ii) by means of oral admissions at the bar; and (iii) in a minute of admissions. However, a party may be taken to have

---

[1] *Law of Evidence in Scotland*, para. 11.2.1, citing Stair, IV, xlv, 5 and Erskine, IV, ii, 33.

impliedly admitted a fact, either by remaining silent when it is arguable that he or she should not have done, or by virtue of a partial averment in the written pleadings. Additionally, both the Court of Session Rules and the Sheriff Court Rules[2] provide for the service of Notices to Admit by one party on another seeking agreement of a specified fact or the authenticity of a document. This procedure is designed to expedite the judicial process and avoid time spent on the unnecessary proof of non-contentious issues.[3]

FORMAL ADMISSIONS

(1) In the closed record

The closed record is intended to be the final statement by the **6.03** parties of those matters which require to be litigated, and "the closing of the record marks the borderline between pleading and Proof".[4] It has been said that: "Admissions on record . . . are, no doubt, equivalent to proof: but averments have no factual significance unless and until they are proved."[5] In other words, what party A chooses to concede in the closed record in response to averments from party B, will be held as proved against A. But what a party avers, with no admission from the other party, must be proved.

Lee v. N.C.B.,[6] is the leading case on the subject in relation to civil cases. It was an action for damages by a labourer in respect of personal injuries which he alleged he had sustained as the result of a breach of statutory duty by his employers, and the failure of a colleague to act with reasonable care towards him. The only evidence of any of this came from the pursuer himself but in corroboration of his evidence[7] he sought to rely on certain of the defender's averments concerning the actions of his colleague. In rejecting the suggestion that a simple unadmitted averment by one party could ever constitute proof for the other party, Lord Sorn[8] ruled that:

---

[2] *i.e.* the Rules of the Court of Session, S.I. 1994 No. 1443 and the Ordinary Cause Rules, S.I. 1993 No. 1956.

[3] The receiving party can counter with a Notice of Non-admission.

[4] Maxwell, *Practice of the Court of Session*, p. 202.

[5] Lord Sorn in *Lee v. N.C.B.*, 1955 S.C. 151 at 160.

[6] *ibid.* See also *Stewart v. Glasgow Corporation,* and *Wilson v. Clyde Rigging*, both noted below.

[7] The requirement for corroboration in civil cases has since been abolished: see Chap. 7.

[8] *ibid.*

"It would introduce the greatest confusion into our practice should we countenance the view that a pursuer in order to supplement deficiencies in his evidence, could select passages from his opponent's averments, construe them as a representation of certain facts, and then treat the result as if it was a judicial admission."[9]

(2) Oral admissions at the bar

6.04　　"In practice admissions are frequently made orally by counsel or solicitors at the bar, and are acted upon by the parties and by the court."[10] Although in theory such admissions are not as formal as those contained in the closed record, they have the same effect. The other party is therefore relieved of the duty of proving the point and the fact admitted finds its way into the formal record of the proof, either in the form of a minute noted by the court as being of consent,[11] or in the notes of evidence. Whereas an admission contained in the closed record will be regarded as final, and as the equivalent of proof, oral admissions at the bar may be rescinded if they are proved to be incorrect.[12]

(3) Minute of admissions

6.05

"A minute lodged in process by a party, or by the parties jointly, is a competent method of recording admissions and is the appropriate method of bringing them to the notice of a jury, who are denied access to the written pleadings."[13]

In both Court of Session civil jury trials and proofs, this procedure is formally recognised by rules 36.7 and 37.4 of the Rules of the Court of Session 1994, and in all forms of action in the sheriff courts, and is in fact positively encouraged.[14] It is particularly prevalent in non-contentious issues such as the medical evidence in actions for personal injuries, in which the extent of the injuries is not disputed, but the cause of them is. Equally it is common in actions of divorce, nullity or separation, in which agreements between the parties on questions relating to children or the financial arrangements may be incorporated in a joint minute under rule 49.27 of the Rules of the Court of Session.[15]

---

[9] See also *Lennox v. N.C.B.*, 1955 S.C. 438.

[10] Walker and Walker, n. 1, para. 11.2.4.

[11] Referred to as such in the interlocutor following the proof.

[12] See *Whyte v. Whyte* (1895) 23 R. 320.

[13] Walker and Walker, n. 1, para. 11.2.2.

[14] Macphail, *Evidence*, Chap. 2.14.

[15] See also s.16 of the Family Law (Scotland) Act 1985, which allows joint minutes of agreement on financial provision in divorce. For cases involving the use of substantial joint minutes, see *Johnstone's Exrs v. Harris*, 1977 S.L.T. (Notes) 10 and *Ross v. B.R.B.*, 1972 S.C. 154. See also *Ribble Paper Mills v. Clyde Paper Mills*, 1972 S.L.T. (Notes) 25.

In matrimonial cases there are frequently joint minutes relating to financial provision on divorce. The general position is governed by s.16(1)(b) and s.16(2)(b) of the Family Law (Scotland) Act 1985. These sections govern the court's power to set aside, or vary, an agreement or any term in an agreement made by the parties to resolve the question of financial provision. The power can only be exercised on granting decree of divorce or within such period as the court may specify.[16]

In actions relating to children it is competent to enter into joint minutes that purport to settle the action and set out the terms of the agreement between the parties in relation to the children. Prior to the Children (Scotland) Act 1995 some reference was generally made to one of the parties having custody and the other access to the child(ren). The intention behind the 1995 Act is to abandon those terms in favour of "residence" and "contact",[17] and to encourage people to think in terms of parental "responsibilities" rather than "rights". The Child Support Act 1991 has caused a similar shift in attitude since many disputes about aliment are now dealt with through the statutory procedures of that Act.

As a general rule, whatever is jointly admitted will normally be taken as final, with no opportunity of reopening the issue.[17a]

IMPLIED ADMISSIONS

In addition to the possibility of a party formally and expressly **6.06** admitting certain facts as part of the pleadings, or in the course of a proof, there is some authority to the effect that admissions may be made by implication. This could occur in two ways. A party might remain silent in the face of an averment from the other party which could easily be denied. Or a party might make averments about some fact which, taken in context, operates as an admission of some fact averred by the other party.

(1) Admission by silence

In relation to this concept of admission by silence the Sheriff **6.07** Court Ordinary Cause Rules 1993 provide, at rule 9.7, that:

"Every statement of fact made by one party shall be answered by the other party, and if a statement made by one party of a

---

[16] In addition to this general power, the court can set aside or vary an agreement in terms of s.16(1)(a) and s.16(3) respectively of the 1985 Act. See *Milne v. Milne*, 1987 S.L.T. 45 and *Horton v. Horton*, 1992 S.L.T. (Sh. Ct) 37.

[17] s.2(1) of the Act.

[17a] See Macphail, *Sheriff Court Practice*, para. 22.42.

fact within the knowledge of the other party is not denied by that other party, the latter shall be held as having admitted the fact so stated."

Rule 9.7 will only apply when the fact in question is within the other party's undoubted knowledge, without the need for any sort of inquiry or investigation. Similar provisions apply in the Court of Session.[18]

(2) Admission from partial averment

6.08 If party A makes an averment which is capable of being interpreted as consistent with an averment made by party B, then it is arguable that A's averment may be taken as an implied admission of B's averment. However, there would seem to be two lines of authority on the point. The mainstream view is illustrated by cases such as *Stewart v. Glasgow Corporation*[19] and *Wilson v. Clyde Rigging and Boiler Scaling Co.*[20]

In *Stewart*, the tenant of a council house sought compensation for the death of her child as the result of an incident allegedly caused by the corroded state of a clothes pole in the back green of her tenement. She wanted to argue that the defenders must have been aware of the state of the pole at the time of the accident. She claimed that this evidence could be found in one of the defender's averments, to the effect that the pole had been inspected and painted five months before the accident. Lord President Clyde in rejecting this submission, relied on the legal principle to the effect that an averment which is not admitted has no evidential value until it is proved, and cannot therefore constitute an admission (see Lord Sorn in *Lee v. N.C.B.* above).

In *Wilson*, a widow sought compensation from the employers of her late husband, who had been killed in the course of loading a cargo of timber into a ship's hold. An important question was whether or not the deceased had been working alone at the time. Apart from eye-witness evidence (which the court on appeal held to be sufficient), the Lord Ordinary (Lord Wheatley) relied on a defence averment to the effect that the deceased had been guiding the load into the hold. Lord Wheatley took this to be an implied admission that the deceased had been alone at the time. On appeal, this approach was firmly rejected, again following the authority of *Lee v. N.C.B.*

An alternative view can be founded upon the qualification offered by Lord Sorn to his judgment in *Lee*, in the subsequent

---

case of *Dobson v. Colvilles Ltd.*[21] In the course of that latter judgment, Lord Sorn observed *obiter* that:

> "If pleaders and pleadings were perfect, it would not be necessary to qualify the passage I have quoted[22] but, as things are, it must be recognised that in practice cases occur in which it is right to treat an averment in answer as equivalent to an admission. Whether this should be done must depend upon the particular case and the particular pleadings and I shall only say that I think we have an example here. The pursuer avers that his hand was injured by the guide wheel. Instead of admitting this and going on to give their own explanation of how the accident came about (as strictly they should have done) the defenders reply with a general denial; but in the explanation which follows they too make an explicit averment to the effect that the pursuer's hand was injured by the guide wheel. The case has been conducted on the footing that this was an agreed fact and, although not formally admitted by the defenders, it would not do now to hold that they had put the pursuer to the proof of it."

Lord Sorn's qualifications were applied in *Lord Advocate v. Gillespie*,[23] a case involving an accident between two vehicles. The Lord Advocate on behalf of the Ministry of Defence raised an action against a contractor, alleging that one of his lorries had forced an RAF vehicle off the road. It was not proved in evidence that the lorry had, at the time, been driven by one of the contractor's employees. However, it was averred on behalf of the MoD that the RAF vehicle had encountered, at the crown of the bend, a lorry belonging to the defender and being driven on the wrong side of the road. In answer, the contractor averred that the lorry had been approached on the bend by an RAF vehicle that was being driven in a reckless fashion.

The sheriff was of the opinion that he was free to choose between Lord Strachan's judgment in *Wilson* and Lord Sorn's qualified view as expressed in *Dobson*, and opted for the latter, regarding it as "the more realistic approach to the problems both of insufficient evidence and improperly drawn pleadings".[24]

---

[21] 1958 S.L.T. (Notes) 30, unreported so far as concerns Lord Sorn's amended opinion, which is, however, reproduced *per* Lord Wheatley in *Wilson*, above, at p. 330.

[22] *i.e.* his own judgment in *Lee v. N.C.B.*

[23] 1969 S.L.T. (Sh. Ct) 10.

[24] at p. 12. And see also *Ellon Castle Estates Co. v. MacDonald,* 1975 S.L.T. (Notes) 66, followed in *EFT Finance Ltd. v. Hawkins,* 1994 S.L.T. 902; and *McNaught v. B.R.B.,* 1979 S.L.T. (Notes) 99.

JUDICIAL ADMISSIONS IN CRIMINAL CASES

6.09 There are three contexts in which a judicial admission may arise in a criminal case. These are (i) as a plea of guilty; (ii) in a joint minute between the prosecution and the defence; and (iii) in the course of a special defence, which may or may not include a partial admission as to the *actus reus*. There are also certain statutory situations in which an accused who fails to challenge an assertion may be taken to have impliedly admitted it.

PLEA OF GUILTY

6.10 According to Macphail: "A plea of guilty is a solemn judicial confession of fact, and if accepted, may result in an immediate conviction."[25] The procedural and evidential consequences of a plea of guilty vary somewhat as between solemn and summary cases, and are now considered separately.

(1) Solemn cases

6.11 Section 77(1) of the Criminal Procedure (Scotland) Act 1995 states that if the accused pleads guilty and the plea is accepted by the Crown, then a written copy of the plea should be signed by the accused, and countersigned by the trial judge. If the plea is to only part of the indictment, and the Crown are not prepared to accept it, then the non-acceptance is also recorded, *per* section 77(2). There is no obligation on the Crown to accept any plea of guilty, not even one which covers the entire indictment,[26] but they cannot thereafter make any evidential use of the fact that the accused was prepared to plead guilty.

In *Strathern v. Sloan*, Lord Justice-Clerk Aitchison observed[27] that: "Where a plea of guilty is tendered and not accepted by the prosecutor, the plea of guilty must under no circumstances be used against the panel, and, where the trial is on indictment, must not be disclosed to the jury."

In solemn cases[28] if the Crown accepts a partial plea of guilty in respect of an indictment which contains more than one charge, and proceeds to trial on the remaining charges, they cannot make use of that plea of guilty as evidence against the accused on the remaining charges.[29] In *Walsh,* the accused was charged on indictment with the theft of three cars, and at the trial diet he tendered a

---

[25] Macphail, n. 14, Chap. 2.26.
[26] *Peter and Smith* (1840) 2 Swin. 492.
[27] 1937 J.C. 76 at 80.
[28] But not in summary cases.
[29] *Walsh v. H.M. Advocate*, 1961 J. C. 51.

plea of guilty to the third charge and pleas of not guilty to the first two. The jury was then empanelled, and the sheriff clerk read out all three charges to them. In charging the jury, the sheriff directed them formally to find Walsh guilty on the third charge, and consider whether or not it was relevant to the issue of his guilt on the remaining charges, using the *Moorov* doctrine.[30] Walsh was convicted on all three charges and appealed.

On appeal, it was held that the jury should not have known about Walsh's plea of guilty, that the third charge should not have been read out to them, and that they should not have been directed to find him guilty. Irrespective of the operation of the *Moorov* doctrine, it was held that the sheriff had misdirected the jury by suggesting that a plea of guilty to charge 3 was of evidential value on charges 1 and 2, and the convictions were therefore quashed.

Macphail[31] argues that the operation of the rule is "unrealistic" in cases in which the *Moorov* doctrine might otherwise be applied. He accepts that in general it is undesirable for a jury to be influenced by being made aware of the accused's plea of guilty to one or more other charges. But he points out that the effect of *Walsh* is to make it "prudent" for the Crown to decline partial pleas when they intend to invoke the doctrine. It can be argued that the outcome is not in the interests of the efficient administration of criminal justice as matters will be taken to trial that would not otherwise need to be.

The effect of a plea of guilty, once signed and countersigned, is as if a formal finding of guilt had been made following trial. The court may proceed to pass sentence following the prosecution's summary of the circumstances of the offence, and the defence plea in mitigation.[32]

The question of whether or not a guilty plea may be withdrawn is dealt with below, since it is common law based, and the only modern authorities are in respect of summary charges.

(2) Summary cases

In summary cases a plea of guilty, if accepted by the prosecutor, **6.12** allows the court to proceed immediately to sentence, following the

---

[30] For which see Chap. 7. The *Moorov* doctrine allows an incident spoken to by only one witness to be corroborated by a witness speaking about another incident where the two incidents are strikingly similar, and appear to form a course of conduct.

[31] n. 14, Chap. 2.28.

[32] Section 77 of the Criminal Procedure (Scotland) Act 1995. In practice, where the plea is partial only, sentence will be deferred until the end of the trial on the remaining charges.

usual representations by the fiscal and the defence agent.[33] As in solemn cases, there is no obligation on the prosecutor to accept any guilty plea, but although the offer of a plea and its rejection will be recorded, the prosecutor may not thereafter make any evidential use of it.

In *Strathern v. Sloan*[34] G and S were charged with the theft of a motor vehicle. At the pleading diet G entered a not guilty plea, but S attempted to plead guilty. The fiscal refused to accept the pleas, and requested a trial diet for both accused. The sheriff refused, and recorded a plea of guilty against S, continuing the case for sentence at a later diet. The prosecution appealed by way of a bill of advocation, and it was held[35] that the fiscal was entitled to lead evidence against S.

In summary cases, it seems that if the prosecutor accepts a partial plea of guilty to certain charges on a complaint, and proceeds to trial on the remainder, he or she may, in some circumstances, make use of these guilty pleas to prove the guilt of the accused on the remaining charges.[36]

This emerged in the case of *McColl v. Skeen.*[37] This was an appeal against conviction for the offence of producing, on request from the police, a forged test certificate for a motor vehicle. The accused had pled guilty to another charge on the complaint, namely using a motor vehicle without a valid test certificate. It was proven that the accused had been unable to produce a test certificate to police officers who had stopped the vehicle. That had led to the police request to produce a certificate at a police station, and the eventual production of a forgery. In the course of finding the accused guilty on the charge of producing a forged test certificate, the trial sheriff made use of the fact that a guilty plea had been entered on the charge of driving the vehicle without a valid current test certificate. The accused appealed, but the appeal was rejected. The High Court made the following observations[38]:

> "The plea of guilty to charge 1 was highly relevant to proof of guilt on charge 2 . . . There is no statutory prohibition which inhibits a sheriff from taking cognisance and account of a

---

[33] Section 144 of the 1995 Act. By virtue of s.146(8), it is not necessary for the prosecutor to prove the accused's guilt of those charges to which he has pled guilty. According to Renton and Brown, *Criminal Procedure*, para. 20–34, acceptance by the Crown of a partial plea is equivalent to desertion *simpliciter* of the rest of the complaint.

[34] 1937 J.C. 76; see above for Lord Justice-Clerk Aitchison's comments on the evidential value of a rejected plea, which covers both solemn and summary cases.

[35] Relying on *Kirkwood v. Coalburn District Co-op.*, 1930 J.C. 38.

[36] *e.g.* under the *Moorov* doctrine.

[37] 1980 S.L.T. (Notes) 53.

[38] at p. 54.

plea of guilty to one charge or two or more in the same complaint when the fact of the admission implied in the plea is, as a fact, relevant to proof of another charge or charges libelled in the complaint."

Some confusion has arisen in recent years over the question of whether, having offered a plea of guilty, the accused may then withdraw it. The authorities suggest that it may only occur when the accused can show that the plea was tendered as the result of trickery or coercion, or because of a genuine misunderstanding.[39] It was held in *Tudhope v. Campbell*[40] that a plea may be withdrawn before the conviction and sentence have been recorded.

The issue in *Tudhope v. Cullen*[41] was whether or not the plea could be withdrawn after the recording of the conviction, but before sentence. The accused, having pled not guilty to an assault charge at the pleading diet, turned up at the trial diet without a solicitor, and pled guilty. Sentence was deferred for a social inquiry report. At the adjourned hearing the accused attempted to withdraw his plea of guilty, claiming that he should have been legally represented at the trial diet, but had been let down by his solicitor. After consideration of the background circumstances, the sheriff refused to allow him to withdraw his plea, but held to the view that in some cases it might be possible, even after conviction, basing his decision on the unreported case of *Tudhope v. MacCauley*.[42]

In *MacCauley* the accused had originally been charged with a variety of road traffic offences. At the pleading diet he pled guilty to one charge and not guilty to the remainder. Sentence was deferred on the charge to which he had pled guilty, but at the trial diet, the accused appeared with a solicitor and requested leave to withdraw the guilty plea, on the grounds that it had been tendered without the benefit of legal advice. The minute of conviction had by that stage been signed by the clerk, and the prosecution argued that *Tudhope v. Campbell* could not therefore be relied upon.

The sheriff concluded that, although the minute referred to a "deferred sentence", this was not to be taken as necessarily implying that conviction had taken place, and that the plea was therefore irreversible. This would be the case where sentence followed immediately upon conviction, but in a case such as this, the sheriff declared that the court should apply "the wider equitable principle that allows a plea of guilty to be withdrawn in a suitable case".[43] Since both parties were in agreement that the

---

[39] See Renton and Brown, n. 33, para. 20–33, and the cases cited there.
[40] 1979 J.C. 24.
[41] 1982 S.C.C.R. 276.
[42] Reported in full in *Tudhope v. Cullen* above. But see *Burns v. Wilson,* 1993 S.L.T. 809.
[43] at p. 280.

equities of the case demanded it, the guilty plea was withdrawn, and a plea of not guilty recorded.

Once sentence has been recorded, however, it would appear that there can be no possibility of a guilty plea being withdrawn.[44]

JOINT MINUTES

6.13 Parties to a civil action may elect to minimise the factual issues between them by admitting certain facts in a joint minute.[45] In criminal cases, in both solemn and summary proceedings, there are provisions to permit the lodging of joint minutes of admissions. The purpose is to speed up the court process by not having to spend time proving non-contentious matters. Section 256 of the Criminal Procedure (Scotland) Act 1995 largely re-enacts, but fortifies, earlier provisions, and permits the lodging in court of minutes of admission and minutes of agreement. Documents and copy documents can be admitted using this mechanism.[46] To encourage the use of these provisions, section 257 places a duty on the Crown and the defence[47] to identify facts which are unlikely to be disputed and which if admitted would avoid the need for oral evidence.[48]

Section 258 goes one step further and entitles a party who considers there are facts that are unlikely to be disputed, to serve on the other party a statement setting out those facts. Unless the receiving party challenges the statement within seven days, the facts "shall be deemed to have been conclusively proved". In terms of section 256(5) parties are not subsequently excluded from leading evidence relevant to any matter contained in the statement. Any document admitted through the joint minute procedure is deemed to have been duly proved.

Joint minutes are appropriate and are frequently used in a variety of situations in which evidence (*e.g.* medical or forensic) is not contentious, or in which the entire evidence of a witness (*e.g.* a police scenes-of-crime photographer) is not challenged. However, the intention behind the 1995 provisions is to go further than agreements relating to formal or expert evidence. It is to seek and obtain evidence from an accused, which, at the pre-trial stage at least, appears uncontroversial. Both the prosecution and defence can use section 256, but the latter may be reluctant to agree

---

[44] *MacNeill v. McGregor*, 1975 J.C. 57.
[45] For the procedure see Maxwell, n. 4, p. 213, and Macphail, *Sheriff Court Practice*, para. 16–28.
[46] s.256(1)(b).
[47] The duty only applies to an accused who is legally represented.
[48] *Quaere* as to whether the admissions need to be in writing. See *Jessop v. Kerr*, 1989 SCCR 417 and the Commentary following the report.

anything other than the most non-contentious evidence on the basis that the accused is entitled to "put the Crown to the test".

Only represented accused have the duty to agree evidence and it may be that solicitors will adopt the cautious approach typical of judicial examination procedures.[49] Although unrepresented accused are to take advantage of section 256, this will inevitably impose additional work on the prosecutor who will have the responsibility of preparing these minutes.

Any minute of admissions or agreement will be strictly construed. In *Evans v. Wilson*,[50] in a trial for alleged drunken driving contrary to the road traffic legislation, the parties lodged a joint minute to the effect that certain numbered productions were doctor's and analyst's certificates under section 10 of the Act. The certificates themselves were not produced, and at the end of the trial, after the completion of the evidence, the defence agent argued that since the certificates were not before the court, there was insufficient evidence for a conviction. The sheriff then instructed the fiscal to lay the certificates before the court, and thereafter convicted the accused. On appeal, the conviction was quashed on two grounds. First, that, since the fiscal had closed his case before the certificates themselves had been lodged in evidence, it was incompetent for the fiscal to have done what he did, even on the instruction of the sheriff. Second, that the joint minute could not remedy the situation, as it simply stated what the productions were, but did not actually admit the facts contained within them.

IMPLIED ADMISSIONS FROM SPECIAL DEFENCES

When an accused lodges a special defence such as self-defence or insanity, there is an implied admission of the *actus reus* of the crime charged. The accused is also seeking to escape the normal consequences of the crime by arguing that there was an absence of the necessary *mens rea* for conviction. The general effect of lodging a special defence is that the Crown is relieved of the burden of proof on the issue of the *actus reus*.[51] There are, though, some exceptions where the Crown is still required to prove the *actus reus*.

In *H.M. Advocate v. McGlone*,[52] an accused charged with a razor assault lodged a special defence of self-defence. Its terms were that: "the panel pleaded not guilty and further that if any wound

6.14

---

[49] Where it is commonplace for an accused to say nothing in response to prosecution questioning on, "the advice of my solicitor".

[50] 1981 S.C.C.R. 60.

[51] For burdens of proof generally, see Chap. 2.

[52] 1955 J.C. 14

was received by [the victim] it was inflicted in self-defence in the course of a struggle in which [the victim] was himself the aggressor". The advocate-depute, for the Crown, objected to this wording, since it was in effect saying: "I did not do it, and if I did, I did it in self defence." The special defence was then reworded to read that "the panel pleaded not guilty and specially that on the occasion libelled he was acting in self-defence, he then having been assaulted by [the victim]". The important concession won by the Crown here, was the implied admission by the accused that he had committed the act.

Like all admissions, however, special defences must be taken subject to the qualifications and excuses contained in them. In *Owens v. H.M. Advocate*[53] in which it was held that the evidential burden on the issue of self-defence rests with the accused, Lord Justice General Normand made the following observation[54]:

> "[The Crown] must prove that the fatal act was the accused's, and that it was deliberate or committed with a reckless disregard of the consequences. The panel relieved the Crown of the first part of the burden by himself admitting the stabbing with a lethal weapon, but attached to his admission the explanation of its being done in self-defence in the circumstances explained by him. The Crown cannot, we think, take advantage of the admission without displacing the explanation or at all events presenting to the jury a not less strong case that shows directly or indirectly that the explanation is false."

IMPLIED ADMISSIONS CREATED UNDER STATUTE

6.15 Section 280(9) of the Criminal Procedure (Scotland) Act 1995 provides that at any trial, it will be presumed that the person who appears in answer to the complaint is the person originally charged by the police, and any contrary assertion must be disposed of by way of a preliminary plea.[55]

By virtue of section 138(4) of, and Schedule 3 to, the Criminal Procedure (Scotland) Act 1995, certain offences when libelled

---

[53] 1946 J.C. 119

[54] at p. 124. The persuasive burden of proving the charge of murder remained with the Crown throughout.

[55] Which is taken as if it were a plea to the competency or relevancy. The significance of this provision as a link in a chain corroborating the identification of the accused emerged in *Smith v. Paterson*, 1982 S.C.C.R. 295, and is further considered in Chap. 7.

against the accused may contain implicit terms regarding the commission of the offence. Any objection taken to these must be as a preliminary plea prior to the tendering of the plea to the charge.[56]

---

[56] See Renton and Brown, n. 33, para. 20–70.

CHAPTER 7

CORROBORATION

INTRODUCTION

7.01 Corroborative evidence means one item of evidence deriving from an independent source that is available to support another item of evidence. The need for corroboration differs as between criminal and civil cases. As a general rule, in criminal proceedings an essential fact cannot be proved by the testimony of one witness alone. Instead, that witness's testimony must be proved by corroborative evidence. Corroboration means that the testimony should be supplemented, supported and confirmed by independent evidence to the same effect from a second source. That second source need not be another witness—it could, for example, be evidence of a documentary nature. As the Scottish Law Commission Report No. 100[1] pointed out, "in practice it [corroboration] is commonly found in a combination of direct testimony and circumstantial evidence".[2]

The need for corroboration in criminal cases reflects a concern that a case should not normally be decided on the basis of the testimony of one witness. The rationale is that corroboration from a separate source provides an independent check on the reliability of the fact in question. This is not a rationale adopted in English law, where there is no general requirement for corroboration, and legislation there in 1994 abolished the need for a judge to give a warning to the jury about the dangers of convicting on the basis of uncorroborated evidence.[3] English law thus operates on the principle that each item of evidence will be assessed on its merits and, if considered reliable by the trier of fact, an appropriate degree of weight attached to it.

---

[1] Report on *Corroboration, Hearsay and Related Matters* (1986).
[2] Quoting Dickson, *Evidence*, paras 1808 and 1811.
[3] Section 32 of the Criminal Justice and Public Order Act. Previously, there had been various circumstances where a corroboration warning was mandatory, including in all cases involving sexual offences. This created unreasonable assumptions about the credibility of complainants in such cases.

140

In civil cases, in both Scotland and England, there is no longer any general rule requiring corroboration. The relevant provisions for Scotland are contained in the Civil Evidence (Scotland) Act 1988.

It is only the "facts in issue" in any case, sometimes described as the essential or crucial facts that require corroboration. Other facts, of which the most frequently encountered are evidential facts that comprise circumstantial evidence, do not require to be corroborated.

ESSENTIAL AND EVIDENTIAL FACTS DISTINGUISHED

The crucial or essential facts of any case are what were referred to **7.02** in Chapter 1 as the *facta probanda,* or "those matters in dispute between the parties".[4] In a criminal case they are "the facts which . . . establish the accused's guilt of the crime charged and must be libelled in an indictment or complaint, expressly or by statutory implication".[5] In a civil case they are "the facts which a party must, or ought to, aver in order to make a case relevant to be sent to proof".[6]

What is, or is not, an essential fact in a case will emerge either in the course of the pleadings in a civil case or, in a criminal case, from the nature of the charge. Essential facts will obviously vary with the substantive law. In *Lockwood v. Walker,*[7] the accused was charged with lewd and libidinous practices with a girl below the age of puberty, and he was acquitted because the only evidence of the girl's age came from the girl herself. As the Lord Justice-Clerk put it[8]: "No doubt our law does not require that every fact in a case shall be proved by the witnesses, but it most certainly does require that every crucial fact shall be so proved."

In *Stewart v. Glasgow Corporation,*[9] a mother sought compensation for the death of her son in an accident involving a clothes pole in a Glasgow drying green. She required to prove that the pole was badly corroded at the time of the accident, and that the local authority must have known this. She lost her case, *inter alia,* because there was no corroborated evidence of the state of the pole at the time. Lord Russell[10] ruled that: "It is true that not every

---

[4] Walker and Walker, *Law of Evidence in Scotland*, para. 1.3.1.
[5] Walker and Walker, n. 4, para. 5.3.1.
[6] *ibid.*
[7] 1910 S.C. (J.) 3. Note that in that case the facts in issue were described as crucial facts.
[8] at p. 5.
[9] 1958 S.C. 28 at 45. See also *Prangnell-O'Neill v. Lady Skiffington,* 1984 S.L.T. 282 at 285. Note that these cases preceded the 1988 Act that abolished the need for corroboration in civil cases.
[10] at p. 46.

part of the evidence of a witness requires to be corroborated but, in the present case, the existence and extent of the corrosion which is claimed to have rendered the pole dangerous is vital to the establishment of the pursuer's case and requires to be affirmatively proved."

The type of evidence that can corroborate essential facts may take several forms. In a criminal case, in the simplest situation, it could be the eye-witness accounts of two independent witnesses, both of whom, for example, saw X hit Y. Or, again in a criminal case, it may take the form of a confession by the accused coupled with a forensic report that links the accused to the crime. Eye-witness accounts, confessions and forensic reports provide direct evidence of the proof of a fact in issue. Such evidence is not always available and a party seeking to prove a particular fact may have to rely on indirect evidence, which is evidence that while not of itself direct evidence of what actually occurred, nevertheless tends to support another item of direct evidence. Evidence that consists of two or more such items of indirect evidence, which are independent of each other, but which point towards the same fact and do not require the support of direct evidence, are referred to as "evidential" facts.

In the vast majority of cases, evidential facts are the same thing as circumstantial evidence, which is considered more fully in its own right in Chapter 8. For example, if A tells the court that she saw X running from the scene of a knife attack; B tells the court that he saw X throw something shiny in the river; and C testifies that she saw blood on X's clothes five minutes later, a powerful case has been established against X that at face value could be sufficient evidence for a conviction. In this example, an essential fact (that X committed a stabbing) could be established without a single piece of direct evidence—the evidence so far adduced has been entirely circumstantial, or evidential.

The significance of this distinction between essential facts and evidential facts is that whereas the former requires to be corroborated, the latter do not. What creates occasional confusion is the practice whereby an evidential fact may be offered in proof of an essential fact, as in the above example, and indeed it is the relevance of the evidential fact to the essential that makes it admissible. This relevance often enhances the reliability of the evidence. So, in the example given above, the case against X is built around three separate items of evidence—the running away, the abandoning of the knife, and the bloodstained clothing—from three separate witnesses. Hume[11] referred to this process as a "concurrence of testimonies", and explained that "the aptitude and coherence of the several circumstances often as fully confirm the

---

[11] II, 384.

truth of the story as if all the witnesses were deponing to the same facts".

An illustration of the use of an evidential fact in corroboration of another item of evidence is afforded by *Patterson v. Nixon*[12] a case of theft by housebreaking in which P had confessed to being near the locus dressed for housebreaking, but denied that he had actually committed it. This partial confession required corroboration, and the police took a tracker dog to the locus. The dog picked up a scent, and when released went straight to P's house, one of six in a block which it could have chosen. It was held that the behaviour of the dog was enough to provide the necessary corroboration.

CORROBORATION IN CRIMINAL CASES

GENERAL

The rule requiring corroboration is only now applicable in criminal **7.03** cases. The classic formulation of the law in this context is that of Lord Justice-Clerk Aitchison in *Morton v. H.M. Advocate*,[13] who stated that:

> "no person can be convicted of a crime or a statutory offence except where the legislature otherwise directs, unless there is evidence of at least two witnesses implicating the person accused with the commission of the crime or offence with which he is charged. This rule has proved an invaluable safeguard in the practice of our criminal courts against unjust conviction, and it is a rule from which the courts ought not to sanction any departure."

The reference to "two witnesses" must not be taken literally, since what is required is two independent items of evidence which may not necessarily be in the form of testimony (*e.g.* a forensic report, or the behaviour of the tracker dog in *Patterson v. Nixon* above), but which point to the crucial fact which needs to be established. Corroboration is evidence that "strengthens, or confirms, or supports a statement or the testimony of a witness".[14]

The Crown must, of course, prove beyond reasonable doubt, that a crime has been committed, and that the accused committed it,

---

[12] 1960 J.C. 42. See also *Norval v. H.M. Advocate*, 1978 J.C. 70; *Little v. H.M. Advocate*, 1988 J.C. 16; and *Kennedy v. F.*, 1985 S.L.T. 22.
[13] 1938 J.C. 50.
[14] *Fox v. H.M. Advocate*, 1998 S.L.T. 335 at 339.

and the facts requiring to be corroborated will vary from case to case. As will be seen in subsequent sections of this chapter, the Crown must always corroborate any identification of the accused as the guilty party, and with rare exceptions any confession the accused is alleged to have made, but otherwise the requirement for corroboration will vary with the charge.

Thus, for example, in most cases the age of the victim is irrelevant, but as was seen above in *Lockwood v. Walker* it is crucial in a sexual offence that is defined by reference to age.[15] In *McCourt v. H.M. Advocate*,[16] M was charged with an offence under the Prevention of Crime Act 1908 that necessitated him being an habitual criminal over the age of 16. M had admitted to a police officer that he was 44, but his conviction was quashed on appeal because there was no corroborating evidence of his age. Similarly, on a charge of "knowingly" making false statements, it must be proved by corroborated evidence that the accused knew the falsity of the statement(s) made.[17]

In many cases there is only one item of direct evidence identifying the accused (*e.g.* only one eye-witness) and the rules of corroboration require some other adminicle of evidence in order to link the crime to the accused. This connecting evidence can take many forms, and over the years the courts have been required to consider a vast variety of items of evidence offered in corroboration.[18] It is even possible for the accused person, by their subsequent words or actions, to provide the evidence necessary to corroborate the evidence of one good witness against them, as happened in *Nisbet v. H.M. Advocate*,[19] in which N was charged with reset. The evidence of the thief to the effect that he had sold the goods to N, and that he had been fully aware of their origin, was held to have been corroborated by police evidence of the "awkward story" which N had given as to how he had acquired them. But evidence of an accused's demeanour cannot be treated as corroboration of his confession.[20]

---

[15] *e.g.* Sexual Offences (Scotland) Act 1976, ss. 3 and 4.
[16] 1913 S.C. (J.) 6, applied in *Herron v. Nelson*, 1976 S.L.T. (Sh. Ct) 42, in which it was held that the fact that D was disqualified from driving was a "crucial" fact which required proof by corroborated evidence for a conviction for driving while disqualified; a simple extract conviction was not sufficient without evidence which linked the accused to the extract.
[17] *Townsend v. Strathearn*, 1923 J.C. 66.
[18] See, *e.g. Douglas v. Pirie*, 1975 J.C 61, *Wright v. Tudhope*, 1983 S.C.C.R. 403, *Proctor v. Tudhope*, 1985 S.C.C.R. 39, *Downs v. Tudhope*, 1982 S.C.C R 563 and *MacNeill v. Wilson*, 1981 S.C.C.R. 80. For cases in which the alleged corroboration was insufficient, see *Reilly v. H.M. Advocate*, 1981 S.C.C.R. 201, *O'Donnell v. H.M. Advocate*, 1979 S.L.T. (Notes) 64, *Ballantyne v. Mackinnon*, 1983 S.C C.R. 97, *Tudhope v. Dalgleish*, 1986 S.C.C.R. 559, and *Smith v. Paterson*, 1982 S.L.T. 437.
[19] 1983 S.C.C.R. 13; see also *Proctor v. Tudhope*, above, (accused running away when challenged), and *Iqbal v. Annan*, 1983 S.C.C.R. 332.
[20] *McGougan v. H.M. Advocate*, 1991 S.L.T. 908.

In the course of a trial, evidence may sometimes be led that **7.04** could corroborate more than one version of events. Thus, in *Fox v. H.M. Advocate*[21] in a charge of clandestine injury, evidence of the complainer's distress which pointed "positively" towards the truth of an essential fact was held to be capable of corroborating her account of events, even though it was acknowledged that the distress might have been consistent with an alternative account put forward by the accused. In arriving at this conclusion, the appeal court in *Fox* disapproved the approach of the then Lord Justice-General Hope in *Mackie v. H.M. Advocate*[22] in adopting the dictum of Lord President Normand in *O'Hara v. Central SMT Co.* to the effect[23]:

> "Corroboration may be by facts and circumstances and proved by other evidence than that of the single witness who is to be corroborated. There is sufficient corroboration if the facts and circumstances proved are not only consistent with the evidence of the witness, but more consistent with it than with any competing account of the events spoken to by him."

Specifically, the appeal court in *Fox* pointed out that corroborative evidence was not a competition to be measured according to whose account it best suited, but instead, whether or not it was capable of corroborating another item of evidence. Thereafter it was up to the jury to decide which account they preferred.

There are certain facts, termed "procedural", that must be proved in the course of a criminal trial, but which do not in themselves prove that the crime was committed or that it was the accused who committed it. Procedural facts do not need to be corroborated. For example, in *Farrell v. Concannon*[24] it was held that only one witness was required to speak to the fact that the accused was advised of his rights before consenting to a medical examination. And in *MacLeod v. Nicol*[25] the same was said to be true of all the preliminary procedure in an alleged drunken driving charge, up to and including the first positive breath test at the locus.[26] In *Hudson v. Hamilton*, it was said that where a tape-recording of an accused's police interview was lodged in court, it was not necessary for a second police officer to listen to the tape to identify it. It was sufficient that the second police officer could confirm that the tape lodged was the tape used.

---

[21] 1998 S.L.T. 335.
[22] 1995 S.L.T. 110 at 118.
[23] 1941 S.C 363 at 379. *O'Hara* was distinguished in *Fox*.
[24] 1957 J.C. 12.
[25] 1970 J.C. 58.
[26] The case was decided under s.2 of the Road Safety Act 1967, now s.7 of the Road Traffic Act 1972, and Lord Justice-Clerk Grant described the whole section as containing matters which were "clearly procedural and incidental".

Where evidence is considered "routine" the Criminal Procedure (Scotland) Act 1995 contains statutory provisions permitting the evidence of only one witness to be sufficient evidence of a fact. In terms of section 280 where a certificate is lodged and signed by an authorised person it is deemed to be sufficient evidence of certain non-contentious issues.[27] In terms of section 281(2) where an autopsy or forensic report is lodged as a production, the Crown, after due notice to the accused and without any objection from him, may call only one pathologist or forensic scientist to give evidence regarding anything contained in their report. It is also now well established that no corroboration is required of the *modus* of a crime or even, apparently, certain elements of any aggravation of it.[28]

Where the Crown allege certain facts rest "peculiarly within the knowledge of" the accused,[29] it is settled law that the prosecution evidence need establish only a *prima facie* case against the accused, and it is then for the accused to produce the evidence which will lead to an acquittal. The clearest examples arise on charges of driving without a licence, or without insurance, and the *prima facie* case against the accused can legitimately consist simply of one item of uncorroborated evidence. Thus, in *Milne v. Whaley*[30] it was held that in such a case, an uncorroborated confession by the accused is sufficient for a conviction.

Where the prosecution adduce as a witness someone who was involved in the crime along with the accused (a *socius criminis*) then the evidence of that person does not require corroboration. The trial judge in a trial on indictment is however entitled to warn the jury to treat such evidence with special care.[31]

Various aspects of corroboration in criminal cases call for closer study. They are:

    (i) corroboration of the identification of the accused;
   (ii) corroboration of alleged confessions by an accused;
  (iii) special suspensions of the normal rule requiring corroboration;

---

[27] A wide range of these issues is covered in Sched. 9 of the Act and includes matters relating to firearms, drugs, immigration, pollution, and road traffic.

[28] See, *e.g. Yates v. H.M. Advocate*, 1977 S.L.T. (Notes) 42 and *Stephen v. H.M. Advocate*, 1987 S.C.C.R. 570; but see *Lynch v. H.M. Advocate*, 1986 S.C.C.R. 244, in which it was held that corroboration was required of the personal violence necessary to convert theft into robbery.

[29] See Chap. 2.

[30] 1975 S.L.T. (Notes) 75.

[31] This is not now mandatory: see *Docherty v. H.M. Advocate*, 1987 J.C. 81.

(iv) corroboration of a series of charges under what is popularly known as the *"Moorov* doctrine"; and

(v) distress as corroboration.

IDENTIFICATION OF AN ACCUSED

The first feature of corroboration to be considered in more detail is **7.05** identification of the accused. No one may be convicted of any criminal offence in Scotland unless there are two independent items of evidence that point to the accused having been the perpetrator. The identity of the accused is a critical element and a simple illustration of the rule can be seen in *Morton v. H.M. Advocate.*[32]

M was charged with an indecent assault upon a woman whom he had allegedly hustled into a close in order to molest her. He was identified by the victim, both at an identification parade and in court, and she was not cross-examined on her identification. The only other items of evidence were, first, that of a neighbour who had seen the assault from within the close, who could not identify the accused, and that of the victim's brother, who spoke only to her distressed state when she arrived home, and to complain of having been assaulted. It was held that M must be acquitted because there was no corroborated evidence that he was the assailant. The rule only comes into play if identification is a live issue. If the accused admits his presence at the *locus*, or admits the *actus reus* but denies *mens rea*, then there will be no need for proof.[33]

The most straightforward form of corroborated identification of an accused is by two eye-witnesses and the recognised procedure is for the witnesses to point to the accused in court as the person to whom they are referring in their evidence.[34] In *Bruce v. H.M. Advocate,*[35] B was charged with wilful fire-raising along with D, and the latter, having pled guilty, then gave evidence implicating B and identifying him. None of the other witnesses in the case was asked to point him out in court, although they referred in their evidence to "the accused James Bruce". In acquitting the accused, Lord Wark on appeal pointed out that, "identification of an accused is not a matter which ought to be left to implication. The proper practice is to have the accused identified directly by persons who are speaking to facts which are material to the charge which is under investigation."

---

[32] n. 13 above.
[33] See *Stewart v. H.M. Advocate*, 1980 S.L.T. 245.
[34] A normal requirement confirmed in *Stewart*, above, at p. 251.
[35] 1936 J.C. 93, approved in *Stewart*, above. See also *Wilson v. Brown*, 1947 J.C. 81.

It is, however, by no means uncommon for the witness to be unable to identify the accused in court, particularly if a long period has elapsed since the incident. It is then that the prosecution are obliged to fall back on evidence that the accused was identified by the witness on an earlier occasion, either in the course of an identification parade, or at the scene of the crime, or shortly after the incident. In all these situations, if it is presented correctly, the court will accept such identification.

The leading case in this area is *Muldoon v. Herron*[36] in which three youths were charged with a breach of the peace. Two witnesses who saw the incident were a Mr and Mrs Miller, who both identified the three accused to the police as soon as they arrived. At the trial, neither was able to identify any of the accused, but both agreed that they had, at the time of the incident, pointed out the culprits to the police. Mrs M gave evidence to the effect that the accused in the dock had not been among those whom she had pointed out to the police, but the sheriff disbelieved her. Two police officers gave evidence that the three accused were all among the group identified by both witnesses shortly after the incident, and on this evidence the sheriff convicted.

On appeal, the conviction was upheld on the grounds that there were two independent items of identification, namely (1) the evidence that Mr M identified the accused shortly after the incident (the act of identification being spoken to by Mr M and the identification of the accused as being those pointed out coming from the police) and (2) the identical evidence of identification by Mrs M, spoken to by police officers, the denial of which on oath by Mrs M the court disbelieved.

The court noted, *obiter*, the evidential role of identification parades. Lord Cameron observed[37]:

> "The practice, which has in recent years become a common feature of trials, of evidence being led without objection both for the Crown and the defence as to what passed at identification parades appears to me to be competent, and I am of opinion that the evidence so obtained is properly admitted and falls well within the scope of the law as it has been developed."

---

[36] 1970 J.C. 30. For the increasing latitude allowed in cases such as this, see *Reilly v. H.M. Advocate*, 1987 S.C.C.R. 68, *Gracie v. Allan*, 1987 S.C.C.R. 364 *Nolan v. McLeod*, 1987 S.C.C.R. 558, and *Ralston v. H.M. Advocate*, 1987 S.C.C.R. 467.

[37] *ibid.* at p. 48. *N.B.* however that his Lordship was not prepared to extend this so as to cover statements of identification given to witnesses other than police officers.

Muldoon was applied in *Bennett v. H.M. Advocate*,[38] a case similar **7.06** to *Muldoon*, but different in one vital respect. In *Bennett*, during the course of an identification parade following a serious assault, B was identified by the victim and by two other witnesses to the assault. None of the witnesses was able to identify the accused at the trial, and the Crown sought to fill the gap by means of the evidence of one police witness as to what had taken place at the identification parade. On appeal, it was held that in *Muldoon* the evidence of two police officers was enough to complete the chain of identification and provide a corroborated case against the accused. However, in *Bennett*, the evidence of the one police officer supplied only one adminicle of evidence, and something further was required to identify the accused as the assailant. In the event there was such evidence, and the conviction was upheld.

In *Howden v. H.M. Advocate*[39] it was established that even if, due to lack of positive identification, it could not be established that an accused committed two separate offences charged, provided it could be established that the offences were both committed by the same person, then it followed that the accused could be convicted of both offences.

In *Muldoon*[40] it was pointed out in passing that "it is not necessary that identity should be established by visual recognition alone". Where a witness has been shown a photograph and identified the accused by name, the witness's evidence may still be admissible.[41] Additionally, an accused may be identified by means of his voice,[42] and as will be seen in Chapter 8, the courts will accept the evidence of tape-recorded conversations.[43] The underlying assumption in such cases is that the voice may be identified as being that of the accused either by persons present at the recording, or presumably by a witness in court identifying the voice.

Identification by build may be admissible if taken in conjunction with other positive identification evidence of the accused.[44] A

---

[38] 1976 J.C. 1. See also *Smith v. H.M. Advocate*, 1986 S.C.C.R. 135 for a case in which *Muldoon* was applied even though the witnesses stated in evidence that they were not certain at the time, but had picked out the accused anyway. It was said to be a matter for the jury whether or not they believed the identification evidence to have been positive and unqualified at the time of the parade. See also *Neeson v. H.M. Advocate*, 1984 S.C.C.R. 72, and *Reilly* and *Gracie*, n. 36 above.

[39] 1994 S.C.C.R. 19, a decision approved by the High Court in *Townsley v. Lees*, 1996 S.C.C.R. 620.

[40] *ibid.* at 45, *per* Lord Cameron.

[41] *Howarth v. H.M. Advocate*, 1992 S.C.C.R. 364.

[42] *McGiveran v. Auld* (1894) 21 R. (J.) 69; see also *Burrows v. H.M. Advocate*, 1951 S.L.T (Notes) 69.

[43] See in particular, *H.M. Advocate v. Swift*, 1983 S.C.C.R. 204, referred to therein.

[44] *Nelson v. H.M. Advocate*, 1989 S.L.T. 215; *Murphy v. H.M. Advocate*, 1995 S.L.T. 725; and see *Ralston v. H.M. Advocate*, n. 36 above, indicated that if there is at least one emphatic positive identification little else is required.

"positive identification" must be expressed by the witness in those terms. Therefore, a comment from a witness that an accused "doesn't look unlike" a person who had threatened him and stolen his car, was in effect a double negative and was held to be insufficient to constitute a positive identification.[45] It is not necessary for there to be two positive identifications of the accused by eyewitnesses, provided overall, there is sufficient evidence of identification.[46]

Identification of an accused can also be made by a variety of types of physical evidence including fingerprints, palm prints, teeth marks, handwriting, ear prints and most recently DNA profiling. These are all considered in detail in Chapter 16.

CONFESSIONS BY AN ACCUSED

7.07 The second feature of corroboration worthy of separate attention is a confession by an accused. An "extra-judicial" confession[47] is a confession made outwith the witness box and not on oath. It is usually, but not always, made to a police officer. It is potentially one of the most powerful items of evidence against an accused, and accordingly it is surrounded by legal safeguards. One of these safeguards is that a confession cannot be the sole evidence against an accused, but before there may be a conviction, this confession must be corroborated by other evidence pointing to guilt.[48] As Lord Justice-Clerk Thomson put it in *Sinclair v. Clark*[49]:

> "an admission of guilt by an accused is not conclusive against him, unless it is corroborated by something beyond the actual admission. One reason for this rule is to ensure that there is nothing phony or quixotic about the confession.[50] What is required in the way of independent evidence in order to elide such risk must depend on the facts of the case, and, in particular, the nature and character of the confession and the circumstances in which it is made."

---

[45] *MacDonald v. H.M. Advocate*, 1998 S.L.T. 37.

[46] *Kelly v. H.M. Advocate*, 1999 J.C. 35.

[47] *i.e.* one made outwith a court of law, normally to a police officer. *N.B.* that even admissions made on oath in court require corroboration: *Milne v. Whaley*, 1975 S.L.T. (Notes) 75, and the same is true of confessions made during judicial declarations: see Renton and Brown, *Criminal Procedure*, para. 18–59. A formal plea of guilty does not require such corroboration.

[48] Which could, of course, be another item of evidence (such as an eye-witness identification) which itself requires corroboration, the two items coming together to form a corroborated case.

[49] 1962 J.C. 57 at 62.

[50] *e.g.* that the accused has not falsely confessed, as happened in *Boyle v. H.M. Advocate*, 1976 J.C. 32.

The confession itself need only be spoken to by one witness,[51] but an accused cannot in law corroborate their own confession, either by confessing to more than one person, or by repeating it on other occasions.[52] A confession, however often made and to whatever number of witnesses, requires corroboration by means of other independent evidence.

However, this evidence need not be very strong. As was seen in *Patterson v. Nixon*,[53] it need be nothing more formal than the actings of a police dog, and more recent cases have served to illustrate that "very little is required to corroborate a confession".[54] The risk of this notion of "very little corroboration" being elevated to a rule was highlighted by Lord Justice-General Hope in *Meredith v. Lees*[55] when he explained that if that were to happen, "there will be a weakening of the principle that there must be a sufficient independent check of the confession to corroborate it". What constitutes a "sufficient independent check" will depend on the circumstances of the case.

Meredith was a case involving allegations of lewd, libidinous and indecent practices towards a four-year-old girl. The accused had given the police a detailed confession of his behaviour. Although the child's description of the events lacked an ideal level of specification and her terminology was somewhat ambiguous, the court undoubtedly took into account her age and that "she was trying to tell the truth". The accused was convicted and appealed on the ground that the child's evidence did not afford sufficient corroboration of the accused's confession. The appeal court refused the appeal pointing to the consistency of the child's account in relation to time, place and circumstance with that given by the accused, combined with the voluntary and genuine nature of the confession. It was held that this consistency constituted sufficient corroboration of the unequivocal confession.

One reason why "very little" corroboration is required is that confessions are statements against interest. As Lord Dunpark explained in *Hartley v. H.M. Advocate*,[56] "the confession of guilt by an accused person is prejudicial to his own interests and may therefore initially be assumed to be true". In *Hartley*, H confessed

---

[51] *Mills v. H.M. Advocate*, 1935 J.C. 77.
[52] *Callan v. H.M. Advocate*, 1999 S.L.T. 1102. For examples of civil cases in which self-corroboration was deemed inadmissible, see *Barr v. Barr*, 1932 S.C. 696 and *Gibson v. N.C.R.*, 1925 S.C. 500.
[53] n. 12 above.
[54] Sheriff Gordon in his commentary on *Cummings v. Tudhope*, 1985 S.C.C.R. 125. See too, *Sinclair v. Clark*, n. 49, and *Lockhart v. Crockett*, 1987 S.L.T. 551.
[55] 1992 J.C.127 at 131.
[56] 1979 S.L.T. 26. Lord Grieve, at 31, observed that: "It is well settled that where, as here, an accused person has, by means of an unequivocal confession, identified himself with an offence, little is required by way of corroboration to meet the requirements of our law."

to the murder of a small boy by drowning him in a burn. At his trial he denied his confession, and claimed that he had simply been working in the area in a local authority gardening squad. It was held that there was "ample" corroboration of his confession from the following facts:

    (i) his work did not require him to go near the burn, although he had said that it did;

    (ii) another young boy described the victim struggling with someone answering H's general description;

    (iii) evidence was led to show that his clothing had been in water that day; and

    (iv) H stayed off his work for the week following the murder.

7.08 Such a collection of cumulative circumstantial evidence may be unexceptionable when dealing with an unequivocal and clear admission of guilt. But great care is obviously required when the circumstances of the confession give rise to doubts, or the accused is of limited intelligence, as was said to be the case in *Hartley*. As Lord Dunpark asserted in that case,[57] one may initially assume that a confession is true, and then "one is not . . . looking for extrinsic evidence which is more consistent with his guilt than his innocence, but for extrinsic evidence which is consistent with his confession of guilt". This is arguably much more necessary when there is doubt about the quality of the confession.

The "extrinsic evidence" in question often comes from information supplied by the accused. This may be either by indicating the location of items connected with the crime, or by disclosing information that only the perpetrator of the crime, or someone present during the commission of it, could have known. This is acceptable if there is no question of the confession being anything other than freely and frankly given, since it then eliminates the possibility of a bogus confession. It does not, however, guarantee the validity of the confession if it is alleged by the accused that the entire confession—together with the "linking" facts—was invented by the police.

Extrinsic evidence supplied by the accused suggests "inside information". This is sometimes described as the "special knowledge" rule, where a confession is almost considered to be self-corroborating. Despite the potential risk of the unreliability of such a confession,[58] the courts regularly accept such evidence as corroboration. One of the most frequently cited examples of this

---

[57] at p. 33.
[58] See Griffiths, *Confessions*, paras 5.63–5.104 for a critical treatment of modern cases dealing with special knowledge.

rule in operation is *Manuel v. H.M. Advocate*.[59] During a confession to a murder Manuel offered to point out to the police the separate spots in a field where he had buried the victim and one of her shoes. His ability to do so later was held to be corroborative of his confession, and this line of reasoning was approved in *Hartley*.

For a confession to be self-corroborating, it is not necessary for it to contain special knowledge that would only be known to a perpetrator, not least because the perpetrator could have disclosed the details to others. Also, the increasing involvement of the media in serious criminal investigations means that over the course of a police enquiry details of the crime can leak out, whether intentionally or deliberately, into the public domain. This appears to the position even if the confession contains details inconsistent with the proven facts.

In *Gilmour v. H.M. Advocate*,[60] the accused gave the police a confession to rape and murder containing details which, allegedly, only the real offender could have known. It also contained discrepancies with the proven facts. In his summary to the jury, the trial judge dwelt only on the consistent facts that could be said to corroborate the confession, stating that the inconsistencies had been effectively rehearsed in the defence speech. It was held on appeal that there was nothing wrong with such an approach, and that when a confession contains both consistencies and inconsistencies, it is for the jury to decide whether or not they feel that the confession is nevertheless corroborated.

At the end of the day, for a court to find that a clear confession has been corroborated, there must be some evidence capable of functioning as corroboration.[61]

STATUTORY EXCEPTIONS TO THE GENERAL RULE IN CRIMINAL CASES

The third feature of corroboration requiring separate study forms **7.09** the statutory exceptions to the general rule. They vary widely in nature, and the law is as laid down for each particular situation. Only a few of the more common examples are given here.

Under section 14(1)(b) of the Road Traffic Act 1960,[62] a provision was enacted whereby a motorist charged with failing to

---

[59] 1958 J.C. 41. See also *Allan v. Hamilton*, 1972 S.L.T. (Notes) 2, *Torrance v. Thaw*, 1970 J.C. 58, *Wilson v. McAughey*, 1982 S.C.C.R. 390, *McAvoy v. H.M. Advocate*, 1982 S.C.C.R. 263, *Annan v. Bain*, 1986 S.C.C.R. 60, *Wilson v. H.M. Advocate*, 1987 S.C.C.R. 217 and *MacDonald v. H.M. Advocate*, 1987 S.C.C.R. 581.

[60] 1982 S.C.C.R. 590.

[61] See *Sinclair v. MacLeod*, 1964 J.C. 19.

[62] Reproduced in s.22 of the Road Traffic Act 1972; see also Road Traffic Regulation Act 1967, s.80(9A).

comply with a traffic sign could be convicted on the evidence of a single witness. It was applied in *Sutherland v. Aitchison*,[63] in which two witnesses spoke to the fact that a car had been driven contrary to a road sign, but were unable to identify the accused as the driver. The accused, the owner of the vehicle, had admitted to the police that he was the driver at the material time, and had given a circumstantial account of what had happened. It was held that the effect of section 14(1)(b) was that he had been lawfully convicted.

These statutory exceptions generally place the burden of proof on a particular issue with the accused. In some such cases, instead of the Crown having to produce a corroborated case that negatives the accused's defence, it is for the accused to produce evidence that prevents a conviction. The question is to what extent that evidence requires to be corroborated. If the burden of proof on the accused is a persuasive one then the defence put forward must be corroborated. If, however, the burden is only evidential, then provided the evidence put forward is credible, it need not be corroborated.

In *Templeton v. Lyons*,[64] L was charged with failing to send his child to school, the charge being brought under an Act which gave the accused the burden of proving any "reasonable excuse" in bar of conviction. L claimed that he was unaware of the truancy, since his wife had intercepted all communications concerning it. Additionally, the attendance officer, who knew him by sight, had on several occasions passed him on the street without comment. In the course of upholding his conviction Lord Wark[65] commented that, "the onus lay upon him to establish by legal proof the excuse which he alleged in explanation of his failure to see that his child attended school, and that he could not do without leading evidence which to some extent corroborated his own evidence".

In *Farrell v. Moir*[66] M, who had been convicted of refusing to give a second breath test or blood or urine sample, pleaded that there was a "special reason" in terms of section 93(1) of the Road Traffic Act 1972 why he should not be disqualified from driving, in that he had only driven the car because the police had ordered him to move it. There was no corroboration of this claim, but the sheriff ruled that M's uncorroborated evidence (which only had to be proved on a balance of probabilities) was sufficient[67]:

"The general principle in Scotland is that where there is an onus on a party to prove any essential fact that must be done

---

[63] 1970 S.L.T. (Notes) 48.
[64] 1942 J.C. 102.
[65] at p. 108.
[66] 1974 S.L.T. (Sh. Ct) 89.
[67] at p. 90. The sheriff observed that there was no earlier authority directly in point.

by corroborated evidence. If this general principle applies to the present case then the accused must fail . . . In my opinion in a proof such as this, when the onus is on the accused, his own uncorroborated evidence, if believed, is sufficient."

The appeal court confirmed this approach, *i.e.* no requirement for corroborated evidence, in *King v. Lees*.[68]

As noted earlier, statutory provisions have also made inroads to the need for corroboration in certain matters classed as "routine evidence" in the Criminal Procedure (Scotland) Act 1995. In routine matters, such as those involving the submission of expert reports and certificates, there is no requirement for corroboration. Sections 281–282 of the Criminal Procedure (Scotland) Act 1995 provides that the evidence of one pathologist or forensic scientist is to be regarded as sufficient to prove any fact or conclusion as to fact contained in any report signed by him and another pathologist or forensic scientist.

The Criminal Procedure (Scotland) Act 1995 provides for dispensing with corroboration through the use of certification of evidence in cases involving drugs, video surveillance, and fingerprints and palmprints. Sections 282–284 detail the procedures that can be used to avoid calling witnesses to court simply to speak to such matters.

THE *MOOROV* DOCTRINE

The fourth feature of corroboration that justifies special attention **7.10** is when a person is accused of a series of offences which are closely connected "in time, character and circumstance" and have "an underlying unity" such that a special rule of evidence applies, known as "the *Moorov* doctrine".[69] Under this doctrine each of the separate offences need only be proved by the evidence of one witness, and each offence then corroborates the other(s) as if the crimes charged were a course of criminal conduct.

This principle, which was recognised by Hume,[70] is now named after the leading case of *Moorov v. H.M. Advocate*, and the facts of that case illustrate the circumstances in which it may be applied. The accused was an employer who was alleged to have committed

---

[68] 1993 S.L.T. 1184, a decision criticised by Sheldon in his article, "Hip Flasks and Burdens", 1993 S.L.T. (News) 33.
[69] *Moorov v. H.M. Advocate*, 1930 J.C. 69, approved *obiter* by the House of Lords in *D.P.P. v. Kilbourne* [1973] A.C. 729. Kilbourne is primarily concerned with the use of similar fact evidence in English law. For further discussion of the associations between these two authorities see Chap. 13.
[70] II, 385, and quoted in Dickson, n. 2, paras 1807–1810.

separate sexual assaults and indecent assaults involving 21 charges and a total of 19 female employees over a period of four years. He was convicted of seven assaults and nine indecent assaults. Corroborative evidence was only available in three of these charges. On appeal to a full bench of seven judges, the conviction was upheld on nine of the original charges, which stretched over a period of some three years, six of these charges resting on the evidence of a single witness. In explaining the circumstances in which such convictions were possible, Lord Justice-General Clyde[71] pointed out that:

> "Before the evidence of a single credible witness to separate acts can provide material for mutual corroboration, the connection between the separate acts (indicated by their external relation in time, character or circumstance[72]) must be such as to exhibit them as subordinates in some particular and ascertained unity of intent, project, campaign or adventure which lies beyond or behind—but is related to—the separate acts."

Put more briefly in the words of Lord Sands[73]: "There must be some special circumstances connecting the incidents in order that it may be held that a course of conduct is established."

The *Moorov* doctrine is not restricted to cases of alleged sexual assault, although given the nature of such offences it is most frequently encountered in this context. Sexual offences tend to occur in private, in the absence of witnesses and the accused frequently puts forward a defence that the victim consented. In such situations, there may be little to support the complainer's account and it is only by demonstrating that there has been a course of conduct involving one or more other victims in similar offences that it becomes possible to use the testimony of each complainer as corroboration for each other.

In *Begg v. Tudhope*,[74] a schoolteacher, B, was accused of indecent assaults on two of his female pupils. The evidence against him consisted of the testimony of the two girls themselves, plus independent evidence of the distressed condition of one of the girls shortly after the incident. On appeal it was held that the evidence of the girl's condition (plus a *de recenti* statement made by her to the witness of her condition) was not capable of corroborating her allegation of assault. Nevertheless, the court upheld the convictions

---

[71] at p. 73.
[72] *N.B.* the interchangeability of these factors, not all of which need apparently be present in each case.
[73] at p. 89.
[74] 1983 S.C.C.R. 32. See also *Scott v. H.M. Advocate*, 1987 G.W.D. 24–871.

because, "as the sheriff accepted the two complainers as credible and reliable . . . he was entitled to apply the principle laid down in *Moorov v. H.M. Advocate* . . . and hence to find the appellant guilty on both charges".[75]

The *Moorov* doctrine has been applied innumerable times and in a wide variety of contexts. For example, it was applied in *McCudden v. H.M. Advocate*,[76] where there were two separate attempts to bribe professional football players; in *H.M. Advocate v. McQuade*,[77] a cases involving six charges of assault by razor, and *Harris v. Clark*,[78] where there were three charges of reset. More recently, the doctrine has been applied in circumstances involving the obstructive driving of a car, based on two distinct charges of a breach of the peace and careless driving under the Road Traffic Acts.[79] The resulting conviction was upheld on appeal as the substance of the charges was the same. The doctrine was also applied in *Thomson v. H.M. Advocate*,[80] a case involving two separate robberies, each spoken to by one witness. However, the conviction was quashed and authority for a fresh prosecution given as the appeal court considered the sheriff failed to direct the jury that they should only convict if they were satisfied beyond reasonable doubt that the two incidents concerned a course of criminal conduct.

It has already been indicated that it is not strictly necessary for **7.11** all three elements of time, character and circumstance to unite in each case to present an overpowering presumption of guilt on the part of the accused. However, where any of them is absent, it may be unsafe to apply the *Moorov* doctrine. The mere fact that the crimes libelled against the accused are similar in nature is not *per se* sufficient to attract the operation of the doctrine.[81] There must be "identity of kind" so that "the crimes are related or connected with each other so as to form part of the same criminal conduct".[82] There is obviously discretion in how that is interpreted.

So far as concerns the gap in time between each of the constituent offences, it will in many ways depend upon the nature of these offences, since: "A man whose course of conduct is to buy houses, insure them, and burn them down, or to acquire ships, insure them, and scuttle them, or to purport to marry women,

---

[75] *per* Lord Stott at p. 40.
[76] 1952 J.C. 86.
[77] 1951 J.C. 143.
[78] 1958 J.C. 3.
[79] *Austin v. Fraser*, 1998 S.L.T. 106.
[80] 1998 S.C.C.R. 657.
[81] See *Ogg v. H.M. Advocate*, 1938 J.C. 152, *McHardy v. H.M. Advocate*, 1983 S.L.T. 375 and *Tudhope v. Hazelton*, 1985 S.L.T. 209.
[82] See *Moorov v. H.M. Advocate* n. 69 above, as applied in *McMahon v. H.M. Advocate*, 1996 S.L.T. 1139.

defraud and desert them, cannot repeat the offence every month, or even perhaps every six months."[83]

It is of course the time period *between* the offences that is significant, and not the time period over which the offences are alleged to have been committed. There are various recent examples of cases where the time period between alleged offences has been a significant factor. In *Coffey v. Houston*[84] a male nurse was convicted of indecently assaulting two girls both aged eleven, in hospital wards in separate hospitals. The time gap was two years and two months, which the court said was "comparatively long" but was not fatal to the conviction given the existence of strong links between the offences which were described as "identical assaults".

By contrast, in *Russell v. H.M. Advocate*,[85] the accused was charged with lewd and libidinous conduct towards two girls who were in a neighbouring household. The alleged offences were three and a half years apart and this was held to be too long for the operation of the *Moorov* doctrine. The court considered various authorities in *Russell* and noted[86] that:

> "Although the interval of time between similar offences is not in all cases critical, it is . . . a most material consideration. Clearly no hard and fast rule can be laid down as far as time is concerned, but it is significant that we were referred to no case where the doctrine was applied in circumstances where there was an interval of three years or more between two similar offences."

This dictum was applied in *Turner v. Scott*,[87] described as "a case on the borderline", where the court held that the *Moorov* doctrine was competent in offences over a period of almost three years, as "there is sufficient coherence in character and circumstance". The Court of Appeal recently affirmed in *Bargon v. H.M. Advocate*[88] that there is no fixed period after which *Moorov* is inapplicable, but in that case the relevant period between offences was three and seven months, and there were said to be considerable differences between the incidents. Thus, it seems that the greater the similarity between offences, the greater the potential for applying the doctrine beyond a strict three year period.

---

[83] *Moorov v. H.M. Advocate*, n. 69 above *per* Lord Sands at p. 89.
[84] 1992 S.C.C.R. 265.
[85] 1990 S.C.C.R. 18.
[86] at p. 24.
[87] 1995 S.L.T. 200.
[88] 1997 S.L.T. 1232.

Although the courts have not provided any specific rationale for applying a three year limitation to the *Moorov* doctrine, justification must be based on the notion that any longer period makes it difficult to sustain an argument that the conduct in question is "a course of conduct".

Whatever flexibility may exist on the question of the time gap, there is no doubt that in order for *Moorov* to be applied, the offences with which the accused is charged must be substantially similar. In *H.M. Advocate v. Cox*,[89] the court refused to apply the doctrine to two charges of incest and a charge of sodomy which were allegedly committed in the family home against stepchildren (two female and one male). The rationale was (a) that sodomy and incest were not the same crimes, and (b) that the two charges of incest were separated by a period of three years. More recently, in *P v. H.M. Advocate*[90] the court affirmed that rape and sodomy were two distinct offences, and where the victims were adults the Moorov doctrine could not apply. However, where the victims were young children subjected to rape and sodomy, as in *P v. H.M. Advocate*, then *Moorov* could be applied, as a course of criminal conduct of sexual abuse could be derived from the fact of sexual penetration of each child. Making such a distinction between adults and children is not particularly convincing, as in cases involving adult victims the fact of sexual penetration is similarly present, and surely it is the nature of the criminal behaviour that is of primary concern to the doctrine, not the status of the victims.

Although the offences charged must be substantially similar, they **7.12** do not require to be precisely the same.[91] As *P v. H.M. Advocate* demonstrates, the courts have been willing to interpret "substantially similar", as cases which include charges of a different name but with a broadly equivalent nature. The important issue is not that "the crimes have a different *nomen iuris*" but that there is an "underlying similarity of the conduct".[92] In *Smith v. H.M. Advocate*,[93] two charges of lewd, indecent and libidinous conduct and one of sodomy led to the application of the *Moorov* doctrine because the court held that there was sufficient relation between the offences to provide a connection of the elements of character and circumstance.[94] In *H.M. Advocate v. Brown*,[95] B was charged

---

[89] 1962 J.C. 27.
[90] 1991 S.C.C.R. 933.
[91] *e.g. H.M. Advocate v. W.B.*, 1969 J.C. 72 and *P.M. v. Jessop*, 1989 S.C.C.R. 324.
[92] *per* Lord Justice-General Hope in *McMahon v. H.M. Advocate*, n. 82 at p. 1142.
[93] 1995 S.L.T. 583.
[94] See also *Carpenter v. Hamilton*, 1994 S.C.C.R. 108 where a charge of indecent exposure was corroborated by a breach of the peace. But in *Farrell v. Normand*, 1993 S.L.T. 793 a charge of indecency was not corroborated by a breach of the peace.
[95] 1970 S.L.T. 121.

with a variety of sexual offences against three stepdaughters (the only witnesses against him) all allegedly committed in the family home within a 21-month period. The time period was held to be short enough to apply the *Moorov* doctrine since only a period of months separated the courses of conduct with each girl. In the case of two of the victims, a course of lewd, etc., behaviour was followed by incestuous intercourse, and it was held[96] that:

> "the evidence in regard to incest can validly be used as corroboration in regard to the charges of lewd practices. The greater here includes the lesser. On the other hand, I do not think the contrary is true. Incest is a very much more serious crime than lewd practices and I think that it would be dangerous to treat evidence that a man had committed lewd practices towards Y as indicative of his guilt of incest with Z ... On the other hand, as I have already indicated, the *Moorov* doctrine could apply the other way round."

That reference to "the greater here includes the lesser" was picked up in *Hutchison v. H.M. Advocate*[97] where it was held that on the basis of the Moorov doctrine an assault charge could provide corroboration for a breach of the peace charge but the reverse was not the case.

In *Hay v. Wither*,[98] the court had to consider whether there was a sufficient connection in character and circumstance in two charges of breach of the peace. In both incidents a teenage boy was sexually accosted in a public place in nearby towns by a man driving a van. It was considered that there was the "necessary nexus" in the offences to apply the *Moorov* doctrine. In contrast, in *Farrell v. Normand*,[99] two charges of breach of the peace involving young girls in the same geographical area were held not to have sufficient similarities. Only one of the charges concerned indecency and it was considered that the conduct complained of in the other charge could not amount to breach of the peace.

While each case is very much determined on its own facts, there is perhaps a detectable shift in attitude in the application of the *Moorov* doctrine in recent years, particularly in cases concerning children, suggesting a willingness to apply the doctrine wherever possible. This may owe something to the greater awareness today of child sexual abuse and to the improvements in arrangements for children giving evidence.

The offences which are used in order to support the *Moorov* doctrine must all be "live" ones, in respect of which a finding or

---

[96] *per* Lord Justice-Clerk Grant at p. 122.
[97] 1998 S.L.T. 679.
[98] 1988 S.C.C.R. 334.
[99] n. 94.

admission of guilt has not yet been entered.[1] It is also essential for the operation of *Moorov* that the accused be clearly identified as the culprit in each of the incidents that are being conjoined for that purpose.[2]

It should be noted in conclusion that while the principle exemplified by *Moorov* finds its most common expression in criminal cases, the rationale underlying it[3] has also on occasions been employed in civil cases in which corroboration is normally required. This is dealt with below.

DISTRESS AS CORROBORATION

The fifth feature of corroboration calling for closer study is the **7.13** extent to which a victim's distress can provide corroborative evidence of an offence. The role of distress in corroborating the essential facts of the crime has been considered in several recent cases. These have not produced a consistency of approach that easily permits a clear exposition of the concept. As the matter does not appear to be entirely settled it is worth recounting the position in some detail.

There was a line of authority stretching from *Yates v. H.M. Advocate*[4] for the proposition expressed by Lord Justice-General Emslie[5] in that appeal that, "evidence as to the condition of the alleged victim of rape is capable of affording corroboration by credible evidence . . . that she has been raped". In cases of rape there is frequently a defence of consent to sexual intercourse. The prosecution have to prove that sexual intercourse occurred against the will of the complainer. In such circumstances, the case law following *Yates* suggested that corroboration for a victim's allegations can be gained from evidence of her distressed condition. For example, In *Gracey v. H.M. Advocate*[6] the appeal court affirmed that, "where evidence has been led that a complainer is in a distressed condition after the alleged rape . . . it is for the jury to assess the evidence and to determine whether they are satisfied that the complainer was exhibiting genuine distress as a result of the alleged rape, or whether they consider that the evidence of distress has been put on or feigned".

---

[1] See *Walsh v. H.M. Advocate*, 1961 J.C. 51.
[2] See *McRae v. H.M. Advocate*, 1975 J.C. 34.
[3] *i.e.* that "the aptitude and coherence of the several circumstances often as fully confirm the truth of the story, as if all the witnesses were deponing to the same facts": Hume, n. 70.
[4] 1977 S.L.T. (Notes) 42. See *Stephen v. H.M. Advocate*, 1987 S.C.C.R. 570 and *Moore v. H.M. Advocate*, 1991 S.L.T. 278.
[5] *ibid.* at 43.
[6] 1987 S.C.C.R. 260 at 263.

The dicta in cases such as *Yates* and *Gracey* were careful to restrict the use of distress as corroboration to cases of rape, where consent was an issue. In *Stobo v. H.M. Advocate*[7] the charge was indecent assault and there was considerable evidence from a number of witnesses of the complainer's distress. On appeal, counsel for the appellant argued that distress might be relevant as an adminicle of evidence but it could never provide corroboration by itself. He criticised the dicta in several cases that suggested distress could corroborate the essential fact of the commission of the crime. The court declined to accept the grounds of appeal, despite little resistance from the advocate depute to the main thrust of the appeal. Lord Justice-General Hope observed that, "I am not persuaded that it is accurate to say that the distressed condition of the complainer cannot in law provide corroboration of her evidence about what was done to her."[8] His point was that distress is circumstantial evidence in the same way that physical injuries or torn clothing would be deemed circumstantial, and he did not think it necessary that any such evidence be "unequivocally referable to the crime libelled before it can be said to corroborate the evidence of an eyewitness".[9]

Stobo was overruled in the five bench decision in *Smith v. Lees*,[10] where the charge was lewd and libidinous practices. In a series of careful opinions, the court concluded that the evidential use made of distress in *Stobo* was wrong and did not fit theoretically with the rule of corroboration in Scots law. The court accepted that "in cases of rape where intercourse is admitted, evidence of distress is capable of corroborating a complainer's evidence that she did not consent".[11] However, in situations such as occurred in Smith, where a 13-year-old girl complained of a sexual assault, it was held distress could not corroborate the specific acts that had allegedly taken place. Instead, distress could only corroborate the fact that *something* had happened and it could lend support to the credibility of the complainer, but it could not corroborate the essential facts of the charge.

It is not just in cases of rape that evidence of distress may be used to support an argument of lack of consent. In *Cullington v. H.M. Advocate*,[12] evidence of distress was used to corroborate lack of consent in regard to sexual conduct (short of rape) where the accused maintained the conduct was indeed with the complainer's consent. C was charged with indecent assault. The only evidence to

---

[7] 1994 S.L.T. 28.
[8] at p. 32J–K.
[9] at p. 33B.
[10] 1997 J.C. 73.
[11] at p. 100.
[12] 1999 G.W.D. 28–1314.

corroborate the complainer was the subsequent distress she exhibited to her boyfriend. It was held on appeal that as the accused's evidence was to the effect that the complainer enthusiastically took part in the sexual activity complained of, then once the jury disbelieved that version they were left with the complainer's account involving use of force.

As in the *Moorov* doctrine, time is of importance and the evidence of distress must not be too remote from the incident complained of. Thus, in *Moore v. H.M. Advocate*,[13] no corroboration was found in evidence of distress exhibited some twelve to thirteen hours after an alleged rape. The court laid emphasis on the fact that during this period the complainer had seen her boyfriend and visited two public houses looking for her handbag without apparently showing signs of distress. However, in *Cannon v. H.M. Advocate*[14] the evidence of a complainer's distress exhibited some twelve hours after a rape was held to be corroborative, when there was evidence that the complainer delayed disclosing her distress until she had the opportunity to speak to a close friend. If corroborative merit is to be found in the distress, then the court must be satisfied that the distress is caused by the offence and no other intervening factor. In *McLellan v. H.M. Advocate*[15] evidence of a child's distress following alleged lewd and libidinous behaviour was held not to be corroborative because it could have been attributable to the child's fear of getting a row from her mother for disobeying an instruction not to go to the house where the alleged assault occurred.

CORROBORATION IN CIVIL CASES

GENERAL RULE

Since April 3, 1989, when the Civil Evidence (Scotland) Act 1988 **7.14** came into force, the requirement for corroboration of the *facta probanda*, or essential facts, in a civil case has been removed. That Act was a result of the recommendations of the Scottish Law Commission in their Report, *Evidence: Report on Corroboration, Hearsay and Related Matters*.[16]

The Scottish Law Commission[17] pointed out that, given modern practice in civil cases: "It . . . may be inconsistent with justice that a

---

[13] 1990 S.L.T. 278.
[14] 1992 S.L.T. 709.
[15] 1992 S.L.T.991.
[16] Report No. 100 published in 1986.
[17] *ibid.*, para. 2.8.

party, though he may have an honest and credible case, must nevertheless necessarily fail if, through circumstances over which perhaps he has no control, corroboration is not available." Accordingly, it recommended[18] that: "The requirement of corroboration in civil proceedings in so far as it still applies should be abolished." This recommendation is now section 1(1) of the Civil Evidence (Scotland) Act.

Prior to the Act there had been other inroads made into the general rule that corroboration was required. The Scottish Law Commission had in an earlier report published in 1965,[19] called for the abolition of the corroboration requirement in all civil cases. Political opposition at that stage restricted the recommendation to dispensing with the need for corroboration in cases of personal injury. This was enacted as section 9 of the Law Reform (Miscellaneous Provisions) (Scotland) Act 1968. This section was replaced by section 1(1) of the 1988 Act but the history of its interpretation is valuable in demonstrating how the courts regard the rule dispensing with the need for corroboration. This section is considered in more detail and the chapter concludes with other illustrations of areas of civil law in which the general rule has been modified.

CIVIL EVIDENCE (SCOTLAND) ACT 1988

7.15 There is still relatively little reported case law arising from the operation of section 1(1) of the 1988 Act. However, where a pursuer has relied on that section there is a clear preference for the liberal approach, which was one of two approaches emerging from the earlier provision contained in section 9 of the Law Reform (Miscellaneous Provisions) (Scotland) Act 1968. By virtue of section 9, and now in terms of section 1(1) of the 1988 Act, the normal rule of evidence requiring that a party provide a corroborated case was dispensed with in claims for damages or *solatium* in respect of personal injuries. The rule applied whether or not the party claiming was the pursuer, and covered any fact in the case which the court is "satisfied" has been established.

It is valuable to consider the case law arising under section 9 of the 1968 Act as it paved the way for interpretation of the equivalent provision in section 1(1) of the 1988 Act. In the first authoritative consideration of section 9, *Morrison v. Kelly & Sons Ltd.*,[20] the Court of Session ruled that it did not eliminate the need

---

[18] *ibid.*, para. 2.10.
[19] Paper No. 4, *Report for Reform of the Law relating to Corroboration.*
[20] 1970 S.C. 65.

for corroboration in those cases in which it is available. In the opinion of Lord President Clyde[21]:

> "There may be cases where owing to the nature of the circumstances corroboration is unobtainable. Such a case may be an appropriate subject for the application of the subsection [2]. But, where corroboration or contradiction of the pursuer's account of the matter is available, a Court would obviously be very slow indeed to proceed on the pursuer's evidence alone . . . How could the Court be satisfied if corroborative evidence was available but without any explanation not produced?"

The ruling might have been regarded by many as a disappointing start for the new section. However, arguably it merely confirmed that a court will always consider the weight of the evidence presented to it, and conversely, the significance of evidence available but omitted. The case itself was not the best candidate for the application of section 9(2) anyway, since the pursuer produced no corroborating evidence, and his own testimony was contradicted by every other witness in the case, including two of his own. In rejecting the pursuer's claim on appeal, the court was doing no more than reflect the weight of the evidence.

Thus, in *McArthur v. Organon Laboratories*[22] conflicting testimony from the pursuer and a key witness in an action of damages prevented the pursuer succeeding. The failure of the case was not due to a lack of corroboration, as it was acknowledged that such corroboration was not required. However, because the judge preferred the contradictory testimony of the eyewitness to the accident to that of the pursuer, the burden on the pursuer to prove the case on a balance of probabilities was not discharged.

A subsequent Outer House ruling in *Thomson v. Tough Ropes*[23] produced a judgment more in keeping with the spirit of section 9. T claimed damages for injuries sustained in the course of her work, allegedly as the result of defective equipment. Although the judge disbelieved T's corroborating witness, B, he did believe the pursuer, and was at pains not to penalise her because of the poor

---

[21] at p. 79. See also *McGowan v. Lord Advocate*, 1972 S.C. 68, in which the only other witnesses in the case apart from the pursuer either were not called or gave evidence contradicting the pursuer. It was held (a) that the pursuer had failed to satisfy the court of his case, and that the question of corroboration did not, therefore, enter into the matter, and (b) that s.9 was in any case primarily intended to cover a case in which there were no eye-witnesses other than the pursuer.

[22] 1982 S.L.T. 425.

[23] 1978 S.L.T. (Notes) 5. See also *Comerford v. Strathclyde Regional Council*, 1987 S.C.L.R. 758.

quality of the evidence from B. Finding that the pursuer's own evidence had established that the accident had occurred as alleged in her averments, Lord Kincraig decided that he could apply section 9 in her favour because:

> "In my opinion, I am entitled to apply s. 9 where the accident occurred in the absence of any credible eye-witness other than the pursuer herself. The fact that there was evidence from an unreliable eye-witness who purported to corroborate the pursuer, should not deprive the pursuer of the assistance of s. 9."[24]

Similarly, in *Ward v. U.C.S. Ltd.*[25] the court found in favour of an uncorroborated pursuer even though at the end of the day it found him to have been contributorily negligent. In a dissenting judgment in *McLaren*, below, Lord Stott ruled that section 9 was intended to prevent the unjust situation in which an honest and reliable pursuer was denied a remedy on a technical rule of law. In the case of *McCallum v. British Railways Board*[26] the court adopted a liberal approach to section 9. Despite a certain lack of corroboration of some aspects and a failure to call potential witnesses, the appeal court said that given the essential facts were proven, the pursuer's apparently credible testimony need not be corroborated.

The Scottish Law Commission[27] argued that section 9(2) had proved useful, and had not led to "a flood of weak claims". It therefore recommended that the principle of the section be extended to all other civil actions, and section 1 of the 1988 Act does precisely this.

The cases since the 1988 Act have confirmed that despite the abolition of the need for corroboration, the pursuer still has to prove his or her case, and where evidence is led that is preferred to the testimony of the pursuer then the case will not succeed. Equally, where witnesses could have been led, but for whatever reason the pursuer chooses not to call them, the court will not necessarily draw adverse inferences. Thus in *Airnes v. Chief Constable of Strathclyde*,[28] the failure of the pursuer to call a witness who was present at the time of the alleged assault for which she was seeking an award of damages, was highlighted in the appeal by the defender against a finding of fault. However, the appeal court

---

[24] at p. 6. A similar view was expressed in *McArthur v. Organon Laboratories Ltd.*, n. 22.
[25] 1973 S.L.T. 182.
[26] 1991 S.L.T. 5. The case dealt with an accident and judgment at first instance that predated the 1988 Act.
[27] *ibid.*, para. 2.10.
[28] 1998 S.L.T. (Sh. Ct) 15.

upheld the award and noted a variety of reasons why it might not be appropriate to call witnesses to an event that occurred some five years previously.

CORROBORATION IN CONSISTORIAL CAUSES

(1) General rule

No decree will be granted in certain consistorial cases, even if **7.16** undefended, unless the pursuer's grounds are established by evidence.[29] In terms of section 8(2) of the 1988 Act this requirement for evidence applies to actions for divorce, separation or declarator of marriage, nullity of marriage, legitimacy, illegitimacy or nonparentage.

Section 8(3) provides that in an action of divorce, separation or declarator of marriage, or nullity of marriage, the evidence required to establish the grounds of an action "shall consist of or include evidence other than that of a party to the marriage". Evidence can come for a source other than another witness, *e.g.* an extract conviction, though even here, a third party will be required to give evidence that the identity of the person to whom the conviction refers is the defender.[30] The reason for retaining the corroboration rule in consistorial cases stems from the courts' reluctance to terminate a marriage except on the strongest of proven grounds.

The demand for corroborated evidence has even survived the reduction of the standard proof in divorce actions from that of beyond reasonable doubt to that of a balance of probabilities.[31] This is so even though "one argument against retaining the need for corroboration is that it sits somewhat uneasily with the concept of proof on a balance of probabilities".[32]

(2) Exceptions to the general rule

Most of the exceptions to the general rule requiring corrobora- **7.17** tion in consistorial cases have been briefly referred to above, but it is convenient to list them again, together with one additional exception that has not yet been touched upon.

---

[29] In any other type of civil action, of course, an undefended action will result in a "decree in absence"; see Scottish Law Commission, *ibid.*, para. 2.11.

[30] *Andrews v. Andrews*, 1971 S.L.T. (Notes) 44

[31] *per* Divorce (Scotland) Act 1976, s.1(6).

[32] Scottish Law Commission, *ibid.*, para. 2.13.

(a) Civil Evidence (Scotland) Act 1988, section 8(4)

7.18   By virtue of this section, the Lord Advocate has the power to prescribe classes of undefended divorce actions in which corroboration is not required. He has so far done so only in respect of two and five-year separations proceeding under "simplified" applications.

(b) Divorce (Scotland) Act 1976, section 3(1)

7.19   Under this provision, a divorce court may "treat an extract decree of separation lodged in process as sufficient proof of the facts upon which such decree was granted". The section excludes adultery-based actions from this rule,[33] but in all other cases, the rule operates not only so as to set up a presumption as regards the facts upon which the earlier findings were based, but also so as to obviate the need for any further corroborating evidence.

(c) Law Reform (Miscellaneous Provisions) (Scotland) Act 1968, section 11

7.20   As noted above, the effect of this section is to make a finding of adultery in earlier matrimonial proceedings admissible in subsequent proceedings involving at least one of the original parties. As with section 3(1) of the 1976 Act, it sets up a rebuttable presumption.

(d) The Moorov doctrine

7.21   This rule, discussed above, whereby each of a series of related incidents may be spoken to by only one witness, and may then be conjoined into a mutually corroborative chain, has spilled over from criminal cases into consistorial ones. In such cases the normal requirement for a corroborated case is regarded as fulfilled.

Thus, in *Whyte v. Whyte*,[34] Mrs W sought a divorce on the grounds of her husband's adultery with a female servant, Y, and it was held that the evidence of another domestic servant, H, of W's indecent behaviour with her corroborated the evidence of Y, and the decree was granted.

The process is subject to the limitations normally imposed when the *Moorov* doctrine is involved. Thus, in *Michlek v. Michlek*[35] the evidence relied on by the wife in a divorce action based on the

---

[33] But they were placed in the same position by virtue of the Law Reform (Miscellaneous Provisions) (Scotland) Act 1968, s.11 anyway, and that is why they were excluded from s.3(1); see below.

[34] (1884) 11 R. 710.

[35] 1971 S.L.T. (Notes) 50.

husband's adultery consisted of (1) his alleged acts of incest with a daughter of the marriage, and (2) his alleged acts of adultery with a stepdaughter. It was held that she was unable to rely on the evidence of each daughter as corroborating the evidence of the other because of an interval of five years that separated the two courses of conduct.

(f) Fatal Accidents Inquiries, Industrial Tribunals and Children's Hearings

Many tribunals and other forms of quasi-judicial proceedings **7.22** have their own statutory rules of procedure that are *sui generis*. These frequently permit a departure from the usual rules of evidence and in each case the statutory framework governing the tribunal in question should be consulted to establish the requirements of evidence.

CHAPTER 8

THE HEARSAY RULE

THE GENERAL RULE

8.01 Hearsay has been defined as: "An assertion other than one made by a person while giving oral evidence in the proceedings is inadmissible *as evidence of any fact asserted.*"[1] The hearsay rule is a common law rule. It has been abolished in civil cases by section 2 of the Civil Evidence (Scotland) Act 1988, and there have been numerous exceptions to the rule formulated at common law and by statute, many of which demand complex and technical interpretation. In criminal cases the rule operates generally so as to restrict evidence given by a witness in court to an account of what *he or she* perceived with one of their senses, *i.e.* what they saw, smelt, heard or touched. Evidence is also restricted to statements of fact, and therefore evidence from a witness of their opinion is normally inadmissible unless the witness is an expert witness.

The hearsay rule renders inadmissible any statement by A which simply repeats something A was told by B, whether or not B is called as a witness. To take a simple example—when an assault is witnessed by A, it is A who is required to give evidence of what was seen, and not B to whom the incident was recounted. The purported evidence of B is "hearsay", and in accordance with the general rule is inadmissible. Nor is the ban restricted to oral accounts that are passed on in this fashion. The hearsay rule applies also to entries in documents whose authors are not available as witnesses to speak to such entries, although, as we shall see, there is a range of statutory exceptions to this application of the rule. It also extends to statements made on previous occasions by persons now giving evidence, at least in so far as such previous statements are offered as evidence of the facts that they contain. What is important to the court is not what the witness may have said in the past, but what is being testified to on oath in the witness box.

---

[1] Cross and Tapper, *Evidence*, (7th ed., 1990) p. 42 (emphasis added) cited approvingly in *Morrison v. H.M. Advocate*, 1990 J.C. 299 at 312.

The remainder of this chapter considers in more detail the nature of a statement described as hearsay and then the various exceptions to the hearsay rule. Finally, the effect of the abolition of the hearsay rule in civil cases is considered.

HEARSAY EVIDENCE DISTINGUISHED FROM ORIGINAL EVIDENCE

A statement will normally only be ruled hearsay and inadmissible **8.02** when it is offered as evidence of the truth of its contents. If a party seeks only to prove the fact that the statement was made, *i.e.* regardless of whether or not it is true, then this fact is not regarded as hearsay and may be proved. As the Judicial Committee of the Privy Council observed in *Subramaniam v. Public Prosecutor*[2]:

> "Evidence of a statement . . . is hearsay and inadmissible when the object of the evidence is to establish the truth of what is contained in the statement. It is not hearsay and is admissible when it is proposed to establish by the evidence, not the truth of the statement, but the fact that it was made."

The facts of that case provide a helpful illustration of this distinction between evidence to establish the intrinsic truth of a statement, and evidence to establish the fact of a statement being made. S was charged with being in possession of firearms without lawful excuse, and his defence was one of duress. S claimed that Malayan terrorists had threatened to kill him if he refused to hold the arms for them. It was held that, regardless of whether or not the terrorists meant to carry out those threats, in support of his defence S could testify to the fact that the threats were made.

The Scottish case of *McLaren v. McLeod*[3] offers another illustration. M was charged with brothel keeping, and evidence was allowed of a conversation overheard by police officers in the premises in question between two people who were not called as witnesses. It was held that evidence of the fact of the conversation was relevant and admissible in that it proved that the conversation occurred and in so doing it cast light on the nature of the premises, and the purpose for which they were being used. Such evidence would not have been admissible had its purpose been to prove the truth of the substance of the conversation.

When a witness speaks to a statement in court simply to prove the fact that it was made, such a statement is known as "original

---

[2] [1956] 1 W.L.R. 965 at 969, on appeal from Malaya.
[3] 1913 S.C. (J.) 61.

evidence", and is distinguished from hearsay, which is the admission of a statement as evidence of the truth of its contents. A defamation action, for example, involves proof that a certain statement was made, as does a claim for misrepresentation, and in both cases the fact that the statement was made may be distinguished from the question of its veracity.

The distinction between a hearsay statement and original evidence is not always easy to draw, as the case law illustrates. Thus, in *Ratten v. R.*[4] the Judicial Committee of the Privy Council admitted evidence of a telephone call by a murder victim, shortly before her death, in which she asked for police assistance. The Privy Council held that evidence of the telephone call was not hearsay, because it was original evidence of (1) the fact that it was not the only call from the house that day, as the accused claimed; and (2) the victim's state of emotion or fear. It is this latter finding which can create confusion since such evidence would only be relevant if it could be regarded as an implied assertion by the victim that she was indeed under threat. This virtually amounts to using the statement as evidence of the truth of its implied contents.

The court noted *obiter* that had the call been regarded as hearsay, it would have been admissible under one of the exceptions to the rule, namely the *res gestae* exception, dealt with below.[5]

The Rationale of the General Rule

8.03 The rationale for the hearsay rule has been summarised by Lord Normand in *Teper v. R.*,[6] who stated that:

> "The rule against the admission of hearsay evidence is fundamental. It is not the best evidence and it is not delivered on oath. The truthfulness and accuracy of the person whose words are spoken to by another witness cannot be tested by cross-examination, and the light which his demeanour would throw on his testimony is lost."

Lord Normand's rationale, which has been endorsed on numerous occasions, comprise five separate elements.

(1) Hearsay statements are not the "best" evidence. They may, however, be the best *which is now available*, hence the exception which is permitted when the maker of the original statement is now

---

[4] [1972] A.C. 378.
[5] As it would be in Scotland. It would also be admissible as a statement by a deceased person. See below.
[6] [1952] A.C. 480 at 486; and for a wider discussion see the Scottish Law Commission's *Report on Hearsay Evidence in Criminal Proceedings*, No. 149, 1995.

dead. In some cases, a hearsay statement may even constitute the best evidence possible. As the House of Lords observed in *Waugh v. British Railways Board*[7] in regard to a report made by eyewitnesses concerning a railway accident, some of whom were available to testify in the subsequent civil action arising from it:

> "It is clear that the due administration of justice strongly requires disclosure and production of this report. It was contemporary. It contained statements by witnesses on the spot. It would be not merely relevant evidence but almost certainly the best evidence as to the cause of the accident."

(2) The maker of a hearsay statement is not on oath when he or she makes it. The argument that hearsay evidence lacks the solemnity of the oath in underlining to a witness the seriousness of testimony in court is no longer convincing. In an increasingly secular Western world the significance of the oath, with its dependency on a belief in religious retribution, is rapidly diminishing, and retaining the offence of perjury for those who lie in the witness box would arguably be just as effective. A separate counter argument is that the closer in time the statement is made to the events to which it relates, the more reliable it may be. This consideration underlies the exception to the general rule permitted in those cases in which the statement is part of the *res gestae*.

(3) There is a risk that a hearsay statement will lose its accuracy through repetition. That may be so but it is a factor the court can take into account through the degree of weight it attaches to the evidence. If the statement in question was made in writing close to the events which it describes, that may enhance its reliability, hence the exception to the rule permitted in the case of public and business records.

(4) There is a risk that hearsay evidence will be manufactured. Whilst this is a possibility, it is one that applies to all evidence.

(5) The court is unable to observe the demeanour of the witness whose evidence is given in hearsay form through the mouth of another, and their words cannot be tested in cross-examination. The argument that hearsay should be excluded because it prevents effective observation of demeanour or cross-examination, merit the same response as the third point, namely that of the weight attaching to such evidence. If the consequence of being unable to interrogate a witness about hearsay testimony is that the particular witness cannot provide a meaningful answer, or is forced to dissemble or remains silent in response to searching questions, then the cross-examination has been effective. The point will have

---

[7] [1980] A.C. 521 at 531. This is an "eyewitness" exception to the general privilege that operates *post litem motam*.

been made—the witness cannot say, because his or her knowledge is limited. Moreover, questions as to that person's demeanour may be asked of the person now testifying.

In the past 20 years or so, much of the rationale underlying the hearsay rule has been critically questioned.[8] The relevance of the hearsay rule to the modern law of criminal evidence has also been examined by the Law Commissions in both English and Scottish jurisdictions.[9] Statutory reform was enacted in Scotland in 1995 and remains as a recommendation in England. In regard to civil cases both jurisdictions have been willing to be radical and have abolished the rule against hearsay evidence, returning instead to a determining principle of relevancy. In England the rule was abolished under the Civil Evidence Act 1968, and the Scottish Law Commission in 1986[10] recommended similar legislation for Scotland, enacted as section 2 of the Civil Evidence (Scotland) Act 1988. That section abolishes the hearsay rule for all "civil proceedings" covered by the Act, including consistorial causes. This permits evidence to be given of any statement made by a person otherwise than in a court of law when that statement would have been admissible had the person making it done so in the form of sworn testimony. The conditions are simply that the statement must be relevant, and the maker must have been a competent witness. At the same time, section 2 continues to permit evidence to be given of the making of such statements where this is relevant as original evidence. "Statements" include all "representations (however made or expressed)", but precognitions are expressly excluded from the operation of section 2.

The Scottish courts have confirmed that there is no fundamental objection under the ECHR to the concept of the admissibility of hearsay evidence.[11]

EXCEPTIONS TO THE HEARSAY RULE

8.04 The remainder of this chapter is devoted to an examination of those exceptions to the hearsay rule that are currently recognised by the criminal courts. In the main they arise from expediency, and may be regarded as simply one manifestation of the best evidence rule, although some are statutory in origin.

---

[8] See, for example, A. Zuckerman, "Law Commission's Consultation Paper No. 138 on Hearsay: The Futility of Hearsay" (1996) Crim.L.R. 4; and J. Spencer, "Hearsay Reform: A bridge not far enough?" (1996) Crim.L.R. 29.

[9] Law Commission Report 245, Cm. 3670, (1997) *Evidence in Criminal Proceedings: Hearsay and Related Topics* (1995); Scottish Law Commission Report, No. 149, (1995) *Hearsay Evidence in Criminal Proceedings.*

[10] *Corroboration, Hearsay and Related Matters,* Memo No. 100, para. 3.37.

[11] *McKenna v. H.M. Advocate,* 2000 J.C. 291 and *H.M. Advocate v. Nulty,* 2000 S.L.T. 528.

STATEMENTS FORMING PART OF THE *RES GESTAE*

A statement that is *res gestae* is a set of words that is so closely **8.05**
connected to a fact or facts in issue, that it is said to form part of
the disputed facts, and is therefore admissible in evidence. It has
been defined as follows:

> "Evidence is admissible of a statement made contempo-
> raneously with an action or event which is, or forms part of,
> the fact or facts in issue by a person present at that action or
> event. The *res gestae* may be defined as the whole circum-
> stances immediately and directly connected with an occur-
> rence which is part of the facts in issue."[12]

Thus, in the case of *Ratten v. R* discussed earlier, the words
heard and subsequently narrated by the telephone operator in the
emergency call, were regarded as *res gestae*, to the close connection
between the fact of the disputed call and the shooting incident. The
res gestae exception is justified on the ground that it represents the
spontaneous reaction of the person who made the statement. The
statement was made before any opportunity existed for reflection,
and is therefore likely to be a genuine indication of what really
happened. The exception covers not only statements but other
physical reactions, such as fainting or vomiting. *Res gestae* statements include the express and implied assertions, not only of the
participants in the incident themselves, but also of those observing
it.

Among the more obvious examples of *res gestae* statements are
the screams and protests of a rape victim, or the use of nicknames
in an unguarded moment by members of a gang of hooded armed
robbers.[13] In *Murray*[14] the accused was charged with the rape of a
girl who was described in the indictment as "of weak and imbecile
intellect" and was thus deemed incompetent as a witness because
of her disability. It was held that her mother might testify as to
"the first statement or exclamation she made" when she returned
home, which was described as a cry of distress.[15]

---

[12] Wilkinson, *Scottish Law of Evidence*, p. 39.

[13] Thus, if one of the accused has the same nickname, the use of it by one of the
gang to another may be employed in evidence to identify the accused by
implication, even if the person who uttered it has never been traced. The
statement will be spoken to by the person (*e.g.* the victim) who heard it being
made.

[14] (1866) 5 Irv. 232.

[15] Although the cry did not strictly accompany the assault, and was therefore more
like a *de recenti* statement (for which see below), the circumstances were such
that the court felt itself entitled to regard it as being part of the *res gestae*.

The statement must be sufficiently close in time to the incident as to form part of it, and must relate to it in some material way. This accords with the rationale of the exception, namely that the statement should be forced instinctively from the maker in the heat of the moment. A statement is therefore only part of the *res gestae*: "providing it is made in such conditions (always being those of approximate but not exact contemporaneity) of involvement or pressure as to exclude the possibility of concoction or distortion".[16]

The facts of *R. v. Gibson*[17] provide a good example of the fine distinctions that sometimes have to be drawn in this area of law. In the trial of G for an assault by stone-throwing, evidence had been admitted of a statement by an eyewitness, now untraceable who had pointed to G's door and stated that: "The person who threw the stone went in there." It was held that this statement should not have been admitted, since it was not part of the *res gestae*.

Lord Normand in *Teper v. R.* described the basic requirements to be met before any statement can be regarded as part of the *res gestae*:

> "It is essential that the words sought to be proved should be, if not absolutely contemporaneous with the action or event, at least so clearly associated with it, in time, place and circumstances, that they are part of the thing being done, and so an item or part of real evidence and not merely a reported statement."[18]

Applying that to the statement in the present case, he ruled:

> "The words were closely associated in time and place with the event, the assault. But they were not directly connected with that event itself. They were not words spontaneously forced from the woman by the sight of the assault, but were prompted by the sight of a man quitting the scene of the assault, and they were spoken to for the purpose of helping to bring him to justice",[19]

and as such they were not part of the *res gestae*. However, as was seen in *Murray*,[20] the courts will allow some latitude of time in those cases in which the statement in question, although not precisely contemporaneous with the incident to which it relates, is nevertheless clearly made under the continuing psychological pressure of that incident.

---

[16] *Ratten v. R.,* n. 4 above.
[17] (1887) 18 Q.B.D. 537 at 538.
[18] n. 6 above at p. 487.
[19] at p. 488.
[20] (1866) 5 Irv. 232.

The case of *O'Hara v. Central S.M.T. Co.,*[21] provides an example of the hearsay rule in civil cases prior to the 1988 Act. In that case, a bus driver accused a pedestrian of having stepped out in front of him, thus causing an accident. Although the accusation was made some minutes after the incident, it "was the first opportunity for the discharge of the driver's pent-up emotion" and was therefore admitted as evidence.[22] The reactive statement of the pedestrian was also admitted as part of the *res gestae*.

Res gestae statements are frequently confused with statements **8.06** made *de recenti*. Whereas the former are part of the commission of the crime, the latter, a *de recenti* statement, is one which is made shortly after the incident to which it related. On those relatively rare occasions when *de recenti* statements are admissible, such as to support lack of consent by the victim in a rape case, they serve only to enhance the credibility of the maker as a witness, and are not evidence of the truth of their contents.[23] It is the fact that the earlier statement was made which is of importance. The admission of such previous consistent statements that were made *de recenti* is merely one example of the more general rule that original (hearsay) evidence will be admitted when it is relevant.

The following are therefore the main points of distinction between *res gestae* and *de recenti* statements.

(1) Statements made *res gestae* are part of the incident to which they refer, whereas statements *de recenti* occur shortly afterwards.

(2) Statements made *res gestae* may be admitted as evidence of the truth of their contents; statements made *de recenti* merely enhance the credibility of the maker, who is now a witness.

(3) Statements made *res gestae* are admissible regardless of who made them; statements made *de recenti* are only admissible when the maker is now a witness giving evidence which is consistent with that contained in the *de recenti* statement.

(4) *De recenti* statements are almost certainly restricted, under modern law, to those circumstances in which the victim of a sexual assault is allowed to show consistency in the denial of consent.

STATEMENTS BY PERSONS NOW DECEASED

At common law, statements by persons now deceased were treated **8.07** as admissible at common law as evidence of the truth of their contents.[24] The rationale of the rule was that it was now the best evidence available to the court of the matters contained in such

---

[21] 1941 S.C. 363.
[22] Walker and Walker, *Law of Evidence in Scotland*, paras 8.10.1–8.10.2.
[23] See *Morton v. H.M. Advocate*, 1938 J.C. 50.
[24] *Irving v. H.M. Advocate,* 1978 J.C.28.

statements. The statutory changes brought about by section 2 of the 1988 Act and section 259 of the 1995 Act affirm the common law position. Before the rule may be invoked the person now deceased must have been a competent witness at the time at which the statement was made.[25] Moreover, the statement will be discounted if at the time when it was made the witness had some self-interest, or was contemplating legal action in connection with the subject matter of the statement. As Lord Watson observed in the *Lauderdale Peerage Case*[26]:

> "the statement of a deceased person, whether oral or written, is not admissible as evidence, when its own terms or the circumstances in which it was made, are such as to beget a reasonable suspicion either that the statement was not in accordance with the truth, or that it was a coloured or one sided version of the truth".

In *William Thyne (Plastics) Ltd. v. Stenhouse Reed Shaw (Scotland) Ltd.,*[27] a company sued its insurance brokers for alleged negligence. The pursuers were under-insured at the time of a fire, and the defenders sought to adduce an internal memorandum from the manager of the relevant office, now deceased, concerning the instructions given to him by the pursuers. They were refused leave to do so because the memorandum had been sent after it was known that the pursuers were holding them responsible for their losses. As such, it "was not a spontaneous account of events written at the time, but a considered version of them after intimation of a prospective claim, and must give rise to a reasonable 'suspicion' that it was a one-sided version of the truth".[28]

Because of the danger of bias creeping in, the courts will likewise reject any statement by a person now deceased that takes the form of a precognition. Rejection is on the grounds that such statements are not the original words of the witness, but have been "filtered through the mind of another".[29]

In *Moffat v. Hunter*[30] the court admitted as evidence statements by a person (now deceased) who had been a witness to a road accident. The statements had been given in his own words to an insurance inspector. The inspector did not proceed by question and

---

[25] See Dickson, *Evidence*, para. 267. *N.B.* that the Scottish Law Commission (Memo No. 46, para. T.08) recommended that the date upon which such competency should be tested is the date upon which the statement is tendered in evidence.

[26] (1885) 10 App. Cas. 692 at 707.

[27] 1979 S.L.T. (Notes) 93.

[28] *ibid.*

[29] *Kerr v. H.M. Advocate*, 1958 J.C. 14, *per* Lord Justice-Clerk Thomson at 19. See too, *Young v. N.C.B.*, 1960 S.C. 6.

[30] 1974 S.L.T. (Sh. Ct) 42.

answer, but simply collected the witness's *verbatim* statement. He had done so five months before the writ was issued, and the witness had no clear idea of the insurance company's interest in the case. It was held that in the circumstances, it was not "tainted by interest" and was not a precognition.

Similarly, in *H.M. Advocate v. Irving*[31] the High Court admitted statements made to the police by the victim in a theft and rape case, who died shortly afterwards, because it was held that her statements were in the form of a straightforward complaint and not by way of precognition. But in *Thomson v. Jamieson*[32] the court rejected a statement made by the (now deceased) driver of a car which had been in collision with the pursuer's motorcycle because it was made to a claims inspector employed by an insurance company at a time when a claim was in prospect, and took the form partly of a question-and-answer session. That was enough, said the court, to make it inadmissible on the ground that it was "akin to a precognition".

The common law also recognised exceptional circumstances in which even a statement originally made in the form of a precognition could be admissible after the maker is dead. Again, these will not be affected by the statutory changes. An example of these "exceptional" circumstances was the "dying declaration or deposition" of a witness in a criminal case who has material evidence to give in the case.[33]

The other possible main exception arises when the statement in question has been given in the form of evidence in another case. In such cases, the statement could be challenged on the basis it derives only from examination and cross-examination and is therefore akin to a precognition, but it has the perceived advantage of having been given on oath. It is therefore arguably the best evidence now available. The authorities are divided as to whether or not the fact that the witness has not been cross-examined by the opposing party in the present case is fatal to its admissibility,[34] but the Scottish Law Commission[35] recommended that this should affect only the weight to be attached to it. The Commission also recommended[36] that if a deceased person's statements are to be admitted, the fact that they are in the form of a precognition should go only to their weight.

---

[31] 1978 J.C. 28.

[32] 1986 S.L.T. 72. See also *Hall v. Edinburgh Corporation*, 1974 S.L.T. (Notes) 14; *Pirie v. Geddes*, 1973 S.L.T. (Sh. Ct) 81; and *Ferrier's Exr v. Glasgow Corporation*, 1966 S.L.T. (Sh. Ct) 44.

[33] Walker and Walker, n. 22, para. 15.5.1. See also Macphail, *Evidence*, Chap. 19.33.

[34] See Macphail, above, Chap. 19.32 and *Hogg v. Frew*, 1951 S.L.T. 397.

[35] Memo No. 46, para. T.11.

[36] *ibid.*, para. T.10.

REPUTATION IN CASES INVOLVING MARRIAGE, LEGITIMACY, PEDIGREE AND ANCIENT RIGHTS

8.08 In cases involving marriage, legitimacy, pedigree and ancient rights, the common law had long recognised exceptions to the general rule against hearsay. Evidence in such cases was permitted under the best evidence rule, on the ground that the events into which the court was then inquiring occurred so long ago that no witnesses remained who could testify in court. The exception was most clearly developed in those cases involving marriage and legitimacy, and rested on the same rationale as that which permits evidence of marriage by cohabitation and repute. Evidence that two persons cohabited, along with a hearsay statement to the effect that local reputation established them as married, may amount to corroborated proof.[37]

The authority for the statement that reputation evidence is admissible in questions of ancient rights rests upon Stair[38] and Erskine.[39] More recently, in *Brook's Executrix v. James*,[40] the House of Lords, considered the legitimacy of a man born in 1868 whose "parents" had not been married until 1871. The court held it to be proved, in the absence of any presumption, by the positive evidence created by the reputation that he had enjoyed at the time as being the legitimate son of the husband. In confirming reputation as an exception to the hearsay rule, their Lordships referred[41] to the fact that: "Where, owing to the passage of time or for other good reasons, there is no other evidence at all, then common reputation ought to be regarded as *prima facie* evidence displacing the onus of proof." The application of the exception to peerage cases was recently confirmed in *Viscountcy of Dudhope and Earldom of Dundee*.[42]

STATUTORY EXCEPTIONS TO HEARSAY IN CRIMINAL CASES

8.09 Significant changes were made to the law following the Scottish Law Commission's 1995 *Report on Hearsay Evidence in Criminal Proceedings*.[43] The Commission's recommendations are in broad measure now incorporated into the Criminal Procedure (Scotland) Act 1995, sections 259 and 260 of which sets out the statutory

---

[37] *De Thoren v. Wall* (1876) 3 R. (H.L.) 28.
[38] IV, xliii.
[39] IV, ii, 7.
[40] 1971 S.C. (H.L.) 77.
[41] *ibid.* at 81.
[42] 1986 S.L.T. (Lyon Court) 2.
[43] Report No. 149 published in February 1995.

exceptions permitting hearsay evidence to be admitted to a court. These are considered in turn.

Section 259

In terms of section 259(1) provided the trial judge is satisfied as **8.10** to four conditions then in certain circumstances, specified in section 259(2), hearsay evidence is admissible. These four conditions are:

(i) that the witness is unavailable;
(ii) that had the maker of the statement given evidence the statement would not be hearsay;
(iii) that the maker of the statement was competent at the time the statement was made;
(iv) that the statement can be proved without recourse to hearsay.

Section 259(2) then specifies the five separate grounds (a) to (e) under which testimony other than oral testimony can be received. These grounds are as follows:

(a) The witness is now dead or unfit or unable to give evidence

As noted above the common law recognised an exception to the **8.11** hearsay rule in regard to statements made by persons who have died before the trial. However, there was some authority that cast doubt on the extent of the exception[44] and the statutory provision now puts the matter beyond doubt. The subsection also permits hearsay from a witness who, "by reason of his bodily or mental condition" is unfit or unable to give competent evidence.

In *H.M. Advocate v. Patterson*,[45] a key prosecution witness died prior to the trial and the Crown applied to have a previous statement made by the deceased admitted as evidence. The defence objected on the ground that the deceased was a known alcoholic and therefore not a competent witness in terms of section 259(1)(c). This argument was rejected by the appeal court which stated that unless a witness was either permanently or temporarily insane, or unable to understand the difference between truth and falsehood, then they would be deemed competent. The condition of alcoholism did not, in itself, render a witness incompetent.

---

[44] Madeline Smith (1857) 2 Irv. 641 at 657–658.
[45] 2000 J.C. 137.

In *H.M. Advocate v. Nulty*,[46] the Crown deserted a rape trial and subsequently raised a fresh prosecution. By the time of the second trial the complainer was mentally unwell and unfit to give evidence. The Crown then sought to use the complainer's previous statement, which took the form of a tape recording. The defence objected to the admission of the tape recording arguing that it would contravene the accused's right to a fair trial in terms of Article 6(1) and 6(3)(d) of the ECHR. This argument was rejected by the appeal court which ruled that there was no overall unfairness to the accused as there were two other safeguards available, namely the requirement for corroboration of the complainer's evidence, and the provisions of section 259(4), which permits a party to challenge the reliability and credibility of any hearsay evidence. In arriving at its decision the court endorsed the approach taken by the European Court of Human Rights in *Doorson v. Netherlands*[47] where it was implied that the question of fairness must be looked at in the round and:

> "No violation of Article 6(1) taken together with Article 6(3)(d) of the Convention can be found if it is established that the handicaps under which the defence laboured were sufficiently counterbalanced by the procedures followed by the judicial authorities."

(b) that the witness is outwith the UK and it is not practicable to secure his attendance or obtain evidence by alternative means

8.12   This exception is essentially to meet the practical and expedient needs of the criminal justice process. It is both inconvenient and potentially unjust to have to delay proceedings simply on account of an absent witness, if the evidence that witness is to give is available in an appropriate form. In *Aslam v. H.M. Advocate*,[48] the appeal court upheld a decision by a sheriff to refuse an application by the Crown to lead, as hearsay evidence, the statement of a witness alleged to be abroad. The sheriff had not been satisfied that the witness was in fact abroad. The appeal court stated that such decisions were a matter for the discretion of the judge at first instance.

(c) that the witness has been sufficiently identified, but cannot be found

8.13   This is another provision to promote expediency. The subsection requires that all reasonable steps be taken to find the witness.

---

[46] 2000 S.L.T. 528.
[47] (1996) 22 E.H.R.R. 330.
[48] 2000 J.C. 325.

(d) that the witness declines to give evidence having been advised that it might be incriminating

The purpose of this provision was to ameliorate the effects of **8.14** the decisions in *Perrie v. H.M. Advocate*[49] and *McLay v. H.M. Advocate*,[50] cases where statements made to third parties by an incriminee were deemed hearsay and inadmissible. The position now is that such statements can be led.

(e) that the witness refuses to take the oath or to give evidence

This provision was intended in part to address the difficulties **8.15** experienced by vulnerable witnesses, especially young children, who might be so intimidated by the court process that they become mute or have limited recall of events once in the witness box. The first application under this subsection was in *MacDonald v. H.M. Advocate*,[51] a case involving various charges of shamelessly indecent conduct towards several children. During the trial, an eight-year-old girl in the course of answering questions put to her by the prosecutor, became upset, then broke down and became unable to answer further questions. The prosecutor successfully applied to the court to regard the child's conduct as a "refusal to give evidence" in terms of section 259 and to lodge as evidence the child's previous statement to a police officer. However, on appeal, it was held that the trial judge had erred in his interpretation of the statute as it only takes effect once a witness has been "directed by the judge to give evidence . . . [and] refuses to do so". In this case the absence of a specific direction to the witness to answer questions was fatal to the admissibility of the previous statement.

Although this decision could be seen as a strict interpretation of the rule and the outcome arguably contrary to the spirit of the legislation, the decision in *MacDonald* was acknowledged by Sheriff Macphail as correctly reflecting the intentions of the Scottish Law Commission (of which he was a member) in its drafting of the clause that was enacted as section 259.[52]

Section 260

In terms of section 260 it is now possible for a prior statement of **8.16** a witness to be admissible at a trial provided three conditions are met. These are (i) that the statement is contained in a document (but not a precognition); (ii) that the witness adopts the statement as his or her evidence; and (iii) that at the time the statement was

---

[49] 1991 J.C. 27.
[50] 1994 S.L.T. 873.
[51] 1999 S.L.T. 533.
[52] See letter to the Editor, S.L.T. 1999 (News) 75.

made the maker was a competent witness. This provision reflects the decision in *Jamieson v. H.M. Advocate*,[53] the ratio of which the Scottish Law Commission recommended be embodied in statute.[54] In *Jamieson* the appeal court upheld the decision of the trial judge to admit in evidence a statement made by a witness to police officers, the terms of which she was unable to recall in court, although she was able to recall having given the police such a statement, and acknowledged its accuracy at the time.

ABOLITION OF HEARSAY IN CIVIL CASES

8.17 The Civil Evidence (Scotland) Act 1988 resulted from the Scottish Law Commission's *Report on Corroboration, Hearsay and Related Matters*.[55] The purpose of the legislation was to promote the inclusion of all relevant evidence and to reduce the effect of exclusionary rules that prevented the court from considering evidence that might be of assistance in reaching decisions. Section 2(1) of the Act provides:

> "In any civil proceedings—
> (a) evidence shall not be excluded solely on the ground that it is hearsay;
> (b) a statement made by a person otherwise than in the course of the proof shall be admissible as evidence of any matter contained in the statement of which direct oral evidence by that person would be admissible; and
> (c) the court, or as the case may be, the jury, if satisfied that any fact has been established by evidence in those proceedings, shall be entitled to find that fact proved by evidence notwithstanding that the evidence is hearsay."

Sections 1 and 2 of the 1988 Act, which respectively abolished corroboration and hearsay, are closely connected in effect and some of the cases emerging to date support this.[56] Many of these cases involve children and in such situations there are always difficult decisions to be made regarding, firstly, the effect on the children of being called as witnesses, and secondly, the risk that the child will not be found to be a competent witness at the proof.

---

[53] 1995 S.L.T. 666.
[54] n. 43 above.
[55] Report No. 100, 1986.
[56] For discussion of some of these cases, see the articles by Lilian Edwards, "Better Seen and Not Heard", 1993 S.L.T. 9, and David Sheldon, "I Heard it on the Grapevine", 1993 J.L.S.S. 292.

Generally, unless a child is found to be a competent witness their testimony will be of no value. The question may then arise as to whether a previous hearsay statement made by the child can be admitted in evidence in place of testimony from the child in court.

This is an issue that has been considered on a number of occasions and was most recently reviewed in 2000 in *MT. v. DT.*,[57] overturning previous established principles. In tracing the history of these statutory provisions the starting point is *F v. Kennedy (No. 1).*[58] This case concerned a referral from a Children's Hearing regarding proof of allegations of sexual abuse against various children. One of the key issues in the case was the competency of one of the children who had appeared as a witness but remained mute. The sheriff had allowed previous statements made by the child to social workers to be admitted as hearsay evidence in terms of section 2(1)(b) of the 1988 Act. This ruling was challenged at appeal on the ground that it had not been established that the child was a competent witness and that even previous statements could not be admitted unless it was also established that, as at the date of the hearing, the child was competent.

The court held that unless a child is confirmed as a competent witness before the judge then any previous statement would be inadmissible.[59] This was on the basis that section 2(1)(b) only permitted hearsay from a witness of whom "direct oral evidence" would be admissible. The Act is silent as to when competency as a witness is to be judged—is it the date of the making of the statement or the date of the proof? The Scottish Law Commission had recommended the latter was more appropriate, but the Second Division in *F v. Kennedy (No. 1)* ruled that competency must be determined as at the date of the proof. The case was remitted back to the sheriff.

A further appeal based on different grounds was made to the Inner House, reported as *F v. Kennedy (No. 2).*[60] It clarified the status of hearsay evidence in situations where a witness is also available to give direct oral evidence. The court ruled that even though direct evidence was given by one of the abused children, this did not prevent hearsay evidence being offered to the court (in this case by two social workers), of what the child witness had said on another occasion.

The issue of competency was also raised incidentally in *M v. Kennedy,*[61] and in his commentary to the case Sheriff Stewart suggests that a hearsay statement should be admissible provided a

---

[57] 2000 S.L.T. 1442.
[58] 1992 S.C. 28.
[59] See too, *Sanderson v. McManus*, 1996 S.L.T. 750.
[60] 1993 S.L.T. 1284.
[61] 1993 S.C. 115.

witness would have been competent at the time it was made, "at least . . . where the incompetence of the witness arises from supervening physical disability". The only difficulty with such a proposal is how competency, even in limited cases, would be established in retrospect.

In *L. v. L.*[62] Lord Hamilton at the Outer House also held that the appropriate point for determining admissibility of a child's evidence was whether the child witness was competent at the time of the proof. His Lordship observed that in his view a child could be determined as competent without adducing the child itself provided another (independent) witness "with appropriate professional qualifications" could testify as to the child's capacity.[63]

8.18   In *Sanderson v. McManus*[64] the House of Lords was also asked to consider the interpretation of section 2(1)(b). In that case an unmarried father was seeking access to his son, born in 1989 and aged four years at the start of the court action. Access was opposed by the child's mother on the basis that the child had made allegations of physical violence against his father. The issue before the appeal court was whether, in arriving at his decision, the sheriff should have taken into account certain statements of the child that were acknowledged to be hearsay, as the child was not called to give evidence. In terms of section 2(1)(b), it was argued that these hearsay statements were admissible. Noting that the statements were not tendered as evidence of the truth of their contents. Lord Hope said[65]:

> "What the witnesses said . . . was not hearsay, because they were describing what they themselves had observed about the child's reactions after the pursuer had had access to him. These consisted partly of actings by the child and partly of things which he said."

The effect of section 2(1)(b) has been considered most recently in *MT. v. DT.*[66] In that case, the First Division had remitted the appeal to a court of five judges who ultimately overruled *F v. Kennedy (No.1)* in entirety and *L. v. L.* in part. The central issue in *MT. v. DT.* was at which of two dates a child, whose evidence was critical to the findings of fact in an action by a father for contact with his daughter, should have been determined a competent witness. Was it at a date in August 1998 when she had made certain statements to a woman police constable, or was it at the

---

[62] 1996 S.L.T. 767.
[63] The case went to appeal on other grounds. See 1998 S.L.T. 672.
[64] 1997 S.C. (H.L.) 55.
[65] at p. 61A.
[66] 2000 S.L.T. 1442.

dates of the proof in 1999? In several previous cases, Lord Hope had suggested that competency should be determined as at the date of the making of the statement and had even suggested how that determination might be carried out. A party would have to:

"[lead] . . . evidence about the child's ability to give a trustworthy account at the time when he made the statement and as to the reason or reasons why that test could not be satisfied when the time came for the child to give evidence."[67]

A five bench decision in *MT. v. DT.*[68] decided that section 2(1)(b) did not embody a competency test (unlike its criminal counterpart section 259 of the Criminal Procedure (Scotland) Act 1995), and therefore there was no requirement to demonstrate competency either at the time of the making of the statement or at the time of the court hearing. It was implicit within the statute that the maker of a statement was a competent and admissible witness and thus, unless there is a separate reason for inadmissibility, any hearsay statement subsequently admitted in the court proceedings will be deemed competent.[69]

In terms of the impact on practice in the obtaining of statements that might subsequently require to be relied upon as hearsay evidence, Lord Bonomy made some comments that, although obiter, are important. He observed that[70]:

"when a child's statement is taken in a 'formal' setting such as by a police officer, it is likely to assist a court considering the statement later if the interviewer has been able to explore the child's understanding in the course of the interview".

With the abolition of the need for corroboration or hearsay in civil cases it is theoretically possible for an uncorroborated pursuer to succeed on the basis of hearsay evidence alone. However, there must still be sufficient evidence to found a case, and, as was pointed out in *Gordon v. Grampian Health Board*, the court has discretion as to how much weight to attach to uncorroborated hearsay evidence.[71] In that case, a reparation action against employers, the only evidence was from the pursuer who relied on a

---

[67] *Sanderson v. McManus*, n. 64, at p. 60B–C.
[68] n. 57 above.
[69] It was observed in *MT. v. DT.* that dicta in earlier cases had caused difficulties in that counsel and solicitors had felt obliged to bring children to court for the purposes of determining competency even if there was no actual intention to take the child's evidence.
[70] at 1460L.
[71] 1991 SCLR 213.

hearsay statement from a colleague. That colleague was cited as a witness but not actually called because the pursuer believed she might be a "hostile witness". The sheriff held that "although there was a bare sufficiency of evidence for the pursuer" he was not satisfied that she had proved her case on a balance of probability. As Sheriff Graham Johnston observed in his commentary to the reported case, while "the Act may well have abolished the *necessity* of corroboration to prove an essential fact, it does not abolish the *desirability* of leading evidence to back up the credibility of a party".[72]

Section 2(1)(b) operates so as to permit the oral evidence of experts who speak to written reports as part of their testimony, but who may not be the authors of these reports.[73] Despite the broad terms of section 2, there is still a prohibition, contained in section 9 against evidence given in precognitions. Whereas a statement is written or prepared by a witness, a precognition "is usually not an account of what the witness has actually said but is the precognoscer's reconstruction or interpretation".[74] As such it is considered to be of less value that a direct account in a statement expressed in the witness's own words. In *Anderson v. J.B. Fraser & Co. Ltd.*[75] it was held that what was said to a precognoscer could be distinguished from what was recorded in a precognition. It is competent therefore to lead evidence from a precognoscer as to what the witness said, but not what was recorded. However, the weight to be attached to such statement may be limited.[76]

DOCUMENTARY EVIDENCE UNDER STATUTE

8.19 On a strict application of the rule against hearsay, all entries in documents would be essentially hearsay in nature, since they represent merely what someone has recorded on an earlier occasion. An entry in a document cannot therefore be evidence of the truth of the facts which it records, and even if the person who made the entry is called, he or she may well not be the person with the knowledge of the truth of the facts recorded. For example, the Registrar of Register of Births, Deaths and Marriages simply records information provided by another person. However, rigid adherence to this principle would make many facts almost unprovable, or at best would delay the process of justice to intolerable

---

[72] *ibid.* at 214.
[73] *Smith's Exrs v. Upper Clyde Shipbuilders Ltd* (in liquidation), 1999 G.W.D. 33–1597.
[74] Wilkinson, n. 12 above.
[75] 1992 S.L.T. 1129.
[76] *Cavanagh v. BP Chemicals Ltd.*, 1995 S.L.T. 1287.

lengths. For this reason, Parliament has on many occasions, and for many different purposes, decreed that entries in documents may be adduced as evidence of the facts that they contain, subject to certain safeguards.

Both the Civil Evidence (Scotland) Act 1988, and the Criminal Procedure (Scotland) Act 1995 make substantial provision for the certification of certain types of documents being provable in evidence without the need for a witness to speak to them. Thus, in civil cases section 5 of the Civil Evidence (Scotland) Act 1988, admits, for the purposes of any "civil proceedings", a document suitably docqueted and purportedly signed by "an officer of the business or undertaking to which the records belong". Such a statement may then be received in evidence without being spoken to by a witness. In terms of section 6, a copy document is similarly admissible if it purports to be authenticated by the person making it. Documents and records are defined in section 9 of the Act and include tapes, disks and computer records.[77]

In criminal cases Schedule 8 to the 1995 Act provides for the admissibility of copy documents and for the certification of documents, primarily business documents, which if properly authenticated are admissible as evidence of any fact or opinion of which direct oral evidence would be admissible. Document is defined very broadly in paragraph 8 to Schedule 8 and includes maps, plans, graphs, drawings, photographs, discs, tapes, and films.

Apart from these major statutory provisions, other statutes render admissible, for the limited purposes specified in each statute, various other records, mainly of a public nature. For example, section 41 of the Registration of Births, Deaths and Marriages (Scotland) Act 1965 renders extracts or abbreviated certificates issued by the relevant registrar evidence of the facts they record, although it is necessary in practice to produce other evidence in order to identify the persons named in the record. Entries in the Registers of Sasines, Inhibitions and Adjudications, the Books of Council and Session and court records are all admissible under statutes applicable to them. There is also general authority for the statement that all public records may be regarded as evidence of the facts which are recorded in them, as may official records kept by a public officer.[78]

---

[77] This replaces an earlier and similar provision contained in s.7 of the Law Reform (Miscellaneous Provisions) (Scotland) Act 1968.
[78] Dickson, *Evidence*, paras 1104, 1204 and 1209.

CHAPTER 9

TYPES OF EVIDENCE

INTRODUCTION

9.01 Evidence can be classified in various ways, including:

    (i) Oral, Real or Documentary
    (ii) Direct or Circumstantial
    (iii) Primary or Secondary

These three classifications are not mutually exclusive, but are simply three separate methods of categorising all items of evidence. Thus all evidence, while being oral, real or documentary, may also be classified as either direct or circumstantial, and as either primary or secondary. Each classification serves a different purpose, and each has its own relevance to the conduct of a case.

ORAL, DOCUMENTARY AND REAL EVIDENCE

ORAL EVIDENCE

9.02 "Oral" evidence is simply the verbal testimony of a witness in court. The law of evidence places great value on the oral testimony of a witness. It is the foundation of our adversarial system. The witness will, ideally, be describing something which he or she has perceived through their own senses—something seen, heard, smelt or felt. If a witness seeks simply to relate what someone else perceived and communicated, then that witness's testimony may well be rejected as hearsay. In criminal cases hearsay evidence is generally inadmissible. In civil cases it is admissible, by virtue of the Civil Evidence (Scotland) Act 1988, but it is not best evidence.

    In certain cases, the main purpose of the witness's testimony lies not in what was perceived. For example, the purpose of an expert witness in many cases is to give testimony in support of a report lodged as a production. In such cases, the entire evidence given by that witness is best regarded as oral evidence. The actual content of oral testimony is, of course, capable of further classification. If, for example, witness W states that she saw A hit B, then in an assault trial this is *direct* evidence. If, on the other hand, W's testimony is to the effect that she saw A running from the scene of the assault, then her evidence is circumstantial. This method of classifying evidence is further considered below and has already been encountered on several other occasions in earlier chapters.

REAL EVIDENCE

"Real" evidence, has been defined as, "a thing, which may be a **9.03** human being, any features of the thing which are significant, and the inferences to be drawn from the existence of the thing or from its significant features".[1]

Real evidence is something tangible and physical, and most such items of evidence are known as "productions". The court is being asked to examine the production and draw its own conclusions from it. Thus, in crimes of violence against a person involving a weapon, the Crown will lodge the weapon, if available, as a production in court, and, if useful, any items of clothing of the victim or accused in order that the court may draw appropriate inferences.

Another type of real evidence is that contained within audio and visual recordings. In *Hopes and Lavery v. H.M. Advocate*,[2] it was held that a tape-recording of an incriminating statement by a blackmailer obtained by "wiring up" the intended victim was "direct" and "primary" evidence. The taping of a confession in a police station was first held admissible in *Lord Advocate's Reference No. 1 of 1983*.[3] In *Bowie v. Tudhope*,[4] the court accepted identification evidence from two police officers who knew the accused and who had picked him out on a video film of a robbery in a shop. It would be competent to allow juries to see such films for themselves

---

[1] Walker and Walker, *Law of Evidence in Scotland*, para. 18.1.1.
[2] 1960 J.C. 104.
[3] 1984 S.L.T. 337. It was held in this case that a written transcript of the confession should normally be supplied to the court. Section 277 of the Criminal Procedure (Scotland) Act 1995 makes provision for the reception by the court of a certificate signed by the person making such a transcript. A copy must be served on the accused not less than 14 days before his trial, and in the absence of any defence objection, not less than six days prior to the trial, the certificate will be regarded as conclusive evidence of the making of the transcript and of its accuracy. Alternatively the oral evidence of the maker will be regarded as having the same effect.
[4] 1986 S.C.C.R. 205.

and form their own conclusions as to the identities of those shown on them.

Real evidence may be offered to a court for a variety of purposes. In some cases, it is made available by one of the parties simply because it features in the case, and is required to prove an essential fact, and not because anything particularly significant may be deduced from its appearance. For example, in a routine shoplifting case, it is expected that the Crown will produce the items stolen but very rarely will they yield any evidence themselves. In a rape case the items of clothing of an alleged rape victim are important because of the body fluid stains identified upon them and examined in the experts' reports, but are not in themselves usually significant.

In some cases, however, the item of real evidence tells an important story in itself. This may be because of certain deductions that the court can make from its appearance, or because of its very existence. In *Sandells v. H.M. Advocate*,[5] the important question was whether a cigarette vending machine wrenched from the wall of a social club and removed from the premises had been stolen by one man or two. The appearance and weight of the machine in question was considered to be a crucial issue in the case. Similarly, as was seen in *Patterson v. Nixon*,[6] the behaviour of a police tracker dog proved sufficiently important to corroborate a partial confession by the accused.

Often, the significance of an item of real evidence is only apparent with the assistance of expert testimony. In a drunk-driving case it is the forensic certificate that accompanies the blood/urine sample which is of significance. The sample—or rather its remains—must always be produced in court, but the focus is on the blood/alcohol reading produced by a small portion of the sample now no longer available because of the destructive nature of the test itself.[7]

Blood tests are used as items of real evidence in a variety of cases. In civil cases they are commonly used in paternity disputes. In *Docherty v. McGlynn*,[8] the lover of a deceased woman sought to show that a child born during her marriage was in fact his child. He relied upon the results of blood tests, the deceased's blood having been taken before her death for other purposes. On the strength of

---

[5] 1980 S.L.T. (Notes) 45.

[6] 1960 J.C. 42.

[7] The same is true for fingerprint evidence (see *H.M. Advocate v. Dennison*, 1978 S.L.T. (Notes) 79) and evidence yielded by dental impressions (*Hay v. H.M. Advocate*, 1968 J.C. 40) and body fluids such as semen (*Preece v. H.M. Advocate* [1981] Crim.L.R. 783). These cases are all considered in Chap. 16.

[8] 1985 S.L.T. 237. The case pre-dated the Law Reform (Parent and Child) (Scotland) Act 1986 which reduced the standard of proof from beyond reasonable doubt to that of a balance of probabilities.

the blood test evidence the court concluded, beyond reasonable doubt, that the deceased's husband could not have been the father of the child, and on a balance of probabilities that the lover could have been. The question of consent to the taking of a blood sample, which was an issue in *Docherty*, is now regulated by statute. Section 6 of the Law Reform (Parent and Child) (Scotland) Act 1986, provides for the obtaining of consent in civil cases relating to "the determination of parentage".

A witness or a party to a civil action is not obliged to submit to a blood test. At common law the court has no power to compel an adult to provide a blood sample to determine paternity whether through blood tests or DNA profiling (otherwise known as genetic fingerprinting).[9] However, section 70(1) of the Law Reform (Miscellaneous Provisions) (Scotland) Act 1990 empowers the court to request a party to proceedings to provide a sample or consent to the taking of a blood sample from a child.[10] Although such blood tests are not compulsory section 70(2) states that the court may draw adverse conclusions from a refusal to provide such a blood sample. In an action of declarator of paternity it has been held that this section extends to the situation where the court may request an executor of a party to provide a blood sample. This occurred in *Mackay v. Murphy*,[11] where the executor was the mother of a deceased soldier. The deceased was a party to a paternity action raised against him. The executor was therefore the alleged grand-mother of the child.

In criminal cases, the police have powers to take certain bodily samples for testing, including DNA profiling. A refusal to provide a blood sample for this purpose on the ground of "needle phobia" will not prevent the police obtaining a warrant authorising a finger prick procedure.[12]

When real evidence is produced in court, it must be formally lodged as a production by whichever party is relying upon it. It must be spoken to by at least one witness (or be covered by joint minute of the parties) in order to make it available as evidence, unless by statute there is no requirement to call such a witness.[13]

When a document in question has relevance simply because of its very existence, it remains an item of "real" evidence. For

---

[9] *Torrie v. Turner*, 1990 S.L.T. 718.
[10] As amended by the Children (Scotland) Act 1995, and see too, section 2(4) of the Age of Legal Capacity (Scotland) Act 1991.
[11] 1995 S.L.T. (Sh. Ct) 30.
[12] *G. v. Lees*, 1992 S.C.C.R. 252.
[13] For example, s.16(1) of the Road Traffic Offenders Act 1988, in the case of a certificate relating to a blood or urine sample taken in the course of a drink-driving investigation. On the requirement for a witness to speak to a production before it becomes evidence, see *Hamilton v. H.M. Advocate*, 1980 J.C. 66. The jury may not necessarily insist on taking a production into the jury room with them, see *Hamilton v. H.M. Advocate*; *Sandells v. H.M. Advocate*, n. 5 above, and *McMurdo v. H.M. Advocate*, 1987 J.C. 61.

example, a document that has been stolen, or forged, and then forms the basis of a criminal charge, would be an item of real evidence when lodged in court. When a document is adduced for its *content* it falls into a separate class of evidence known as "documentary" evidence.

DOCUMENTARY EVIDENCE

9.04 "Documentary" evidence may be defined as, "any written or printed matter expressed in words and also drawings, plans and maps".[14] Various statutes provide their own definition. For example, section 9 of the Civil Evidence (Scotland) Act 1988 defines a "document" so as to include, in addition to the items listed above, photographs, discs, tapes and films. Schedule 8 to the Criminal Procedure (Scotland) Act 1995 extends the definition of a document to also include "a sound track on which sounds or other data are recorded . . . a negative, disc or other device in which one or more visual images are recorded." In *Rollo v. H.M. Advocate*,[15] a prosecution under the Misuse of Drugs Act 1971, the court extended the definition of document to an electronic notepad, holding that the essence of a document is not its form but the information recorded on it. In practice, many mechanical recordings are now accepted as evidence of their contents, and since this is precisely the function of documentary evidence, the supposed distinction between real and documentary evidence may be largely academic. However, where a document is adduced in evidence under a statutory provision operating as an exception to the hearsay rule the distinction is still necessary.

An early definition of documentary evidence was provided in *Jacobs v. Hart*,[16] which ruled that a "writing" cannot come within the definition of "documentary" evidence, until there is some fact within it which the contents tend to prove. A document that is shown to the witness solely for the purposes of identification is classified as a production only. A document that is relied on or referred to for its terms in court, must either be incorporated in civil pleadings or "noted" by the court during the course of a criminal trial. This is so that in the event of any appeal, the appeal court has available to it all the evidence upon which the first

---

[14] Wilkinson, *The Scottish Law of Evidence*, p. 7.
[15] 1997 J.C. 23.
[16] (1900) 3 Adam 131 at 140.

instance judgment was based.[17] The distinction between the two depends on the purpose of the document in court. As Lord McLaren explained in *Jacobs v. Hart*[18]: "Is it necessary that the judge should read the contents of the writing produced, or is it only shown to the witness for the purposes of identification?"

Some forms of documentary evidence are subject to special rules, most of which are dealt with in other chapters. For example, some forms of documentary evidence fall within categories that may be "judicially noted". These were considered in Chapter 4, and include Acts of Parliament and statutory instruments. Documents that prove the record of a previous conviction, or of a finding of adultery in a previous divorce action may be used in a later case without need for further proof.[19] If not admitted for this purpose, then the document is not admissible *in causa* in the case itself, but a previous conviction may be used in considering sentence in a criminal case. In certain circumstances a document that comprises a statement may be admissible as evidence of its contents as an exception to the hearsay rule.[20] However, where a party wishes to found on a document and its contents then that document, if available, should be lodged as a production. It will not be sufficient to lodge a copy of the document or to provide oral testimony of the contents of the original document.[21] In some limited circumstances, when such a document amounts to a prior statement it may be used to discredit a witness by demonstrating the inconsistency of his or her evidence, although it never becomes evidence in its own right (see Chapter 10).

PROVING PRIVATE DOCUMENTS

Private documents may be defined as those that are not maintained **9.05** or compiled for public or official purposes, but which are used in support of a private action between two parties. Typically, a document could be used in a court action to prove the existence of an obligation or to prove the existence of a defence or counterclaim.

For the purposes of the law of evidence a document can have "self-proving" status and be valid if it complies with the statutory requirements of subscription set out in the Requirements of Writing (Scotland) Act 1995. This statute, which came into force

---

[17] Lord MacLaren in *Ogilvy v. Mitchell* (1903) 4 Adam 237 at 245. For the suggested best procedure in a criminal case, see Renton and Brown, *Criminal Procedure*, para. 14–75.
[18] (1900) 3 Adam 131 at 140
[19] See Chap. 5.
[20] See Chap. 8.
[21] *Japan Leasing (Europe) plc v. Weir's Trustee (No. 2)*, 1998 S.C. 543.

on August 1, 1995, made radical changes to the law relating to the authentication of deeds.[22] Authentication is the process of prescribing the formalities of execution of documents. Section 2 of the Act provides for a new type of "self-proving" status. Provided a document is subscribed by the grantor, signed by one witness and contains details of the witness's name and address, it will have self-proving status. In terms of section 1, writing is required for the effective constitution of certain types of contracts: *i.e.* those relating to heritage, wills, gratuitous unilateral obligations (except where undertaken in the course of a business), and trusts (where the trustor is the sole trustee). Even if the statutory requirements for subscription are not met, then in some cases it may be possible to apply to the court under section 4 for certification of self-proving status.

A document which is not self-proving in terms of the Act or which has not been certified as such by a court, may be proved to be authentic by means of any competent evidence available and acceptable to the court. Such evidence may well be that of the person who made the documents[23] or someone who saw it being compiled. Equally, a document that is not self-proving may be challenged as to its authenticity by any admissible means available to the party challenging it, and it is not necessary to do so by means of an action of reduction.

Section 11(1) of the Requirements of Writing (Scotland) Act 1995 abolished the previous rule of evidence that in relation to certain types of contract, *i.e.* loans of a limited amount, obligations of relief and innominate and unusual contracts, proof was restricted to the writ or oath of the defender. Such contracts may now be proved by any competent and admissible means.

CHALLENGING THE TERMS OF A PRIVATE DOCUMENT

9.06 As indicated above, when two parties have chosen to record the terms of an agreement in writing, it is regarded as the best possible evidence of what they agreed. Consequently it is not normally open to either of them, at some later date, to adduce any evidence that will have the effect of varying, adding to or contradicting the clear written terms of that agreement. This is sometimes referred to as the "parole evidence rule",[24] and its rationale was explained in the leading case of *Inglis v. Buttery*[25]:

---

[22] See Rennie and Cusine, *The Requirements of Writing (Scotland) Act 1995.* and Walker and Walker, n. 1, Chap. 22.

[23] *i.e.* compiled it, but not necessarily as the person in possession of the facts recorded in it.

[24] See Walker and Walker, n. 1, para. 27.2.1.

[25] (1878) 5 R. (H.L.) 87 at 102.

"Where parties agree to embody and do actually embody their contract in a formal written deed, then in determining what the contract really was and really meant, the court must look to the formal deed and to that deed alone. This is only carrying out the will of the party."

A previous agreement may, of course, be cancelled by a later one which is expressed to have such an effect or which is so regarded in law,[26] but otherwise the general rule is that once completed, a written agreement stands alone on its own terms.

There is a long list of recognised exceptions, to this general rule which are considered in detail elsewhere.[27] The following are among the best known.

(1) Evidence to show that the document is not valid

It is permissible to prove that the document is not the valid **9.07** record that it purports to be. Such categories include documents allegedly obtained by improper execution, fraud, essential error and fear, etc.[28]

(2) Evidence to show that the document is not operative

Evidence is admissible to show whether or not a document is **9.08** operative. For instance, a question may be raised as to whether a prior condition has been purified,[29] or ceased to be operative, perhaps because it has been rendered impossible.

(3) Evidence to show that the document does not reflect the parties' intentions

In *Hotson v. Paul*,[30] an action over a bond, extrinsic evidence was **9.09** admitted to show that the bond did not record the correct amount advanced, even though the parties could not agree what the correct amount was. Similarly, where a pure clerical error has led to the parties' agreement not being correctly recorded, parole evidence can be led to show what the parties had really agreed.[31]

---

[26] *e.g.* "novation" in the law of contract, and the superseding of missives by the formal disposition itself: see *Lee v. Alexander* (1883) 10 R. (H.L.) 91 at 96.

[27] *e.g.* Gloag and Henderson, *Introduction to the Law of Scotland*, Chap. 6.

[28] See Gloag on *Contract*, p. 365, and *Stewart v. Kennedy* (1890) 17 R. (H.L.) 25.

[29] *e.g. Abraham v. Miller*, 1933 S.L.T. 161.

[30] (1831) 9 S. 685. See too, *Irons v. Partick Thistle Football Club Ltd*, 1997 S.L.T. 983.

[31] *Krupp v. Menzies*, 1907 S.C. 903.

(4) Evidence to supplement a silent point in a document

9.10   In some cases, extrinsic evidence may be admitted to supplement a document where some aspect of its terms has been left silent. This has been permitted, for example, in cases in which a collateral agreement exists separate from the main one. This situation might arise in the context of missives and the sale of heritage. Provided the collateral agreement is clear and distinct from the main agreement, evidence will be permitted of its existence.[32] Similar exceptions apply in relation to extrinsic evidence that assists in the interpretation of a document, upon which the document itself is silent,[33] or which establishes whether the grantee of a deed was acting in a personal or a representative capacity.[34] Customs of trade may also be proved, where they were intended to apply and are not inconsistent with the document.[35]

(5) Evidence to clarify a latent ambiguity

9.11   The clear terms of a contract or other agreement will be enforced by the courts, even though they may contain an obvious ("patent") ambiguity, such ambiguity being resolved wherever possible by reference to the rest of the document. Where, however, the ambiguity is "latent" (*i.e.* it does not appear manifest from the wording of the document, but only comes to light when the parties attempt to implement it), then extrinsic evidence will be permitted in an effort to resolve the conflict.[36] There is also case authority for the suggestion that the distinction is not always maintained, and that even patent ambiguities may be resolved by recourse to extrinsic evidence.[37]

(6) Incorporation of other writings

9.12   On occasions, a document may indicate, expressly or by implication, that it is intended other documents or writings be read in association with it. For example, a contract of employment may specifically refer to a pension scheme to which an employee will be subject, details of which are available in another document. Or, a testator may incorporate further instructions given to his or her executors in a separate paper into the body of the will. In such cases evidence may be led of those other documents.[38]

---

[32] *Jamieson v. Welsh*, 1900 3F. 176; *Winston v. Patrick*, 1980 S.C. 246; and *Porch v. MacLeod*, 1992 S.L.T. 661.

[33] See, *e.g. Laird & Co. v. Rutherford* (1884) 12 R. 294.

[34] See, *e.g. Renison v. Bryce* (1898) 25 R. 421.

[35] *Tancred Arrol v. Steel Co. of Scotland* (1890) 17 R.(H.L.) 31.

[36] See, *e.g. Cathcart's Trs v. Bruce*, 1923 S.L.T. 722; *McDonald v. Newall* (1898) 1 F. 68; and *Nasmyth's Trs v. N.S.P.C.C.*, 1914 S.C. 76.

[37] See *e.g. Robertson's Trs v. Riddell*, 1911 S.C. 14.

[38] *Inglis v. Harper* (1831) 5 W. and S. 785.

DIRECT AND CIRCUMSTANTIAL EVIDENCE

THE DISTINCTION DEFINED

"Direct" evidence may be defined as evidence which leads directly **9.13** to proof of a fact or facts in issue (*facta probanda*), while "circumstantial" evidence is evidence which has an indirect effect. Walker and Walker describe circumstantial evidence as "evidence of facts from which the fact in issue can be inferred".[39] Thus, for example the evidence of W to the effect that she saw A hit B is, in an assault case, direct evidence of that assault. On the other hand W's statement to the effect that she saw A running away from the scene of the assault on B is circumstantial evidence that A committed the assault, as it proves a fact which itself tends to suggest another fact, which is the fact in issue (*i.e.* the assault). W's statement that she saw A running amounts to indirect evidence of the assault.

Circumstantial evidence has played a prominent role in several of the civil cases already examined. In *Stewart v. Glasgow Corporation*,[40] the pursuer wanted to prove that a clothes pole in a council drying green was known by the landlords to be in a dangerously corroded state at the time of a fatal accident. Evidence was led to show that it must have been in a poor state five months previously, when it was inspected and painted. Such evidence was circumstantial only. In *Bark v. Scott*[41] the court held that in assessing a driver's capability at a given time, it was competent to consider how the vehicle was being driven shortly before, and shortly after that time.

One striking example of circumstantial evidence leading to a conviction in a criminal case was the behaviour of the police dog in *Patterson v. Nixon*.[42] Also, the remarkable set of evidential facts tending to prove the accused's complicity in a robbery in *Norval v. H.M. Advocate*,[43] which Lord Emslie described as "a chain of circumstantial evidence". Evidence of handwriting, fingerprints and dental impressions is, as explained in Chapter 7, also circumstantial in identifying the accused as the culprit in a criminal trial. As such it can be powerful evidence requiring little corroboration. Circumstantial evidence can be adduced by either party, and the court may be left to establish the truth from a string of items of circumstantial evidence, some more compelling than others. For example, the Crown in a criminal case may possess several items of circumstantial evidence that point strongly towards the guilt of the accused.

---

[39] n. 1, para. 1.5.2.
[40] 1958 S.C. 28.
[41] 1954 S.C. 72.
[42] 1960 J.C. 42.
[43] 1978 J.C. 70.

However, quality is always preferable to quantity (subject to any need for corroboration) and variable weight will attach to circumstantial evidence. If the Crown case is founded on only circumstantial evidence it may take little for the accused to raise a reasonable doubt. As Walker and Walker point out[44]: "Even if the accused's fingerprints are found in the premises which have been broken into, the jemmy used was his, and the stolen goods were found hidden in his bedroom, he must be acquitted of the theft if he was in prison when it occurred."

PRIMARY AND SECONDARY EVIDENCE

THE DISTINCTION DEFINED

9.14 "Primary" evidence is the best form of evidence available in support of a particular fact or issue, while "secondary" evidence is, by definition, something less than the best. Thus, the best evidence that A hit B comes from B, and anyone else who happened to witness the assault, while evidence given by W to the effect that B told her what had happened is clearly not the best evidence that can be produced, and will in fact normally be rejected under the hearsay rule.

Similarly, when A sues B, alleging that she possesses certain rights against B under a written contract, then the best evidence in support of that claim is the original of that contract, and not a copy. Once again, where it is alleged that W stole various items from a supermarket, the original items form the primary, or best, evidence, while a photograph of them is inevitably second best.

The distinction between primary and secondary evidence arises from the "best evidence" rule. The application of this rule has become less rigid in recent years as it has given way to the sort of guiding principles restated by the Scottish Law Commission in their *Report on Hearsay Evidence in Criminal Proceedings*.[45] Broadly these were that rules of evidence should aim to achieve reasonable expedition and a reasonable degree of certainty, while avoiding needless expense. The Commission noted that the best evidence rule was rarely applied today.[46] Nonetheless the rule still has some significance and many other rules of evidence have originated from it. A good example is the hearsay rule, which in its pure form rejects "second-hand" evidence, but whose common law exceptions are permitted precisely because they are the best *available* evidence.

---

[44] n. 1, (first edition) para. 9(a).
[45] Report No. 149 published in February 1995 paras. 2.26–2.31.
[46] at para. 3.5.

There is also the rule that in the case of a document which is relied upon as establishing a right of one party against the other, then only the original will do, unless the party relying upon it can "prove the tenor" of it in a separate action. The hearsay rule is considered in an earlier chapter, but the remaining applications of the best evidence rule in civil and criminal cases are examined below in more detail.

BEST EVIDENCE RULE IN CIVIL CASES

As noted earlier in *Stewart v. Glasgow Corporation*,[47] a crucial issue **9.15** in the case was the allegedly corroded condition of a clothes pole in a local authority drying green. Several times during the proof pointed reference was made to the fact that the pole itself was not produced, most notably when the court rejected the evidence of an "expert" witness who had not even examined the pole, but tried to rely upon the verbal description given by another expert who had examined it.

Similarly, in *McGowan v. Belling & Co.*,[48] a claim for injuries sustained in a house fire hinged upon the allegedly defective state of an electric fire, which was never made available for inspection at any time after the fire, and was not lodged as a production. An attempt to adduce expert evidence based on an examination of an appliance, allegedly identical to the one involved in the accident, was rejected on the ground that the best evidence rule required the production of at least the appliance that had been examined. The court considered it unreasonable for the offending fire not to have been produced, as it was still in existence. In its absence, the court held that "an oral description of its condition . . . was inadmissible and any expert evidence based on its alleged condition was also inadmissible".[49] In all such cases, clearly it is for the court to assess how much the failure to adduce potential evidence detracts from the overall case of the party who should have adduced it.

The clearest application of the best evidence rule in civil cases is the rule that when a document is fundamental to a claim being made by one of the parties, then the original of that document must be produced. If the original cannot be produced then the

---

[47] n. 40 above.
[48] 1983 S.L.T. 77.
[49] *ibid.* at 78.

problem can only be overcome if the parties accept a copy of the original, or if section 6 of the Civil Evidence (Scotland) Act 1988 applies. Section 6 (1) provides that a copy document properly authenticated by the person making the copy shall be deemed a true copy.[50] If the parties agree that a copy is sufficient then their acceptance should be incorporated into a joint minute, or an admission is required on record to the effect that a document quoted *ad longum* in the averments is genuine.

The absence of an original document is fatal to the party seeking to establish the point evidenced by the document, (if a joint minute or an admission cannot be secured), unless the party can prove the contents of the document by means of an action of "proving the tenor" of it, or unless the document was lost or destroyed while in the hands of the other party.[51]

When the missing document does not constitute the foundation of a party's claim (but is, for example, simply an adminicle of evidence of it), then it is the normal practice for secondary evidence of its terms to be admitted in proof. This is only so if the absence of the document is satisfactorily explained, or if it is in the custody of some person beyond the jurisdiction of the court who refuses to give it up. Whether or not a party will succeed in adducing such secondary evidence will depend upon the circumstances of the case.[52]

BEST EVIDENCE RULE IN CRIMINAL CASES

9.16 In criminal cases the effect of the best evidence is that any production relied on by the Crown must be lodged in court if its absence would be prejudicial to the accused. However, where no such prejudice would arise, and where production would be totally impracticable, then the court may dispense with it. There are, for example, practical problems in the case of very large, fixed or perishable items.

The rule was considered in *Hughes v. Skeen*,[53] in which H was charged with the theft of 78 newspapers from a consignment of 102 which had been left for collection in a common close. The

---

[50] *McIlveney v. Donald*, 1995 S.C.L.R. 802.

[51] For modern examples of the continuing applicability of this rule, see *Scottish & Universal Newspapers Ltd. v. Gherson's Trs*, 1987 S.C. 27; *Crichton v. Wood*, 1981 S.L.T. (Notes) 66; and *Inverclyde D.C. v. Carswell* (Sh. Ct), 1987 S.C.L.R. 145.

[52] e.g. *Eliott v. Galpern*, 1927 S.C. 29; *Young v. Thomson*, 1909 S.C. 529; and *Ritchie v. Ritchie* (1857) 19 D. 505.

[53] 1980 S.L.T. (Notes) 13. See also *McLeod v. Woodmuir Miners Welfare Society Social Club*, 1961 J.C. 5; *MacIver v. Mackenzie*, 1942 J.C. 51; and *Friel v. Leonard*, 1997 S.L.T. 1206.

newspapers themselves were not produced in court, and on appeal against conviction the defence alleged that although H had not been prejudiced by the non-production of the newspapers, the best evidence rule required that they be produced unless to do so was impracticable. The appeal was rejected on the grounds that in the circumstances it was impracticable to produce the papers, and that to have done so would have served no useful purpose anyway. The High Court stated that:

> "in a criminal trial the best evidence rule applies to the extent that where it is both convenient and practicable, productions which are referred to, or to be referred to, must be produced or an adequate explanation furnished for their non-production".[54]

One of the most common reasons for not lodging potential productions is the fact that they are perishable. In *Anderson v. Laverock*,[55] salmon seized from the accused were destroyed prior to the trial. Although the court accepted that it was not practicable or convenient to retain the fish, it was held that the accused should have been informed of the intention to destroy the fish. The failure to do so had materially prejudiced him and the conviction was quashed. In such circumstances therefore, the accused should at least be given the opportunity to examine the items, and perhaps take photographs, where the condition of the items is crucial to the case.

In *Kelly v. Allan*,[56] the issue of "material prejudice" to the accused from the failure to produce an item central to the case arose in the context of a stolen vehicle. Whereas it is normal practice not to produce motor cars which are allegedly stolen, in *Kelly* the charge was reset of a motorcycle which despite missing registration plates, frame and engine numbers was nevertheless identified by the true owner to the police. K did not deny being in possession of the cycle, and did not challenge police witness descriptions of its condition when found in his possession. He did not deny that it belonged to the true owner. The Crown did not produce the motorcycle at the trial, and they did not even produce photographs. An appeal against conviction was rejected on the grounds that in the circumstances, the failure caused no "such

---

[54] *ibid.*
[55] *ibid.*
[56] 1984 S.C.C.R. 186. See also, *Tudhope v. Stewart*, 1986 J.C. 88, another recent case in which lack of material prejudice to the accused seems to have been regarded as the main test of whether or not failure to lodge a production was fatal.

material prejudice as to lead to the conclusion that his conviction represented a miscarriage of justice".[57]

An application of the best evidence rule, in relation to original documents, arose in an interesting context in *Nocher v. Smith*,[58] a case involving illegal possession of drugs found during a police raid under a search warrant. The warrant itself was not produced at the trial, although it had been shown to N before the search took place. The defence argued that since the whole of the evidence subsequently discovered depended for its legality on the validity of the warrant, and since the best evidence of a document is the document itself, the absence of the warrant among the Crown productions was fatal to any conviction. In rejecting this argument the High Court declared:

> "We are in no doubt that in a case of this nature it is desirable that the warrant should be produced, but that does not necessarily mean that its non-production here was *per se* fatal to the acceptance of the evidence of the police officers as to what they found as a result of the search."

The distinction between primary and secondary evidence, and the suggestion that the best evidence rule renders the latter inadmissible, continues to appear in a variety of contexts in criminal cases.[59] However, it is clear from recent case law that unless there is significant prejudice to the accused resulting from a failure to produce best evidence, the admissibility of "less than best" evidence will often be sufficient.

---

[57] n. 56 above at 189. And sometimes not even parts of cars—see *Morrison v. Mackenzie*, 1990 G.W.D. 4–174, where tyres alleged to be defective in a prosecution under the Road Vehicles (Construction and Use) Regulations 1986 were not produced in court. The appeal court upheld the sheriff's view that it was unnecessary to produce the tyres given the inconvenience for the Crown and that there was no resulting prejudice to the accused. For a commentary on this and best evidence in criminal cases, see Duncan Nicol, "Best Evidence in Criminal Cases", 1990 S.L.T. (News) 149.

[58] 1978 S.L.T. (Notes) 32.

[59] e.g. *Hamilton v. H.M. Advocate*, 1980 J.C. 66 (written confession); *H.M. Advocate v. Dennison*, 1978 S.L.T. (Notes) 79 (fingerprint "lifts"); *Hamilton v. Grant*, 1984 S.C.C.R. 263 (photographs of fingerprints); *H.M. Advocate v. Swift*, 1983 S.C.C.R. 204 (tape-recording of confession); and *McLeod v. Fraser*, 1987 S.C.C.R. 294 (computer printout of blood/alcohol reading).

CHAPTER 10

THE COURSE OF A TRIAL OR PROOF

INTRODUCTION

The remaining chapters of this book are concerned with the **10.01** process by which evidence is heard in court. Although this is a book on evidence, the rules of procedure determine how evidence is led and some account must be given of these general rules. It is intended here to provide an outline only of the rules of procedure. For more detailed analysis reference should be made to specific texts on civil and criminal procedure.[1]

THE ORDER OF TRIAL AND PROOF

(1) Criminal trials

In criminal cases the rules of evidence have to be applied in the **10.02** separate contexts of solemn and summary procedure. The main distinguishing feature of these two contexts, which has consequences for the evidential rules applicable, arises from the presence of a jury in solemn procedure, and from the duty that places upon the presiding judge to ensure fairness. The actual order in which the evidence is heard is the same in both types of case, and begins when the Crown call their first witness. Unlike the system in England and Wales, there are no opening speeches by either the prosecution or the defence.

In virtually all criminal trials the persuasive burden of proof is on the Crown, and it is therefore the obligation of the Crown to lead their witnesses first. Each witness for the Crown will first of all be examined "in chief" by whoever appears for the Crown, after which the witness is available for "cross-examination" by the defence. Before leaving the witness box, it is also possible that the witness

---

[1] *e.g.* Macphail, *Sheriff Court Practice*, Maxwell, *Court of Session Practice*; Renton and Brown, *Criminal Procedure*.

may be "re-examined" by the Crown. After leading all their witnesses, but before closing the Crown case, the fiscal or advocate depute will place before the court any record of judicial examination of the accused[2] and any joint minute agreed with the defence. They will have ensured that any productions relied upon by the Crown which are not admissible in their own right have been spoken to by at least one witness.

After the Crown have closed their case, it is the turn of the defence to call their witnesses, beginning always with the accused if he or she is to give evidence. The roles are then reversed, with the defence agent examining the witnesses in chief, and the Crown subjecting them to cross-examination, the defence having the right to re-examine where appropriate. Once the defence has led their last witness, and has no further evidence to offer the court, the normal procedure is for the Crown to sum up their case, leaving the defence with the traditional "last word" by way of defence summary. In solemn trials, the final word comes from the presiding judge who is responsible for giving the "charge to the jury" summarising the law and the available evidence, before the jury retire to reach a verdict. In summary trials the sheriff or justice (in district court cases) may adjourn to consider the evidence before coming to a conclusion. In both types of case, either side may seek to place additional evidence before the court after the formal close of their case, or apply to have a witness recalled after they have left the witness box. These possibilities are considered below.

(2) Civil proofs

10.03   In a civil proof, the order of leading evidence is similar to that described if one substitutes "pursuer" and "defender" for "Crown" and "defence" respectively. It is the general rule that the party bearing the "ultimate burden" in a civil case is the one who must lead evidence first, and this will normally be the pursuer. Most civil cases are heard before a single judge but in some cases there is a proof before a jury of twelve. In a civil jury trial, it is the normal practice for counsel for each party to address the jury in general terms concerning what it is hoped to prove before calling witnesses.[3] Otherwise the procedure is as described for criminal cases, with each party examining their witnesses in chief, having them cross-examined, and then re-examining them where appropriate.

(3) Judicial questioning

10.04   It is also possible, at any stage of either a criminal trial or a civil proof, that the judge will wish to ask questions of his or her own, either to clarify a matter which remains obscure, or perhaps to

---

[2] Criminal Procedure (Scotland) Act 1995, ss.35–39.
[3] See Hajducki, *Civil Jury Trials*, 4.16–4.23.

open up another line of inquiry which seems pertinent. Little formal objection is likely to be raised to such a course in a summary criminal trial, or during a civil proof without a jury, but where the judge is sitting with a jury, the greatest tact and impartiality must be observed if an appeal is to be averted. The parties ought to be offered an opportunity to cross-examine on any new points raised by such questions from the bench.[4] The role of the judge in overseeing fairness and in acting at all times with impartiality will be an important ingredient of fulfilling Article 6 of the ECHR, the right to a fair trial.

OBJECTIONS TO EVIDENCE

At any stage of a trial or proof, the flow of examination and cross-examination may be halted by an objection by one of the parties to a question being asked of the witness, or to an entire line of questioning which is being embarked upon. Two questions then arise under the law of evidence. First, can a party who does not object immediately be said to have impliedly accepted the admission of that evidence? Second, must a trial judge make a decision there and then, or can evidence be allowed in "under reservation" of the question of its admissibility? **10.05**

(1) Implied acceptance by silence

(a) Criminal cases

In summary criminal cases, the position is largely governed by section 192(3) of the Criminal Procedure (Scotland) Act 1995. This section states that in a case in which the accused is legally represented, no appeal may be based on the admission or rejection of an item of evidence unless the appropriate objection "shall have been timeously stated" at the trial. The High Court in *Skeen v. Murphy*[5] explained the effect of this rule: "[U]nless objection to the **10.06**

---

[4] See, *e.g. McLeod v. H.M. Advocate*, 1939 J.C. 68 and *Livingstone v. H.M. Advocate* (Court of Criminal Appeal 2213174), reported in *Tallis v. H.M. Advocate,* 1982 S.C.C.R. 91 in Sheriff Gordon's commentary, and *Nisbet v. H.M. Advocate*, 1979 S.L.T. (Notes) 5. For an example of the same principle in action in a civil case, see *McCallum v. Paterson*, 1969 S.C. 85. For the policy to be followed in summary criminal cases, see *Elliot v. Tudhope*, 1987 S.C.C.R. 85, and for an example of "unjustified" interference in such a case, see *Cooney v. H.M. Advocate*, 1987 S.C.C.R. 60.

[5] 1978 S.L.T. (Notes) 2. *N.B.* that this was a Crown appeal in which the High Court held that the defence failure to object to the late service of the analyst's certificate, etc., in a drink driving case was fatal to the suggestion that the sheriff could not consider them in evidence. The section clearly covers appeals against acquittal as well as conviction. See also *Tudhope v. Stewart*, 1986 S.L.T. 659.

. . . admission of evidence is timeously taken, it cannot be subsequently taken, and, if not, such evidence becomes part of the evidence *in causa.*" However, failure to object to evidence that is *per se* incompetent[6] would not bar an appeal.

There is no equivalent of section 192(3) in solemn cases. However, there are frequent successful appeals against conviction arising from a decision by a presiding judge to admit evidence that is inadmissible, even in the absence of defence objections. Therefore, whether or not the defence object at the time, the wrongful admission of some items of evidence may be fatal to a conviction. A failure to object does not therefore necessarily bar an accused from using the admission of such evidence as a ground of appeal.[7]

In summary proceedings, when either party requests it, objections to the admission of evidence must be noted in the record, in terms of section 157 of the Criminal Procedure (Scotland) Act 1995. An equivalent rule for solemn cases, in terms of section 93 of the Act, requires that such objections are noted in the shorthand record, though in practice most judicial proceedings are now taped.

(b) Civil cases

10.07   In summarising the position in regard to civil cases in 1987, Macphail[8] noted that:

> "It is . . . thought that the rule now generally observed in practice in the courts in Scotland . . . is that a pursuer may not found on a ground of liability which has not been averred and has been the subject of evidence to which no timeous objection has been taken."

---

[6] See Walker and Walker, *Law of Evidence in Scotland*, para. 12.6.4. See also *Handley v. Pirie*, 1976 J.C. 65, *McLeary v. Douglas*, 1978 J.C. 57 and *Robertson v. Aitchison*, 1981 S.C.C.R. 149. See also Renton and Brown, n.1, para. 31–09 and Macphail, *Evidence*, Chap. 8.40.

[7] But see *McAvoy v. H.M. Advocate*, 1982 S.C.C.R. 263, in which the failure by the defence to object timeously to the admission of a statement by a witness which revealed that A had a criminal record was taken into account as part of the circumstances surrounding the case, but the appeal finding was that, overall, there had been no "miscarriage of justice". Sheriff Gordon, commenting at p. 275, pointed out that, "it is not safe for counsel or solicitor to 'sit back and wait for the Crown to make a mistake' as the professional lore used to have it." In other words, even in solemn cases objections should be made timeously.

[8] n. 6, Chap. 8.40.

He did, however, acknowledge that there was authority[9] for the view that the failure of the other party to object timeously to the admission of evidence, which in effect opened up matters not on record, could amount to its admission. In civil cases, the prudent course for the challenging party is to object to the evidence in question as soon as it is sought to admit it, even in a jury trial.[10]

(2) Evidence heard "under reservation as to its admissibility"

(a) Criminal cases

In summary cases, until recently, it was considered that the better practice, where possible, was for the sheriff to admit the evidence *ab initio*, but to reserve the question of admissibility until the end of the trial.[11] In solemn cases the approach that had developed was that questions of admissibility were dealt with as soon as they were raised, and frequently within the hearing of the jury. One of the most important of such issues that arises in practice is the question of the admissibility of a confession. The ruling in *Thompson v. Crowe*[12] is to the effect that in summary cases a judge may determine admissibility as objections arise, and in solemn cases a judge may be obliged to determine such questions outwith the presence of the jury. **10.08**

(b) Civil cases

The general rule in civil cases heard without a jury now seems to be for the judge to allow the evidence in "under reservation" of the question of its admissibility. This permits the issue to be debated later, and also ensures that the evidence is on record for any subsequent appeal court to consider.[13] A failure to follow such a practice will have the effect in some cases of depriving the court of the evidence for all time, and can lead to a successful appeal.[14] **10.09**

The position is different, however, when there is a jury. In such cases, there is a risk that if a decision on admissibility is not made as soon as the point is raised, the jury will be led to rely on the evidence thus admitted, and may not be swayed by any subsequent

---

[9] Notably *McGlone v. British Railways Board*, 1966 S.C. (H.L.) 1, and *O'Donnell v. Murdoch Mackenzie & Co.*, 1966 S.C. 58, 1966 S.C. (H.L.) 63. See also *Brown's Exr v. North British Steel Foundry Ltd.*, 1967 S.L.T. (Notes) 111, and *Gibson v. B.I.C.C.*, 1973 S.L.T. 2, in which the House of Lords criticised the Scottish closed record system for its rigidity.

[10] See, *e.g. McDonald v. Duncan*, 1933 S.C. 737.

[11] *Clark v. Stuart*, 1950 J.C. 8 at 11.

[12] 2000 J.C. 173, dealt with more fully in Chap. 15.

[13] See, *McDonald v. Duncan*, n. 10 and Hajducki, n. 3, at 4.32–4.35. But see also *McGowan v. Mein*, 1976 S.L.T. (Sh. Ct) 29, for a case in which the sheriff saw good reason for departing from this practice.

[14] As in *Baretdji v. Baretdji*, 1985 S.L.T. 126.

instruction by the presiding judge to ignore what they have heard. According to *McDonald v. Duncan*[15] the appropriate procedure is that, "if an objection is taken to the admissibility of evidence, it is for the judge there and then to decide that question and not to hold it up until the conclusion of the whole proof, and then to give a pronouncement on it". This rule still applies in civil jury cases.[16]

Examination in Chief

10.10 Examination in chief is the process whereby counsel or the solicitor for a party elicits from a witness called by that party evidence which it is believed will be favourable to that party's case. It should be noted though that the Crown have a duty to elicit all evidence having a bearing on the case, and not just that which is apparently favourable to them. This belief will be based on information provided by the witness at an earlier date, in the course of a "precognition". However, experience shows that for various reasons, witnesses do not always live up to their early promise. In such situations, the agent for the party calling them may, in varying degrees of desperation, attempt to encourage them to refresh their memories from notes taken at the time. An agent may also ask a witness a "leading question", or put to the witness statements made by them on a previous occasion, or indeed deal with the witness as if they were a "hostile" witness called by the other party.

Refreshing Memory

10.11 It is a cardinal principle of the law of evidence that when a non-expert witness gives oral testimony, he or she should speak from personal memory of something which they experienced with one of their senses. It may therefore seem odd to suggest that a witness may refresh their memory by reference to notes. Nevertheless, this has become the standard practice in many types of situation, and the only prerequisite would seem to be that the notes to which the witness refers must either have been made or dictated to someone else at, or shortly after, the time of the events to which they refer.[17]

There are two familiar examples of this process. First, police officers in a criminal trial frequently refer to their notebooks in order to testify as to precisely what the accused said when cautioned and charged. Second, doctors in the civil proof will usually refer to their notes in order to advise the court of the

---

[15] n. 10, *per* Lord Anderson at 744. See also *McCallum v. Paterson*, 1969 S.C. 85.
[16] Hajducki, n. 13, *loc. cit.*
[17] See, *e.g.* Walker and Walker, n. 6 para. 12.7.1.

precise nature of the pursuer's injuries shortly after the accident. It would seem, however, that refreshment of memory is competent in any case in which the necessary conditions are satisfied.[18] The fact that the witness has had recourse to such an *aide-mémoire* may, of course, affect the weight to be attached to their evidence.

The documents from which the witness refreshes his or her memory do not themselves become documentary evidence in the case—rather they become part of the witness's oral testimony. In the words of Lord Justice-General Clyde in the leading case of *Hinshelwood v. Auld*[19] speaking of the witness who uses notes in order to refresh his memory:

"If . . . when he gives his evidence, he requires to look at the notes in order to enable him to give his account of what occurred, then the notes become part of his oral evidence. They are—so to speak—read into his oral testimony, as a material part of the foundation on which that testimony rests."

If a witness does rely on notes to refresh memory and give oral testimony, then the notes must be made available to the other party. As Lord Justice-General Clyde pointed out in *Hinshelwood*[20]: "In such a case considerations of fairness compel the production of the notes . . . it is obvious that the cross-examiner becomes entitled, not only to see them, but to use them in cross-examination." He added the proviso that, "if the witness does not use his notes to refresh his memory in the witness-box, the notes possess no evidential quality whatever, and production of them cannot be compelled by the cross-examiner". This latter point was affirmed in *Deb v. Normand*,[21] where a police officer had referred to his notebook to refresh his memory before the trial but did not use the notebook while he was in the witness box. He was held entitled to refuse to produce the notebook.

The type of note to which a witness may validly refer in the course of oral testimony must serve simply to *refresh* memory, and may not be used as a total substitute for it. If the witness has no recollection of the events in question then he or she should not be giving oral testimony in the first place, since:

"It is essential to this kind of evidence . . . that the witness have some recollection upon the matter to which the [note]

---

[18] *e.g.* the witness to a road accident who writes down the number plate of the offending vehicle, or the housebreaking victim who makes a list of what is missing.

[19] 1926 J.C. 4 at 7–8.

[20] *ibid.* at 8. See also *Niven v. Hart* (1898) 25 R. (J.) 89.

[21] 1997 S.L.T. 107.

refers; for if his memory is a total blank on it, the document is not made part of his deposition, but comes under the rules as to the admissibility and production of written evidence."[22]

In cases in which the note is being used to refresh the witness's memory, and is incorporated into his or her oral testimony, it is proper practice for it to lodged as a production,[23] though it need not be in a form that would make it admissible *per se*. But a note that represents a witness's only recollection of events must be lodged to even have a chance of being considered admissible.[24]

LEADING QUESTIONS

10.12 A "leading" question is one that either suggests the desired answer, or takes for granted a crucial fact that has yet to be proved. For example, if, in an assault charge the witness complainer is asked by the prosecutor, "He hit you, didn't he?", that would be an example of a leading question which suggests a desired answer. If, before the fact of assault had been established by evidence, the same witness is asked "What did you do after he hit you?" that would be an example of a leading question which took for granted that a crucial fact had yet to be proved.

The general rule is that, whereas leading questions are permissible when put to a witness in cross-examination, they may not be asked of a "witness-in-chief" (*i.e.* a witness called by one's own party). In practice, however, it is acceptable for the agent calling a witness to "lead" him or her through the introductory part of their evidence (name, address, occupation, presence at the locus, etc.) until the point is reached at which the evidence to be given by that witness is likely to be disputed by the other party. Exceptionally (and normally by prior agreement between the agents) a witness may be led through all, or a large portion of, the evidence, where it is uncontroversial and the parties have not arranged in advance for a joint minute to cover it. A typical example is the evidence of a police photographer speaking to photographs taken of the locus, or of a casualty doctor speaking to injuries sustained by a road accident victim.

When a leading question is improperly put, it should be objected to. However, the damage may well have been done if the witness

---

[22] Dickson, *Evidence*, para. 1778. See also *McGowan v. Mein*, 1976 S.L.T. (Sh. Ct) 29.

[23] See *Hinshelwood v. Auld*, n. 19. See too the Criminal Procedure (Scotland) Act 1995, s.157, which states that such statements are not documentary evidence, and need not be lodged as productions, in summary cases.

[24] *H.M. Advocate v. McPherson*, 2 Broun 450.

has given the desired answer before an objection is made. Walker and Walker[25] suggest that the form of the question and answer should be recorded, in order to assist an appeal court to assess the reliability of that evidence. Modern practice tends to leave the question of the weight to be attached to a witness's testimony firmly in the hands of the judge at first instance, who can make allowances for the fact that the witness was "led".

PREVIOUS CONSISTENT STATEMENTS BY THE WITNESS

Because of the primacy of oral testimony, special rules have **10.13** developed for the admissibility of statements made by a witness before a civil proof or criminal trial. In civil cases, section 3 of the Civil Evidence (Scotland) Act 1988 provides that a previous statement made by a witness is admissible "in so far as it tends to reflect favourably or unfavourably on that person's credibility". In criminal cases, there is a general prohibition against the admissibility of previous statements other than in specific exceptional circumstances. The reasoning is twofold: first, if a previous statement is related by the witness, it simply duplicates his or her present testimony; and second, if related by someone else, it is usually struck at by the hearsay rule. The position varies depending on whether or not the previous statement is consistent with what the witness is now saying in the witness box. In both cases there is a recognition that evidence is always admissible of the fact that a statement was *made*, as opposed to evidence of the contents of that statement. This reflects the distinction made in the hearsay rule regarding original evidence and "hearsay".

(1) Criminal cases

(a) De recenti statements

A previous statement may be admitted if it has been made *de* **10.14** *recenti*. These types of statements arise in a limited class of cases, namely those in which an accused person is charged with an assault, particularly a sexual assault. In such cases, it is competent to offer support for the complainer's testimony by leading evidence to show that the complainer first made his or her allegations against the accused shortly after the event, and usually to a close trusted friend or relative. This type of early statement—known as a *de recenti* statement[26]—is taken to provide positive evidence in support of the credibility of the complainer. The absence of any early complaint has become regarded as a point in favour of the defence.

---

[25] n. 6, para. 12.5.3.
[26] And as such a recognised exception to the hearsay rule: see Chap. 8.

De recenti statements can themselves be used in support of the witness's credibility. In *Morton v. H.M. Advocate*,[27] M was accused of dragging his victim up a close and sexually assaulting her. Among the items of evidence unsuccessfully offered by the Crown as corroboration was the fact that shortly after the assault, the victim went home to her brother in a distressed condition and complained of being assaulted. Speaking of the practice of allowing such evidence to be heard in assault cases, Lord Justice-Clerk Aitchison[28] stated that:

> "the Court will allow the evidence of complaints or statements *de recenti* made by the injured party, for the limited purpose of showing that the conduct of the injured party has been consistent and that the story is not an afterthought, and, in the case of assaults upon women, to negative consent. A complaint *de recenti* increases the probability that the complaint is true and not concocted, and the absence of complaint where sexual offences are alleged is always a material point for the defence. But it must be clearly affirmed that the evidence is admissible as bearing on the credibility only, and the statements of an injured party, although made *de recenti* of the commission of a crime, do not in law amount to corroboration . . . A statement of the injured party *de recenti* is nothing but the statement of the injured party, and is not evidence of the fact complained of."

Such statements are only admissible when they are made as soon after the alleged assault as is reasonable in the circumstances.[29] The *de recenti* rule was applied in *Begg v. Tudhope*,[30] which demonstrated that one potential use for such a statement is to supply the credibility required of a victim in order that her statement may be used as a foundation for the application of the *Moorov* doctrine.

(b) Reply to caution and charge

10.15 In current criminal practice, even in summary cases, it is normal policy for police officers to relate to the court what the accused said when cautioned and charged. In many cases this is incriminating and constitutes a confession. In all cases it is admitted as an

---

[27] 1938 J.C. 50, considered more fully in Chap. 7.
[28] *ibid.* at 53.
[29] See *Anderson v. McFarlane* (1899) 1 F. (J.) 30, and *Hill v. Fletcher* (1847) 9 D. 7. Although both these cases were civil cases they involved allegations of a criminal offence.
[30] 1983 S.C.C.R. 32. Here, there was an attempt to use the girl's complaint to a teacher shortly after the alleged event as corroboration of her oral testimony, on the grounds that it was admissible as part of the *res gestae*.

exception to the hearsay rule in so far as it is offered as evidence of the truth of its contents.

(c) Mixed statements

Where the accused is relying on evidence derived from a **10.16** previous statement that he or she gave, and that statement is mixed, in that parts of it are exculpatory while other parts are incriminating, then that prior statement can be admitted. However, in such circumstances the court must have regard to the whole contents of the statement—both exculpatory and incriminatory.[31] As the court explained in *Morrison v. H.M. Advocate*,[32] "it would be unfair to admit the admission without also admitting the explanation"[33] and it was then for the jury to decide which, if any, parts of the statement they accepted as true.

The court in *Morrison* also reinforced the general rule that:

> "[a] prior statement of an accused which is not to any extent incriminatory is admissible for the limited purpose of proving that the statement was made, and of the attitude or reaction of the accused at the time when it as made".

(d) Evidence of previous identification

A fourth situation when a previous statement may be admitted **10.17** arises when a witness at a trial identifies the accused in court and states that identification was also made of the accused on an earlier occasion, *e.g.* at an identification parade. When the witness identifies the accused again when in the dock, then the evidence of previous identification (*e.g.* during a formal identification parade) would seem to be superfluous; nevertheless it seems to be a practice that "has existed without objection for many years".[34]

The practical effect is probably to bolster the credibility of the witness on a crucial matter central to any subsequent conviction. There are times though when a witness, who may have picked out the accused in an identification parade, is unable subsequently to identify the accused in court as the person the witness believes committed the crime. In such circumstances the law permits other witnesses (usually police officers) to give evidence that on an earlier occasion it was the accused who was picked out by the witness. Provided the witness confirms that an identification was

---

[31] *Morrison v. H.M. Advocate*, 1990 J.C. 299 (a seven bench decision).
[32] *loc. cit.*
[33] at p. 313. See too, *Hoy v. H.M. Advocate*, 1997 S.L.T. 26.
[34] Macphail, n. 6, Chap. 19.60.

made earlier, then there is considered to be corroboration of the identification of the accused.

The Scottish Law Commission pointed out that the courts in England have now held this type of evidence to be inadmissible hearsay. Nonetheless, the rule has been extended on several occasions. In *Muldoon v. Herron*[35] it was held that even if the witness at the trial denies having identified the accused previously, if the police give evidence to the effect that identification did occur, the evidence of the police can be relied on as evidence of who in fact was identified. The rule also extends to identification by description given previously to the police.[36]

(e) Section 260 Criminal Procedure (Scotland) Act 1995

10.18   The Criminal Procedure (Scotland) Act 1995 enacted a statutory provision that was intended to embody the *ratio* of the decision in *Jamieson v. H.M. Advocate (No 2)*.[37] The Scottish Law Commission had recommended that the principle emerging in *Jamieson* be given legislative effect.[38] In *Jamieson* a witness stated in court that she could not remember details of an assault. As part of her examination-in-chief by the Crown she acknowledged that she had made an earlier statement to the police about the incident and that the prior statement was a true statement. A police officer to whom the witness had given the original statement then gave evidence regarding its content. The accused was convicted and appealed on the ground that the police officer's evidence was inadmissible hearsay.

The court applied the principle in *Muldoon v. Herron* which they declared to be "of wider application and . . . not confined to identification evidence".[39] In this case the court considered there were two separate and primary sources of evidence, namely, (i) the evidence of the police officer as to what was said to him by the witness; and (ii) the evidence of the witness that she had made a statement to the police officer and that what she said to him at the time was true.

(2) Civil Cases

To bolster the credibility of a witness

10.19   The position with regard to previous statements in civil proceedings is less strict than in criminal proceedings. Since the abolition of the hearsay rule in terms of section 2 of the Civil Evidence

---

[35] 1970 J.C. 30, also discussed in Chap. 7.
[36] *Frew v. Jessop*, 1990 S.L.T. 396.
[37] 1994 S.C.C.R. 610
[38] Report No 149, *Report on Hearsay Evidence in Criminal Proceedings*, published in 1995, at paras 7.39–7.40.
[39] *per* the Lord Justice-General at p 618.

(Scotland) Act 1988, it is admissible to lead evidence of the *content* of a witness's previous statement. It had always been possible to lead evidence of the making of the statement. As indicated above, section 3 permits the use of previous statements both to support or attack a witness's credibility and to lead evidence of the contents of the statement. As in criminal cases though, statements in precognitions remain inadmissible.[40]

When it is alleged that a witness is now giving fabricated evidence, and in particular that it is a recent fabrication, at common law, evidence may be led to show that the same witness told the same story much earlier in the history of the case, in order to negative such an allegation.[41] The evidence of a previous consistent statement can be produced in re-examination, by calling additional witnesses either before the party's case is closed or before the final speeches. The reason for admitting the previous statement is to show that the witness is a more credible or reliable witness by virtue of being consistent with their story.

THE HOSTILE WITNESS

If a witness does fail to live up to early promise regarding the **10.20** testimony given, there are various salvage options open to the party who cited the witness, once this fact becomes apparent. The subtle refreshment of memory, the tactical use of leading questions, and the introduction of previous consistent statements can, however, achieve only so much, and on some occasions the agent for the party calling the witness may realise that the witness is doing more harm than good to the case.

There may be many reasons for this, not the least being a hopelessly optimistic precognition, and it by no means follows that the witness is now lying, or has been "got at" by the other party. However, the agent for the party calling the witness has to make a fairly urgent decision on how to deal with the situation, and reduce the effect of any damaging evidence which that witness has given. One tactic may be to put to that witness, where this is permitted, the fact that on a previous occasion he or she made a statement that was inconsistent with the one that is now being made. Another is to switch to cross-examining the witness rather than conducting an examination-in-chief. In the course of the cross-examination the agent can suggest to the witness that he or she is acting out of bias,

---

[40] s.9 of the Civil Evidence (Scotland) Act 1988.
[41] *Barr v. Barr*, 1939 S.C. 696, *Gibson v. N.C.R.*, 1925 S.C. 500, and, most importantly, *Burns v. Colin McAndrew and Partners*, 1963 S.L.T. (Notes) 71, which imposed the prerequisite that the witness's credibility must first be impugned.

fear, self-interest, etc. In England, such a witness is termed a "hostile" witness and although the term is not officially recognised in Scotland the effect is the same.

It is for each party to decide how best to use a witness, and when and if to change tactic whenever the circumstances warrant.[42] Leave of the court is not required.[43] In *Avery v. Cantilever Shoe Co.*[44] Lord President Normand explained the Scottish procedure as follows:

> "[It] is for the counsel to make up his mind, subject to the Court's seeing that the witness has fair play, how he will examine his witness, and for the counsel at the end of the day to lay his submissions before the Court, having in view his own method of handling the witness, and, if he so chooses, to ask the Court to disbelieve the witness, provided that he has given him a fair opportunity of answering any charge of unreliability or untruthfulness which may emerge from his evidence."

The rule applies to both civil and criminal cases. Thus, in *Manson v. H.M. Advocate*,[45] a prosecution witness appeared hesitant and reluctant to give evidence, then admitted in response to a question from the advocate-depute that she had in fact been threatened by M's wife. The question and answer were held to be quite permissible. The questions put to such a witness are only of use in testing his or her credibility. When they concern the character of the witness, they may be kept to a minimum by the court on the grounds that they concern issues that are only "collateral" to the matter in hand. This point is considered further below.

CROSS-EXAMINATION

PURPOSE AND FUNCTION

10.21 Cross-examination has been described as follows[46]:

---

[42] See Macphail, n. 6, Chap. 8.17. *N.B.* that s.3 of the Evidence (Scotland) Act 1852, and s.263(4) of the Criminal Procedure (Scotland) Act 1995, which permits the putting of previous inconsistent statements to witnesses, and which are dealt with below, do not restrict such questioning to cross-examination of the other party's witnesses.

[43] Unlike the position in England, where leave of the court must be sought to treat the witness as "hostile".

[44] 1942 S.C. 469 at 471.

[45] 1951 J.C. 49. See also *Frank v. H.M. Advocate*, 1938 J.C. 17.

[46] Lord Avonside in *Hartley v. H.M. Advocate*, 1979 S.L.T. 26.

"[cross-examination] consists in questioning an adverse witness in an effort to break down his evidence, to weaken or prejudice his evidence, or to elicit statements damaging to him and aiding the case of the cross-examiner".

Skilful cross-examination therefore has a dual function, testing and "neutralising" evidence given by a witness for the "other side" but also seeking favourable evidence for one's own party. It is sometimes necessary to lay the ground for a particular line of argument that is to be developed later by putting certain questions to a witness under cross-examination.[47] Cross-examination is both a skill and an art and the lawyer embarking on a cross-examination should be aware of the need for ethical practice to ensure proper treatment of witnesses whilst the evidential objectives are achieved.[48] This section is primarily concerned with those rules of evidence which control the cross-examination of a witness called for the other party, but these same rules can also be applied to a witness of one's own, who is now being regarded as "hostile".

THE RIGHT TO CROSS-EXAMINE

The general rule, in both civil and criminal cases, is that every **10.22** party may cross-examine every witness who is called by the other party, and may also, if wished, examine that witness in chief. In civil cases, this is established by section 4 of the Evidence (Scotland) Act 1840. In criminal cases the rule is now applied in both solemn and summary cases by section 263 of the Criminal Procedure (Scotland) Act 1995.

The primary purpose of each section seems to be to allow the opposing party to treat a witness called by the other side as a witness of his or her own, although it also has the effect of confirming each party's right to cross-examine every such witness. In terms of the legislation, it is necessary for the witness to be called and sworn in before the opposing party has this right. However, in criminal trials it has become the practice for the defence to be allowed to call, and examine in chief, any witness who appears on the Crown witness list, but who is not called and sworn by them.[49] Separate from the rights of parties to cross-

---

[47] See *Lee v. H.M. Advocate*, 1968 S.L.T. 155 at 157.
[48] See the Code of Conduct for Criminal Work in *Parliament House Book*, F839. It exhorts solicitors "at all times to comply with good professional practice and the ethics of the solicitors' profession as set out in practice rules, other codes of conduct and textbooks on professional ethics." Advocates are under a similar obligation.
[49] Section 67(6) of the Criminal Procedure (Scotland) Act 1995 allows any party (including a co-accused) to examine *in causa* any witness listed by another party. See *Todd v. H.M. Advocate*, 1984 S.L.T. 123 and *Hunter v. H.M. Advocate*, 1984 S.L.T. 434.

examine, the presiding judge in a criminal trial has a right to put questions to a witness, and even though that right should be used sparingly it may serve to elicit new evidence. In *McLeod v. H.M. Advocate*[50] it was held that the party against whom such evidence operates should, in such a case, have a further right to cross-examine, and Macphail[51] argues that the same rule should apply in civil cases.

Problems can arise in connection with the order in which each of the parties may cross-examine a witness called by one of the other parties, where there is more than one. Taking civil cases first, the normal situation involving a multiplicity of parties will be one in which there is more than one defender, each of whom has interests that are conflicting and each of whom is separately represented.

In such a case, each of the pursuer's witnesses will be cross-examined by each of the defenders in turn, in the order in which they appear in the "instance" of the closed record. The first defender's witnesses will be cross-examined first by the remaining defenders in the same order, and then finally by the pursuer. The second defender's witnesses will be cross examined by the remaining defenders, then the pursuer, and then the first defender and so on,[52] forming a circular order of cross-examination. In *Boyle v. Olsen*,[53] the Court of Session was faced with an unusual situation in which there was more than one pursuer, and it was held that each pursuer might cross-examine, not only the defender's witnesses, but also the witnesses for the other pursuer.

In criminal cases in which there is more than one accused, and each is separately represented, it was established in *Young v. H.M. Advocate*[54] that the evidence of each accused is admissible against the others, and that therefore, "once one of the accused goes into the witness-box in support of his separate defence, the door opens for a general cross-examination by his co-accused for the purpose of vindicating their own separate defences".[55]

Young v. H.M. Advocate also confirmed the right of the Crown to cross-examine a co-accused after the remaining accused have done so. Exactly the same procedure is observed in regard to the remaining witnesses called for each accused, so that "in the trial of

---

[50] 1939 J.C. 68.

[51] n. 6, Chap. 8.24.

[52] As Sheriff Macphail explained, Chap. 8.25: "In a civil action by P against D1, D2 and D3, where the defenders have conflicting interests and are separately represented, P and his witnesses are cross-examined by D1, D2 and D3; D1 and his witnesses are cross-examined by D2, D3 and P; D2 by D3, P and D1; and D3 by P, D1 and D2." In such cases, it seems from *Ayr Road Trustees v. Adams* (1883) 11 R. 326 that all such evidence will be regarded as evidence *in causa*.

[53] 1912 S.C. 1235, a salvage case in which two pursuers conjoined their actions.

[54] 1932 J.C. 63.

[55] *ibid*. at 74. See s.266 of the Criminal Procedure (Scotland) Act 1995.

X, Y and Z, X and each of his witnesses are in turn examined by
X's advocate then cross-examined by Y, Z and the prosecutor.
Accused Y is then examined by his own advocate and crossed by X,
Z and the prosecutor".[56]

The order in which each of the accused is allowed to take part in
this rotating system seems to be the order in which each appears
on the complaint or indictment, and "this is determined by the
Crown on what may be alphabetical, chronological or tactical
grounds; or it may be simply a matter of chance".[57] The presiding
judge has a discretionary right to alter this order, in the interests of
justice or clarity.[58]

IMPLICATIONS OF FAILURE TO CROSS-EXAMINE

It is not essential to cross-examine every witness in a criminal trial **10.23**
or civil proof, and it will be a question of tactics as to when the
opportunity to cross-examine is foregone. There are various circumstances, however, when failure to cross-examine creates
difficulties.

In civil cases the position was summed up by Lord Justice-Clerk
Cooper in *McKenzie v. McKenzie*,[59] who, while conceding that it
should not be necessary for a party to put every fact averred in the
case to every witness called for the other party, nevertheless
observed:

> "[The] most obvious principles of fair play dictate that, if it is
> intended later to contradict a witness upon a specific and
> important issue to which that witness has deponed, or to
> prove some critical fact to which that witness ought to have a
> chance of tendering an explanation or denial, the point ought
> normally to be put to the witness in cross-examination. If
> such cross-examination is omitted, the witness may have to be
> recalled with the leave of the Court, possibly on conditions as
> to expenses; and in some circumstances the omission may
> cause fatal damage to the case."

One situation where a failure to cross-examine can "cause fatal
damage to the case" arises when a party, by allowing a witness to
go unchallenged, effectively permits the court to regard that
witness as credible on that point. But this process does not

---

[56] Macphail, *loc. cit.*
[57] *ibid.*
[58] *Sandlan v. H.M. Advocate*, 1983 S.L.T. 519.
[59] 1943 S.C. 108 at 109. See also *Harringon v. Milk Marketing Board*, 1985 S.L.T. 342
for an example of a case in which failure to cross-examine was nearly fatal.

dispense with the need for the other party to provide sufficient corroboration for their own case. In other words, failure to cross-examine does not operate as a corroborating factor.[60]

In criminal cases, the position is dominated by the fact that the burden of proof is on the Crown to prove the accused guilty beyond reasonable doubt, and that unless this burden is discharged there can be no conviction. The defence lawyers are not obliged to cross-examine all or any of the Crown witnesses, but the risk that is run in not doing so, of course, is that those witnesses will be believed.[61]

The question of the evidential significance of a failure on the part of the Crown to cross-examine defence witnesses arose in *Young v. Guild*,[62] when neither the accused nor his witness (his wife) were cross-examined by the procurator fiscal. On appeal, it was argued that this failure amounted to an acceptance by the Crown of the defence version of events (an assault) and that the Crown should not then have sought a conviction. It was held that while such a failure might well have "an impact on the weight and value of the evidence", it could not operate as a bar to conviction. The court took its lead from *McPherson v. Copeland*, and ruled[63] that:

> "It was for the sheriff to decide at the end of the day on all the evidence before him whether a conviction should result or not. If the unchallenged evidence of the appellant and his wife had even cast a reasonable doubt in his mind about convicting, that would have been enough to warrant an acquittal."

In short, while the Crown, by not cross-examining, run a serious risk that the defence witnesses will be believed, they are still entitled to a conviction if they are not believed. Also, at the end of the day, the Crown must produce a corroborated case against the accused, and it was established in *Morton v. H.M. Advocate*[64] that they may not do so solely on the basis that a witness giving evidence of a crucial fact has not been cross-examined on that fact by the defence.

PREVIOUS INCONSISTENT STATEMENTS

10.24 Earlier in this chapter we considered the admissibility of previous statements that were consistent with what is now being said by the witness. We saw that in civil cases a previous statement made by a

---

[60] *Stewart v. Glasgow Corp.*, 1958 S.C. 28.
[61] *McPherson v. Copeland*, 1961 J.C. 74.
[62] 1985 S.L.T. 358.
[63] at p. 360.
[64] 1938 J.C. 50.

witness is admissible in regard to determining credibility; while in criminal cases there is a general prohibition against the admissibility of previous statements other than in specific exceptional circumstances. In contrast, in criminal cases when there is a suggestion that the witness made a previous statement that is *inconsistent* with the evidence now being given in the witness box, a different approach is taken. In criminal proceedings the position is governed by section 263(4) of the Criminal Procedure (Scotland) Act 1995. That section provides that a witness may be examined as to whether he or she has previously made a statement different from the evidence given at the trial. Evidence can be led at the trial to show that a different statement was made previously.

The fact that a witness has on a previous occasion made a statement that is inconsistent with the one now being made on oath, is clearly of considerable significance, primarily to show that the witness is unreliable. Where this occurs, the witness may be cross-examined regarding the apparent inconsistency. A party seeking to prove a witness's previous inconsistent statement must first of all lay a basis for this by putting to the witness the fact that it was made, and giving him or her the opportunity to confirm or deny that fact. Only if it is denied can the evidence of the previous inconsistent statement be led.[65] As is the position with previous consistent statements, this rule does not extend to precognitions.[66]

A statement made to a police officer at a time when the maker is only a potential witness is not regarded as a precognition,[67] nor is a statement made to a friend.[68] Indeed, in both civil and criminal cases the current trend seems to be to allow witnesses to be challenged on the basis of any previous inconsistent statement made other than in the traditional precognition situation.[69]

In conclusion, the principal function of previous inconsistent statement evidence is to suggest to the court that the witness is not reliable and that the testimony now being given should be ignored.

---

[65] See *Gall v. Gall* (1870) 9 M. 177, *Mactaggart v. H.M. Advocate,* 1934 J.C. 33, and *Paterson v. H.M. Advocate,* 1998 J.C. 183.

[66] See Chap. 8. Precognitions given on oath before a sheriff are statements that can be put to a witness. See *Coll, Petr,* 1977 J.C. 29, in particular Lord Justice-Clerk Wheatley at pp. 32–33.

[67] *Aitchison v. Simon,* 1976 S.L.T. (Sh. Ct) 73, also shows that a false denial that such a statement was made can form a satisfactory basis for a perjury charge. See too *Hall v. H.M. Advocate,* 1968 S.L.T. 275.

[68] *Green v. H.M. Advocate,* 1983 S.C.C.R. 42.

[69] See, *e.g. Dorona v. Caldwell,* 1981 S.L.T. (Notes) 91, and *Low v. H.M. Advocate,* 1987 S.C.C.R 541, in which the statement was later used as the basis for a perjury charge.

CROSS-EXAMINATION AS TO CREDIBILITY

10.25 The previous section considered previous inconsistent statements as a means of attacking the credibility of a witness. In relation to criminal proceedings the Scottish Law Commission canvassed views on whether a prior inconsistent statement might be admissible of its content.[70] They reported that "the weight of opinion was against such a radical reform of the law".[71] One powerful reason against admitting such a statement was the consideration that an "accused could be convicted on the basis of prior statements attributed to witnesses by police officers, even though the witnesses denied having made such statements".[72]

Cross-examination can also be used to put to witnesses questions that are designed to undermine their credibility and show that they are of such poor character generally, that they should not be believed. Cross-examination cannot, however, be used to attack the character of a witness, because the general rule, discussed in Chapter 13, is that character evidence is "collateral" evidence. It is considered marginal and not central to the court's enquiry. As such it is not relevant to the essential facts, and evidence regarding it will be inadmissible. If a witness is shown to have a personal interest in the outcome of a case then that may well affect that witness's credibility but it does not generally disqualify them from testifying.[73]

Evidence suggesting some dubiety about the witness's credibility is regarded as an exception to the general rule that credibility is collateral. But the party attacking credibility is normally only permitted to raise the suggestion that the witness is not to be believed, and leave it at that.[74] It is not permissible to pursue the point and rebut any denial with additional evidence.

RE-EXAMINATION — PURPOSE AND FUNCTION

10.26 The precise purpose and function of re-examination was summarised by Wilkinson[75] as being:

> "to give the party who has adduced the witness an opportunity of clearing up difficulties or ambiguities which may

---

[70] Report No 149, *Report on Hearsay Evidence in Criminal Proceedings*, 1995.
[71] at para. 8.11.
[72] *ibid.*
[73] Evidence (Scotland) Act 1840, s.1; Criminal Procedure (Scotland) Act 1995, s.265(3).
[74] as in *Falconer v. Brown* (1893) 21 R. (J.) 1.
[75] *The Scottish Law of Evidence*, p. 161.

have emerged from cross-examination or to seek to repair the damage which cross-examination may have done".

Re-examination is simply a second chance to examine on matters arising from cross-examination. The normal rules of examination-in-chief must be observed, and in particular no leading questions should be put. Re-examination should be confined to matters already covered in cross-examination, though the permission of the judge may be obtained to raise new matters. In such circumstances the authorities seem to be in favour of permitting further cross-examination.[76] In criminal cases such an approach would certainly be in keeping with the spirit of *McLeod v. H.M. Advocate*,[77] which laid down a general rule that evidence against an accused (from whatever source it originates) is something upon which the accused should always have the right to cross-examine. This applies whether it comes from a witness during examination-in-chief or from the subsequent examination.

FURTHER EVIDENCE

INTRODUCTION

After every witness has been taken through the process of exam- **10.27** ination in chief, cross-examination and re-examination, it may come to light that there is further evidence that might have been taken, but was not. It may be, for example, that a later witness gives evidence that indicates that an earlier witness may not be as credible as was believed at the time, and it may be desired to put this suggestion to the earlier witness. Alternatively, a fresh line of evidence may have been opened up by a later witness, which it is felt might usefully be explored with a witness who has already testified. Or it may simply be the case that the agent for the party calling the witness forgot to ask that witness an important question.

In these circumstances, leave can be sought from the court to recall a witness, or to call completely new witnesses who can supply fresh evidence relevant to the case, but which has only emerged during the case. These witnesses may sometimes be called by the court itself, or they may be called by one of the parties. Such action may be necessary either before or after the close of the case for the party seeking to adduce the fresh evidence. The purposes for which such additional evidence is permitted will vary from case to case.

---

[76] See, *e.g.* Walker and Walker, n. 6, para. 12.2.1, and Macphail, n. 6, Chap. 8.34. See also *Gunn v. Brown*, 1987 S.L.T. 94.
[77] 1939 J.C. 68.

RECALL OF A WITNESS

10.28 A clear distinction may be drawn between the common law rules relating to the recall of a witness who has already testified, and the corresponding statutory rules. At common law, a witness may only be recalled by the presiding judge *ex proprio motu*, or at the request of one of the parties. The recall may be at any stage of the trial or proof, even after both parties have closed their case, but the recall is only ever permitted for the limited purpose of clearing up some ambiguity in that witness's evidence.[78] The recalled witness is classed as the judge's witness, and must be questioned only by the judge. When a witness is recalled in this way, at least in a criminal case, then by analogy with the facts in *McLeod v. H.M. Advocate*,[79] either party may claim the right to cross examine on any new evidence elicited by such questions as may be put by the judge.

This common law rule is obviously very restrictive in its operation, and offers no assistance to a party who wishes to recall a witness to ask specific questions. However, there is statutory regulation of the position. Section 4 of the Evidence (Scotland) Act 1852 deals with the civil position, and section 263(5) of the Criminal Procedure (Scotland) Act 1995 with the criminal position. Both sets of provisions depart considerably from the common law rule, in that the recalled witness remains the witness of the party recalling him or her, and the questions which may be put are not limited simply to those which resolve ambiguities. In addition, the party wishing to invoke the section may do so at any time up to the close of their case. Thus in *Todd v. MacDonald*,[80] the Crown was allowed to recall a witness in order that he might identify the accused when this was vital to a conviction, and the question had been overlooked in chief.

The injustice which could arise from such an interpretation became most obvious in *Lindie v. H.M. Advocate*,[81] which gave rise to a good deal of criticism,[82] and the Thomson Committee[83] recommended a whole new approach to fresh evidence which becomes available in a criminal case after the parties have closed their cases. The current statutory provisions are contained in

---

[78] For confirmation of this principle in solemn criminal cases, see *Lindie v. H.M. Advocate*, 1974 J.C. 1 at 6, and for summary cases see *Todd v. MacDonald*, 1960 J.C. 93 at 95 and 96. For examples of the limitations imposed by the common law rules in civil cases, see *Gairdner v. Macarthur*, 1915 S.C. 589 and *McFarlane v. Raeburn*, 1946 S.C. 67.

[79] n. 50.

[80] n. 78 at p. 96.

[81] 1974 J.C. 1; a decision based on s.4.

[82] See, *e.g.* G.H. Gordon, *"Lindie v. H.M. Advocate"* (1974) 19 J.L.S. 5 and Macphail, *Evidence*, Chaps 8.56 and 8.58.

[83] Cmnd 6218, paras 43.05 to 43.13; Recommendations 120 to 123.

section 268 of the Criminal Procedure (Scotland) Act 1995. This section allows witnesses to be recalled where a party wishes to lead fresh or additional evidence. Various statutory conditions must be met, dealt with below. The position in criminal cases therefore now is that:

(i) *before* the close of the case, either party may seek leave to recall a witness under section 263(5).

(ii) *after* the close of the case, either party may seek leave to adduce additional evidence, including where necessary the recall of a witness, when the conditions of section 268 are satisfied.

These latter provisions may now be considered in the broader context of "fresh" evidence generally.

FRESH EVIDENCE

The recall of a witness is simply one means by which a party in **10.29** either a civil or a criminal case may seek to introduce fresh evidence. As was seen above, there are restrictions placed even upon that limited method of raising fresh issues, and it might never have been allowed at all had it not been for the intervention of statute.

There are many reasons why a party may discover, at the last possible moment, that evidence is now available which was not available earlier, or that evidence is now required to rebut issues raised by the other party that no one could reasonably have anticipated. The rules of evidence that deal with this type of situation differ as between criminal and civil cases.

(1) Criminal cases

The position in criminal law is now governed by the effects of **10.30** sections 268 and 269 of the Criminal Procedure (Scotland) Act 1995. These sections permits the introduction of "additional evidence" after the close of a party's case, but before the speeches begin.[84] The procedure under section 268 is open to either party, who must make a motion to that effect to the judge who may only grant the motion where:

(i) the new evidence is material, and either it was not reasonably available at the time or its materiality could not reasonably have been anticipated (section 268);

---

[84] Ironically, if the facts of *Lindie* above, were to recur, there would still be no statutory remedy, since in that case the speeches had begun.

(ii) it is accepted that at the time when the party closed their case, *either* the additional evidence now being introduced was not available and could not reasonably have been made available, *or* the materiality of such evidence could not reasonably have been foreseen by the party now wishing to introduce it.

Separately, under section 269, the Crown may, with the leave of the court:

(iii) lead additional evidence for the purpose either of contradicting defence evidence which could not reasonably have been anticipated, or of proving that a witness who has given evidence[85] has in the past made a statement inconsistent with the one given during the trial.

The reason for the introduction of this rule under section 269 is, of course, that the Crown will not be in a position to put to a defence witness the fact that he or she has made such a statement, or to bring evidence "in replication" of fresh matters raised by the defence, until after the close of its own case. It would clearly lead to injustice if, purely because of the order in which a criminal trial is conducted, the defence were in a procedural position to counter all the evidence led by the Crown, but the Crown did not have a similar right *vis-à-vis* the defence case.

The judge may permit the additional evidence to be led notwithstanding that a witness must be recalled,[86] and in a solemn case notwithstanding that a witness or a production will now be introduced who or which was not on the original lists served by the parties, and the requisite notice was not given concerning them. In all cases, if the motion is granted, the judge may adjourn or postpone the trial before allowing the additional evidence to be led.

An integral component of the current approach to fresh evidence, is contained in section 269 of the 1995 Act which provides that in both solemn and summary cases, the prosecutor alone may, after the close of the defence case but before the commencement of the speeches, move for leave to call additional evidence for the purpose *either* of contradicting evidence led by the defence which could not reasonably have been anticipated by the Crown, *or* of providing evidence that a witness who has given evidence, gave a previous inconsistent statement on some prior occasion.

---

[85] *N.B.* not necessarily a defence witness, although presumably the Crown can deal effectively at the time with any such issues as may arise in the course of examining one of their own witnesses.

[86] For a case in which the test of evidence "reasonably available" was applied, see *Salusbury-Hughes v. H.M. Advocate,* 1987 S.C.C.R. 38.

The High Court considered the effect of these statutory pro- **10.31** visions (whilst enacted in a previous form in section 149A of the Criminal Procedure (Scotland) Act 1975) in *Sandlan v. H.M. Advocate*.[87] *Sandlan* appeared first on an indictment for theft, along with K. Sandlan was cross-examined by counsel for K, in respect of his movements on the day in question. He claimed to have visited a certain shop on that day, and he was pressed for further details of this in his subsequent cross-examination by the Crown. The Crown then applied for, and were granted, leave under section 149A to lead evidence in replication to show that the visit to the shop in question had in fact occurred two days earlier. S was then allowed to give further evidence to rebut the evidence led in replication, and to call his own solicitor as a witness. It was held on appeal that the operation of section 149A was not restricted to evidence led in chief by the defence, but could in fact apply to evidence elicited from the defence during the course of cross-examination. It is not clear from the report of the case whether this related only to the cross-examination by the Crown, or was thought to extend to cross-examination by a co-accused, and the court also made it clear that the point was being decided *obiter*.[88] No adverse comment was made on the fact that S was allowed to lead further evidence to rebut the Crown evidence in replication, even though, as Sheriff Gordon points out in his commentary to the reported case[89]: "This procedure could theoretically go on for ever."

Fresh evidence may also be heard by the High Court in the course of hearing an appeal from either solemn or summary proceedings.[90] The test for admitting new evidence is a strict one. It must be "important and reliable" and "likely to have had a material part to play in the jury's determination of a critical issue at the trial".[91] Two of the most recent and controversial cases are those of *Church v. H.M. Advocate*[92] and *Elliott v. H.M. Advocate*.[93] These two cases were heard within a fortnight of each other. *Church* was heard first and hailed as a breakthrough in the application of the section in allowing additional evidence to be heard. In the meantime, the appeal in *Elliott* was remitted to a full bench who disapproved the decision in *Church*, rejected the liberal

---

[87] 1983 S.L.T. 519.
[88] See Lord Hunter, *ibid.* at 93. *N.B.* that the possibility of the Crown making use of s.149 appears not to have been considered.
[89] 1983 S.C.C.R. 71 at 96.
[90] ss. 106 and 175 respectively of the Criminal Procedure (Scotland) Act 1995.
[91] *Stillie v. H.M. Advocate*, 1992 S.L.T. 279 *per* the Lord Justice-General at 284c, interpreting the forerunner statutory provision to s.106, namely s.228 of the Criminal Procedure (Scotland) Act 1975, and approving *dicta* in *Cameron v. H.M. Advocate*, 1988 S.L.T. 169.
[92] 1995 S.L.T. 604.
[93] 1995 S.L.T. 612.

implication of section 228 made there, and restated the traditionally strict approach to the question of whether additional
evidence "was not and could not reasonably have been available at
the trial".[94]

(2) Civil cases

10.32   In civil cases, the position with regard to the admissibility of
fresh evidence is far more piecemeal. There is no general rule
covering all civil cases, but certain exceptions have been recognised
in which the "interests of justice" require that evidence "in
replication" of evidence already led should be admitted. In Court
of Session cases,[95] the common law position in both Outer House
first instance and Inner House reclaiming cases is that fresh
evidence may be led after the close of the proof only if it could not
have been made available previously by the exercise of reasonable
diligence. This normally means that no warning of it could have
been gleaned from a careful study of the closed record.[96]

In cases in which the Court of Session is hearing appeals from
decisions of the sheriff court, the Inner House has the power under
section 72 of the Court of Session Act 1868 to hear additional
evidence "if necessary" in the interests of justice.[97] In the sheriff
court itself, a sheriff conducting a proof has no power to hear fresh
evidence after the proof has closed, but the sheriff principal can
hear such evidence in any case appealed to him in terms of section
27 of the Sheriff Courts (Scotland) Act 1907. Such examples as
arise in practice are normally in the nature of *res noviter*, which,
again, could not reasonably have been anticipated at the time of
the original proof.[98] Once new evidence comes to light after a civil
jury trial has been concluded, the only way of dealing with it would
appear to be via a new trial.[99]

---

[94] See the articles by M. Scott, "The Cases of *Church* and *Elliott*", 1995 S.L.T.
(News) 189, and P. Ferguson, "Fresh Evidence Appeals", J.L.S.S. 1995, 264.
[95] For which, generally, see Maclaren, *Court of Session Practice*, p. 562.
[96] Maxwell, n. 1, p. 559.
[97] See *Gairdner v. Macarthur*, 1915 S.C. 589.
[98] See, *e.g. McFarlane v. Raeburn*, 1946 S.C. 67 (alibi not disclosed in closed record
for affiliation and aliment action).
[99] Hajducki, n. 3, 6.38–6.40.

CHAPTER 11

COMPETENCE AND COMPELLABILITY OF WITNESSES

INTRODUCTION

Witnesses are "competent" to give evidence on oath or under **11.01** affirmation when they are permitted by law to testify; and are "compellable" when they can be *forced* to testify under threat of a charge of contempt of court.[1] The general rule is that every person who is capable of giving intelligible evidence is both a competent and a compellable witness.[2] Although most witnesses are required to take an oath before testifying, a witness may choose, for religious or other reasons, to "affirm".[3] The distinctive position of children is dealt with below.

The fact that a person is of bad character, has previous convictions, or even has an interest in the outcome of the case does not prevent them from testifying, since "moral turpitude or interest is a ground of criticism not of the admissibility of the witness but of the reliability of his evidence".[4] It is quite possible though that such a person would find their credibility being attacked.

Despite the wide applicability of the general rule that everyone is both competent and compellable as a witness, there are some classes of persons who are not fully competent as witnesses, and there are others who, while competent, are not compellable. This chapter concentrates on these exceptions to the general rule that still exist. Unless indicated to the contrary, the principles discussed apply equally to civil and criminal cases. The additional complication arising from the fact that some witnesses may claim a "privilege" against answering certain types of question is considered in Chapter 12.

---

[1] See *H.M. Advocate v. Airs*, 1975 J.C. 64.
[2] Walker and Walker, *Law of Evidence in Scotland*, para. 13.1.1.
[3] See ss. 1(1), (3) and 5(1) of the Oaths Act 1978.
[4] *Dow v. McKnight*, 1949 J.C. 38 at 56. This case contains a comprehensive summary of the development of Scots law in this area. For the possibility of attacking a witness's *credibility* on the grounds of bad character, etc., see Criminal Procedure (Scotland) Act 1995, s.265(1)(a).

231

WITNESSES OF LIMITED COMPETENCE

MENTAL INCAPACITY

11.02 The fact that a person is mentally ill, or is suffering from mental incapacity does not, by itself, render that person incompetent as a witness. The test in all cases is whether or not the witness understands the difference between truth and falsehood, appreciates the duty of telling the truth, and can give coherent testimony.[5] It is a question of degree in the circumstances, and, for example, the man who is convinced that he is the reincarnation of John the Baptist may be a perfectly reliable witness to an assault in a bus station.

The decision on the competency of a witness is that of the presiding judge, if necessary after hearing evidence on that point.[6] Once a determination is made on competency, the witness is either sworn in the normal way, or simply admonished to tell the truth. The nature and extent of the disability may of course affect the weight to be given to that witness's evidence. Thus, in *H.M. Advocate v. Stott*,[7] where a night attendant was on trial for the murder of a patient in a mental asylum, testimony was given by another patient. The court heard conflicting medical evidence. One view was that the witness had a reliable memory, while another view was that he suffered from gross delusions. In his charge to the jury the judge commented that the witness had given a perfectly distinct account of what he had seen but that he was "obviously insane". He advised them that since it was impossible to tell how much of the witness's evidence was a reliable product of his memory, and how much emanated from a diseased mind, they should not rely on that evidence except in so far as it was corroborated by other witnesses.

WITNESSES WITH COMMUNICATION DIFFICULTIES

11.03 In principle, there is no bar to the admissibility of testimony from witnesses who are disabled in a way that inhibits their communication skills. The only problem that arises is the physical one of obtaining evidence from the witness. The witness who has a hearing or speech impediment is a perfectly competent witness, though it may be that they will require assistance to communicate their evidence to the court. Any witness who testifies should do so

---

[5] Dickson, *Evidence*, paras. 1550–1554.
[6] *Black* (1887) 1 White 365.
[7] (1894) 1 Adam 386.

on oath. It is competent to use an interpreter, including experts in sign language[8] or, a witness may be able to give replies to questions in writing. The interpreter must also make a declaration *de fidele administratione*.[9] A witness will only be deemed incompetent if all reasonable attempts at communication are fruitless.

CHILDREN AND OTHER VULNERABLE PERSONS

In the last decade increasing concern has been voiced regarding the **11.04** treatment of witnesses within the legal, and specifically criminal justice, system. It is a truism to say that the judicial process is dependent upon members of the public being willing to appear as witnesses. Equally it is trite to observe that best evidence is more likely to be available from witnesses who are treated with respect and protected from intimidation. The advent of the Human Rights Act coupled with the activities of organisations such as Victim Support has encouraged a climate of political change as is apparent from various government publications looking at the position of witnesses.[10] Article 3 of the ECHR states, *inter alia*, that no one shall be subjected to inhuman or degrading treatment. It is certainly arguable that some of the treatment experienced by certain witnesses, notably complainers in rape and sexual assault cases, could be characterised as "degrading" and thus in breach of Article 3. Initially, protective domestic measures were focused solely on children but recently these measures have been extended to persons described as "vulnerable". The remainder of this section considers various matters relating to the competency of vulnerable witnesses, starting with children.

Competency of children

There is no prescribed age below which a child is incompetent to **11.05** give evidence. In *Millar*,[11] a child of three was allowed to testify concerning a sexual assault upon her, where she had made a *de recenti* statement, but in *Thomson*,[12] in the absence of a *res gestae* statement, a child of three was rejected as a witness in a murder trial.

The test to be applied in determining competence is whether the child has a sufficient understanding of the concept of truth, an

---

[8] Experts in sign language used by the deaf: see *H.M. Advocate v. Wilson*, 1942 J.C. 75.

[9] Macphail, *Sheriff Court Practice*, para. 16.65.

[10] See for example, *Towards a Just Conclusion — vulnerable and intimidated witnesses in Scottish criminal and civil cases*, 1998 and *Redressing the Balance — Cross-examination in rape and sexual offence trials*, 2000.

[11] (1870) 1 Coup. 430.

[12] (1857) 2 Irv. 747.

understanding of the duty to tell the truth, and is able to give coherent testimony. Extreme youth may detract from the weight to be attached to the resultant evidence. The judge has a duty to establish the competence of the child, and may hear evidence to assist in making the decision.

Competence has to be established in two stages. First, the court has to be satisfied that the child knows the difference between truth and lies, and second, the child must be admonished to tell the truth.[13] Where a child remains mute throughout the proceedings these requirements cannot be met.[14] Simply asking the child the question, "Do you understand the difference between telling the truth and telling a lie?" may well be insufficient, as the judge has to demonstrate that the steps taken to determine competency could yield enough information to enable such a determination to be made.[15] The competence of children as witnesses has gained prominence in recent years due to the frequency of cases referred to the sheriff court for proof of grounds of referral from the Children's Hearings system. Historically, it had been left to the discretion of the judge whether or not to administer the oath to child witnesses,[16] but modern cases have clarified the position. It is now settled that children under 12 should be admonished to tell the truth, while children aged between 12 and 14 should be sworn by the judge if he or she is satisfied that the child understands the nature of the oath, and it is expected that children over 14 will be sworn.[17]

As was discussed in Chapter 8 in regard to hearsay statements, competency has also created debate in the determination of exactly when the child must be deemed competent. Is it at the time the hearsay statement was made, or is it at the point at which the child could give evidence in court, a possible time difference of months, or even years? At common law, the admissibility of hearsay evidence from children is limited and is a matter that invariably would involve the child being examined for competency during the course of a proof or trial. As we saw, statutory provisions have affected both the civil and the criminal position. In regard to the former, the decision in *MT. v. DT.* [18] ruled that section 2(1)(b) of

---

[13] *Rees v. Lowe*, 1990 J.C. 96, followed in *Kelly v. Docherty*, 1991 S.L.T. 419.

[14] *F v. Kennedy*, 1993 S.L.T. 1277.

[15] *Per* Lord Prosser in *A.R. v. J.G.R.*, a referral from a Children's Hearing, decided December 30, 1998, listed at www.scotcourts.gov.uk.

[16] *Anderson v. McFarlane* (1899) 1 F. (J.) 36.

[17] See Dickson, n. 5, paras 1548–9, *Rees v. Lowe*, and *Kelly v. Docherty*, n. 13, and *M v. Kennedy*, 1993 S.C. 115. Also, Macphail, *Evidence*, Chap. 8.03. Where a child of 13 was not tested as to competency it was held that no objection could be taken subsequently to his evidence, as an objection had been not made timeously during the trial; *Jardine v. Howdle*, 1997 S.C.C.R. 294.

[18] 2000 S.L.T. 1442

the Civil Evidence (Scotland) Act 1988 does not embody a competency test. Thus, statements made by a child can be admitted into court, notwithstanding that the child is not present or examined in court for competency. The position differs in criminal cases, where in terms of the interpretation afforded to section 260 of the Criminal Procedure (Scotland) Act 1995 by *MacDonald v. H.M. Advocate*,[19] a child's hearsay statement can only be used as evidence if the child is present and, having been ordered by the judge to testify, refuses or is unable to do so.

Measures to facilitate children's evidence

The frequency with which children are appearing in court as **11.06** witnesses has led to increasing awareness that the formal procedures of the judicial process are not conducive to assisting children to give evidence. This is particularly so when the nature of the evidence being given is of a difficult or embarrassing nature. It is also felt that it is especially intimidating for children in cases of physical or sexual abuse to have to give their evidence in a witness box placed a short distance from the alleged perpetrator. In 1990 the Scottish Law Commission published their report on *Evidence of Children and Other Potentially Vulnerable Witnesses.*[20] A number of recommendations were made, many of which have been enacted in legislation.

For some time prior to the 1990 Report many judges had tried to alleviate the formality of the court setting by removing wigs and gowns, clearing the court of unnecessary personnel and by rearranging the furniture so that the judge was not in a distant and elevated position. However, it had been recognised that these voluntary practices did not go far enough. Following the publication of the Scottish Law Commission's Report, the Lord Justice-General issued a *Memorandum on Child Witnesses*[21] that suggested a variety of measures that could be taken to improve the position. The objective was to ensure that "so far as is reasonably practicable . . . the experience of giving evidence by all children under sixteen causes as little anxiety and distress to the child as possible in the circumstances".[22] In addition to the three practices mentioned earlier which some judges had adopted, the Memorandum also suggested permitting the child to be accompanied by a relative or other supportive person to sit alongside the child while giving evidence.

---

[19] 1999 S.L.T. 533.
[20] Report No. 125.
[21] Reproduced in H. Dent and R. Flin, *"Children as Witnesses"* at pp. 148–150.
[22] Dent and Flin, *loc. cit*, para. 2.

Protective measures for children and vulnerable witnesses

11.07   The Law Reform (Miscellaneous Provisions) (Scotland) Act 1990 enacted a major recommendation to assist child witnesses arising from the Scottish Law Commission's 1990 Report, namely the option of giving evidence by live television link. That recommendation was subsequently embodied in section 271 of the Criminal Procedure (Scotland) Act 1995. That section was further amended by section 29 of the Crime and Punishment (Scotland) Act 1997, which extended the statutory protection offered to children to "vulnerable persons". The definition now contained in section 271(12) of a "vulnerable person" is any child; any person over the age of 16 who is suffering from a mental disorder; and any person who is suffering from "significant impairment of intelligence and social functioning". Although the Act makes no specific provision regarding the assessment of this last criterion, it would seem that expert evidence of some sort would be necessary in order for an application to then be made for appropriate protective measures to be taken to facilitate the giving of evidence.

Section 271(7) states that a court may authorise the giving of evidence by a vulnerable witness by live television link "on cause shown". The court must have regard to three separate considerations: the possible effect on the vulnerable person if the application was not granted; whether the vulnerable person would be "better able to give evidence" if the application was granted; and the views of the vulnerable person. In considering whether to grant such an application the court may take into account the four factors set out in s. 271(8). These are:

(1)   the nature of the alleged offence;

(2)   the nature of the evidence the vulnerable person is likely to give;

(3)   any relationship between the vulnerable person and the accused; and

(4)   where the vulnerable person is a child, his or her age and maturity.

As noted above, one of the factors that may be taken into account by the court in determining an application for a TV link on behalf of a child who is vulnerable, is their age and maturity. In the first reported case on the matter, *H.M. Advocate v. Birkett*,[23] an application was made on behalf of five children to allow their evidence to be given by live TV link. Three of the children had witnessed an attempted murder of their mother. The court permitted evidence by TV link in the case of only one of the children as

---

[23] 1993 S.L.T. 395, determined under the earlier provision for CCTV link in terms of section 56 of the Law Reform (Miscellaneous Provisions) (Scotland) Act 1990.

he was said to be frightened of the accused. In the case of the other children the court ruled that cause had not been shown in terms of the Act, but that a subsequent application could be made nearer the time if the circumstances changed. This is the only factor which relates to the personal characteristics of the child witness, and it has been noted that the decision in *Birkett* suggests that the mere narrative of a child's age and a reference to a "traumatic event" is not in itself sufficient to "show cause" for granting an application under section 271.[24]

In the second reported case, *Brotherston v. H.M. Advocate*,[25] **11.08** three children gave evidence by means of a live television link. The quality of the resulting evidence was much criticised by the defence during the trial and several aspects of the judge's charge to the jury formed grounds of appeal. In particular, an appeal was taken against the judge's observation that evidence by CCTV link was obviously of less value than direct evidence. The appeal court said that the use of a TV link required a balancing of two interests— fairness to the accused, and avoiding undue distress to the child. In this instance the court considered that the jury had been sufficiently alerted to the risks of this mode of giving evidence.

Indirectly there is additional protection for children (and other "vulnerable" witnesses) in that section 259 of the 1995 Act permits hearsay evidence of a witness to be led in court in circumstances where that witness has refused or is unable to give evidence. In *Macdonald v. H.M. Advocate*,[26] a case involving a child witness, it was held that a "refusal" can only occur after a judge has directed a child to answer, and the child has then refused to do so. The court stated that a "refusal" was not just an inability or difficulty in giving evidence.

The issue of protective measures for child witnesses has been considered in several cases before the European Court of Human Rights.[27] Child witnesses are given explicit recognition in Article 6 of the ECHR in that "the press and public may be excluded from all or part of the trial . . . where the interests of juveniles . . . so require". The explanatory memorandum to the Council of Europe's *Recommendation on the Intimidation of Witnesses and the Rights of the Defence* states that "the welfare of the child witness must, in general, be the paramount concern over other interests, even the interests of justice".[28]

---

[24] Gordon in his Commentary to the case report of *H.M. Advocate v. Birkett,* in 1992 S.C.C.R. 850 at 854.

[25] 1996 S.L.T. 1154 at 1156. This case was also determined in terms of the earlier statutory provisions of the 1990 Act.

[26] n. 19.

[27] *e.g. X. v. Austria*, Application No. 1128/70, 15 Yearbook, 264.

[28] (R. (97) 13) at para. 100.

Section 271(1) of the 1995 Act also permits a vulnerable person to give evidence on commission.[29] This is a procedure whereby the court appoints a commissioner (either an advocate or solicitor of five years' standing) to take evidence from the vulnerable person, whose responses to questions asked by the commissioner are recorded on videotape and witnessed by the accused in a separate room. In determining an application made for a vulnerable person to give evidence on commission, the court has to have regard to the same considerations in section 271(8).

Finally, another measure designed to protect vulnerable witnesses is contained in section 271(6) which permits the use of a screen to conceal the accused from a vulnerable witness. The screen must be of a design to allow the accused to watch and hear as the witness gives evidence.[30] An application for the use of a screen can be made at any time including during the trial.[31]

So far the response by the courts to these protective provisions has been modest. Although screens appear to be in quite frequent use, the Scottish Courts Administration statistics for 1998 reveal that only one application was made that year to permit evidence to be given on commission. These statistics also indicate that 13 applications for live TV link were made in sheriff courts throughout Scotland. Eleven of these were from Glasgow, one from Haddington and one from Falkirk. The figures do not distinguish between the three statutory sections under which applications can be brought. All but one of these applications was granted. No comparable figures are available for the High Court, as apparently no such statistics are kept.

In terms of section 45 of the Children and Young Persons Act 1937, the court has certain power in regard to any proceedings relating to indecent or immoral conduct in which a person under 16 is called as a witness. The presiding judge can order the courtroom to be cleared of all persons from the courtroom except the parties and their legal advisers, other persons directly concerned with the case, officers of the court and the press.

JUDGES, JURORS AND ARBITERS

11.09 When judges are acting in their official capacity their competency as witnesses varies depending on their status as a judge. In *Muckarsie v. Wilson*,[32] it was held that a judge of the Supreme

---

[29] For details of the procedures involved generally in taking evidence on commission see Maxwell, *Practice of the Court of Session*, and Macphail, n. 9, paras 15.18–15.24.

[30] Formerly a provision contained in s.34 of the Prisoners and Criminal Proceedings (Scotland) Act 1993.

[31] *H.M. Advocate v. McGrattan*, 1997 G.W.D. 10–407.

[32] 1834 Bell's Notes 99.

Court could not be called as a witness to evidence given before him.[33] However, judges of the lower courts are competent witnesses to cases heard by them,[34] notably when the testimony of a witness heard by the judge results in a subsequent perjury charge.[35] The distinction would seem to be based on the twin considerations of the dignity of the office and the fact that senior judges are often sitting with a jury.[36]

When judges are acting in their private capacity, as members of the public, they are perfectly competent witnesses to anything they may see or hear. For example, a judge involved in a road traffic incident would obviously be competent to give evidence as to the facts of that incident.

Jurors may not testify to matters which arise in the jury room,[37] whether in civil[38] or in criminal[39] cases, although in all other matters they remain competent witnesses, *e.g.* to an incident occurring during the trial.

It seems that whereas a decree-arbitral[40] must "stand or fall on its own merits",[41] arbiters are competent witnesses on any matter that could form the basis of a challenge to their awards,[42] even though otherwise evidence of the testimony heard by them is incompetent.[43]

PROSECUTORS AND DEFENCE SOLICITORS

According to the rule laid down in *Mackintosh v. Wooster*[44] **11.10** procurator fiscals are perfectly competent witnesses to any matter on which they can assist the court, provided that they are not also conducting the case, and preferably, have had no personal involvement in its preparation. Best professional and ethical practice dictates that any suggestion of a conflict of interest should be avoided. In *Ferguson v. Webster*,[45] Lord Deas noted that:

---

[33] But he could to a physical incident such as a disturbance.

[34] *Monaghan* (1844) 2 Broun 131.

[35] *e.g. Davidson v. McFadyean*, 1942 J.C. 95.

[36] See Macphail, n. 17, paras. 3.08–3.13.

[37] At least, not so far as concerns their deliberations; see *McGuire v. Brown*, 1963 S.C. 107 at 109 and 112.

[38] *Pirie v. Caledonian Ry.* (1890) 17 R. 1157 at 1161.

[39] Hume, II, 429.

[40] The final ruling of an arbiter, which *quoad* the parties has the force of law.

[41] Macphail, n.17, Chap. 3.15; and see Davidson, *Arbitration*, para.18.18.

[42] *e.g.* bias, failure to exhaust remit, etc.

[43] See *Black v. John Williams & Co.*, 1923 S.C. 510; 1924 S.C. (H.L.) 22 at 28. For an example of a case in which the arbiter's evidence was heard in an action for the reduction of his award, see *Glasgow City and District Ry. v. MacGeorge* (1886) 13 R. 609.

[44] 1919 J.C. 15.

[45] (1869) 1 Coup. 370 at 375. The effect of *Mackintosh* is that the only strict bar arises when the prosecutor is actually presenting the case.

"It would be the duty of anyone so situated to decline from the outset all interference, either official or judicial, in a case in which he knew he had important testimony to give from his own personal knowledge."

In contrast, it is possible for a defence solicitor, while actually conducting a client's case, to testify to matters within his or her knowledge.[46] In terms of section 265(2) of the Criminal Procedure (Scotland) Act 1995, where a solicitor, who is or has been an agent for an accused, is called to testify, the accused cannot insist on the confidentiality of certain matters on the grounds of agent-client privilege. If an accused wanted to preserve the confidentiality of the relationship then he or she would have to forego the opportunity of citing the solicitor as a witness.

HEADS OF STATE

11.11 There is no direct authority on the competence of the monarch as a witness, but the general assumption seems to be that the monarch is competent, but not compellable, as a witness.[47] The remainder of the Royal Family is taken to be both competent and compellable.[48] In terms of section 20 of the State Immunity Act 1978, foreign heads of state, their families and domestic retinue, have the same basic privilege as foreign diplomats, in that they are competent but not compellable as witnesses.[49]

PERSONS PRESENT IN COURT DURING PREVIOUS EVIDENCE

11.12 At common law, there was an absolute bar against the hearing of testimony from a witness who had been in court prior to giving evidence, and had therefore heard some of the previous testimony.[50] This rigid rule has now been partly amended by section 3 of the Evidence (Scotland) Act 1840, which applied to all cases until 1975 (and still applies in civil cases) and now applies to criminal cases by virtue of section 267 of the Criminal Procedure (Scotland) Act 1995.

---

[46] *Campbell v. Cochrane*, 1928 J.C. 25. The rule extends to defence advocates; see Renton and Brown, *Criminal Procedure*, para. 24.154.
[47] See Macphail, n. 17, Chap. 3.04–3.06.
[48] Wilkinson, *Scottish Law of Evidence*, p. 154.
[49] Their status is confirmed by a certificate from the Foreign Office: *ibid.*, s.21.
[50] See Dickson, n. 5, para. 1599.

In terms of section 3 of the 1840 Act the court has a discretion to admit the evidence of any witness who has been present "without the permission of the court" and "without the consent of the party objecting", when it can be shown that the witness's presence in court was not the result of "culpable negligence or criminal intent" and that "injustice will not be done by his or her examination". The burden of proof on each of these issues rests with the party seeking to adduce the witness.[51]

The effect of section 267(1) of the 1995 Act is that the court may, on the application of any party to either solemn or summary proceedings, permit a witness to be in court during the proceedings of any part of them before giving evidence, if the court is satisfied that this would not be contrary to the interests of justice. These provisions apply when permission is being sought in advance for a witness to be present during proceedings.

Where a witness has been in court without permission and a party wishes to call that witness to give evidence then section 267(2) gives the court discretion to admit the evidence provided: (1) the witness's presence in court was not as a result of culpable negligence or criminal intent; and (2) that the witness has not been unduly instructed or influenced by what has taken place; and (3) that there will be no injustice by his being heard.

It was established in *Campbell v. Cochrane*[52] that parties, their advocates and agents may testify even though they have been present during the whole of the prior evidence, and this applies equally to the accused.[53] It is well established[54] that in the absence of any objection, an expert witness may be allowed to remain in court during the hearing of other testimony, except the opinion part of other experts' testimony.[55]

When a witness is allowed to remain in court after giving testimony, but is then recalled, it seems that current practice is to reject any objection to the recall on the ground that the witness has heard some of the testimony, and has almost certainly heard that part of it which has led to the recall.[56]

---

[51] *Macdonald v. Mackenzie*, 1947 J.C. 169 at 174. *N.B.* also pp. 175 and 176, where it was held to be the duty of the judge to question the competence of any witness who has been present in court where this is apparent to him.

[52] n. 46 above. The fact that a party has heard prior testimony can, however, be the subject of judicial comment; see *Perman v. Binny's Trs*, 1925 S.L.T. 123.

[53] *H.M. Advocate v. Ferrie*, 1983 S.C.C.R. 1.

[54] See, *e.g. H.M. Advocate v. Laurie* (1889) 2 White 326.

[55] See Renton and Brown, n. 46, para. 24.164 and *H.M. Advocate v. Laurie*, above.

[56] See *Dyet v. N.C.B.*, 1957 S.L.T. (Notes) 18, where the justification for permitting the recall was that it was in the interests of justice to do so.

Witness Competent but not Fully Compellable

Introduction

11.13 As has already been noted, the guiding general rule is that a witness who is competent is also compellable[57]:

> "If a competent witness, who has knowledge of the circumstances to be inquired into, is present in court, I can see no inherent objection to his being compelled to give evidence, whether he be a party or not, if the court decides that this is desirable in the interests of justice with a view to the ascertainment of the facts."

This ruling, made *obiter*, arose in the context of a witness who had not been cited, but it appears to reflect the modern view.[58] In civil cases, section 1 of the Evidence (Scotland) Act 1852 renders competent, witnesses who appear without citation, and a similar rule exists in criminal cases by virtue of section 265(1)(d) of the Criminal Procedure (Scotland) Act 1995.

It follows from this that a witness called for one party in a civil case, but not examined by that party, may be called by the other party. This was the point established in *McDonnell v. McShane*,[59] in which the witness in question was the defender in an affiliation and aliment action. It was ruled that he could be called as a witness by the pursuer, even though he had not been cited as a witness, since citation simply serves the purpose of securing the attendance of the witness, and thereafter he or she is compellable for either side if competent.

A similar ruling for criminal cases was laid down in *Todd v. H.M. Advocate*.[60] T objected to the fact that evidence given by a witness for a co-accused, L, was used against her, arguing that evidence by a witness for one co-accused was not, at common law, admissible against another accused when they were running separate defences. On appeal, it was held that the law of evidence had developed and broadened over the years, to the point at which a co-accused may be called as a witness for another accused.

---

[57] Sir Allan G. Walker, Q.C., co-author of Walker and Walker, *Law of Evidence in Scotland* (1st ed.), in *McDonnell v. McShane*, 1967 S.L.T. (Sh. Ct) 61.

[58] See, *e.g.* Macphail, n.17, Chap. 3.31, and Wilkinson, *loc. cit.*, n. 48.

[59] *McDonnell v. McShane*, n. 57.

[60] 1984 S.L.T. 123.

The general rule for both civil and criminal cases would therefore seem to be that a person who has appeared in court as a
witness, whether cited as such or not,[61] is available as a witness for
either side, and is compellable to give such evidence in the
interests of justice.

DIPLOMATS AND CONSULAR OFFICIALS

Under the Diplomatic Privileges Act 1964, the head of a diplo- **11.14**
matic mission based in the United Kingdom, and members of the
diplomatic staff, while competent to give evidence if they wish,
cannot be compelled to do so. The same privilege extends to the
families and staff of diplomats, and to the families of members of
staff, provided in every case that they are not also citizens of the
United Kingdom and colonies. The qualification of any given
person to claim this form of diplomatic immunity is determined by
a certificate from the Foreign Office.

Under the Consular Relations Act 1968 and the Diplomatic and
Other Privileges Act 1971, similar rules apply to full-time consular
officials. All part-time consular officials and their staff, however,
are both competent and compellable, except in relation to matters
covered by their diplomatic work. Equally, they are competent but
cannot be compelled to act as expert witnesses on the law of their
home countries.

BANKERS

In criminal proceedings, by virtue of section 6 of the Bankers **11.15**
Books Evidence Act 1879, a bank official is competent but not
compellable as a witness in matters relating to entries in the bank's
books. This extends to appearances or to production of any bank
book or record, unless ordered by the court to do so for "special
cause" as shown by the party wishing to call him. Where it is
necessary to call a bank witness to testify that a copy of an entry in
the bank's records is an authentic copy of the original, sections 4—
5 provide that he is compellable for that purpose. In civil proceedings the position is broadly the same as section 7(2) of the Civil
Evidence (Scotland) Act 1988 extends the effect of section 6 of the
Bankers' Books Evidence Act 1879 to civil matters.

---

[61] But *N.B.* The requirement in solemn criminal cases for both parties to give notice
to the other of the witnesses they intend to call, *per* s.67 of the 1995 Act. There
are also exceptions in the case of the accused where he or she intends to give
evidence, and co-accused who plead guilty during the course of the trial. These
are dealt with later.

PARTIES AND THEIR SPOUSES IN CIVIL CASES

11.16 As was explained earlier, there has been a gradual erosion of the old common law rule whereby a party to a civil action was incompetent as a witness, and the rule was formerly abolished by section 3 of the Evidence (Scotland) Act 1853. It was also held in *Campbell v. Cochrane*[62] that the fact that such parties have been present in court and have therefore heard the testimony prior to their own does not disqualify them as witnesses.

Section 3 did not specifically state whether or not a party was compellable as a witness, and indeed in the normal course of things such a question will not arise. It will arise, however, when the party in question is forced into the witness box by the other party, which is what happened in *McDonnell v. McShane*.[63] The court held that in such circumstances the party was compellable, and this accords with the general rule that competence implies compellability. It is consistent with "the trend which seeks to remove artificial or illogical restrictions from the law of evidence".[64]

The parties' spouses were also granted competence as witnesses under section 3, while at the same time they were given a privilege against testifying to matters characterised as "any matter communicated (to each other) during the marriage", more commonly known as "marital communications". The wording of the section has given rise to some doubts as to the compellability of the spouse in circumstances other that those comprising marital communications.[65]

THE ACCUSED: GENERAL

11.17 There are three contexts in which the accused person in a criminal trial might enter the witness box, namely:

(1) as a witness for himself or herself;
(2) as a witness for a co-accused; and
(3) as a witness for the prosecution.

The accused may be a competent witness, subject to certain safeguards, in all three cases, but special problems surround the compellability of the accused in each case.

---

[62] n. 46 above.
[63] n. 57 above.
[64] Lord Justice-Clerk Wheatley in *Todd v. H.M. Advocate*, n. 60. See also Macphail, n. 17, Chap. 3.31.
[65] Macphail, n. 17, Chap. 4.03–4.06.

THE ACCUSED AS A WITNESS ON HIS/HER OWN BEHALF

At common law, the accused had no status as a witness in his or **11.18** her own trial, and had to be content with an unsworn judicial declaration from the dock. In 1898 the accused was made a competent witness in his or her own defence on any charge. The current law is in section 266(1) of the Criminal Procedure (Scotland) Act 1995 which states that the accused is a competent witness for the defence at every stage of the trial, whether he is tried alone or with a co-accused. Section 266(11) requires that where the accused is to be called as a witness by the defence, he must be the first witness called unless the court directs otherwise.[66]

When giving evidence, the accused is sworn, or affirms, in the normal way, testifies from the witness box, and is liable to a perjury charge if he or she gives false evidence.[67] In solemn cases, although the defence must give advance notice to the Crown of their intention to call all other witnesses, they need not do so in the case of an accused, who may testify at the trial without prior intimation.[68]

Although the right to make an unsworn judicial declaration was lost in 1898, the Criminal Justice (Scotland) Act 1980 introduced the concept of judicial examination and the current provisions are contained in section 35(4) of the Criminal Procedure (Scotland) Act 1995. This permits an accused who appears on petition before a sheriff to advance a defence or make any other comment in response to questions put by the prosecutor.[69]

The accused is not on oath during judicial examination, and has the right to refuse to answer any questions put by the Crown, as they try to establish a preliminary response to the charge(s) against the accused. However, a record of the proceedings (subject to deletions called for in advance by either party, and agreed by the court after hearing both sides) is read out at the trial. This creates the potential for introducing to the jury a statement by the accused on which he or she cannot be cross-examined if they decline to go into the witness box. This practice was condemned by Lord Justice-Clerk Wheatley in *Hendry v. H.M. Advocate*[70] as "illegitimate", who observed that "the sooner it is stamped out the better". Even so, the appeal court was obliged to hold that such a statement could be used to bolster the credibility of other, independent evidence.

---

[66] See Macphail, n .17, Chap. 5.16–5.19.
[67] *H.M. Advocate v. Cairns*, 1967 J.C. 37.
[68] *Kennedy v. H.M. Advocate* (1898) 2 Adam 588.
[69] For further details of this procedure, see Renton and Brown, n. 46, paras. 12.15–12.28.
[70] 1986 S.L.T. 186.

Section 266 states that the accused may only be called as a witness for himself upon his own application and it follows that in the formal sense, an accused can never be compelled to give evidence on his own behalf. There may however be dangers in such a course of action, since adverse implications might be drawn from silence on the part of an accused.

Until April 1, 1996 the failure of the accused to give evidence was not something upon which the Crown could comment. However section 32 of the Criminal Justice (Scotland) Act 1995 repealed those provisions in the Criminal Procedure (Scotland) Act 1975 that prohibited comment.[71] The entitlement now to comment is an encroachment on the so-called "right to silence" since any Crown comment is likely to be adverse.

In a solemn trial the judge is entitled to comment adversely on an accused's failure to give sworn testimony, though if such comment is excessive it can give rise to grounds for appeal, and a reasonable balance should be struck.[72] In some cases adverse comment may be unavoidable if justice is to be done to both sides. There are cases in which an accused is expected to give an innocent explanation of circumstances that imply guilt,[73] and silence in such cases is an invitation to the jury to draw the most adverse inferences it wishes from the unchallenged prosecution evidence.

11.19   The guidelines to be followed in cases in which evidence ought reasonably to be expected from the accused are those laid down by Lord Justice-General Normand in *Scott v. H.M. Advocate*,[74] who advised trial judges that:

> "Although a comment of the kind is, in my view competent, it should be made with restraint and only when there are special circumstances which require it; and, if it is made with reference to particular evidence which the panel might have explained or contradicted, care should be taken that the evidence is not distorted and that its true bearing on the defence is properly represented to the jury."

It is an unsettled point whether or not a co-accused can comment on the failure of an accused to give sworn testimony, although the authorities seem to be in agreement that such comment should be allowed.[75] If an accused fails to testify, there cannot then be any

---

[71] ss. 141(1)(b) and 346(1)(b).

[72] *Stewart v. H.M. Advocate*, 1980 J.C. 103.

[73] See *McHugh v. H.M. Advocate*, 1978 J.C. 12 and *H.M. Advocate v. Hardy*, 1938 J.C. 144; see also Lord Justice-Clerk Grant in *McIlhargey v. Herron*, 1972 J.C. 38, who pointed out that "the silent defender does take a risk". See also *Dorrens v. H.M. Advocate*, 1983 S.C.C.R. 407 at 411.

[74] 1946 J.C. 90 at 98. See also *Knowles v. H.M. Advocate*, 1975 J.C. 6.

[75] See Macphail, n. 17, para. 5.34, and Renton and Brown, n. 46, both of whom quote the analogous English authority of *R. v. Wickham* (1971) 55 Cr.App.R. 199.

cross-examination by a co-accused, and it would seem to be only fair to allow the frustrated co-accused the right to comment on this.

In the course of giving evidence on his or her own behalf, it is quite possible that the first defender (D1) will give evidence which is adverse to, or even incriminatory of, the second defender (D2). The common law rule that the evidence of D1 is not admissible against D2 unless they are running a joint defence was ignored in practice for many years, and was finally laid to rest in *Young v. H.M. Advocate*.[76] It is obviously of crucial importance to every accused to have the right to cross-examine a co-accused who gives evidence. *Young v. H.M. Advocate* arguably only applied when the two accused were running separate defences, and perhaps only when D1 gave evidence adverse to D2. For this reason, section 266(8)(b) of the Criminal Procedure (Scotland) Act 1995 states that an accused may "ask a co-accused any question in cross examination if that co-accused gives evidence".[77] The effect of this is to place on the widest possible basis the right of D1 to cross examine D2 when and if he gives evidence on his own behalf. It is not necessary for the defences of each to be separate, or for D2 to say a single word against D1. The very fact that he gives evidence on his own behalf allows D1 to cross-examine him, along of course with the Crown.

When more than one accused appears on the same charge(s), and any one of them gives evidence, then *quoad* the remainder, the evidence of each becomes the evidence of a *socius criminis*. However, it is incompetent and improper to issue the *cum nota* warning to the jury in respect of that evidence because of the prejudicial effect which it may have on a person whose guilt has yet to be established.[78] This is true even though there is evidence to incriminate a co-accused.[79] If an accused pleads guilty to, or is convicted of, the charges in which he or she is *socius criminis* before the end of the trial, and thereafter gives evidence for the Crown, then the warning may be administered,[80] but not until. It is competent to proceed to trial against an accused who is charged with an offence while acting along with another, even though that other person has been previously acquitted of the charge.[81]

---

[76] 1932 J.C. 63. This case also established the right of Dl to cross-examine D2 in order to vindicate his own defence. See also *Lavery v. H.M. Advocate*, 1979 S.L.T. (Notes) 4.

[77] Alternatively, *per* s.266(8)(a), he may call him as a witness with his consent, but he cannot do both.

[78] *Martin v. H.M. Advocate*, 1960 S.L.T. 213.

[79] *Slowey v. H.M. Advocate*, 1965 S.L.T. 309.

[80] *Wallace v. H.M. Advocate*, 1952 J.C. 78 at 84; see now *Docherty v. H.M. Advocate*, 1987 S.L.T. 784.

[81] *Howitt v. H.M. Advocate*, 2000 J.C. 284.

The remaining issues which are likely to arise from the position of the accused as a witness for him or herself, namely questions of privilege, and cross examination as to character and previous convictions, are dealt with in later chapters.

THE ACCUSED AS A WITNESS FOR A CO-ACCUSED

11.20 At common law, D1 could not competently be called as a witness for D2,[82] but that position was changed by statute in 1980 and the current provisions are contained in section 266(9)(a) of the Criminal Procedure (Scotland) Act 1995. This states that "the accused may, with the consent of a co-accused, call that other accused as a witness on the accused's behalf."[83] It is clear that while D1 may be competent as a witness for D2, he cannot be compellable while the two remain co-accused, *i.e.* still facing a verdict on charges on a complaint or indictment in which they are both named.

That is as far as the law goes while the two remain as co-accused, but the position is more complicated if and when one of the accused has the charges withdrawn, or pleads guilty, after the start of the trial. This is because of the effect of section 266(10) of the 1995 Act which states that:

> "The prosecutor or the accused may call as a witness a co-accused who has pleaded guilty to or been acquitted of all charges against him which remain before the court (whether or not in a case where the co-accused has pleaded guilty to any charges, he has been sentenced) or in respect of whom the diet has been deserted; and the party calling such co-accused as a witness shall not require to give notice thereof, but the court may grant any other party such adjournment or postponement of the trial as may seem just."

In such circumstances, the accused is not just competent as a witness, but also compellable.[84] Before the subsection may operate, however, it is necessary for all the charges which the former accused faced at the start of the trial diet to have been disposed of by either a guilty plea or an acquittal or a desertion of the diet by

---

[82] See Renton and Brown, n. 46, para. 24–21.
[83] It will be recalled that by subs. (9)(b) in each case, he may also cross-examine him if he gives evidence, but he may not do both.
[84] In accordance with the normal rule that competence implies compellability, and by contrast with the wording of s.266(9)(a) above.

the Crown.[85] It is not necessary for the accused to have been convicted or sentenced.

The point arose in *H.M. Advocate v. Ferrie*,[86] in which a number of accused persons appeared in an indictment on a number of charges. One of them, Y, pled guilty to part of one charge, and the Crown accepted it by withdrawing the remaining charges against him from the indictment, the jury being directed to record a not guilty verdict on the remainder of the charge to which Y had partially pled guilty. Sentence on him was postponed until the end of the trial and he was held in custody. The Crown then sought leave to call him as a witness against the remaining accused, who objected on the ground that he had not pled guilty to all the charges that remained against him at the time of the making of the plea. It was held that the point at which the subsection was to be applied was the moment at which the former co-accused was called as a witness, and at that time he had pled guilty to the only charge that remained against him.

Before a person can be classed as the "co-accused" of another for the purposes of section 266(9) it is necessary for them both to appear at a trial diet on the same complaint or indictment. Even if they began in this position when first charged, D1 will no longer be classed as the co-accused of D2 if their trials have been separated as the result of some earlier diet prior to trial. In such cases, each will be a competent and compellable witness for the other in their separate trials, whether or not their respective cases have been disposed of.[87] Where the trial proceeds by solemn procedure the potential witness must appear on the witness list of the accused for whom he or she will be testifying.

It was held in *Monaghan v. H.M. Advocate*[88] that when D1 is originally charged along with D2 on an indictment, but pleads guilty by the accelerated procedure available under section 76 of the 1995 Act, D1 remains a "co-accused" and qualifies to be called as a witness for a co-accused by virtue of section 266(10).

The final possibility involving the appearance of an accused as a witness for a co-accused, is when the charges against one of two

---

[85] Unless the Crown desert these charges *simpliciter*, the accused giving evidence for a co-accused enjoys a privilege against answering questions which are incriminating, even in respect of charges which have been withdrawn. The accused will, however, come within the purview of the subsection because he or she will have pled guilty to all the charges "remaining before the court", a phrase clearly intended to make allowance for withdrawals by the Crown.

[86] 1983 S.C.C.R. 1. *N.B.* that this was a case in which the former accused was called by the Crown, but the point at issue is the same for both types of case.

[87] *Morrison v. Adair*, 1943 J.C. 25. In such a case, of course, the accused called as a witness will enjoy a privilege against self-incrimination in respect of the charges still outstanding against him.

[88] 1983 S.C.C.R. 524, another case in which the co-accused was in fact called for the Crown.

original co-accused are dropped by the Crown prior to the commencement of the trial. In such a case the person concerned is at common law a competent and compellable witness for the remaining accused. In solemn cases that person must appear on the defence witness list, and, unless the Crown have deserted *simpliciter*, may refuse to answer any questions which could be incriminating *quoad* those charges.

No co-accused giving evidence on behalf of another co-accused can be classed as *socius criminis*, a term which is confined to witnesses giving evidence *against* another accused, and probably to those who do so as Crown witnesses.[89]

THE ACCUSED AS A WITNESS FOR THE PROSECUTION

11.21 For as long as a person remains on trial on charges which have yet to be proved or admitted, they can never be a competent witness for the prosecution, either against themselves or against a co-accused. However, as noted earlier, since *Young v. H.M. Advocate*[90] an accused giving evidence on their own behalf may well assist the prosecution by giving evidence adverse to a co-accused upon which the prosecution may rely.

The process of judicial examination was introduced in 1980 and is now embodied in sections 35 and 36 of the Criminal Procedure (Scotland) Act 1995.[91] These two sections provide for an accused person arrested for a serious crime to be brought before a sheriff on petition and given an opportunity to make a "judicial declaration" regarding the charges. The accused is invited to make any comments in respect of (i) any of the charges in the petition; (ii) any defence he or she wishes to put forward; or (iii) any confession which he or she is alleged to have made to the police.

In this sense the accused may turn out to have given evidence at the behest of the Crown. Although there is a theoretical right to remain silent on this occasion, this is qualified by section 36(8) of the 1995 Act. That subsection provides that an accused's silence may be made the subject of adverse comment by the Crown, the judge or any co-accused if, at the subsequent trial any matter is raised (such as a defence of alibi or incrimination) which might appropriately have been raised at the judicial examination.[92]

---

[89] *Slowey v. H.M. Advocate*, n. 79 above.

[90] n. 76 above, and in practice since before then.

[91] For details of this process see Renton and Brown, n. 46, paras. 12.15–12.28.

[92] *e.g. Alexander v. H.M. Advocate*, 1989 S.L.T. 193 where nothing was said at the judicial examination on the instructions of the accused's solicitor. When a defence of alibi was put forward at the trial, it was held competent for the trial judge to comment on this in his charge to the jury, leaving them to assess what weight to attach to the accused's evidence.

Aside from sections 35 and 36, an accused may become a witness for the Crown if they cease to be an accused, by virtue of having pled guilty or had the charges deserted, but then find they are called as a prosecution witness against a former co-accused. Alternatively, as explained above, the trials of an accused and a co-accused may be separated so that each is a competent and compellable witness for the Crown at the trial of the other.[93]

As noted earlier, when, during the course of a trial an accused pleads guilty to all remaining charges, or where such charges are dropped by the Crown, or where the Crown accepts a partial plea of guilt, the situation is covered by section 266(10) of the 1995 Act. In such circumstances, the former co-accused may be called as a witness by either a continuing accused *or* the prosecution. He is then, in the circumstances envisaged by the sections, both competent and compellable for the Crown. All that was written previously concerning the statutory provisions in regard to a former accused testifying for a former co-accused applies equally *quoad* evidence given by such a person for the Crown. The main distinction between the two situations is that when a former accused gives evidence for the Crown following a guilty plea, then in accordance with the definition in *Wallace v. H.M. Advocate*,[94] his or her evidence must be treated as that of a *socius criminis* whether or not they have been sentenced.

Moreover, when D1 appears as a witness for D2, in circum- **11.22** stances in which the Crown have not deserted the charges against D1 *simpliciter*, a privilege may be claimed against answering any incriminating question in relation to the offences charged. This cannot arise when the accused appears for the Crown in those cases in which the Crown has given up the right to prosecute in respect of these charges. This occurs whenever an accused is called specifically as a *socius criminis* in respect of those charges that the remaining accused still faces. The *socius* in such cases is said to have an "immunity" against further prosecution, and this operates to all intents and purposes like a desertion *simpliciter*. The same rule applies when the Crown have secured D1 as a *socius criminis* witness by a separation of trials. If, however, D1 is not specifically called as a *socius criminis* the immunity does not apply, and D1 will require to fall back on the privilege against self-incrimination.

The immunity was expressed by Hume thus: "By the very act of calling him as a witness, the prosecutor discharges all title to molest him for the future with relation to the matter libelled."[95] The modern interpretation of this is more restricted. In *O'Neill v.*

---

[93] See *Morrison v. Adair*, n. 87 above.
[94] n. 80. But see *Scott v. H.M. Advocate*, 1987 S.L.T. 389 and *Docherty v. H.M. Advocate*, n. 80 above.
[95] Hume, II, 366–367.

Wilson,[96] a police officer, O'Neill, was charged with assaulting M, but claimed immunity on the ground that on an earlier occasion, as a witness for the Crown, he had given evidence against M on a charge of assaulting him, O'Neill. It was held on appeal (a) that the immunity from prosecution applies only to a person expressly called as a *socius criminis* in the crime with which the then accused is charged, and (b) that such immunity covers only the charges contained in the "libel" in support of which he has given evidence.

The position, in those cases in which D1 is called by the Crown as a witness against D2 while certain charges remain outstanding against D1 (in that they have not been deserted *simpliciter*), would therefore seem to be as follows. If D1 is called as a *socius criminis* and the charges which remain against D1 are also the charges faced by D2, then D1 acquires immunity from further prosecution on such charges, and cannot claim the privilege against self-incrimination. In all other cases, D1 has no future immunity, but may claim the privilege. D1 remains, however, otherwise compellable as a witness.

When D1 is called to testify for the Crown against D2 in terms of section 266, D1 need not appear on the Crown witness list, although the court may grant "such adjournment or postponement of the trial as may seem just". In all other cases, the normal witness notice must be given.

THE SPOUSE OF AN ACCUSED

GENERAL

11.23 At common law the spouse of an accused remains incompetent as a witness for all purposes, except in those cases in which he or she is the "victim" of the crime with which their spouse is charged. In that event the spouse is both competent and compellable for the Crown, but no one else. The most obvious applications of this rule are in cases of physical assault, but it may also be applied in offences against property, such as theft[97] and forgery.[98] The term "spouse" is restricted to a married person and does not include cohabitees.[99] It has been held in England that a divorced spouse is competent to testify to matters pre-dating the marriage and can only be cross-examined as to credit with regard to matters that arose during the marriage.[1]

---

[96] 1983 J.C. 42.
[97] *Harper v. Adair*, 1945 J.C. 21.
[98] *Foster v. H.M. Advocate*, 1932 J.C. 75.
[99] *Casey v. H.M. Advocate (No.1)*, 1993 S.L.T. 33.
[1] *R. v. Ash* (1985) 81 Cr.App.R. 294.

The common law rule has been amended by various complex statutory exceptions that are currently contained in section 264 of the Criminal Procedure (Scotland) Act 1995[2]:

> "(1) The spouse of an accused may be called as a witness—
>   (a) by the accused;
>   (b) by a co-accused or by the prosecutor without the consent of the accused.
> (2) Nothing in this section shall—
>   (a) make the spouse of an accused a compellable witness for a co-accused or for the prosecutor in a case where such spouse would not be so compellable at common law;
>   (b) compel a spouse to disclose any communication made between the spouses during the marriage.
> (3) The failure of the spouse of an accused to give evidence shall not be commented on by the defence or the prosecutor."

Each aspect of this section is now considered in turn.

THE SPOUSE AS A WITNESS FOR THE ACCUSED

Section 264(1)(a) confirms that, without exception, the spouse is a **11.24** competent witness for the accused. Any doubt that might have remained as to compellability was removed in *Hunter v. H.M. Advocate*,[3] in which H was charged with assaulting and then murdering his daughter. His wife appeared on the Crown witness list against him, but was not called. The accused, who had lodged a special defence incriminating his wife on the assault charge only, sought to call her as a witness for himself. The trial judge ruled that she need not answer any questions put to her by his counsel if she did not wish. On appeal, it was held that although the omission of the evidence had not led to a miscarriage of justice (since the evidence in question would only have been to the effect that H had hitherto been a loving father to the child), the trial judge had erred in his ruling. The wife was said to be a compellable witness for the accused because[4]:

---

[2] The complex nature of these provisions is well documented by Macphail, n. 17, Chap. 6.

[3] 1984 S.L.T. 434. The case dealt with the statutory provisions that preceded those in the 1995 Act.

[4] at p. 437. *N.B.* that had she been asked questions concerning her alleged involvement in the assault, in line with H's original special defence, she would have been able to claim a privilege against answering any question which might incriminate her: see below.

"The provisions of section 143[5] are symptomatic of the development of the principle that, subject to appropriate safeguards, all relevant evidence should be available to the court at a criminal trial in the interests of justice."

In a case where a spouse is not compellable, but nevertheless elects to give evidence, then they must answer every question put to them, even if that means incriminating their accused spouse. In other words, having agreed to go into the witness box, a spouse cannot then be selective about the questions answered.[6] The only matters in respect of which a spouse cannot be compelled to testify once in the witness box (apart from answering questions which might be self-incriminating in any future charge) are, as indicated by subsection (2)(b), those covered by the "marital communications" privilege.

THE SPOUSE AS A WITNESS FOR A CO-ACCUSED

11.25 Section 264(1)(b) makes it clear that while a spouse is always a competent witness for a co-accused, they cannot be compelled to testify except in a case in which they would have been compellable at common law. This is somewhat misleading, since, there never was any circumstance in which a spouse was compellable at common law for a co-accused, and the confusion seems to have arisen from the desire of the draftsman to include the possibility of a spouse testifying for a co-accused along with the possibility of him or her testifying for the Crown.[7]

A spouse can choose to testify for a co-accused if they so wish. The "privilege" against testifying is for the spouse to claim or reject. The difficult position for a spouse of a co-accused who is called as a witness for the prosecution was considered in *Bates v. H.M. Advocate*.[8] In that case the wife of a co-accused was asked certain questions in cross-examination by the accused. The witness declined to answer. On appeal it was held that while she could not be compelled to give evidence, if she chose to go into the witness box, then she must answer all questions put to her.

Once again, the privilege against disclosure of marital communications is preserved by section 264(2)(b).

---

[5] Now s.264 of the 1995 Act.
[6] *Bates v. H.M. Advocate*, 1989 S.L.T. 701.
[7] And, as already explained, there are common law cases in which she is compellable for the Crown.
[8] n. 6 above.

THE SPOUSE AS A WITNESS FOR THE PROSECUTION

As noted above, section 264 is just as applicable to a spouse called **11.26** by the Crown as it is to a spouse called by a co-accused. The one exception is in cases in which a spouse may be said to be the "victim" of the crime with which the other spouse is charged. In such circumstances the victim spouse is compellable under the Act because he or she is compellable at common law. Once again though, marital communications remain protected from disclosure.

COMMENT ON THE FAILURE OF A SPOUSE TO TESTIFY

Section 264(3) prevents any comment being made by either the **11.27** Crown or the defence on the failure of a spouse to testify. Reference to *McHugh v. H.M. Advocate*[9] suggests that some departures from that rule may be tolerated in practice, provided that overall there is no miscarriage of justice. Additionally, Sheriff Gordon[10] suggests that the accused might be permitted to comment when the Crown might have called the spouse but did not (*e.g.* where she is the alleged victim) and of course the subsections do not prevent the trial judge from making comment, provided presumably that this is not excessive and becomes damaging to an accused.[11]

---

[9] n. 73 above.
[10] In his commentary on s.29 of the Criminal Justice (Scotland) Act 1980.
[11] *Knowles v. H.M. Advocate*, 1975 J.C. 6.

CHAPTER 12

PRIVILEGE AND IMMUNITY

INTRODUCTION

12.01 When a witness is said to possess a "privilege" against answering a certain question or a series of questions, this means that the law recognises the right not to answer such questions. This applies even if the questions are relevant and competent, and even though the witness may otherwise be compellable. For example, as was seen in Chapter 11, a spouse is normally both competent and compellable as a witness for their spouse, but even so, he or she cannot be forced to disclose the contents of a "marital communication" as such communications are accorded a privileged status.

If a witness is able to claim a privilege against answering questions then the normal penalty for refusing to answer a competent question as a compellable witness, namely, a charge of contempt of court, cannot be enforced. As the information which the witness is refusing to disclose is frequently highly relevant to the matters under consideration by the court, the recognition of such a privilege by the law is clearly a matter of balancing the promotion of confidentiality against the interests of justice.

The general rule is that the privilege is that of the witness who is being called upon to testify, and he or she may waive that privilege if so wished. If the witness does waive the privilege, the other party has no right to object but may object if the privilege is wrongfully upheld, depriving that party of vital evidence which it was intended to call.[1] It is not certain whether the courts can make use of the same information which the privileged witness would have given as evidence, when that evidence comes from another source, for example, a third party who overhears a conversation between spouses. There appears to be no general rule, and such matters are resolved from case to case.

---

[1] *Kirkwood v. Kirkwood* (1875) 3 R. 235 at 236.

Privilege Against Self-Incrimination: Witnesses other
THAN THE Accused

It is a fundamental proposition within Scots law that a person **12.02**
cannot be forced to incriminate themselves. This is a principle
affirmed in the European Convention of Human Rights now
incorporated into domestic law via the Human Rights Act 1998. In
Saunders v. United Kingdom the European Court of Human Rights
stated that "the right not to incriminate oneself, like the right to
silence, was a generally recognised international standard which lay
at the heart of the notion of a fair procedure under Article 6 of the
convention."[2] This right is not explicit in terms of Article 6, but as
the *Saunders* judgement reinforces, it is integral to fair treatment.

The privilege against self-incrimination arises from what was
once described as "a sacred and inviolable principle . . . that no
man is bound to [in]criminate himself"[3] and its extent was summarised by Walker and Walker[4] as being that: "A witness is
entitled to refuse to answer a question if a true answer may lead to
his conviction for a crime or involves an admission of adultery." An
untrue answer can lead to a perjury charge.[5] With the exception of
an accused who gives evidence at their own trial, this section of the
chapter deals with all witnesses, in both civil and criminal cases,
who are asked on oath any question which might incriminate them
in respect of certain matters.

It will be noted that the privilege is against answering the
particular question which has such an effect, and the general rule
does not prevent the question being asked in the first place. In
general, it is for the witness to claim the privilege if and when the
question is put. However, there are two statutory exceptions to this
general rule, under which the question may not even be asked.
These are section 2 of the Evidence (Further Amendment)
(Scotland) Act 1874, which deals with questions which tend to
show that the witness has been guilty of adultery; and section 266
of the Criminal Procedure (Scotland) Act 1995, which applies to
questions asked of an accused in a criminal trial. Macphail has
suggested[6] that a new statutory rule should be enacted which
prevents the question even being asked. But this assumes the
questioner is aware that the question has incriminatory implications, and this may not always be the case. Moreover, a witness
may not realise that he or she has a privilege against answering a
particular question. Therefore, it is regarded as the duty of the

---

[2] (1996) 23 E.H.R.R. 313.
[3] Lord Gillies in *Livingstone v. Murray* (1830) 9 S. 161 at 162.
[4] *Law of Evidence in Scotland,* para. 12.13.1.
[5] *Graham v. H.M. Advocate,* 1969 S.L.T. 116.
[6] Macphail, *Evidence,* Chap. 18.05.

judge to advise the witness of the privilege when a particular question seems likely to lead towards an incriminating answer.[7]

At present there is no procedure for determining whether an answer is genuinely incriminatory. Thus, if all that is required is that the witness states an objection, without need for further inquiry, then many awkward questions may be avoided by the unscrupulous or the unwilling witness. As was observed by Lord Stephen in *R. v. Cox and Railton*,[8] "the secret must be told in order [that the court may] see whether it ought to be kept".

A witness may not succeed in claiming a privilege against answering a particular question, perhaps because of a lack of awareness of the existence of the privilege, or because the answer is denied privilege by the trial judge. Additionally, a witness may elect to waive the privilege. In such circumstances, the answer given becomes admissible for all purposes, even if the witness is a party to the action.[9] For example, in *O'Neill v. Wilson*,[10] it was affirmed that a failure to warn a witness of his or her privilege does not affect liability to subsequent prosecution. However, if a statement were forced from a witness by a denial of the privilege, it would be classed as "involuntary", and therefore inadmissible as a confession.

12.03 The privilege, as originally formulated, seems very wide in its application, but in practice it has been reduced to the point that it is best considered as a privilege against answering questions which would incriminate the witness *quoad* a criminal offence. In particular, the following limitations on the privilege are recognised.

(1) It is not applicable when the witness is no longer "in peril" of conviction of the offence revealed by the answer, if given. If, for example, an accused has already pled guilty, or been convicted of the offence in question, or has been granted immunity by the Crown because he or she is to be used as a *socius criminis* witness by them, then the witness may no longer refuse to testify as to guilt.[11] A finding of not guilty will also rob the witness of privilege because the matter is then *res judicata* and a desertion *simpliciter* by the Crown will presumably have the same effect.

(2) A witness cannot, in all probability, claim the privilege against answering a question that will reveal the commission of an offence under foreign law. Although many consider that in principle the privilege should extend to such questions, the point

---

[7] Lord President Inglis in *Kirkwood v. Kirkwood*, n.1.

[8] (1884) 14 Q.B.D. 153 at 175.

[9] Lord President Inglis in *Kirkwood v. Kirkwood*, n.1.

[10] 1983 J.C. 42. In *Graham v. H.M. Advocate*, n. 5, it was held that a witness who is not advised of his privilege, and who then goes on to give a false answer to the question, cannot hide behind the failure to advise him of his privilege in any subsequent perjury trial.

[11] *MacMillan v. Murray*, 1920 J.C. 13.

remains unsettled under Scots law.[12] The House of Lords in the English appeal case of *Rio Tinto Zinc v. Westinghouse Electric Corporation*[13] allowed the privilege to be invoked against disclosure of documents which might expose the defenders to various fines under EC Regulations but *quaere* whether, given the terms of the Treaty of Rome, this could be regarded as a matter of "foreign law" anyway.[14]

(3) With the exception of adultery, the privilege may not be claimed in respect of any question, the answer to which might expose the witness to a civil action. This creates an area of uncertainty in those cases in which a future action, although civil in form, can result in penalties that are quasi-criminal in nature. An example is the system of fines which operates as the penalty for breaches of EC Regulations, and as the *Rio Tinto Zinc* case shows, the English courts are prepared to extend a statutory privilege in such circumstances. However, there does not appear to be any specifically Scots law on the point.

(4) The privilege does not extend to those questions which might incriminate the witness's spouse, although English law has been extended to incorporate such a privilege in terms of their Civil Evidence Act 1968, s.14(1)(b). It has been argued that it is "repellant" to force a witness to incriminate his or her spouse,[15] but Macphail has observed that "[i]t may be . . . that the matter is of small practical importance" in Scotland,[16] and any such extension could not, of course, include the evidence of a spouse testifying at the trial of her husband, whether for the Crown or the defence.[17]

(5) The privilege may now be limited in its application to allegations of adultery. As the broader rule was formulated at a time when adultery was a criminal offence, Wilkinson has argued that when adultery ceased to be a crime, the privilege should have ceased to apply to questions concerning adultery.[18] However, section 2 of the Evidence (Further Amendment) (Scotland) Act

---

[12] See, for example, Macphail, n. 6, Chap. 18.13 who concedes the practical difficulty of the presiding judge having to become acquainted with the law in question.

[13] [1978] A.C. 547.

[14] See also *H.M. Advocate v. Entwhistle* (1980), unreported, *per* Macphail, n. 6. Chap. 18.13A, in which a witness in the High Court was allowed the privilege against answering questions that might render him liable to prosecution in England.

[15] By the Law Reform Committee for England and Wales, whose report led to the 1968 Act.

[16] n. 6, Chap. 18.12.

[17] See Chap. 11.

[18] *The Scottish Law of Evidence*, p. 93. The privilege was abolished quoad allegations of adultery in England by virtue of Civil Evidence Act 1968 s.16(5). Macphail advocates a similar fate for the rule in Scotland, n. 6, Chap. 18.18.

1874, preserved the privilege in statutory form in "any proceedings", and prevented such questions even being asked of the witness.

12.04   In *Sinclair v. Sinclair*,[19] an undefended divorce action in the sheriff court on the grounds of the defender's adultery, it was held that there could be no objection to the use of affidavits in which both the defender and the paramour admitted adultery, on the ground that the witnesses were not warned of the privilege. It was held that there was no rule of law which required a prospective witness deponing by affidavit to receive such a warning, and no evidence in the present case that the statements had been anything but voluntary. Any suggestion of lack of consent could be countered by including a clause in the affidavit acknowledging that the witness has been warned of his or her right not to incriminate themselves as to adultery.

(6) In certain cases, the privilege is removed by statute in circumstances where the personal right to privacy from self-incrimination is outweighed by the wider public interest in securing justice. Among the more common examples of this situation is section 172 of the Road Traffic Act 1988, which requires a potential witness/accused to answer police questions concerning the identity of the driver of a motor vehicle owned by the witness. The answers are subsequently admissible in evidence in court proceedings.

This fairly commonplace provision was challenged in the case of *Brown v. Stott*,[20] a case that was ultimately adjudicated by the Judicial Committee of the Privy Council,[21] to whom there is now a right of appeal in criminal cases under the Scotland Act 1998. In *Brown* the Crown challenged the High Court's decision that Miss Brown's obligation to incriminate herself under road traffic legislation (by identifying herself to the police as the driver of a car when she was suspected of being drunk) was an infringement of her Convention right to a fair trial under Article 6. The Judicial Committee quashed the declaration made by the High Court on the ground that Article 6 did not confer absolute rights in circumstances where the state was justified in curtailing the rights of an individual in the broader public interest.

Noting that there was no suggestion of coercion or compulsion in seeking an answer to the question posed under the road traffic legislation, Lord Kirkwood considered the statutory provision met the test of proportionality sought in the jurisprudence of the European Court of Human Rights in striking the balance between the general interests of the community to be protected against drunk drivers, and the rights of a suspect to a subsequent fair trial.

---

[19] 1986 S.L.T. (Sh. Ct) 54. But see *Cooper v. Cooper*, 1987 S.L.T. (Sh. Ct) 37.
[20] 2000 S.L.T. 379.
[21] 2001 S.L.T. 59.

Another quite common example is to be found in the Bank-ruptcy (Scotland) Act 1985. In terms of section 47(3), a bankrupt must answer "all lawful questions" which may be put to him in his public examination, even if they incriminate him in a crime, subject to the important proviso that his answers may not be used against him in any subsequent criminal proceedings. Many other statutes contain similar provisions where it is felt that public interest outweighs private privilege.[22]

When a witness claims the privilege against self-incrimination no adverse inference should arise against the witness.[23] But it is always possible that asserting a privilege may affect the credibility of the witness, since, according to Dickson, "an innocent man is far more likely to answer with an indignant denial than to avail himself of his privilege".[24]

PRIVILEGE AGAINST SELF-INCRIMINATION: THE ACCUSED

Since 1898 an accused person has possessed the right to give sworn **12.05** testimony at his or her own trial, a right which is now to be found in section 266(1) of the Criminal Procedure (Scotland) Act 1995. Clearly though, an accused cannot be allowed to claim the normal witness privilege against self-incrimination which was discussed earlier. It would not make sense if the accused could give evidence-in-chief, and then refuse to answer any questions in cross-examination on the grounds that they tended to incriminate.

On the other hand, the accused is entitled to be protected from questions which are designed to show the commission of offences beyond those charged. Forcing such disclosures would be highly prejudicial to the balance between these two interests is now found in sections 266(3) and (4) of the Criminal Procedure (Scotland) Act 1995 which respectively provide as follows:

> "(3) An accused who gives evidence on his own behalf in pursuance of this section may be asked any question in cross-examination notwithstanding that it would tend to incriminate him as to the offence charged.
>
> (4) An accused who gives evidence on his own behalf in pursuance of this section shall not be asked, and if asked shall not be required to answer, any question tending to show that he has committed, or been convicted of or been charged with, any offence other than that with which he is then charged, or is of bad character, unless . . ."

---

[22] See, *e.g.* Explosive Substances Act 1883, s.6(2), and Representation of the People Act 1983, s.141(1) and (2).

[23] Macphail, n. 6, Chap. 18.05.

[24] Dickson, *Evidence,* para. 1790.

Each section then goes on to prescribe certain circumstances in which an accused may forfeit the "shield" of subsection (4), and these are examined in more detail later. These provisions offer a shield to the accused against certain incriminating answers and to this extent an accused is treated more favourably than normal witnesses who may, subject to the general privilege, be asked questions that impugn their credibility as a witness.

MARITAL COMMUNICATIONS

12.06 Once spouses were rendered competent witnesses in law the question arose as to the extent of the privilege. Could one spouse claim a privilege against answering questions that related to communications made by the other spouse during the course of the marriage? The intention of the legislature seems to have been to preserve the sanctity of marital communications. If there is to be such a rule it is arguably no longer justifiable or consistent to privilege only communications in marital relationships, as opposed to other forms of intimate relationships. The civil and criminal provisions relating to marital communications are quite different and are considered separately.

(1) Criminal cases

12.07   In criminal cases, the privilege against disclosing marital communications is contained in section 264(2)(b) of the Criminal Procedure (Scotland) Act 1995 which states (reproducing the privilege first introduced in 1898[25]) that nothing shall "compel a spouse to disclose any communication made between the spouses during the marriage".

(2) Civil cases

12.08   In civil cases the privilege against disclosing marital communications is contained in section 3 of the Evidence (Scotland) Act 1853, which states that:

> "nothing herein contained shall in any [civil] proceeding render any husband competent or compellable to give against his wife evidence of any matter communicated by her to him during the marriage, or any wife competent or compellable to give against her husband evidence of any matter communicated by him to her during the marriage."

A problem created by the wording of this section arises from the use of the phrase "competent or compellable", as the phrase

---

[25] *Hunter v. H.M. Advocate,* 1984 S.L.T. 434 at 437.

implies that the spouse was not even competent to give such evidence, whether or not he or she wished to. This in effect makes the privilege that of the other spouse as the party who would be entitled to invoke the privilege by insisting that their spouse was not competent to answer questions put to them. The logical conclusion of this interpretation would support an argument that the evidence could not be given even if both parties wished. This anomalous situation has been abolished in England in terms of section 16(3) of the Civil Evidence Act 1968. Macphail has recommended that it also be abolished in Scotland on utilitarian grounds, or at least reduced to the point at which it becomes the privilege solely of the communicator and not the recipient.[26]

It is clear that in such cases, the privilege is that of the witness spouse alone, and he or she is free to waive it if so desired.[27]

(3) General

In both criminal and civil cases, the privilege appears to apply to **12.09** any form of communication, written, oral or other.[28] However, as discussed, some exceptions have been recognised to the right to claim the privilege, as in civil cases in which the court is investigating the behaviour of one spouse towards another. For example, in *Mackay v. Mackay*,[29] a letter written by a husband confessing adultery was held not to be privileged, thus allowing the wife, who would not otherwise have been competent, to relate its contents. There are also some statutory exceptions such as section 47(3) of the Bankruptcy (Scotland) Act 1985.

Even if a particular witness claims a privilege, the court can hear from an alternative source the same evidence that is covered by the privilege. For example, a witness who overheard the privileged conversation, or a third party who intercepted a privileged letter.[30] The privilege relates only to the spouse as a witness, and not to anyone else. It is unclear whether or not the privilege ends with the marriage, and whether for, example, a former spouse can claim the privilege in respect of a communication made during the existence of the marriage. Dickson[31] claims that the privilege survives death or divorce but some modern observers challenge this view, on the grounds both of utility and the wording of the relevant sections.[32]

---

[26] n. 6, Chap. 4.06–4.07.
[27] See *H.M. Advocate v. H.D.*, 1953 J.C. 65, a criminal case but the principle would also be applicable to civil cases.
[28] See Walker and Walker, n. 4, para. 13.10.2.
[29] 1946 S.C. 7.
[30] See Walker and Walker, n. 4, para. *loc. cit.*
[31] n. 24, para.1660.
[32] See, *e.g.* Wilkinson, n. 18, p. 103; Clive, *Husband and Wife*, para. 18–017, and Macphail, n. 6, Chap. 4.10. See too the position in England, *R. v. Ash* (1985) 81 Cr.App.Rep. 294.

The wording of each section clearly envisages that one of the spouses is a party to the action in which the privilege is claimed.

MARITAL INTERCOURSE

12.10 A rather curious privilege was introduced into Scots law by virtue of the Law Reform (Miscellaneous Provisions) Act 1949, s.7, which enacts that:

> "(1) Notwithstanding any rule of law, the evidence of a husband or wife shall be admissible in any proceedings to prove that marital intercourse did or did not take place between them during any period.
>
> (2) Notwithstanding anything in this section or any rule of law, a husband or wife shall not be compellable in any proceedings to give evidence of the matters foresaid."

This statutory provision was intended primarily to overrule the decision in the English case of *Russell v. Russell*,[33] which had never been adopted into Scots law anyway[34] and was therefore unnecessary in Scotland. The privilege has never apparently been judicially considered in Scotland,[35] even though it is drafted widely enough to apply not only to all civil proceedings, but to criminal proceedings as well. Ironically, the privilege has been abolished in relation to civil proceedings under English law by virtue of section 16(4) of the Civil Evidence Act 1968 and its abolition in Scots law would seem to be long overdue.[36]

PRIVILEGES IN AID OF LITIGATION

LEGAL ADVISER-CLIENT PRIVILEGE

12.11 Since at least the days of Stair[37] communications passing between a legal adviser and a client have been privileged from subsequent disclosure in evidence. This is because "it is essential for the administration of justice that persons should be able to consult their legal advisers freely without the subject matter of their discussions being under risk of disclosure".[38]

---

[33] [1944] A.C. 57, in which it was held that a spouse could not give such evidence of non-access as would tend to render illegitimate a child born in wedlock.
[34] See *Brown v. Brown*, 1972 S.C. 123.
[35] Macphail, n. 6, Chap. 4.12.
[36] Macphail, n. 6, Chap. 4.13.
[37] IV, xliii.
[38] Wilkinson, n. 18, p. 94.

The privilege reflects the fundamental relationship of trust between legal advisers and their clients and thus the need for confidentiality in their dealings. Communications in the normal course of business are protected—the privilege is not confined to circumstances where litigation is in contemplation. The privilege, or confidentiality, covers solicitors and advocates, and their clerks and other staff.[39] It is, however, most commonly referred to as "the solicitor and client privilege", and is limited to qualified legal advisers. It does not extend, for example, to accountants giving legal advice in the course of their work.[40] The privilege appears to be that of the client, so that the legal adviser may disclose the communication if so authorised by the client, and the privilege is lost if the client calls that legal adviser as a witness.[41]

The absoluteness of the privilege was recently affirmed in the English case of *R. v. Derby Magistrates' Court, ex p. B*[42] where the House of Lords declined to permit a person accused of murder access to solicitors' files that might have assisted him in the preparation of his defence. Refusal was on the ground that these files were confidential between the solicitor and his client (a person previously acquitted of the murder) and the privilege attaching to that relationship was paramount. Lord Taylor observed[43]:

> "Legal professional privilege is thus much more than an ordinary rule of evidence . . . It is a fundamental condition on which the administration of justice as a whole rests."

Before the privilege will cover a particular communication, it must have been made in circumstances in which the relationship of legal adviser and client was at least in contemplation between the parties. It is uncertain what the precise position is when a solicitor receives the communication and then declines to act. In *H.M. Advocate v. Davie*[44] such evidence was admitted under reservation, although it was unnecessary to consider the point on appeal. However, doubts have been expressed as to whether this represents Scots law,[45] and it does not apply in England, where the privilege is invoked as soon as the relationship is fairly in contemplation.[46]

At the other end of the time scale, the privilege ends when the relationship ends, and communications made afterwards are not

[39] Macphail, n. 6, Chap. 18.20.
[40] Dickson, n. 24, para. 1665.
[41] Evidence (Scotland) Act 1852, s.1.
[42] [1995] 4 All ER 526.
[43] at pp. 540–541.
[44] (1881) 4 Coup 450.
[45] Macphail, n. 6, Chap. 18.21. See too, R. Black, "A Question of Confidence" (1982) 27 J.L.S.S. 299, 389.
[46] *Minter v. Priest* [1930] A.C. 558.

covered. However, communications made during the relationship continue to attract the privilege.[47] The privilege likely survives the death of the legal adviser and in some cases the death of the client.[47a] When the communication relates to some item of property in which the client's executors have an interest, it seems that the privilege transfers to the executors, but cannot be invoked to deny a third party rights in the succession.[48]

12.12 There are various limitations to the extent of the privilege, and they are as follows:

(1) The privilege covers only those matters formally communicated by the client to the legal adviser, and arguably not those facts which the latter may observe for himself or herself. As Wilkinson explained: "A solicitor must refuse to say whether his client confessed to a crime but must answer if asked whether he came to him wearing blood-stained clothing."[49]

(2) The privilege does not apply when the very matter into which the court is inquiring is whether or not the communication was made. Thus, in *Anderson v. Lord Elgin's Trustees*[50] the question arose as to whether or not the pursuer had delayed in bringing his action, as the defenders averred, and it was held to be competent to adduce correspondence between the defenders and their solicitors which referred to an earlier claim.

(3) The privilege will not cover communications that reveal the true nature of the relationship between the parties where this itself is in dispute. In *Fraser v. Malloch*[51] for example, the pursuer raised an action against a solicitor who had acted for a client in a previous action, claiming that the solicitor had done so without instructions. The pursuer was allowed to recover correspondence passing between the solicitor and the alleged client in order to shed further light on the relationship.

(4) The privilege will not cover communications which have passed between a solicitor and a client who is alleged to have performed some illegal act, when it is also alleged that the solicitor was directly involved in the carrying out of the illegal act. In *Micosta S.A. v. Shetland Islands Council*[52] the pursuers brought an action against the local authority for alleged abuse of statutory powers. They successfully obtained commission and diligence to recover certain documents amongst which was a sealed envelope containing correspondence that had passed between the defenders

---

[47] Dickson, n. 24, para. 1664.
[47a] Walker and Walker, n. 4, para. 10.2.2.
[48] See *Mackenzie v. Mackenzie's Trs*, 1916 1 S.L.T. 271.
[49] n. 18 at p. 95. See too, *Stair Memorial Encyclopedia*, para. 682, but this approach is considered indefensible by Walker and Walker, n. 4, para. 10.2.3.
[50] (1859) 21 D. 654. See also *Kidd v. Bunyan* (1842) 5 D. 193.
[51] (1895) 3 S.L.T. 211 (O.H.).
[52] 1983 S.L.T. 483, especially at 485.

and their law agents. Although the pursuers alleged the documents related directly to the alleged abuses, and were indicative of the defenders' state of mind at the time, the court sustained the defenders' arguments that the correspondence was privileged and could not be opened up. The court stressed that such privilege would not apply if the legal advisers had been directly involved in the action complained of[53]:

> "the only circumstances in which the general rule will be superseded are where fraud or some other illegal act is alleged against a party and where his law agent has been directly concerned in the carrying out of the very transaction which is the subject-matter of inquiry."

There is, however, a valid distinction between a communication made in the furtherance of an unlawful purpose, which is not privileged, and a request for legal advice afterwards on possible defences to a particular action, which is privileged. Requests for advice as to the legality of a contemplated course of action will also attract the privilege.

(5) In terms of section 47(3) of the Bankruptcy (Scotland) Act 1985, a bankrupt person must answer all questions posed during his public examination, and cannot generally claim privilege on the grounds of confidentiality against disclosure of communications with another person. However, the bankrupt person need not disclose matters communicated with his or her legal adviser, unless that adviser is also called for examination.[54]

There are many statutory provisions, including section 37(6) of **12.13** the Restrictive Trade Practices Act 1976, and section 3(2) of the Data Protection Act 1984, that preserve the legal adviser/client privilege even though it might be argued that it is in the public interest that all the client's dealings be brought into the open. However, Macphail points out that EC Regulations are not so protective, and that on at least one occasion the legal adviser/client privilege has been waived aside in the interests of the enforcement of the Treaty of Rome.[55]

There remains the question of whether or not the court may make use of privileged communications that have become available from another source, such as the overheard conversation or the intercepted letter. There is no Scottish authority on the position when the information is obtained illegally, although Macphail is of the opinion that such material should be subject to the normal rules relating to illegally obtained evidence.[56]

---

[53] n. 52 at p. 485 *per* Lord President Emslie.
[54] McBryde, *Bankruptcy*, para. 11–24.
[55] n. 6, Chap. 18.20. See too *AM & S Europe Ltd v. Commr of the European Communities* [1983] Q.B. 878.
[56] n. 6, Chap. 18.22.

In *McLeish v. Glasgow Bonding Co. Ltd.*[57] privileged information that became available through an innocent mistake was held admissible for the purposes of cross-examination. This ruling is not a helpful precedent for those supporting the rationale of the privilege as promoting public confidence in the legal system together with the fair and proper administration of justice.

COMMUNICATIONS *POST LITEM MOTAM*

12.14 A communication *post litem motam* is a communication made in circumstances in which it is in the mind of a party that litigation may be pending. Any such communication, whether between legal adviser and client or anyone else and a potential party, is generally privileged.

This privilege is clearly wider in scope than the legal adviser/client privilege, and is not limited simply to situations in which a writ has been issued. In one sense, however, it is narrower than the legal adviser/client privilege in that the latter covers all communications made at any time, while for a communication to be *post litem motam* it must be made at least when litigation is in contemplation. Thus, it was held in *Admiralty v. Aberdeen Steam Trawling and Fishing Co.*[58] that a communication *post litem motam* is one made not "merely after the summons has been raised, but after it is apparent that there is going to be a litigious contention".

In *Johnstone v. National Coal Board*,[59] a case concerning an industrial accident claim, the rationale of the privilege was described by the Lord President:

> "after an accident and even before any claim has been made, each party having a possible interest should be entitled to pursue his own investigations into the cause of the accident, free from the risk of having to reveal his information to the other side".

In *More v. Brown & Root Wimpey Highland Fabricators Ltd*[60] it was held that the privilege operated so as to prohibit the pursuer's recovery of photographs taken by the defenders' safety officer shortly after the accident. A similar ruling was given in *Anderson v. St Andrews Ambulance Association.*[61] In distinguishing between

---

[57] 1965 S.L.T. 39.
[58] 1909 S.C. 335 at 340.
[59] 1968 S.C. 128 at 133, quoting Lord Walker in *Young v. N.C.B.*, 1957 S.L.T 266 at 268 and adopted in *More v. Brown & Root Wimpey Highland Fabricators Ltd*, 1983 S.L.T. 669 at 670.
[60] *ibid.*
[61] 1942 S.C. 555 at 557. See too *Hepburn v. Scottish Power*, 1997 S.C. 80.

those communications which are made *post litem motam* and those which are not, Lord Hunter in *Marks & Spencer v. British Gas Corporation (No. 1 Corp)*[62] ruled that:

"the contrast is between reports which are designed to put the person concerned in possession of the true facts, on the one hand, and reports made in contemplation of judicial proceedings, on the other".

A communication *post litem motam* does not cease to have confidential status on the completion of the case for which it was prepared.[63]

There is one type of post-accident report which forms an exception to the general privilege normally afforded to statements *post litem motam*. There is no privilege attaching to a report made to an employer by an employee who was present at the scene of an accident, if that report was made at or about the time of the accident. This is so even though it may be very likely that litigation will result. Thus, the exception has been applied in situations where litigation was clearly in contemplation, including reports made to insurance companies containing lists of potential witnesses.[64] The rationale of the exception appears to be that:

"if such a report is made as part of routine duty, and as a record of the reporter's immediate reaction before he has had the time, opportunity or temptation to indulge in too much reflection, it may well contain an unvarnished account of what happened and consequently be of value in the subsequent proceedings as a touchstone of truth".[65]

As such it is similar to the underlying rationale for admitting *de recenti* statements. This overlooks, however, the primary reason for allowing privilege to attach to communications *post litem motam* in the first place, and the exception has been criticised as anomalous.[66]

A party who seeks to rely on one item in a course of correspondence or other communications passing between themselves and another party, may thereby be taken to have waived any privilege

---

[62] 1983 S.L.T. 196 at 197.
[63] *Hunter v. Douglas Reyburn & Co. Ltd*, 1993 S.L.T. 637.
[64] *MacPhee v. Glasgow Corp.*, 1915 S.C. 990.
[65] Lord Justice-Clerk Thomson in *Young v. N.C.B.*, n. 59 at 270. This rationale was also approved in *More v. Brown & Root Wimpey*, n. 59, in which the exception was affirmed as still representing the law of Scotland.
[66] See Macphail, n. 6, Chap. 18.26. A proposal to abolish this exception was, however, rejected by the Scottish Law Commission (Memo No. 46, para. S.26).

which might otherwise have been claimed in regard to the entire course of correspondence. Thus, in *Wylie v. Wylie*[67] a pursuer founding on one letter passing between his solicitor and himself was held to have waived his privilege in respect of other letters in the same course of correspondence passing at about the same time and dealing with the same legal action. The rationale appears to be that of preventing a party from selecting only favourable items from a wider collection, with the risk of distortion which might result.[68]

COMMUNICATIONS IN AID OF SETTLEMENT OF LITIGATION

12.15 A general privilege exists in respect of communications passing between the parties to an action and their respective solicitors with a view to settling that action out of court. These communications may also be covered by the solicitor/client privilege. This is true even if the communication consists of, or includes, an admission. The privilege was said by Dickson to arise from "mutual concessions".[69] It is clearly in everyone's interests that extra-judicial settlements should be encouraged in this manner. The result of the existence of the privilege is that concessions may be offered by either or both parties to a dispute without fear that they may be used against them in court should the attempted settlement fail.[70]

The existence of the privilege explains the tendency of solicitors attempting to settle a dispute to head their correspondence "without prejudice", a phrase which in recent years has evolved into a much more substantial disclaimer intended to cloak the author(s) in privilege. The effect of the phrase has been considered in two Outer House decisions. In *Bell v. Lothiansure Ltd*[71] Lord McCluskey held that the general rule applied and that nothing written or said under the cloak of "without prejudice" should be looked at unless both parties consented.

---

[67] 1967 S.L.T. (Notes) 9. The privilege waived was both solicitor/client and *post litem motam*.

[68] See *Marks & Spencer v. British Gas Corporation (No. 1)*, 1983 S.L.T. 196, in which the defenders were not allowed to waive confidentiality on part only of a report when this was not clearly severable from the rest of the report. In England there is recent authority that privilege may be claimed for part only of a document, see. *G.E. Capital Corporate Finance Group Ltd v. Bankers Trust Co.* [1995] 2 All E.R. 993.

[69] See Dickson, n. 24, para. 305.

[70] Both the Civil Evidence (Family Mediation) (Scotland) Act 1995 and the Industrial Tribunals Act 1996 grant privilege re certain statements made to mediators and ACAS officers, respectively.

[71] 1990 S.L.T. 58.

In *Daks Simpson Group plc. v. Kuiper,* Lord Sutherland,[72] in distinguishing *Bell,* said that, "if offers, suggestions, concessions or whatever are made for the purposes of negotiating a settlement, these cannot be converted into admissions of fact". However, he went on to say that if someone made a clear and unequivocal admission or statement of fact, then "I see no objection in principle to a clear admission being used in subsequent proceedings."[73] Both this case and *Gordon v. East Kilbride Development Corporation*[74] suggest a fairly strict approach will be taken to the application of the privilege. In *Gordon,* Lord Caplan observed that the privilege should only apply "where the communication in question is clearly eligible for it".[75]

The phrase "without prejudice" may not, in any event, cover the entire correspondence between the parties, where such correspondence shows that one of the parties was prepared to settle on terms which have subsequently been awarded by the court. In such circumstances Macphail argued that fact should be brought to the attention of the court when determining expenses.[76]

Privilege is strictly applied only to those matters which are the subject of the negotiations in hand, and may not be extended to any other matter which may appear in the correspondence. In *Ware v. Edinburgh District Council*[77] the distinction was made that:

"the words 'without prejudice' inserted in correspondence may not cover with the cloak of confidentiality all portions of a particular letter which do not strictly relate to a proposed settlement . . . Nevertheless, they do cover actual negotiations and, in particular, negotiation figures for a settlement."

The privilege may apparently be invoked by either party to the dispute, whether that party was the maker or the recipient of the communication.

COMMUNICATIONS IN SETTLEMENT OF MATRIMONIAL DISPUTES

One special form of negotiation for settlement may arise from a **12.16** matrimonial dispute, for example in an offer of terms for a separation agreement. When such communications arise between legal advisers and their clients, then they are part of the wider

---

[72] 1994 S.L.T. 689 and see *Richardson v. Quercus,* 1999 S.L.T. 596.
[73] at p. 692B–C and D.
[74] 1995 S.L.T. 62.
[75] *ibid.* at 64C.
[76] See Macphail, n.6, Chap. 18.28.
[77] 1976 S.L.T. (Lands Tr.) 21 at 24.

privilege considered above.[78] Section 1(1) of the Civil Evidence (Family Mediation) (Scotland) Act 1995 privileges "what occurred during family mediation". Various exceptions are set out in section 2 and the ethos of the Act is to encourage a frank exchange of views in mediation without concern that anything said can be used in subsequent court proceedings.

OTHER CLAIMS TO PRIVILEGE

GENERAL

12.17 There are many other professional relationships that could be regarded as "confidential", and occasionally a court may be presented with the refusal of a particular witness to disclose the contents of a particular statement made to him or her on the grounds that it was made "confidentially". Two such examples are communications between doctors and their patients and between bank managers and their customers.

However, with rare exceptions, all such claims to confidentiality have been rejected by the Scottish courts, and the only privileged communications which exist are those which have already been considered in this chapter. There are a few rare statutory exceptions to this rule such as provided for in the Bankers' Books Evidence Act 1879. Two further situations that have given rise at common law to debate regarding possible privileged status are considered below.

JOURNALISTS

12.18 Journalists are sometimes put in a position where they feel bound by conscience to retain confidentiality, often in the interests of future goodwill with informants. The legal position of such a witness is that while he or she may remain silent until ordered by the court to speak, they must then disclose the communication or face a charge of contempt of court. This is so even though the breach of confidence may thereby expose the witness to civil legal action for breach of confidence.

The consequence of a refusal to disclose a confidential source was apparent in *H.M. Advocate v. Airs*.[79] A journalist on the *Daily*

---

[78] But see Macphail, n. 6, Chap. 18.31, in which it is argued that there can be no strict comparison between the settlement of commercial disputes and the settlement of matrimonial disputes, because the latter involve issues about which the court must learn the truth, if necessary by admission, particularly when the welfare of children is in dispute.

[79] 1975 S.L.T. 177.

Record was fined £500 for contempt of court for refusing to disclose details of a conversation he had allegedly had with one of the accused in the "Tartan Army" trial. It was held that, except in the rare instance in which a judge may excuse a witness from answering on the ground of conscience (unlikely to occur when the evidence was highly material to the case), no one could be excused from the duty to answer a competent and relevant question.

In the words of the High Court[80]:

> "Now that all possible causes of misapprehension have been dispelled, any witness, including any journalist witness, who declines to answer a competent and relevant question in court must realise that he will be in contempt and be liable to incur severe punishment."

This view may have to be tempered in future cases where journalists claim a privilege. In 1995 the European Court of Human Rights found the United Kingdom to be in breach of the Human Rights Convention for imposing a fine on a journalist who refused to reveal his source of information.[81] Certainly the English courts deal with claims of privilege from journalists on a regular basic, and there is a limited privilege offered to journalists (applicable to Scotland) through section 10 of the Contempt of Court Act 1981.[82]

The possible consequence of a civil claim for breach of confidence arose in *Santa Fe International Corp. v. Napier Shipping S.A.*[83] In this case S were suing N for alleged infringement of a patent, and called for recovery of certain documents which had passed between N and third parties. N refused, on the ground that to do so would reveal certain technical information which they were bound by contract with those third parties not to reveal. N argued that disclosure would render them liable to an action for breach of contract. In holding that N must yield up the documents, it was emphasised by the court that except in "special circumstances", private promises of confidentiality must yield to the public interest in justice and truth.

CLERGY AND PENITENT

There is some authority for the proposition that a privilege exists **12.19** in the "confessional" situation in which a parishioner gives confidential information to his or her spiritual mentor. Macphail described an unreported case in 1960 in which the High Court

---

[80] *ibid.* at 181.
[81] The case of the journalist Bill Godwin, reported in *The Scotsman*, March 28, 1995.
[82] See *John v. Express Newspapers* [2000] 1 W.L.R. 1931 and *R. v. Central Criminal Court, ex p. Bright,* [2001] 1 W.L.R. 662 for insight into the English approach to this issue. See, too, Cross and Tapper, *Evidence*, pp. 465–467.
[83] 1985 S.L.T. 430.

upheld the confidentiality of the Catholic confessional in a homicide trial.[84] However, the position is not clear, and even Macphail acknowledged that the case was "of little practical importance".[85] The same view was taken by the Scottish Law Commission who refused to recommend that the privilege be formalised.[86] Instead, it was suggested that each case be taken on its merits in the exercise of a general judicial discretion to uphold confidences except where the interests of justice dictate otherwise. In England there is some support for the creation of such a privilege.[87]

PUBLIC INTEREST IMMUNITY

DEFINITION AND EXTENT

12.20 In some circumstances it is argued that public policy requires that certain information remain confidential. In such cases the person or body holding that information may claim an immunity against disclosing it in a court of law. This rule was formerly known as "Crown privilege", as it was most frequently claimed by Ministers on behalf of the Government, but is today generally described as public interest immunity. The privilege is much wider merely than Government departments, and has been held to extend to local authorities, police authorities and similar bodies. The underlying rationale of the immunity is that in some circumstances private justice must be subordinated to national security or to confidentiality of official records. The appropriate procedure is for the public officer responsible for authorising or withholding disclosure to grant a certificate, or other document, in which the court is advised of the general ground upon which immunity is being claimed—such as national security or confidentiality.

Typical of circumstances in which the immunity has been considered appropriate was *Duncan v. Cammell Laird & Co. Ltd,*[88] an English case in which the Minister of Defence, during wartime, successfully resisted the production of plans of a British submarine in an action for damages by the relatives of those who had died in it. The court agreed that the Minister who claimed Crown privilege had ultimate discretion and it was held that his certificate was conclusive. This approach was not adopted unequivocally as part of the law of Scotland. In *Glasgow Corporation v. Central Land*

---

[84] n. 6, Chap. 18.38 and 18.39.
[85] at Chap. 18.42.
[86] Memo No. 46, para. S. 32.
[87] Cross and Tapper, n. 82, at p. 463.
[88] [1942] A.C. 624.

Board[89] the House of Lords held that the Scottish courts have the power to go behind a ministerial certificate and decide for themselves whether or not a particular item of evidence is deserving of immunity, after weighing private interests against public. In *Conway v. Rimmer*[90] the House of Lords agreed that the correct approach was for the court (not a Minister) to evaluate the competing public interests involved. These twin interests are, first, the public interest in refusing to disclose documents in order to prevent harm to the national interest or to the proper functioning of the public service, and second, the public interest in producing the documents to enable the proper administration of justice. The effect of *Conway* was to bring the law of England into harmony with that of Scotland. English authority since 1968 has therefore possessed additional weight in Scotland.[91] However, as the Scottish Law Commission observed: "Although this power to overrule ministerial directions is now recognised in both jurisdictions, courts on both sides of the Border have been slow to exercise it."[92]

There are two types of case in which the immunity may be claimed. The first arises when the document or information called for contains items which it is believed should be withheld (the so called "contents" cases). The second arises where the document itself, while perhaps not containing anything immediately sensitive, belongs to a class of documents which is normally withheld (the "class" cases). Both are, however, subject to the same tests, and in recent years there has been an expansion in the type of document or other information that may be subject to the immunity. As was observed in *D. v. N.S.P.C.C.*,[93] "the categories of public interest are not closed and must alter from time to time whether by restriction or extension as social conditions and social legislation develop." However, the distinction between the categories of "classes" and "contents" may be becoming of less significance. In *D*, immunity was successfully sought against disclosing the identity of the person who had made a complaint to the N.S.P.C.C. concerning D's ill-treatment of his child. A similar ruling was made in *Rogers v. Secretary of State for Home Dept.*,[94] in which the pursuer sought damages for defamation in respect of a report on him sent by the police to the Gaming Board. Disclosure of the report was refused on the ground that its production might jeopardise the working of the public service. The approach adopted by the current leading authority in England is that each application for immunity should

---

[89] 1965 S.C. (H.L.) 1.
[90] [1968] A.C. 910 at 990, in which the English authorities are extensively reviewed.
[91] See Macphail, n. 6, Chap. 18.54. See too, for a review of the position in England, L.J. Simon Brown, "Public Interest Immunity" (1994) *Public Law*, 579.
[92] *Law of Evidence*, Memo No. 46, S. 39.
[93] [1978] A.C. 171 at 230.
[94] [1973] A.C. 388.

be determined on its merits and not depending on whether it belongs to a particular class of documents.[95]

Although there is little authority in Scotland, in *Strathclyde R.C. v. B.*[96] a local authority was unsuccessful in its claim to the immunity in relation to a social work file. The success of a claim for privilege will depend largely upon the extent to which the party seeking disclosure can show that the information required is vital to the case. The stronger the private interest in disclosure, the stronger must be the public interest against it. In *Park v. Tayside Regional Council*[97] a foster mother who claimed she had contracted hepatitis B from a child she had fostered, sought to recover hospital and social work records relating to the child. Noting that there had been no case in Scotland in which public interest privilege had been extended beyond departments of national government or of the Lord Advocate, Lord Sutherland went on to say that in this case, "the public interest in seeing justice done far outweighed the public interest in favour of confidentiality".[98]

12.21   The nature of the remedy sought, and the moral worthiness of the party seeking disclosure, may also have a bearing.[99] In particular, courts in recent years have displayed a reluctance to go behind the appropriate certificate claiming immunity in cases in which a former accused or suspect is seeking a civil remedy against a police authority. Thus, in *Friel, Petitioner*[1] the "victim" of a fruitless police search under warrant to search for stolen goods sought to bring a civil action against the person who had informed on him to the police. To do this F required to know the identity of the informant, and he petitioned the court for an order for recovery of the relevant police records. This was opposed by the Chief Constable and the Lord Advocate on the ground that the document in question fell within a class of documents which must be withheld in the interests of crime detection. Against this it was argued that if such claims were upheld, members of the public in F's position would find themselves denied access to the courts. It was held that in such cases the Lord Advocate's objection to disclosure could only be overridden by another public interest which was more pressing. This might take the form of the interests of justice to the

---

[95] *R. v. Chief Constable of West Midlands, ex p. Wiley* [1995] 1 A.C. 274.
[96] Unreported, *per* Macphail, n. 6, Chap. 18.54C.
[97] 1989 S.L.T. 345.
[98] at p. 348D.
[99] Compare, *e.g. Norwich Pharmacal Co. v. Customs and Excise Commrs* [1974] A.C. 133 with *Alfred Crompton Amusement Machines Ltd v. Customs and Excise Commrs* [1974] A.C. 405, the difference between which appears to have been the fact that in the first case, the party whose identity would have been revealed by disclosure was himself a wrongdoer, while in the second he was not.
[1] 1981 S.L.T. 113, also reported sub. nom. *Friel v. Chief Constable of Strathclyde*, 1981 S.C. 1.

individual. The denial to an individual of the possibility of bringing a civil action for malicious slander was held in *Friel* not to outweigh the general public interest in law enforcement.

Friel was followed in *P. Cannon (Garages) Ltd v. L.A.*[2] when the court refused to order the production of a blood sample taken from an alleged drunken motorist, or of his relevant certificates, for use in a civil action by the owner of a car damaged in the resulting accident. Here again the Lord Advocate opposed production on the "class" argument, and it was held that the private interest involved did not generate sufficient public interest to outweigh the public interest in the administration of criminal justice.

An interesting observation concerning the use of "public interest immunity" documents arose in *Anderson v. Palombo*[3] in which A, a police officer, sought damages for defamation against P, who had allegedly made an unfounded complaint concerning his behaviour. In his averments, A made reference to previous unfounded complaints by P against police officers, and a history of incidents in which P had proved abusive and uncooperative with the police. P sought to have these averments struck out as irrelevant and incapable of proof because the relevant police records relating to them would be immune from disclosure. In allowing proof before answer, Lord MacDonald observed that this would not necessarily be the case, as circumstances can clearly have a bearing on the balance between public and private interests.

The immunity applies as much in criminal cases as in civil actions, but in criminal cases the interests of justice to the individual accused must weigh heavily against any routine denial of information simply because that information belongs in a "class" which is normally immune. In *Rogers v. Secretary of State for Home Department*[4] for example, it was observed *obiter* that the police would not be entitled to protect the identity of an informer when his identification might establish the innocence of an accused. A conviction in these circumstances, *i.e.*, the refusal of a police officer to disclose the identity of an informer, was quashed in *Thomson v. Neilson*.[5]

The interests of justice to the individual also played a prominent role in the *Matrix Churchill* trial mentioned in Chapter 1. The defendants in this trial risked imprisonment having been prosecuted in 1992 for alleged breaches of export regulations during the Iran/Iraq war in the 1980's. Their defence was that the relevant government departments were well aware of their activities and in effect condoned them as two of the defendants who worked for the

---

[2] 1983 S.L.T. 50.
[3] 1984 S.L.T. 332.
[4] n. 94 above.
[5] (1900) 3 F. (J.) 3.

export company were also agents for MI5 and MI6. The trial collapsed after the judge's partial quashing of the public interest immunity certificates claimed by various government ministers and after one of the ministers confirmed under cross-examination the accuracy of the defendants' claims.[6] In cases such as these there are obviously competing interests between the needs of the individual and the wider interests of the state. The impact of the Human Rights Act has already been felt in this area and it is predictable that further challenges under this legislation will be made.[7]

---

[6] For background to this unreported case see I. Leigh, "Matrix Churchill, Supergun and the Scott Inquiry" (1993) *Public Law*, 630 and also the series of articles after the publication of Sir Richard Scott's Report into the arms to Iraq affair: (1996) *Public Law* 357–527.

[7] *Edwards v. U.K.*, 1993 T.L.R. 20 and *Rowe and Davis v. U.K.*, 2000, T.L.R. 147.

CHAPTER 13

CHARACTER EVIDENCE

INTRODUCTION

For the purposes of the law of evidence, a person's "character" **13.01** includes not only their known disposition from previous actions, but also their general reputation in society.[1] Character evidence is classed as a "collateral" issue in all but a minority of cases, and as a general rule is inadmissible.[2] The reason for excluding collateral issues is that:

> "Experience shews [sic] that it is better to sacrifice the aid which might be got from the more or less uncertain solution of collateral issues, than to spend a great amount of time, and confuse the jury with what, in the end, even supposing it to be certain, has only an indirect bearing on the matter in hand."[3]

There are, of course, some cases in which the character of one of the parties constitutes the main issue in a trial or proof, in which case it will no longer be considered as collateral, but will be provable as a main issue. In cases of alleged defamation of character, for example, it is the reputation of the pursuer, but not specific acts performed by him or her, which is the main issue. In *C. v. M.*[4] the defender was allowed to adduce evidence to show that the pursuer was well known for having "a loose and immoral nature", but could only cross-examine as to credibility in regard to *specific* acts of adultery as fair notice of those allegations had been given.

A person's character may be a main issue in a criminal action, as for example when an accused is charged with driving while

---

[1] Wilkinson, *Scottish Law of Evidence*, p. 22, citing *R. v. Rowton* (1865) 34 L.J.M.C. 57.
[2] Dickson, *Evidence*, para. 6.
[3] Lord President Robertson in *A. v. B.* (1895) 22 R. 402 at 404.
[4] 1923 S.C. 1.

disqualified by reason of a previous conviction. In *Wallace v. Mooney*,[5] W sued M, a police constable, for an assault arising from his forcible ejection from a racecourse. M had instructions to remove all persons of bad character, and it was held that he could adduce evidence of W's bad character to justify his actions.

In the vast majority of cases however, both civil and criminal, a person's character, using the term in its broadest sense, is not a main issue. As a collateral issue, it is something that may only be proved in evidence in exceptional circumstances where it is felt that it has a material bearing on at least one of the main issues, permitting it to be treated as an exception to the general rule against admissibility. These exceptional circumstances are examined in the remainder of this chapter as follows:

1. Similar fact evidence in criminal cases.
2. Similar fact evidence in civil cases.
3. Character of victim of crime.
4. Character of witness.
5. Character of a criminal accused.
6. Character of other persons.

SIMILAR FACT EVIDENCE IN CRIMINAL CASES

13.02 Similar fact evidence has been defined as:

> "evidence of the character or of the misconduct of the accused on other occasions . . . tendered to show his bad disposition, (which) is inadmissible unless it is so highly probative of the issues in the cases as to outweigh the prejudice it may cause".[6]

The acceptance of similar fact evidence in criminal cases is an exception to the general rule that a person's previous behaviour is not relevant to the assessment of their guilt or innocence in a criminal trial. The rationale behind admitting similar fact evidence is that it may be reasonable to take into account a person's behaviour on a previous occasion provided:

> "it be relevant to an issue before the jury, and it may be so relevant if it bears upon the question whether the acts alleged to constitute the crime charged . . . were designed or accidental, or to rebut a defence which would otherwise be open to the accused".[7]

---

[5] (1885) 12 R. 710.
[6] Cross and Tapper, *Evidence*, p. 335.
[7] *Makin v. Attorney-General for New South Wales* [1894] A.C. 57 at 65.

The origins of similar fact evidence are usually located in the case of *Makin v. Attorney-General for New South Wales*.[8] Mr and Mrs Makin were charged with the murder of a baby that been unofficially fostered by them in return for money, and whose body had been found buried in the back yard of their house. Their defence was that the baby had died accidentally or of natural causes. In order to rebut this defence the prosecution led evidence of three separate discoveries of corpses. First, the discovery of the bodies of three other babies at the Makins' house, second, evidence of the remains of another seven babies at a house previously occupied by the Makins; and third, the remains of two more babies at yet another house the Makins had occupied. The prosecution also adduced evidence from a number of women who had given up their babies to the Makins for fostering and had never seen the babies again. The accused had initially insisted that they had only fostered one baby. On appeal to the Privy Council, it was held that the prosecution could adduce this similar fact evidence of past misdeeds to negative the defence put forward by the accused and to challenge their assertion of accidental or natural death.

In cases such as *Makin*, the admissibility of evidence of previous misdeeds of the accused is admitted on two grounds. First, because of the similarity of circumstance, which is highly suggestive of the accused's guilt of the offence with which he or she is now charged; and second, because it negatives some innocent explanation of the present charge which the accused is putting forward. The first of these must be treated with care as often such evidence is highly relevant to the case in hand but nonetheless is excluded due to its prejudicial effect, especially where there is a risk of a jury attaching too great a probative value to it.[9]

The rule emerging from *Makin* has had a complex history under English law,[10] and has only made rare appearances in Scotland. It was referred to in submissions in the Scottish case of *H.M. Advocate v. Joseph*.[11] In *Joseph*, details of a fraud committed by J abroad were held to have been properly libelled in an indictment in Scotland in order to show the fraudulent intent with which the present offence had been committed. Lord Murray declared that it was settled that:

> "evidence in regard to another incident of a similar character may be admitted in proof of a crime charged notwithstanding that this evidence may incidentally show, or tend to show, the

---

[8] *ibid.*

[9] See *D.P.P. v. Kilbourne* [1973] A.C.729 and *D.P.P. v. Boardman* [1975] A.C. 421.

[10] For which see Cross and Tapper, n. 6 at pp. 335–347, and *R. v. Selvey* 1970 A.C. 304.

[11] 1929 J.C. 55. See too *Nelson v. H.M. Advocate*, 1994 J.C. 94 at 101.

commission of another crime, provided there be some connection or 'nexus' which in the opinion of the court is sufficiently intimate between the two 'incidents'."

13.03 This reference to a "nexus" between incidents is, of course, similar to the rationale of *Moorov v. H.M. Advocate*.[12] The link between the present charge and the previous act must be as strong as that required for the operation of the *Moorov* doctrine, although that may not be very much.[13] There is however, one key distinction. Under the *Moorov* doctrine, two or more similar charges on the same complaint or indictment are spoken to by only one witness (in respect of each) in order to produce a corroborative course of criminal conduct. In the *Makin* type of case reference is being made to behaviour on the part of the accused that is *not* now charged[14] largely to rebut some defence that the accused is raising to the present charge. Thus, in *Joseph* Lord Murray stated[15]:

> "I am of opinion that it is the law in Scotland, as in England, that it is open to the prosecution to prove any facts relevant to the charge, notwithstanding that they may show or tend to show the commission of another crime, if they show or tend to show that the act charged was *done of design and did not arise by accident, or if they tend to rebut a defence of innocence.*"

The concept of similar fact evidence has developed much more substantially in English law compared to Scots law. There is a range of dicta to the effect that it is not possible to have a definitive list of categories when similar fact evidence will be relevant. Nor is it possible to define the degree of probative value required before similar fact evidence will be admissible, beyond stating that it "requires a strong degree of probative force".[16] This "strong degree" might be derived from evidence of conduct that offers such "striking similarity" to other crimes committed by the accused that it would offend against common sense to exclude it from probation.[17]

For example, evidence that *only* shows the accused to be of bad disposition will be inadmissible. To be admissible the evidence must do more than infer that the accused has a propensity to commit a crime of the type charged. Thus in *R. v. B,*[18] evidence

---

[12] 1930 J.C. 68, considered in Chap. 7.
[13] See *Reynolds v. H.M. Advocate*, 1995 S.C.C.R. 504.
[14] And may never have been charged, as in *Makin* itself.
[15] n. 11, at p. 57 (emphasis added).
[16] *D.P.P. v. Boardman*, n. 9 above.
[17] *loc. cit.*
[18] [1997] 2 Cr. App. R. 88, CA.

produced at trial of pornographic magazines in B's possession was held by the House of Lords to be improperly admitted insofar as they were intended to suggest B had committed the indecent assaults of his two grandsons with which he was charged. The magazines and other related evidence merely proved propensity to commit the crime, which did not meet the criterion for admissibility of similar fact evidence.[19]

Remarkably, the rule appears to have featured little in Scots law since *Joseph*, and when it has the evidence has been adduced to show motive or intention.[20] In any future case in Scotland there could be recourse to recent English authorities, where, as already noted, it has arisen frequently, although care would be required as the rule has evolved so differently in the two jurisdictions.[21] The modern test in England of admissibility of similar fact evidence can be broadly stated as dependent on its relevance and its probative value.[22] Given that similar fact evidence is potentially very prejudicial, it will only be admissible if the "nexus" between the present crime and the previous act is sufficiently strong. The evidence must obviously be relevant to an issue before the jury, and it will not be admitted if its prejudicial value outweighs its probative value. The most recent consideration of this balance between prejudice to the accused and probative value occurred in *R. v. Z.*[23] In this case Z was charged with rape. He had faced four previous allegations of rape. On three of these occasions he had been acquitted and on one occasion he had been convicted. In each case he had put forward a defence that the woman had consented to sexual intercourse, or at least that he had believed that she had consented. The Crown wished to bring evidence from those four complainants to negate Z's defence, arguing that such evidence was admissible under the similar facts rule. The trial judge accepted the evidence came within the scope of the similar facts rule but held that evidence of the three acquittals was inadmissible due to the double jeopardy rule.[24] The House of Lords ultimately ruled in favour of the Crown on the ground that evidence of the previous acquittals

---

[19] See *H.M. Advocate v. Pritchard* (1865) 5 Irv. 88 for a case in which it was held that an accused's previous misconduct gave rise to a motive for murder, and was admissible as evidence of such.

[20] See, in particular, *Griffen v. H.M. Advocate*, 1940 J.C. 1, and also, *Booth v. Tudhope*, 1986 S.C.C.R. 638 and *McIntosh v. H.M. Advocate*, 1986 J.C. 169.

[21] See Cross and Tapper, n. 6, pp. 335–347. Also, *D.P.P. v. Boardman*, n. 9 above; *R. v. Wilson*, 1973 58 Cr.App.Rep. 169; and *Thompson v. R.* [1918] A.C. 221.

[22] See Keane, *The Modern Law of Evidence*, Chap. 16, and Cross and Tapper, n. 6, pp. 348–357 for detailed discussion.

[23] [2000] 3 All E.R. 385.

[24] The effect of the double jeopardy rule is that a person cannot be tried twice for the same offence. The trial judge ruled the previous conviction evidence did not of itself establish "a sufficiently cogent picture" (p. 389) to be admitted as similar fact evidence.

was being led, not to put the accused on trial on a second occasion or to seek to punish the accused, but simply to lead evidence to demonstrate the behaviour of the accused towards other complainants on previous occasions as that was relevant to his defence of consent. There was therefore no infringement of the double jeopardy rule and the testimony was admissible as similar fact evidence.

SIMILAR FACT EVIDENCE IN CIVIL CASES

13.04 There is no equivalent rule to *Makin* in civil cases, and the general rule is that what may or may not have happened in other incidents is of no relevance in the present action, not even if it sheds light on the character of one of the parties.

As noted above, in *A. v. B.*,[25] a pursuer seeking civil damages for rape was not allowed to adduce evidence of the defender's alleged attempts to rape two other women, on the grounds that such evidence was collateral and irrelevant. It was considered by the court that the allegations were being presented, not because these other women were complaining of rape, but "merely . . . to lend some probability to the pursuer's case".[26]

Similarly, in *H. v. P.*,[27] where the main issue in a slander action was whether or not H had committed adultery with P, it was held that P could not lead evidence to show "instances of H's unchastity with other men" as such evidence relating to third parties was irrelevant. In both cases, however, it was held that such questions might be put to test the party's credibility as a witness, provided that fair notice had been given. This remains the case today, although doubts have been expressed about the current value of such a practice,[28] and the Scottish Law Commission has recommended the abolition of cross-examination on issues of chastity which cannot be tested by evidence in chief.[29]

There is authority to the effect that a party's behaviour on some previous occasion may be relevant to the case in hand, and provable in chief, when it appears to form a "course of conduct" with the behaviour currently in issue. *Whyte v. Whyte*[30] is regarded as an early example of this principle in action, when, in an action for divorce on the grounds of adultery with a female servant, Mrs W was allowed to adduce evidence of W's indecent behaviour with another female servant.

---

[25] n. 3 above.
[26] n. 3, at p. 404.
[27] (1905) 8 F. 232.
[28] See Macphail, *Evidence,* Chap. 16.05, and *Duff v. Duff,* 1969 S.L.T. (Notes) 53.
[29] Memo No. 46, para. Q.04.
[30] (1884) 11 R. 710.

Another example was *Roy v. Pairman*,[31] although like *Whyte* it may be regarded as a special case in an area of law in which corroboration is difficult to obtain. Of more general application is the authority of *Knutzen v. Mauritzen*,[32] in which K, in an action for damages against M for the delivery of poor quality goods, was allowed to adduce evidence that another delivery from the same consignment, made to a third party, was also of poor quality. Although *Knutzen* did not relate strictly to a question of character, the principle involved is the same. Where the similar fact (or similar act) belongs in what may fairly be called the same course of conduct with an alleged act into which the court is now inquiring, it may be sufficiently relevant to transform itself from a mere collateral issue into a main issue which may be proved by evidence in chief.

THE CHARACTER OF A WITNESS

The character of a witness, in all but a few exceptions, is regarded **13.05** as purely collateral, going only to his or her credibility as a witness. Collateral matters are not central to the primary matters into which the court is enquiring. As such character is not relevant to the essential facts and evidence regarding it will be inadmissible.

Evidence suggesting some dubiety about the witness's credibility is regarded as an exception to the general rule that credibility is collateral. The effect is that while questions relating to character may be put to the witness to test credibility, the matter may not be pursued by means of evidence in chief. Questions may be put to witnesses that are designed to undermine their credibility and show that the witnesses are of such poor character generally, that they should not be believed. But the party attacking credibility is normally only permitted to raise the suggestion that the witness is not to be believed, and leave it at that. It is not permissible to pursue the point and rebut any denial with additional evidence.

It is not therefore permissible to produce extracts of previous convictions that relate to a witness.[33] However, in some recent cases courts have been prepared to allow questioning on issues that may have had a bearing on the credibility of a witness, particularly in the wider interests of criminal justice.[34] That said, a party

---

[31] 1958 S.C. 334, in which P's admitted act of intercourse with R after she had become pregnant was held to be admissible on the issue of his alleged intercourse with her *before* conception.

[32] 1918 1 S.L.T. 85. See also *Morrison v. McLean's Trs* (1862) 24 D. 625.

[33] See *Kennedy v. H.M. Advocate* (1896) 23 R. (J.) 28, and *Dickie v. H.M. Advocate* (1897) 24 R. (J.) 82 at 83.

[34] e.g. *Green v. H.M. Advocate*, 1983 S.C.C.R. 42; *Marshall v. Smith*, 1983 S.C.C.R. 156; and *Williamson v. H.M. Advocate*, 1979 J.C. 36.

seeking to test the credibility of a witness will not be permitted to make "vague suggestions against the character of a witness by a series of insulting questions".[35]

Cross-examination as to credibility generally

13.06 While the character or disposition of a witness may be relevant in assessing veracity and credibility, it is always subject to the broader rule that it is normally irrelevant and inadmissible. The older authorities cite a previous conviction for perjury as an example of poor character that may be used to discredit a witness.[36] Apart from perjury or some other specific previous conviction, there are a few other isolated cases that arise when the interests of justice permit that the general behaviour, or even personality, of a witness be taken into account. Similarly, there are a few situations where the character of a victim or complainer in a criminal case can be examined.[37] When that victim gives evidence it can be almost impossible to distinguish between evidence which shows that the victim is unreliable as a witness and evidence which goes to the very credibility of the allegation, and hence the guilt of the accused.

In *Green v. H.M. Advocate*,[38] G and another had been convicted of rape. Their defence was consent and there was evidence that the complainer had been sniffing glue on the day of the incident. Subsequent to conviction a successful application was made to have the appeal court consider fresh evidence, not available at the trial, relating to the complainer's character.[39] The appeal court heard that she had on previous occasions made false allegations of rape, was suffering from a psychiatric disturbance which led her to fantasise, and had admitted to a third party that the present allegations were false. It was held that this fresh evidence cast such grave doubts on the credibility of the complainer, and had such serious implications for the original defence of consent, that the accused must be acquitted on the grounds of a miscarriage of justice.

---

[35] *e.g.* as in *Falconer v. Brown* (1893) 21 R. (J.) 1 at 4.

[36] Walker and Walker, *Law of Evidence in Scotland*, para. 12.13.2 and Dickson, n. 2, para. 1618. *N.B.* that not even this may be proved by additional evidence when denied by the witness: see *Carey v. Tudhope*, 1984 S.C.C.R. 157.

[37] Even when deceased; see *H.M. Advocate v. Kay*, 1970 J.C. 68, *H.M. Advocate v. Cunningham* (cited by Macphail, n. 28, Chap. 16.07). In *Cunningham*, proof by means of extract convictions was allowed, while in the same case, evidence in chief was permitted of previous assaults by the deceased upon the accused.

[38] n. 34. See also *Marshall v. Smith*, n. 34, but see *Allison v. H.M. Advocate*, 1986 J.C. 22.

[39] The application was in terms of the Criminal Justice (Scotland) Act 1980, Sched. 2, para. 1, which has now been replaced by Criminal Procedure (Scotland) Act 1995, s.106(3).

Cross-examination as to personal interest

One of the most important impediments to a witness's credibility **13.07** could be the fact that he or she has some sort of personal interest in the outcome of the case. This may be in the form of a personal relationship, present or former, to one of the parties or the accused, or it may be that the witness has a financial stake in the subject matter of the action. As a general rule, however, the relationship of a witness to a party in an action does not disqualify him or her from testifying.[40]

The type of background circumstances which cannot be ignored include allegations that the person giving evidence in a criminal trial also took part in the criminal activities with which the accused is now charged. Such persons are known as *sociis criminis*,[41] and in a jury trial, the presiding judge is entitled to draw the jury's attention to the potential question mark against the credibility of the evidence of any *socius criminis*. However, such a warning is not obligatory.[42]

In *Manson v. H.M. Advocate*,[43] a Crown witness who appeared hesitant and reluctant to give evidence eventually admitted, under cross-examination by her own counsel, that she had been threatened by the accused's wife. It was held that such cross-examination was valid provided that the jury were carefully directed that such matters go only to the credibility of the witness. This type of personal bias regarding the outcome of a case is likely to become more prevalent, given the increasing impact of witness intimidation.[44]

THE CHARACTER OF THE VICTIM OF CRIME

General

On some occasions, the character of the victim of a crime can be **13.08** a material issue, whether the victim is called as a witness or not. This could arise, for example, when an accused on an assault

---

[40] Evidence (Scotland) Act 1840, s.1; Criminal Procedure (Scotland) Act 1995, s.265(3).

[41] Defined in *Wallace v. H.M. Advocate*, 1952 J.C. 78, *per* Lord Keith at 83 as being anyone who has been convicted of, or pleaded guilty to, the offence with which the accused is charged or who gives evidence, on his own admission, as an accomplice in that crime.

[42] In *Docherty v. H.M. Advocate*, 1987 J.C. 81, the practice of giving what is usually referred to as the *cum nota* warning was stated to be a matter of discretion for the trial judge. Corroboration is not required if the witness is believed. Note that an accused still on trial cannot be treated as *socius criminis*.

[43] 1951 J.C. 49. See also *Williamson v. H.M. Advocate*, 1978 S.L.T. (Notes) 58.

[44] See the Council of Europe Recommendation No. R (97) 13, *Intimidation of Witnesses and Rights of the Defence*.

charge pleads self-defence, or an alleged murderer pleads provocation. The general rule in all such cases is that if the character in
question is materially relevant to the defence, then it is admissible.
When the character evidence consists of the victim's behaviour at
the time of the alleged offence, then no special notice is required,
but if the accused intends to attack his victim's character on
general grounds, then it is.[45]

Until recently, it was believed that while an accused might lead
evidence of specific acts of violence by the victim on the occasion
into which the court is inquiring, and evidence concerning the
victim's character generally, he might not cite specific acts of
violence on other occasions.[46] However, doubt has been cast on
this proposition by the High Court in *H.M. Advocate v. Kay*,[47] in
which K was charged with the murder of her husband, the
indictment also libelling previous indications of malice and ill-will
on the part of the accused towards the deceased. Her special
defence of self defence took the form of a belief on her part that
she was about to be assaulted by the deceased, and she was allowed
to lead evidence of previous assaults upon her by the deceased.
Lord Wheatley[48] ruled that:

> "I consider that it would be unfair to allow detailed evidence
> by the Crown in support of that part of the indictment which
> alleges that the accused had previously evinced malice and ill
> will towards the deceased, without allowing the accused the
> opportunity of proving in turn by detailed evidence that she
> had reason to apprehend danger from the deceased."

The Scottish Law Commission,[49] in approving this ruling, widened
it as follows:

> "We do not see how an accused can readily prove that the
> victim was a violent person unless he is permitted to cite
> specific violent actings on the part of that person . . . The
> arguments against allowing such evidence are that it prolongs
> criminal trials and can also confuse juries. We do not
> consider either of these arguments sufficiently weighty to
> justify the *status quo*, and propose that in cases of murder or
> assault the accused should be entitled by citing specific acts of

---

[45] See Walker and Walker, n. 36, para. 7.7.1, and *Dickie v. H.M. Advocate*, n. 33.
[46] Walker and Walker, *loc. cit.*; Wilkinson, n. 1, p. 30.
[47] 1970 J.C. 68.
[48] n. 47 at p. 69.
[49] Memo No. 46, para. Q.05. See also *H.M. Advocate v. Cunningham* (1974),
  unreported, cited in Macphail, n. 28, Chap. 16.07, in which an accused in a
  similar position to *Kay* was allowed to prove the deceased's previous conviction
  for culpable homicide.

violence to prove that the injured person was of a violent or quarrelsome disposition."

This argument is equally applicable to battered women who kill, of whom there have been a number of recent highly publicised cases.[50] Such women find the traditional defence of self defence unsuitable for their particular circumstances and instead, often plead the defence of diminished responsibility. It is essential to this defence that evidence is admitted regarding the alleged violent characters of their deceased partners.

Evidence of the character of the complainer in a sexual offence

One of the most controversial applications of the law in relation **13.09** to the character of a victim is the use made of sexual character evidence of a victim of rape or sexual assault. A person's sexual morality is irrelevant in most cases except, it seems, in certain sexual offences where examination may be permitted in assessing whether or not a victim is a credible witness. Under common law an accused could attack his victim's general reputation for chastity. According to Dickson[51] this represented the only exception to the general rule forbidding character evidence and was justified:

> "while so much depends on the truth of her statements, and there is so great risk of her story having been concocted in a fit of jealousy, or with the view of extorting money, or covering her shame when discovered in a voluntary connection, that a full inquiry into her character is requisite to enable the jury to estimate her credibility".

Mounting public concern surrounding the alleged abuse of this rule led to statutory reform in 1985.[52] The Law Reform (Miscellaneous Provisions) (Scotland) Act 1985, section 36 (now section 274 of the Criminal Procedure (Scotland) Act 1995) was intended to regulate questions that might be asked by defence counsel in rape cases relating to the general sexual character of the complainer. In terms of section 274(1), no complainer in any of the cases covered by the legislation may be cross-examined[53] as to their previous good character in sexual matters, as to whether or not they are a prostitute, or as to whether or not they have previously engaged

---

[50] See, for example, *R. v. Ahluwalia* [1992] 4 All E.R. 889, and *R. v. Thornton (No. 1)* [1992] 1 All E.R. 306.

[51] Dickson, n. 2, para. 1622.

[52] Macphail, n. 28, Chap. 16.09. Such questioning is admissible at common law *per Dickie v. H.M. Advocate*, n. 33, in so far as it reflects upon the credibility of the witness.

[53] Nor may any such evidence be led in chief.

with any person in any sexual behaviour[54] which does not form part of the subject-matter of the charge. In terms of section 274(4) none of these restrictions apply to questions being put by the Crown.[55]

All of these prohibitions can be modified in the circumstances prescribed in section 275, namely:

> (i) that such questions must be asked in order to explain or rebut evidence adduced, or to be adduced, otherwise than by or on behalf of the accused,[56] or
>
> (ii) that the questions relate to other sexual behaviour which took place on the same occasion as the behaviour with which the accused is charged, or are relevant to the defence of incrimination,[57] or
>
> (iii) that it would be contrary to the interests of justice to exclude such questions.[58]

Before such questions may even be put in cross-examination, the accused must make special application during the course of the trial, but outwith the presence of any jury, the complainer, any person cited as a witness and the public. The court has a wide discretion to allow or to limit the extent of such questioning. In *Bremner v. H.M. Advocate*[59] the appeal court refused to interfere with the trial judge's refusal to allow the complainer to be questioned about her relationship with the accused that had ended some eight months before the rape.

Many observers have cast doubt over the effectiveness of the legislation in protecting the character of the complainer from attack. Research carried out in 1992 found that in 32 per cent of sexual offence trials the defence made an application to lead evidence of the previous character of the complainer and in 85 per cent of these cases the applications were at least partially successful. The research also found that there was a high incidence (24 per cent of cases) of breach of the prohibition against leading character

---

[54] *N.B.* not just the accused.

[55] Presumably to the accused, but conceivably to the complainer herself, or to any of the Crown witnesses.

[56] *e.g.* if the complainer alleges that she was a virgin at the time of the offence, or if medical evidence is led for the same purpose.

[57] *e.g.* the accused alleges that certain sexual familiarities were permitted prior to an alleged rape, or that he was only one of several men who had intercourse with the complainer with her consent, or that in fact someone else committed the act in respect of which he is charged.

[58] A significant discretion, that arguably subverts the primary aim of the legislation.

[59] 1992 S.C.C.R. 476.

evidence.[60] These findings, coupled with public distaste at a number of well-publicised cases where complainers were subjected to gruelling cross-examination by the accused representing himself, led to the publication of a pre-legislative Consultation Paper, by the Scottish Executive, entitled *Redressing the Balance: cross-examination in rape and sexual offence trials*.[61] The Executive are considering legislation to restrict the rights of accused to represent themselves where that exposes the complainer to personal cross-examination by the accused, and also to strengthen the sexual history and character provisions designed to protect a complainer from irrelevant intrusion into their sexual past.

The treatment of victims of rape and sexual assault is frequently cited as one explanation for the under reporting of such offences, and for the proportionately poor rate of convictions, as compared to other offences.[62] Witnesses who give testimony regarding their assaults are often bitter about their experience in court and feel let down by the apparent inability of the rules of evidence to regulate effectively the admissibility of sexual history evidence.[63] The provisions of the Human Rights Act will undoubtedly impact on this area of the law in two major ways. First, Article 3 ECHR accords certain rights to victims, *i.e.* the right not to be subjected to inhuman or degrading treatment. Thus, excessively intrusive, irrelevant cross-examination relating to sexual history of a type that humiliates and degrades witnesses may contravene the Act.[64] Second, Article 6 provides, in the context of the right to a fair trial, that an accused has the right to defend himself in person and concerns have been expressed that this would prevent legislation prohibiting an accused from representing himself, including personally cross-examining a complainer. However, such legislation has now been enacted in England and is discussed as an option in the consultation document *Redressing the Balance* referred to above.

---

[60] Brown *et al., Sexual History and Sexual Character Evidence in Scottish Sexual Offence Trials*, 1992, Scottish Office Central Research Unit Papers. See also the text, *Sex Crimes on Trial* by the same authors.

[61] Published in 2000. See too the Sexual Offences (Procedure and Evidence) (Scotland) Bill, published in July 2001. Action to increase the protection of victims in England has already been taken under the Youth Justice and Criminal Evidence Act 1999.

[62] *e.g.* J. Temkin, *Rape and the Legal Process*, 1987, Sweet & Maxwell, London; S. Lees, *Carnal Knowledge—Rape on Trial*, 1996, Hamish Hamilton, London and see the criminal justice statistics Statistical Bulletin available at www.scotland.gov.uk.

[63] See for *e.g.*, G. Chambers and A. Millar, "Investigating Sexual Assault" (1983) Scottish Office Research Unit; G. Chambers and A. Millar, "Prosecuting Sexual Assault" (1986) Scottish Office Research Unit; L. Ellison, "Cross-examination in rape trials" (1998) Crim LR 605; J.Temkin, "Prosecuting and Defending Rape: perspectives from the Bar" (2000) JLS (27(2) 210–248.

[64] See *e.g. R. v. Brown* [1998] 2 Cr. App. Rep. 364.

THE CHARACTER OF A CRIMINAL ACCUSED

GENERAL

13.10 The character of a criminal accused obviously raises special issues. On the one hand, it is crucial to a fair trial that the court (and particularly a jury) should not be influenced in its decision as to the accused's guilt of the offence now charged by evidence of the accused's misdeeds on previous occasions. On the other hand, it is equally important that an accused should not be allowed to make false claims to having a good character, or to malign the character of those who are testifying against him or her, without the court being advised of their true character. At the same time, there may be some incident in the accused's past which cannot logically be ignored, given the nature of the present charge, whether the accused has put character in issue or not.

At common law, it is always open to an accused to put their own character in issue. This will normally take the form of evidence of good character, which an accused is entitled to raise as an issue.[65] This right predates the 1898 Act which first made the accused a competent witness in his or her own defence, and it therefore follows that such evidence may take the form, not only of testimony by the accused, but also of testimony from other character witnesses called by the defence.[66]

There is however a risk attaching to the defence strategy of raising character as an issue. If an accused person gives evidence of their own character then the prosecution have a statutory right to cross-examine on that matter. If on the other hand, the accused declines to go into the witness box, but arranges for other witnesses to speak to their good character, then the normal rule is that, while the prosecution can cross-examine, they have no separate right to lead evidence which they may have concerning the accused's character. The presiding judge, but not the prosecution, may however comment on an accused's failure to testify.[67]

On rare occasions it may be necessary for an accused person to use their *bad* character in their own defence, as for example where an alibi defence consists of the fact that the accused was in prison at the material time. The choice of raising bad character is that of the accused and, as discussed below, must not be as a result of a prosecution attack on character.[68]

Until fairly recently, the main problem concerning the character of an accused person related to the restrictions placed upon the

---

[65] Dickson, n. 2, para. 15.
[66] Or conceivably from prosecution witnesses, by means of cross-examination.
[67] Criminal Procedure (Scotland) Act 1995, s.266.
[68] See *Carberry v. H.M. Advocate,* 1975 J.C. 40 at 46.

prosecution against cross-examining on character when the accused had chosen to testify. A number of cases have seen a gradual erosion of these restrictions, and where the prosecution successfully argue that an accused's character is relevant to the issues in hand, then they have been allowed to adduce evidence of character in chief, regardless of whether or not the accused chooses to give evidence. Additionally, there is the situation where one accused attacks the character of a co-accused in order to exculpate him or herself. These and other issues are considered below.

PROSECUTION EVIDENCE IN CHIEF OF THE ACCUSED'S CHARACTER

The general rule is that the prosecution may not, in the course of **13.11** their own evidence in chief, lead evidence of the bad character of the accused as evidenced by past misdeeds, or by any other inference.[69] This rule is embodied in statute in section 101(1) (solemn proceedings) and section 166(3) (summary proceedings) of the 1995 Act which provide that no reference should be made to previous convictions of an accused in the course of a trial.[70]

The apparent strictness of these rules is, however, tempered by a line of cases in which previous convictions have been placed before the court accidentally, and it has been held that no substantial prejudice occurred to the accused and that the conviction could stand. Thus, in *H.M. Advocate v. Corcoran*[71] Lord Anderson ruled that:

> "Where a witness in good faith, and in answer to a competent question fairly put by the prosecutor, incidentally discloses the existence of a prior conviction, I do not think that a contravention of the statute takes place."

This view was endorsed *obiter* in *Carberry v. H.M. Advocate*,[72] while in *Johnston v. Allan*[73] the same view was taken of a previous conviction contained on a computer printout from the DVLC which was handed to the sheriff in error, with no improper motive on the part of the fiscal depute.

These rulings appear to proceed upon the basis that there was no deliberate attempt by the prosecution to prejudice the accused,

---

[69] Dickson, n. 2, para. 15. Neither may a co-accused: see *Slane v. H.M. Advocate*, 1984 S.L.T. 293.

[70] And see *Forsyth v. H.M. Advocate*, 1992 S.L.T. 189 where there was held to have been a miscarriage of justice though not based on statutory provisions.

[71] 1932 J.C. 42 at 49.

[72] 1975 J.C. 40 at 46; this case is considered below.

[73] 1984 S.L.T. 261; see also *O'Neill v. Tudhope*, 1984 S.L.T. 424 and *Moffat v. Smith*, 1983 S.C.C.R. 392.

and that there was no active intent to lay the previous conviction before the court. However, in most cases this will not reduce the prejudicial effect for the accused, and the more important question on appeal should be whether or not this prejudice was material.

The consequences of a deliberate breach of either section will normally be an acquittal on appeal, or a desertion of the diet *ex proprio motu* by the presiding judge. An example of this was *Smith v. H.M. Advocate*,[74] in which a police witness, asked in chief if he recognised the accused, not only acknowledged him but gratuitously informed the court that he knew him as a housebreaker. The subsequent conviction was quashed.

In *Cordiner v. H.M. Advocate*,[75] C was charged on an indictment libelling three charges. On the date upon which one of these was alleged to have occurred, C had been serving a prison sentence in respect of a previous conviction, and he intimated this to the Crown in his special defence of alibi. This could have been readily confirmed by the Crown, who instead allowed the special defence to be read to the jury, and then later in the trial withdrew the only charge to which it related. The convictions *quoad* the remaining charges were quashed, the Crown having conceded that forcing C to disclose his prison sentence was equivalent to the prosecution having laid a previous conviction before the court.

Distinct from those cases examined above in which breach of the sections was held to have been accidental, there are two competent exceptions to the statutory rule contained in the 1995 Act.

(1) When disclosure is competent in support of a substantive charge

13.12 Provisos to both sections 101(2)(b) and 166(8)(b) of the 1995 Act allow previous convictions to be disclosed in circumstances in which it is competent to do so "in support of a substantive charge".[76] This is because in certain exceptional circumstances, the Crown cannot effectively libel the charge(s) against an accused without making reference to a previous conviction. For example, a charge of driving while disqualified by its very nature implies a previous motoring offence, and the Crown cannot obtain a conviction without proving both the disqualification and the offence

---

[74] 1975 S.L.T. (Notes) 89. See also *Graham v. H.M. Advocate*, 1984 S.L.T. 67, in which an accused charged with assaulting his wife and various other offences was acquitted on appeal after a police witness read out a reply to caution and charge which consisted of the words: "That cow's got me the jail again!" The appeal court went so far as to accuse the fiscal depute of having engineered the breach of the statute without justification. See also *McCuaig v. H.M. Advocate*, 1982 J.C. 59 and *Binks v. H.M. Advocate*, 1984 J.C. 108.

[75] 1978 J.C. 64; *N.B.* however that the defence must make timeous objection to any breach of the section: *Jackson v. H.M. Advocate*, 1982 J.C. 117.

[76] See *Russell v. H.M. Advocate*, 1993 S.L.T. 358, a case decided under the previous statutory provisions.

which gave rise to it.[77] In such cases, because the disclosure of the conviction is a pre-requisite of the current charge it is regarded as an essential exception to the general rule. Disclosure should be with the minimum of prejudice to the accused, reflecting the wording of the proviso to each of the sections, which refers to such evidence being led "in support of" the charge.[78]

Two examples of this exception in operation are *Varey v. H.M. Advocate*[79] and *Murphy v. H.M. Advocate*.[80] *Varey* was charged with prison-breaking, and the indictment libelled the length of the sentence he had been serving and the offence for which it had been imposed. Despite a defence challenge, the court held that the indictment was relevant, since it was essential to the Crown case to prove the date and length of the sentence, and the fact that such detention proceeded upon lawful cause.

In *Murphy*, M was charged with perverting the course of justice. He had given his solicitor false information concerning his private life. That information was then used in mitigation of sentence on two separate occasions. M had previous convictions, which he had admitted on each occasion, and the Crown called as witnesses the sheriff and justice who had sentenced him on each occasion, to testify that but for the false representations the sentences would have been more severe. It was held that disclosure of the previous convictions was admissible as the Crown could not competently narrate the charges without including reference to these convictions.

The right to adduce evidence of an accused's previous convictions in support of a charge may also occasionally be found in statute. For example, section 19 of the Prevention of Crimes Act 1871 allows a prosecutor who has proved an accused's possession of stolen property to adduce evidence of previous convictions implying dishonesty, if they are less than five years old, in support of the *mens rea* of guilty knowledge.

(2) Where disclosure is relevant to a defence raised by the accused

On rare occasions, the Crown cannot adequately rebut a defence **13.13** put forward by the accused without revealing that he or she has previous convictions, and in such cases it seems that they may be permitted to do so. For example, in *Carberry v. H.M. Advocate*[81] a statement led in evidence in which the accused admitted to being

---

[77] *Moffat v. Smith*, n. 73 above.
[78] The difficulty in *Moffat v. Smith*, n. 73, was the fact that although obliged to libel one previous conviction, the Crown had inadvertently proved two.
[79] 1986 J.C. 28.
[80] 1978 J.C. 1.
[81] n. 68 above.

"in Barlinnie" was held in the particular circumstances of the case to be admissible.[82]

The principle embodied in sections 101 and 166 extends to exclude disclosure of A's previous convictions by a co-accused B. This was established in *Slane v. H.M. Advocate*,[83] in which S was on trial with two others. During the course of the Crown case, counsel for a co-accused, M, asked a Crown witness questions expressly designed to show that S had a criminal record. It was held that although this was not technically a breach of section 160, it was contrary to its spirit, since "those accused of crime are entitled to enjoy the presumption of innocence throughout their trial and . . . information as to their criminal past should not be disclosed to the court or the jury".[84] Holding that ordinarily, such an "inexcusable" breach of procedural ethics would give rise to a miscarriage of justice, the appeal court nevertheless upheld the resulting conviction because of the weight of the other evidence against S.

CROSS-EXAMINATION OF THE ACCUSED ON ISSUES OF CHARACTER

13.14 As explained above, a criminal accused is in an anomalous situation when he or she exercises the right provided in section 266 of the 1995 Act to give sworn evidence in their own defence. On the one hand, an accused is not allowed to claim the normal privilege against self incrimination which an ordinary witness may claim, and subsection (3) takes away this privilege in regard to the offence(s) presently charged. On the other hand, the effect of disclosing to the trial court that the accused has previous convictions, or has misbehaved in the past, would be unduly prejudicial to a fair trial unless the accused has raised the issue of character, or has maligned the character of Crown witnesses. This is the case even if character evidence is being adduced merely to impugn the accused's credibility as a witness, since an accused's character is virtually indivisible in such circumstances. Evidence tending to impugn credibility as a witness will invariably also suggest guilt of the charge. As was explained above, an accused who puts his or her own good character in issue cannot, however, complain if the prosecution then lead evidence to contradict that, and section 101(2) and 166(8) of the 1995 Act expressly permit this.

Section 266(4)(b) permits the prosecution the option of cross-examining the accused as to character if evidence of good character has been given by the accused:

---

[82] See too, *Gemmill v. H.M. Advocate*, 1979 S.L.T. 217.
[83] n. 69 above—the first direct case on the point; see Sheriff Gordon's commentary at 1984 S.C.C.R. 77 at 80.
[84] n. 69 at p. 79.

"(4) An accused who gives evidence on his own behalf in pursuance of this section shall not be asked, and if asked shall not be required to answer, any question tending to show that he has committed, or been convicted of, or been charged with, any offence other than that with which he is then charged, or is of bad character, unless—

   (a) the proof that he has committed or been convicted of such other offence is admissible evidence to show that he is guilty of the offence with which he is then charged; or

   (b) the accused or his counsel or solicitor has asked questions of the witnesses for the prosecution with a view to establishing the accused's good character or impugning the character of the complainer, or the accused has given evidence of his own good character, or the nature or conduct of the defence is such as to involve imputations on the character of the prosecutor or of the witnesses for the prosecution or of the complainer; or

   (c) the accused has given evidence against any other person charged in the same proceedings."

Only when the accused has brought himself within one of the circumstances listed above may the prosecution cross-examine on his character,[85] and even then it is the proper practice for them to seek the leave of the court before doing so.[86] Otherwise, it will be noted, such questions may not even be asked.

A breach of subsection (4) will normally lead to a successful appeal if not carefully corrected by the trial judge in a solemn case when charging the jury, and will be almost certainly fatal in a summary trial. In *McLean v. Tudhope*,[87] M was charged with a breach of the peace, and in the course of being cross-examined he stated that he was an honest man. Without seeking the leave of the court, the fiscal depute then referred to a previous conviction, and in re-examination M was obliged to give details of it by way of a damage limitation exercise. On appeal, it was held that since the case turned on credibility, the reference to the previous conviction required the conviction to be quashed.[88]

---

[85] *N.B.* that "character" for the purposes of subs. (4) is not restricted to previous convictions.

[86] *O'Hara v. H.M. Advocate*, 1948 J.C. 90. This case was over-ruled in relation to other aspects by *Leggate v. H.M. Advocate*, 1988 S.L.T. 665.

[87] 1982 S.C.C.R. 555.

[88] The fact that M had apparently put his character in issue appears not to have been considered: see Sheriff Gordon's comment on the case, n. 87 at p. 557.

13.15   An almost identical provision to subsection (4) in England[89] has led to many test cases and much controversy. The position in Scotland was settled by the full bench decision in *Leggate v. H.M. Advocate*.[90] This decision overruled previous authority governing the circumstances in which an accused would lose the statutory immunity against attacks on character. *Leggate* is best considered in the light of the previous case law, both English and Scottish.

Section 266(4) makes the general position clear—the accused shall not be asked any question "tending to show" that he has committed, been convicted of or even charged with previous offences. In *Jones v. D.P.P.*[91] it was held that the words "tending to show" must be interpreted as meaning "tending to show for the first time". The effect of this is that if the court becomes aware of, for example a previous conviction, by other means,[92] then the accused may be cross-examined on it.

In *Maxwell v. D.P.P.*[93] it was held that even though the accused may throw away his immunity by giving evidence of the type prescribed by (a), (b) and (c) of subsection (4), the prosecution may even then only adduce such evidence of his character as is relevant in the circumstances. In particular, the House of Lords doubted whether there would be many cases in which the fact that the accused had been charged with a previous offence but acquitted would be relevant to the present charge. In *Stirland v. D.P.P.*[94] it was held that "charged" meant "charged in court", and the court in that case went on to rule that a person's "character" is indivisible, so that once an accused's character is in issue, all relevant aspects of it may be considered.[95]

Also, in *Jones v. D.P.P.*,[96] the House of Lords pointed out that the statutory protection refers only to questions asked in cross-examination, and does not prevent the question being put to an accused by his or her own solicitor or counsel during examination-in-chief. When this occurs, of course, the prosecution may then cross-examine on it, because such later questions will not "tend to

---

[89] Under the Criminal Evidence Act 1898, which applied in Scotland until 1975. See Cross and Tapper, *Evidence*, p. 430.

[90] 1988 J.C. 127.

[91] [1962] A.C. 635; which considered the equivalent provisions in English law; followed in *Dodds v. H.M. Advocate,* 1988 J.C. 21.

[92] *e.g.* if the accused makes reference to it, or even if a prosecution witness refers to it by accident: see *H.M. Advocate v. Corcoran*, n. 71.

[93] [1935] A.C. 309. See *Lowson v. H.M. Advocate*, 1943 J.C. 141, and *Lindie v. H.M. Advocate*, 1974 S.L.T. 208; 1974 J.C. 1.

[94] [1944] A.C. 315; [1944] 2 All E.R. 13.

[95] On which point see *Leggate v. H.M. Advocate*, n. 86, discussed below.

[96] [1962] A.C. 635; [1962] 1 All E.R. 569; followed in *Dodds v. H.M. Advocate*, 1988 S.L.T. 194.

show for the first time" that the accused has a "past". In *McLean v. Tudhope*[97] it was also demonstrated that when an accused is forced to go into detail concerning a previous conviction only because of an inadmissible question in cross-examination by the Crown, this does not homologate the asking of the original question so as to make it admissible.

If the accused uses section 266(4) to set up their own good character or to attack the character of others, the prosecution cannot attack the accused's character unless the presiding judge permits this in terms of subsection 5. In all cases except under section 266(4) the prosecution must seek the leave of the court, outwith the presence of the jury, before proceeding to cross-examine the accused as to character. But a co-accused against whom evidence has been given is not affected by these restrictions.[98]

(1) Subsection (4)(a): Accused's character relevant to the charge

As noted earlier, there are circumstances in which, notwithstand- **13.16** ing the general rule against adducing evidence of the accused's character in chief, the prosecution may rely on such evidence when it is "relevant" to the charge that the accused now faces. Subsection (4)(a) allows the Crown to cross-examine the accused along these lines, but it may be superfluous in this context, given the *ratio* of *Jones*, that subsection (a) does not apply when the court has already learned of the accused's bad character by other means.

Thus, in cases such as *Varey v. H.M. Advocate*[99] and *Murphy v. H.M. Advocate*,[1] the prosecution could presumably not only adduce evidence of the accused's previous convictions in chief, but could cross-examine on them if the accused has chosen to give evidence. *Quaere* whether or not this will be the case when the accused's character is relevant only to his defence,[2] but given the ratio of *Jones*, above, once the court is aware of the character in question anyway, there would seem to be nothing to prevent cross-examination on it.

When "similar fact evidence" is relevant under the rule in *Makin v. Attorney-General for New South Wales*,[3] cross-examination on it would seem to be permitted under subsection (4)(a).

---

[97] 1982 S.C.C.R. 555.
[98] See *McCourtney v. H.M. Advocate*, 1977 J.C. 68 at 72.
[99] n. 79 above.
[1] n. 80 above.
[2] As in *Carberry v. H.M. Advocate*, n. 72 and *Gemmill v. H.M. Advocate*, n. 82.
[3] n. 7 above.

(2) Subsection (4)(b): Accused gives evidence "of his own good character"

13.17   When an accused sets out to establish his or her good character, either by cross-examining witnesses for the prosecution concerning it, or by giving such evidence on oath then the Crown are entitled, with the leave of the court, to counter such evidence.[4] The Crown may cross-examine the accused as to character to show that the position is other than the accused would have the court believe. It is uncertain whether or not, if the accused denies the accusations made against him, the Crown may go on to prove them by recalling a witness or calling fresh evidence altogether. Section 266(4)(b) only operates when the accused gives evidence. Section 270 of the Criminal Procedure (Scotland) Act 1995 covers the situation where the accused declines to go into the witness box, but nonetheless makes good character an issue. In the event that the accused attacks Crown witnesses in cross-examination or seeks to set up his or her good character through defence witnesses called for this purpose, the Crown can retaliate by leading evidence of the accused's previous misconduct including previous convictions.

Problems can arise when good character evidence is obtained by co-accused A from co-accused B or from B's witness. B may then wish to cross-examine A as to B's good character. Since A has "set up" his character it is only fair to allow B to set the record straight by cross-examining A as to his misdeeds in the past. This is particularly true where the two are running what is popularly known as a "cut-throat" defence (*i.e.* each is incriminating the other) and the issue of credibility is crucial. There is, not surprisingly, no direct authority on the point, since in most such cases each accused will go on to give evidence against the other, and thus invoke subsection (4)(c).

(3) Subsection (4)(b): "Nature and conduct of defence involves imputations on character of prosecutor, prosecution witnesses or complainer."

13.18   The basic rules of fair play suggest that when the accused sets out, either in chief or in cross-examination,[5] to impugn the character of the prosecutor[6] or the Crown witnesses or the complainer,[7] then the court should also be advised of any stains on the accused's own character. At the same time, an accused is entitled to a fair opportunity to develop a genuine defence, and

---

[4] See Walker and Walker, *Law of Evidence in Scotland,* paras 13.4.2–13.14.4.
[5] *N.B.* that there are no restrictions on the form that such evidence may take.
[6] See *H.M. Advocate v. Grudins,* 1976 S.L.T. (Notes) 10.
[7] The addition of the complainer to this list is an extension of the statutory provisions as contained in ss. 141 and 346 of the 1975 Act.

that may, incidentally, involve imputations against the prosecution witnesses. A balance has to be struck between these two considerations.

Until the case of *Leggate*[8] the practice was to grant an accused whose defence necessarily involved casting aspersions on the character of Crown witnesses some degree of statutory immunity.[9] This immunity protected the accused against a character attack, and/or the disclosure of previous convictions, if the accused gave evidence. *Leggate* was a full bench decision that overturned a line of case authority from *O'Hara v. H.M. Advocate* in 1948,[10] including a five judge decision in *Templeton v. McLeod*.[11]

The appeal court in *Leggate* decided that when an accused attacks the character of a Crown witness, even if this is necessary to establish his defence, he does not retain any immunity from attack on his own character. It was recognised that there might be situations where this was unduly prejudicial to an accused so the trial judge has discretion to ameliorate the consequences of an attack on character. Section 266(5) requires the prosecution to apply to the court for permission to cross-examine on character. The application must be made outwith the presence of the jury. The judge can refuse leave to cross-examine the accused on his character.

The search for a balance between developing a genuine defence and imputations against Crown witnesses has produced a confusing and often contradictory series of cases in England, culminating in *Selvey v. D.P.P.*[12] In that case the House of Lords refused to exclude the possibility of cross-examination on character of an accused who could not mount a fair defence without impugning the character of prosecution witnesses.

In *H.M. Advocate v. Grudins*[13] it was held that subsection (4)(c) does not apply, and the accused does not lose the statutory protection when the character which is being attacked is not that of a witness. In *Grudins*, the accused on a murder charge did not lose her immunity when she attacked the character of the deceased. The wording of subsection 4(b) indicates that the statutory protection is not lost if the accused attacks the character of a defence witness who proves "hostile".

---

[8] 1988 J.C. 127.
[9] In terms of ss. 141(1)(f) and 346(1)(f) of the 1975 Act.
[10] 1948 J.C.90.
[11] 1985 J.C. 112.
[12] [1970] A.C. 304.
[13] n. 6, applying the previous provisions contained in the 1975 Act.

(4) Subsection (4)(c): "Accused gives evidence against a co-accused"

13.19   Section 266(4)(c) applies in respect of any two accused who appear on the same complaint or indictment, regardless of the charges against them. When subsection (4)(c) comes into play an accused may be cross-examined as to character not only by the prosecution but also by a co-accused. When one co-accused attacks the character of another co-accused or the witnesses of a co-accused, then, by virtue of subsection (4)(c) the statutory protection will be lost.

In *Murdoch v. Taylor*[14] the House of Lords, in an English case, held that giving "evidence against" a co-accused could consist of either giving evidence which supports the prosecution's case against him in some material respect, or giving evidence which undermines the defence being put forward by that co-accused. In addition, it held that such evidence could be given either in chief or in the course of being cross-examined, and that it was not necessary for the accused to have any hostile motive, since the test of whether or not evidence is given "against" a co-accused is objective and not subjective.

Both rulings were adopted in *Burton v. H.M. Advocate*.[15] The court added that there was no distinction to be drawn between the case in which an accused gave evidence against a co-accused expressly, and that in which an attack on the co-accused might be inferred from the evidence given, or arose by implication. In *Sandlan v. H.M. Advocate*[16] it was held that an accused who has been incriminated by a co-accused has a right to cross-examine that accused on the incriminating evidence. This may entail a second cross-examination. And in *Todd v. H.M. Advocate*[17] it was held that evidence by one co-accused is evidence *in causa* generally, and may be used against another co-accused even if not intended for that purpose.

In *McCourtney v. H.M. Advocate*[18] it was held that once an accused has given evidence against a co-accused in terms of subsection (4)(c), the judge has no discretion to exclude the disclosure of that accused's bad character. This is because when one accused gives evidence against another, he "is in the same position as a witness for the prosecution so far as the co-accused is concerned, and nothing must be done to impair the right of a person charged to discredit his accusers".[19]

---

[14] [1965] A.C. 574.
[15] 1979 S.L.T. (Notes) 59. Some doubts were cast, *obiter*, on the accuracy of the first interpretation in *Sandlan v. H.M. Advocate*, 1983 J.C. 22.
[16] n. 15 above.
[17] 1984 S.L.T. 123.
[18] 1977 J.C. 68.
[19] Cross and Tapper, n. 6, pp. 373–374.

CHARACTER OF OTHER PERSONS

GENERAL

Occasionally it can become important for the court to consider the **13.20** character of a person who is not a party to the case, nor a witness, nor the victim of a crime. Provided that such evidence is relevant, it may apparently be admitted.

In *Gracie v. Stuart*,[20] a reset trial, it was held that the Crown could prove that the person from whom the accused admitted having obtained a stolen watch was in fact a dealer in stolen watches. In *MacPherson v. Crisp*,[21] a charge of brothel-keeping, the Crown were allowed to show that two women, not cited as witnesses, but who had been observed entering the accused's premises, were known to be prostitutes.

---

[20] (1884) 11 R. (J.) 22.
[21] 1919 J.C. 1.

CHAPTER 14

CONFESSION EVIDENCE

INTRODUCTION

14.01 Confession evidence plays a very significant role in daily practice within the criminal courts. According to Griffiths[1]: "Confession evidence is one of the commonest types of evidence tendered in the Scottish courts and it has a major place in the general law of criminal evidence." The confession that has been unfairly obtained may still be true, but it is contrary to public policy, and unsafe, to rely on any confession so obtained. Such a confession is therefore ruled inadmissible.

A confession should, strictly speaking, be referred to as an "extra-judicial" admission because it is a statement made by a person against their own interest outside a court of law. The term "confession" is used to describe a statement of admission made by someone who later becomes the accused in a criminal trial. An admission by someone who later becomes a party to a civil action rarely carries such serious consequences as an admission made in the criminal context, but it may still constrain the lines of proof or defence open to such a party. When such confessions or admissions are made formally in court, as part of the judicial process, they are known in both civil and criminal cases as "judicial admissions". These were considered in Chapter 6, and it will be recalled that they are binding upon the maker once they are made.

Extra-judicial admissions and confessions, however:

> "are not by themselves conclusive against the party making them as in the case of judicial admissions. Evidence of them is relevant either because it may throw light on the party's credibility as a witness, or as an adminicle of evidence in the cause, and must be considered along with all the other evidence led."[2]

---

[1] D. Griffiths, *Confessions*, 1994, p. 1.
[2] Walker and Walker, *Law of Evidence in Scotland*, para. 9.1.2.

The statements are admissible in evidence because they are made against the interests of the person making them, and are therefore more likely than not to be true.[3] When the party who made the statement in question also gives evidence in the case, then this admission or confession may clearly have relevance to that person's credibility as a witness if it conflicts with the evidence which is now being given. Where the party does not give evidence, then the admission or confession may be admissible as an exception to the hearsay rule.

In criminal cases, confessions can normally never be the sole evidence in a case, because of the general rule which requires corroboration, but their precise probative value will vary from case to case. Thus, in *Buick v. Jaglar*,[4] Sheriff Wilkinson observed that:

> "It is true, no doubt, that a statement against interest, made coolly and after reflection, is stronger evidence against its maker than a statement made by a person who is in a greatly distressed condition. It is also no doubt true that such a statement is stronger evidence if it never be contradicted or it be contradicted only after a long interval than if it is contradicted shortly after it is made."[5]

ADMISSIONS AND CONFESSIONS BY WITNESSES IN PREVIOUS CASES

A witness who gives evidence in a case but not as a party to it, may **14.02** make statements or admissions while on oath in the witness box. Any confessional statement made by that witness is regarded as an extra-judicial admission or confession for the purposes of any later case to which he or she is a party, and in which that statement is relevant.[6] Where possible, of course, the witness should be warned before giving such evidence of any privilege against self-incrimination that may apply.

In *Banaghan v. H.M. Advocate*[7] B was charged with sending a threatening letter, and the Crown were allowed to adduce evidence of the fact that in a previous civil action to which B had not been a party, he had admitted to having been the writer of the letter. In

---

[3] Dickson, *Evidence*, para. 297.
[4] 1973 S.L.T. (Sh. Ct) 6 at 8.
[5] See also Lord Kincraig in *Liquid Gas Tankers Ltd. v. Forth Ports Authority*, 1974 S.L.T. (Notes) 35, who approved the statement in Walker and Walker, (1st ed.) n. 2, para. 30, that "in each case the probative weight to be attached to . . . an admission must depend upon the circumstances of the particular case."
[6] Dickson, n. 3, para. 288.
[7] (1888) 15 R. (J.) 39; (1888) 1 White 566.

Edmison,[8] the same rule was applied in regard to a confession of guilt made by E at the criminal trial of another person charged with that offence. It is because of the admissibility of such statements in later cases that the need exists for a privilege against self-incrimination. It has been held that even though some formal record of the case in which the admission was made may be available, such as the transcript or the judge's notes, reliable oral evidence may prove the making of the statement.[9]

IMPLIED ADMISSIONS AND CONFESSIONS

14.03 At common law an admission or confession may sometimes be implied. This might occur from a person's silence or other reaction when confronted with an allegation that would ordinarily call for some sort of reply, such as a denial. As Dickson noted: "Admissions may be implied from a party remaining silent when statements to his prejudice are made in his presence".[10] However, because it would conflict with the right of a person not to make an incriminating statement, the principle is not applied merely because an accused remains silent in the face of a charge or accusation, or offers a flat denial.[11]

This does not, however, eliminate the possibility of the court inferring some sort of confession from the fact that an accused reacted in a particular way to a statement made in his or her presence and/or hearing which could be said to call for a response. For this reason "statements made in the presence of an accused" are regularly admitted as an exception to the hearsay rule in order to cast light on the accused's reaction to them, be it silence or some action such as bursting into tears or turning pale.

One special form of this process arises when two accused persons are interviewed by the police, and one of them makes an incriminating statement which the other "adopts" by failing to deny it. In *Annan v. Bain*,[12] for example, two suspects who had been chased to a standstill by police officers from the point at which they had abandoned a stolen car, made statements there and then. One of them made a reference to a "white car" (which only the thieves might have been expected to know) and the other was held to have adopted this reference by silence. It proved crucial in providing corroboration.

---

[8] (1866) 1 S.L.R. 107; (1866) 5 Irv. 519.
[9] See *McGiveran v. Auld* (1894) 21 R. (J.) 69 at 72.
[10] Dickson, n. 3, para. 368.
[11] See Walker and Walker, n. 2, para. 9.6.2, and *Robertson v. Maxwell*, 1951 J .C. 11 at 14.
[12] 1986 S.C.C.R. 60. See however *H.M. Advocate v. Davidson*, 1968 S.L.T. 17, where the point was made that the police will not be permitted to force two accused into this sort of confrontational situation.

Such implied admissions by adoption must however be approached with care, and in particular very close regard must be had to the context in which the original statement was made. Thus, in *Hipson v. Tudhope*,[13] H had been a passenger in a stolen car that had been chased by police after it failed to stop. The car collided with a railing and stopped, and when the police asked whose car it was, another accused, in the presence of H, stated that it was stolen. It was held on appeal that the failure of H to dissociate himself from this confession did not amount to a new confession by him. The court said that in view of his explanation that he did not know the car to be stolen when he accepted a lift in it, he could not be convicted of reset.[14]

The common law protection against self-incrimination has been modified by a number of statutory exceptions, including the Road Traffic legislation. One of the frequently invoked provisions is section 172(2)(a) of the Road Traffic Act 1988 which provides that a person requested by the police must supply details of the driver of a vehicle. The competency of this section in regard to whether it may compel a person to make an incriminating statement, and thus its compatibility with the Human Rights Act 1998, has recently been tested in the case of *Brown v. Stott*.[15] B was questioned by police whilst under suspicion of having stolen a bottle of gin from a supermarket. The officers smelt alcohol on her breath and asked her how she had got to the supermarket. She indicated she had driven her car. Her admission, as required by the statute, was subsequently challenged at trial on the ground that it breached the Convention right to a fair trial contained in Article 6 of the ECHR. This contention was upheld by the Court of Criminal Appeal, a decision then appealed by the Lord Advocate to the Privy Council, who reversed the decision and upheld Brown's conviction.

While it was acknowledged that there was a general right not to incriminate oneself, it was accepted this was not an absolute right[16]:

> "Limited qualification of these rights is acceptable if reasonably directed by national authorities towards a clear and proper objective and if representing no greater qualification than the situation calls for."

According to Lord Bingham, the admission of being the driver of a car was not in itself an offence without some other facts being proven to point to an offence having been committed. Moreover, all car drivers understood they were subject to a "regulatory

---

[13] 1983 S.L.T. 659.
[14] See also *Clark v. H.M. Advocate*, 1965 S.L.T. 250.
[15] 2001 S.L.T. 59, *per* Lord Bingham.
[16] at p. 70 H–I.

regime" that was necessary given the potential of cars to cause grave injury. In those two contexts, the requirement of section 172 was not disproportionate.

In a similar vein, Lord Kirkwood argued[17] that while the right to a fair trial under Article 6 was absolute (the question of what is "fair" being a moot point) the right implied in Article 6 not to incriminate oneself was not absolute:

> "It is a right which is capable of being limited by law to some extent, always provided that the limitation is shown to be necessary to protect the legitimate interests of the community."

The reasoning in this decision suggests that ECHR challenges to regulatory regimes such as other road traffic measures including speed cameras, and CCTV in public places will be unsuccessful.

FORM OF CONFESSIONS

14.04 There is no distinction made between oral confessions and those that are in writing or in some other form, such as incriminating behaviour. All such activities are considered as "statements" against interest and are subject to the same rules of admissibility. A written statement may well appear more reliable, but such statements may be challenged on the ground that they did not emanate from the accused, or that they are not in his or her own words. A court will regard as inadmissible a statement that has simply been prepared by a third party for signature by the accused.[18]

In regard to behaviour as an indicator of guilt, the English case of *R. v. Voisin*[19] provides a vivid illustration. In that case the police were investigating the murder of a woman whose body was found in a parcel with a scrap of paper upon which the words "Bladie Belgiam" were written. V. was asked to write down the words "Bloody Belgian" and he wrote "Blaidie Belgiam". He was subsequently convicted. In *Manuel v. H.M. Advocate*[20] the conduct of M in being able to lead the police to the scene of the crime and point

---

[17] at p. 85 C.

[18] Which is often the case with confessions made to police officers. A precognition will also fail the admissibility test: see *Carmichael v. Armitage*, 1983 J.C. 8, in which the High Court rejected as inadmissible a declaration made by A before a sheriff which had been prepared for him by his solicitor, since the court viewed it as being more in the nature of a precognition than a statement by the accused himself.

[19] [1918] 1 K.B. 531.

[20] 1958 J.C. 41. See, too, *Chalmers v. H.M. Advocate*, discussed below as an example of incriminating conduct.

out where a shoe belonging to the victim was buried constituted a "confession".

VICARIOUS ADMISSIONS AND CONFESSIONS

General rule

As a general rule, an admission or confession made by co- **14.05**
accused A in a criminal trial will not be admissible against co-accused B, and similarly in a civil case when A and B are co-defenders or pursuers. There are two well recognised exceptions to this general rule. First, where it is shown that the accused were acting in concert, and second, when the statement by A was made in the presence of B, and might reasonably be regarded as having required some response from B.

"Concert" means simply that the accused were acting together with a common purpose. Before any confession by A will be admissible against B it must relate to that common purpose. There are relatively few cases on the point,[21] but an example of the principle in operation was *H.M. Advocate v. Docherty*.[22] D was charged with corruption in the public office which he occupied, his alleged corrupter being a person J who was dead by the date of the trial. The Crown sought to adduce evidence of incriminating statements made by J in the furtherance of corrupt acts involving D. It was held that if the jury came to the conclusion that D and J were acting in concert, then since D would be answerable for actions performed by J it was permissible for the jury to be made aware of J's contemporaneous statements concerning those actions. In short, J's statements were part of the *res gestae*, and D was bound by them in so far as the two were acting in concert.

As noted earlier, a statement made by A in the presence of B may be regarded as having been adopted by B if he fails to dissociate himself from it.[23] However, this will not apply when the second accused has been compelled to listen to the statement in question against his will. In *H.M. Advocate v. Davidson*,[24] D had been cautioned and charged and placed in a police cell. Shortly afterwards he was brought to the charge bar to hear what a co-accused, C, said when cautioned and charged. He was given no reason for being there, and was not warned of what was to happen, or the consequences for him. It was held that the subsequent confession by C was inadmissible against D in these circumstances,

---

[21] See, however, *Young v. H.M. Advocate*, 1932 J.C. 63.
[22] 1980 S.L.T. (Notes) 33, quoting Walker and Walker, n. 2, para. 37.
[23] See *Annan v. Bain*, n. 12 above.
[24] 1968 S.L.T. 17.

as it amounted to a breach of D's fundamental right to remain silent after caution and charge.

Where co-accused A and B are not acting in concert, and A has not made any statement in the presence of B to which a reply could properly be expected, then the general rule applies, and B is not incriminated by anything said by A.[25] In *Jones v. H.M. Advocate*[26] the High Court, reaffirmed this general principle, emphasising the need for trial judges to make it plain to juries that in normal cases, a confession by one accused is not admissible against any other.

ADMISSIBILITY OF CONFESSIONS

General Rule

14.06 A confession by an accused person carries a great deal of weight. This is so even if the accused subsequently declines to give evidence at his or her own trial. A confession is potentially one of the most powerful items of evidence that can be adduced against an accused for the reason given earlier, *i.e.* it is a statement against interest. It is therefore assumed that a person would only make such a statement if it were true. There could however be alternative explanations, such as fabrication or suggestibility, either of which may be motivated by numerous factors.[27] Because of the highly prejudicial nature of a confession, and the numerous instances of miscarriages of justice based on false confessions, courts are rightly wary of confessions, all the more so now in the context of the European Convention of Human Rights.[28]

Voluntary Statements

14.07 The law is concerned to ensure that confessions are genuinely voluntary, and various tests of admissibility of confessions have been developed over the years by the courts. To a large extent the tests focus on the procedures surrounding the obtaining of a confession and the degree to which these procedures are deemed fair. One of the tests most influential in the modern development of the rules regarding admissibility was laid down by Lord Justice-General Thomson in *Chalmers v. H.M. Advocate*[29]:

---

[25] See, *e.g. Black v. H.M. Advocate*, 1974 J.C. 43 and *Murray v. H.M. Advocate* 1996 S.L.T. 648.

[26] 1981 S.C.C.R. 192.

[27] For discussion see G. Gudjonsson, *The Psychology of Interrogations, Confessions and Testimony*, 1993.

[28] See *Magee v. United Kingdom* (2000) 8 B.H.R.C. 646.

[29] 1954 J.C. 66.

"there comes a point in time in ordinary police investigation when the law intervenes to render inadmissible as evidence even answers to questions which are not tainted by such methods.[30] After that point is reached, further interrogation is incompatible with the answers being regarded as a voluntary statement, and the law intervenes to safeguard the party questioned from possible self-incrimination . . . Once [the] stage of suspicion is reached, the suspect is in the position that thereafter the only evidence admissible against him is his own voluntary statement. A voluntary statement is one which is given freely, not in response to pressure and inducement and not elicited by cross-examination. This does not mean that if a person elects to give a statement it becomes inadmissible because he is asked some questions to clear his account of the matter up, but such questions . . . must not go beyond elucidation."

Lord Thomson's dictum made the status of "suspect" a particularly significant stage in the police investigative process and laid down quite strict rules regarding what kind of questions could be asked of a suspect to elicit admissible answers. The strictness of these rules has been eroded by a series of cases, of which the first important one was *Miln v. Cullen*[31] where following a road traffic accident C was asked whether he was the driver of one of the vehicles involved in the collision. After confirming he was the driver, C was cautioned and charged. This admission was objected to at trial on the ground of unfairness in that C had not been cautioned prior to answering the question, yet he was clearly under suspicion at the time. Rejecting this argument, Lord Wheatley said[32]:

"fairness is not a unilateral consideration. Fairness to the public is also a legitimate consideration . . . it is the function of the court to seek to provide a proper balance to secure that the rights of individuals are properly preserved while not hamstringing the police in the investigation of crime."

Many subsequent cases have considered the appropriate interpretation of "fairness" which remains one of balance in all the circumstances.[33]

---

[30] The reference to "such methods" was to bullying, pressure and third degree methods alluded to in an earlier passage in Lord Thomson's opinion.

[31] 1967 J.C. 21.

[32] at pp. 29–30.

[33] *e.g. Jones v. Milne*, 1975 J.C. 16; *McGlory v. McInnes*, 1992 S.L.T. 501; and *Miller v. H.M. Advocate*, 1997 S.C.C.R. 748.

The Fairness Test

14.08 The modern test of "fairness" in determining admissibility of confessions was expressed by Lord Justice-General Emslie in *Lord Advocate's Reference (No. 1 of 1983)*[34] as follows:

> "A suspect's self-incriminating answers to police questioning will indeed be admissible in evidence unless it can be affirmed that they have been extracted from him by unfair means. The simple and intelligible test which has worked well in practice is whether what has taken place has been fair or not . . . In each case where the admissibility of answers by a suspect to police questioning becomes an issue it will be necessary to consider the whole relevant circumstances in order to discover whether or not there has been unfairness on the part of the police resulting in the extraction from the suspect of the answers in question. Unfairness may take many forms."

The "many forms" of unfairness referred to by Lord Emslie fall broadly into two categories: the procedures surrounding the obtaining of the confession, and the effect of any specific characteristics of an accused that might render him or her especially vulnerable. For a confession to be fairly obtained it must have been given voluntarily, and thus the fairness test incorporates the criterion of volition. There is no finite list of criteria that must be satisfied before a statement can be said to be "voluntary". However, if challenged, the Crown must be able to demonstrate that the police followed the correct procedures, and that the state of mind and physical health of the accused was taken into account. These two aspects are illustrated in the case of *H.M. Advocate v. Gilgannon*,[35] a case of attempted rape.

In *Gilgannon* the court rejected G's confession to the attempted rape as inadmissible, because it was unreliable. G was examined by a police surgeon a few hours prior to the confession. The police surgeon considered G to be mentally subnormal. The police themselves were unaware of this assessment, and they simply noted the contents of a statement which G volunteered to make. Nevertheless, and despite the fact that the police behaviour could not be faulted, the confession was rejected because, "it comes as an at least possibly if not probably incomplete narrative from one who is not only mentally subnormal but unable to give a coherent and complete and therefore accurate account of an incident in which he himself played a principal part".[36]

---

[34] 1984 J.C. 52 at 58. See too, *Brown v. H.M. Advocate*, 1966 S.L.T. 105.
[35] 1983 S.C.C.R. 10.
[36] Lord Cameron at p. 12.

Lord Cameron gave[37] as the underlying reason for rejecting the confession the fact that:

"I am not . . . prepared to accept the rigid proposition that the matter of fairness is confined to the detailed circumstances in which the voluntary statement is obtained; that is the questioning itself or the pressures put on the maker of the statement. The mental or physical state of the maker may well be an important and relevant circumstance in determining the issue of admissibility. Once, as here, a suspect is under arrest even before he has been formally charged he is under and is entitled to the protection of the court and therefore it is proper that the circumstances in which the statement is taken should be regarded as well as the manner itself in which the statement is obtained and elicited. The physical or mental state of an accused at the time of making a statement may be such as to make it unfair on him."[38]

In order for a statement to be voluntary the suspect must under- **14.09** stand the question being asked. Thus, in *H.M. Advocate v. McSwiggan*,[39] a man who was being questioned regarding allegations of incest thought he was being questioned regarding impregnating the woman. His reply to questions was that "he had taken precautions". This response was ruled inadmissible as McS was said to be "intellectually not that bright", and therefore not capable of appreciating the import of the question or the consequences of his reply. Other vulnerable accused persons include those who are very young or of limited intelligence.[40] In *Hartley v. H.M. Advocate*[41] the court warned that the confession of a young person of limited intelligence must always be examined with particular care.

Accused persons who are not considered vulnerable are still entitled to fair treatment. The types of unfair treatment that have rendered a confession inadmissible in the past are "third degree" forms of interrogation[42] and so-called "questions" which were little removed from aggressive assertions of guilt designed to "break" the suspect into a confession.[43] One of the most recent illustrations of this emerged in *Codona v. H.M. Advocate*,[44] a case that attracted

---

[37] Lord Cameron at pp. 11–12.
[38] Lord Cameron quoted *H.M. Advocate v. Aitken*, 1926 J.C. 83 and *H.M. Advocate v. Rigg*, 1946 J.C. 1 as his authorities.
[39] 1937 J.C. 50.
[40] See *B v. H.M. Advocate*, 1995 S.L.T. 961 where the accused was said to be mentally impaired and suggestible.
[41] 1979 S.L.T. 26. Note that the confession in that case was nevertheless admitted.
[42] *H.M. Advocate v. Friel*, 1978 S.L.T. (Notes) 21, and *Boyne v. H.M. Advocate*, 1980 J.C. 47.
[43] *H.M. Advocate v. Mair*, 1982 S.L.T. 471.
[44] 1996 S.L.T. 1100.

the comment that the strict rule set out in *Chalmers* had been revived.[45] C, a 14-year-old girl, was accused of murder while acting with others. She was interviewed, in the presence of her father, by two female police officers. The interview was taped and lasted three and a half hours, of which one hour was a break. The tape revealed however that C was subjected to what was described as police pressure in that the interviewing officers often asked questions simultaneously, and repeatedly told the girl that she was inconsistent and they did not believe her. The appeal court rejected the confession as unfair in not having been given voluntarily. Undoubtedly the factors of C's age and the length of the interview impacted on the issue of fairness.

Threats or inducements will also be classed as unfair, and will deprive any subsequent confession of any utility that it might have had as an item of evidence. In *Black v. Annan*,[46] an admission by B to the police was held to be inadmissible as the Crown had not proven it was fairly obtained in circumstances where B claimed he was threatened with being detained in custody over the weekend unless he "co-operated". Similarly, if a suspect is unwittingly tricked or induced into making an incriminating statement then it is unlikely that the statement will meet the test of being voluntary and fair.[47] Where suspects are "encouraged" to make statements that will be unfair unless they can be shown to be genuinely voluntary.[48]

Confessions may be regarded as unfair, in the absence of overt aggression, threats or incentives, if there is any suggestion of pressure. In *Balloch v. H.M. Advocate*,[49] B made a highly incriminating statement to police officers after several hours of questioning. During the interrogation B had come under strong suspicion of guilt, and, shortly after being shown, for a second time, the clothing and belongings of the deceased, with whom he had lodged, he confessed. The statement was made without caution, and after B was asked if he was sure he was telling the truth. In upholding the trial judge's decision to allow the confession to be put to the jury, Lord Justice-General Wheatley stated that:

> "a Judge who has heard the evidence regarding the manner in which a challenged statement was made will normally be justified in withholding the evidence from the jury only if he is satisfied on the undisputed relevant evidence that no

---

[45] Editor's comment in the report at 1996 S.C.C.R. 300.
[46] 1996 S.L.T. 284.
[47] See, *e.g. H.M. Advocate v. Davidson* n. 12; *Tonge v. H.M. Advocate,* 1982 J.C. 130 and *H.M. Advocate v. Campbell,* 1946 J.C. 80.
[48] *Fraser and Freer v. H.M. Advocate,* 1989 S.C.C.R. 82.
[49] 1977 S.C. 23. See too the importance of "fairness" in the decision in *H.M. Advocate v. B. and M.,* 1991, S.C.C.R. 533.

reasonable jury could hold that the statement had been voluntarily made and had not been extracted by unfair or improper means".[50]

Balloch marked an important procedural departure from the **14.10** hitherto accepted practice by which objections to confessions were considered. *Chalmers v. H.M. Advocate*[51] had laid down a procedure that became known as a "trial within a trial".[52] The procedure was invoked when the defence challenged the admissibility of evidence on the ground of it having been obtained by improper methods. It was the practice for the jury to then be asked to withdraw, and for the trial judge to determine the admissibility of the statement by means of a trial within a trial. Only if the evidence was deemed admissible was the returning jury allowed to consider its value as an item of evidence. The practice was frequently criticised in later years,[53] and increasingly ignored. In *H.M. Advocate v. Whitelaw*[54] Lord Cameron ruled that:

"Now since the case of *Chalmers* there has been a growing feeling that, as it is both the right and the duty of the jury to hear and pass judgment on all the relevant evidence, evidence as to statements of a possibly incriminating character alleged to have been made by an accused person is prima facie of the highest relevance and the jury's function should not be in fact usurped and, unless it is abundantly clear that the rules of fairness and fair dealing have been flagrantly transgressed, it would be better for a jury seised of the whole evidence in the case and of all the circumstances, under such guidance as they should receive from the presiding judge, themselves to take that decision as to the extent to which, if at all, they will take into account evidence of statements given by a suspect after due caution."

The rationale for avoiding the trial within a trial procedure was explained by Lord Emslie in *Lord Advocate's Reference (No. 1 of 1983)*,[55] in which he reminded all trial judges that:

"a judge who has heard all the relevant undisputed evidence bearing upon the admissibility of answers by a suspect, under

---

[50] n. 49 at p. 28.
[51] n. 29 at p. 80.
[52] A similar procedure operating in English law is usually referred to as *voire dire*.
[53] See, *e.g. Thompson v. H.M. Advocate*, 1968 J.C. 61, and *Hartley* n. 41 above.
[54] 1980 S.L.T. (Notes) 25 at 26, approved in *Tonge v. H.M. Advocate*, n. 47 *and Lord Advocate's Reference (No. 1 of 1983)*, n. 34 above.
[55] at pp. 69 and 341.

caution, to police questioning, will normally only be justified in withholding the evidence of the alleged answers from the jury if he is satisfied that no reasonable jury could hold upon that evidence that the answers had not been extracted from the suspect by unfair or improper means".

In other words, judges were to be careful not to usurp the fact-finding function of the jury. Judges remained in charge of determining what evidence was legally admissible, while juries were responsible for deciding how much weight to attach to any individual item of evidence. The difficulty with this approach was identified by Lord Justice-General Roger in *Thompson v. Crowe*[56]:

> "In effect it robs the concept of admissibility of evidence of all real content in those cases where evidence of the statement is actually admitted and the jury are told it is for them to decide whether they can take it into account. But another important consequence of the approach is that the court no longer takes responsibility for decisions on admissibility except in the most extreme cases where the only possible reasonable view is that the evidence is inadmissible."

Balloch was overruled by *Thomson v. Crowe* by a bench of five judges. The opinion recounted the history of the trial within a trial procedure, noting its importance in upholding the principle against self-incrimination, and concluded that some criticisms of the procedure had been "misconceived". According to the Lord Justice-General, the arguments that the procedure could unduly lengthen trials, inconvenience jurors and distort evidence led for a second time before a jury, had to give way to the general duty on a judge to ensure a fair trial.[57] The discharge of that duty might require a trial within a trial to be held to give an accused a proper opportunity to object to the admissibility of certain evidence, and to do so without also being obliged to give evidence in the trial as a whole.

Eavesdropping

14.11   If accused persons fall into a trap of their own making then the resulting confession will be admissible. This situation arises in cases sometimes described as "eavesdropping" cases. When police officers overhear a conversation between an accused and another person, perhaps a co-accused, then that conversation will be

---

[56] 2000 J.C. 173 at 190.
[57] at p. 198B–E. See too, the 10-point summary of "practical conclusions" at p. 202 offering a procedural guide for the future.

admissible provided it has been made voluntarily and not as a result of any entrapment. Where there is a suggestion of entrapment then it is likely the evidence will be inadmissible.

In *H.M. Advocate v. O'Donnell*[58] an accused in a police cell shouted certain incriminating remarks to a co-accused in another cell, which were overheard by police officers. At trial, it was held that the officers could testify as to the contents of the remarks made by the accused. This was considered fair because the remarks had been made voluntarily, no inducement had been offered to the accused to make them, the officers listening in to them had done so spontaneously and had not been deliberately listening in, and indeed did not even have any knowledge of O'Donnell's involvement in the case. In coming to this conclusion, the sheriff felt that he could not rely on the conflicting authority of *H.M. Advocate v. Keen*,[59] where, in similar circumstances, the statement was rejected as evidence. Sheriff Macphail, in *O'Donnell* noted that the decision in *Keen* was unhelpful as the report lacked argument and reasoning.

Keen was not in any event followed in *Welsh and Breen v. H.M. Advocate*.[60] The Thomson Committee[61] preferred the approach taken in *Welsh and Breen* and *O'Donnell*, and recommended that such overheard conversations be put to the accused at judicial examination.[62] The Scottish Law Commission[63] also upheld the view expressed in *O'Donnell*, and it would seem that the courts are no longer prepared to carry fairness to the accused to the length of ignoring safe and highly relevant evidence.[64] The decision in *O'Donnell* was approved in *Jamieson v. Annan*[65] where an incriminating conversation between two accused who shouted to each other whilst held in adjoining police cells was admitted as it was regarded as voluntary and spontaneous and in the absence of inducement, trap or unfairness.

---

[58] 1975 S.L.T. (Sh. Ct) 22 at 28. *O'Donnell* was approved in *Jamieson v. Annan*, 1988 S.L.T. 631.

[59] 1926 J.C. 1.

[60] November 15, 1973, High Court, unreported but referred to in Macphail, *Evidence*, Chap. 20.22 and *O'Donnell*, n. 58 above.

[61] Cmnd. 6218 (1975), para. 7.20.

[62] at para. 8.18b. Note that s.36 of the Criminal Procedure (Scotland) Act 1995 makes provision for this.

[63] Memo No. 46, para. T.45.

[64] By the same token, the courts will also accept as evidence the contents of prisoners' correspondence that has been intercepted: *H.M. Advocate v. Fawcett* (1869) 1 Coup. 183, approved by the Scottish Law Commission, n. 63, para. T.46. See also *Ming v. H.M. Advocate*, 1987 S.C.C.R. 110.

[65] 1988 S.L.T. 631.

Entrapment

14.12 Eavesdropping is to be distinguished from entrapment. Confessions obtained by eavesdropping are generally admissible, while confessions obtained through entrapment are not admissible. Whereas the former arises fortuitously, the latter is deliberate and, especially in circumstances involving organised crime may be carefully designed. Although each case is obviously decided on its merits, there is some basis for the argument that the courts are willing to tolerate a measure of deception in police practices where the context is the investigation of organised crime.[66]

An example of the "fortuitous" confession is *H.M. Advocate v. Campbell.*[67] C offered to give an interview to a journalist in return for money, and when the meeting took place in a public house, the journalist was accompanied by a plain clothes police officer who did not reveal his identity until after C had made certain incriminating statements. It was held that these statements were inadmissible because they had been obtained by a trick.[68] This is not necessarily a view that would be adopted today. Certainly the statements could be argued to have been given voluntarily, and without any inducement.

There are obviously some situations in which for operational success the police have to work undercover, possibly using surveillance techniques to gather intelligence about known criminals or criminal activities. Some of these operations are specifically authorised by legislation, such the Interception of Communications Act 1985 which regulates telephone tapping and other types of bugging devices. To undertake surveillance lawfully the police must obtain appropriate warrants, and, as with standard search warrants, acting beyond the warrant is likely to render any evidence obtained inadmissible. Any action taken by the police must also be compatible with Article 8 ECHR which protects the right to respect for private and family life, home and correspondence. Article 8(2) permits interference with this right provided conducted lawfully and when it is necessary for reasons of national security and public safety including the prevention of crime. The 1985 Act was a response to a finding in *Malone v. United Kingdom*[69] that U.K. legislation in the area of secret surveillance of communications was obscure and insufficiently precise.

---

[66] See A. Ashworth, "Police and Deceptive Practices" (1998) 114 L.Q.R., 108, for a review of the position in England.

[67] 1946 J.C. 80.

[68] And similarly, see *H.M. Advocate v. Graham*, 1991 S.L.T. 416 where evidence obtained through police officers "wiring up" a third party was held inadmissible because had equivalent questions been asked in a police station then a caution would have been required.

[69] (1984) 7 E.H.R.R. 14.

The next section considers in more detail the procedural stages involved in obtaining a confession, the observance of which are often indicative of the admissibility of a confession.

STATEMENTS MADE PRIOR TO CHARGE

There are basically two situations in which an accused makes an **14.13** extra-judicial statement, or confession, prior to actually being charged with an offence. The first is where the police are merely carrying out inquiries into the offence, and the accused has not yet become a suspect. The second is when suspicion has begun to harden against a person, but the point has not yet been reached when the police ought fairly to caution the suspect and formally charge him or her with the offence. At both stages the accused is entitled to remain silent, unless detained under the Criminal Procedure (Scotland) Act when a person is obliged to supply their name and address.[70] However, an accused's failure at this stage to give an innocent explanation of, *e.g.* possession of recently stolen property, may create problems of credibility at any later trial.[71]

The need for a caution

At the earliest stages of a criminal investigation, the police **14.14** should not be hampered in their work by having to take into account the fact a person they are now questioning may subsequently turn out to be an accused. For that reason the mere fact that an accused is charged following questioning does not render his or her answers to those questions inadmissible.[72] In *Costello v. MacPherson*,[73] for example, it was held that police officers were perfectly entitled to stop a person seen carrying goods in suspicious circumstances and question him as to his possession of them. His answers to those questions were admissible.

In *Thompson v. H.M. Advocate*,[74] while T was being kept at the police station and blurted out, without prompting or caution: "It was her or me", his subsequent full confession, after caution, was held admissible. Generally though, when suspicion has begun to harden on the accused, it is expected that the police will administer a caution to their suspect. At common law although there is no prescribed formula of words that must be used, it is important to convey certain information to the suspect. A suspect should be told that they are not obliged to speak, but that if they do, their

---

[70] Criminal Procedure (Scotland) Act 1995, ss. 13(1)(b) and 14(9).
[71] See *Cryans v. Nixon*, 1955 J.C. 1.
[72] *Chalmers v. H.M. Advocate*, n. 29 at p. 81, *per* Lord Thomson.
[73] 1922 J.C. 9.
[74] 1968 J.C. 61.

statement will be recorded and may be used in evidence in any subsequent trial. While there is no defined point at which the caution must be administered, the absence of such a caution in circumstances in which a court later feels that it should have been given, may render any subsequent statement inadmissible.

The dangers of failing to observe the rules scrupulously are well illustrated in *Tonge v. H.M. Advocate*[75] in which T and two others were detained under section 2 of the Criminal Justice (Scotland) Act 1980[76] on a charge of rape. At the start of his detention T was given the statutory caution in terms of section 2(7),[77] but he was not given the common law caution. Later in the course of his detention, and without caution, T was accused of the crime by investigating officers, whereupon he made an incriminating statement. The High Court ruled that T's alleged confession should not have been left to the jury. They found that the allegation made against him amounted to a charge of rape, and that: "To charge an accused person without cautioning him is to put pressure upon him which may induce a response."[78] Best practice suggests that all statutory detainees should ideally receive the full common law caution.

Lord Cameron summarised the requirements of the common law in regard to suspects in a police station[79]:

> "It is of course well established that police officers are entitled to question a suspect as to his possible complicity in a crime which they are investigating, and that his replies will be admissible in evidence if they have not been extracted or compelled by unfair or improper means including threats, intimidations, offers of inducements, or cross-examination designed or intended to extract incriminating replies, but it is equally well recognised that in the case of one on whom suspicion of responsibility or complicity has centred, in order that his replies should be admissible in evidence, it is proper practice that any further questioning should be preceded by a caution in common form."

The Lord Justice-General[80] issued the following warning:

---

[75] n. 47 above. See also *Wilson v. Robertson*, 1986 S.C.C.R. 700.
[76] Now s.14 of the Criminal Procedure (Scotland) Act 1995.
[77] Namely that he was obliged by law to say nothing apart from giving his name and address.
[78] at p. 140.
[79] at p. 147.
[80] at pp. 145–146.

"I would strongly urge police officers throughout Scotland who proceed to accuse a detainee or to question him or to take from him a voluntary statement, to rely not at all upon the efficacy of the warning described in section 2(7), and to appreciate that if any use is to be made in evidence of anything said by a detainee in these circumstances the ordinary rules of fairness and fair dealing which have been developed by the common law should be strictly observed. The wise course will be, inter alia, to administer to the detainee in the events which I have mentioned a full caution in common law terms. The omission to give such a caution will, by itself, at the very least place the admissibility of anything said by the detainee in peril."

When an accused is given a caution in relation to one charge and questioned about other related charges, the answers to the related charges will be admissible provided there is no unfairness to the accused.[81]

So far as concerns the wording of the caution, there are two important constituents, neither of which may be omitted. The accused must be left in no doubt that he or she has the right to remain silent. In *H.M. Advocate v. Von*[82] a confession was rejected after the accused was told merely that any answers he gave to police questions might be used in evidence, and he was not advised that he need not say anything to incriminate himself. At the same time, informing an accused of the right to remain silent is insufficient by itself if the accused is not also warned of the potential evidential significance of anything that is then said.

The need for a charge

Very shortly after the administration of the caution, and prefer- **14.15** ably along with it,[83] the accused should be charged. It will otherwise be regarded as unfair for the police to continue to extract incriminating information from an accused once they have collected sufficient information to make him or her a chargeable suspect.[84] Once a person reaches this stage, then as Lord Cameron pointed out in *H.M. Advocate v. Gilgannon*,[85] the accused acquires new status in which he is "under and . . . entitled to the protection of the court". It was, however, suggested in *Johnston v. H.M.*

---

[81] *Wilson v. Heywood*, 1989 S.L.T. 279, distinguishing, *Tonge*, n. 47, because in that case there had been no caution at all of one of the suspects.

[82] 1979 S.L.T. (Notes) 62. See also *H.M. Advocate v. Docherty*, 1981 J.C. 6.

[83] Certainly not before it: see *Tonge*, n. 47 above.

[84] But see *H.M. Advocate v. Penders*, 1996 SCCR 404, and *Miller v. H.M. Advocate*, 1998 SLT 571 as to status, if any, of being a "chargeable suspect".

[85] n. 35 above.

Advocate[86] that to continue to question a suspect prior to a charge is acceptable, even if the suspect has been arrested, provided there is no unfairness. Johnston was arrested at the scene of a crime where a murder had been committed. His answers to police questioning after his arrest both at the locus and later on tape at the police station were held admissible even though he had not been charged, as the appeal court considered that there was no unfairness in the procedures. It was observed that had the police used their powers of statutory detention instead of arrest then they would have been entitled to question J for up to six hours.

STATEMENTS MADE AFTER CHARGE

14.16 Once a person is formally charged, their immediate reaction to the charge is admissible,[87] but no further statements will be admissible unless they are totally spontaneous. In particular, there may be no more police questions designed to elicit new incriminating material from the accused. Where practicable, even a spontaneous statement should be interrupted by a repeated caution, and taken down by officers unconnected with the case.[88] Particular care must be taken when the accused is mentally subnormal,[89] or in some other way vulnerable, and any suggestion that pressure or inducements have been applied to persuade the accused to make further statements will render any such statement inadmissible.

Once charged an accused should if possible be granted the services of a solicitor, but a failure to do so is not necessarily fatal, being simply one factor to be taken into account when assessing the overall "fairness" of the circumstances in which the confession was made.[90] In *Paton v. P.F.*, [91] P was detained under section 14(1) of the Criminal Procedure (Scotland) Act 1995, interviewed and made a confession. The police had informed P's solicitor of his detention but the solicitor had not attended at the police station.[92] P's complaint was that he had not been told that he was entitled to

---

[86] 1994 S.L.T. 300.
[87] Conveyed to the court by police witnesses who recite to the court what the accused said "when cautioned and charged".
[88] See *Tonge v. H.M. Advocate*, n. 47 at p. 137; but see also *Aiton v. H.M. Advocate*, 1987 J.C. 41, *Custerson v. Westwater*, 1987 S.C.C.R. 389 and *MacDonald v. H.M. Advocate*, 1987 S.C.C.R. 581. No adverse inference may be drawn from the fact that the accused exercises his right of silence: *Robertson v. Maxwell*, 1951 J.C. 11; *Douglas v. Pirie*, 1975 J.C. 61.
[89] *H.M. Advocate v. Gilgannon*, n. 35 above.
[90] *H.M. Advocate v. Cunningham*, 1939 J.C. 61. See too, *H.M. Advocate v. McCrade and Stirton*, 1982 S.L.T. (Sh. Ct) 13.
[91] Reported November 24, 1999 at www.scotscourts.gov.uk.
[92] Notification having been made in terms of s.15(1)(b) of the 1995 Act giving the detainee a right to have "some person" informed of his detention.

have a solicitor present at his interview if he so wished, and that this omission amounted to a breach of Article 6(1) and 6(3) of the European Convention on Human Rights. These provisions afford an accused a "fair and public hearing . . . to defend himself in person or through legal assistance of his own choosing". The issue before the appeal court was whether P could receive a fair trial (the alleged breach of the ECHR having been raised as a preliminary point at the pleading diet of the case). The court rejected P's argument that there had been a breach of Convention rights. It noted that the right conferred by Article 6(3) was one among several comprising the concept of a fair trial,[93] and that it was left to the domestic jurisdiction to decide how best to give effect to the Convention rights.

Although it is preferable for any reply to caution and charge to be noted verbatim in the notebook of the police officers to whom it is made, oral evidence from those officers as to what the accused said is admissible as direct evidence.[94] Tape-recorded confessions have been approved since the decision in the *Lord Advocate's Reference (No. 1 of 1983)*.[95] The court ruled that tape-recorded evidence is subject to the normal admissibility tests applied to all confessions, and that while inadmissible parts of the transcript of such interviews[96] must be deleted in just the same way as they must be erased from the original tape, the remainder of the transcript can be presented to the jury.

CONFESSIONS MADE TO OTHER PERSONS

So far it has been assumed that a confession made by an accused **14.17** person has been made to police officers. In fact many officials have the power to interview persons suspected of contravening various statutory provisions. These officials include H.M. Customs and Excise, H.M. Inspectors of Taxes and DSS officials. Criminal accused who are assisting the police with their inquiries, or who have been detained pending a court appearance, sometimes make statements to persons in authority such as prison officers or police surgeons.

Provided an official is not acting *ultra vires, i.e.* he or she does have a statutory right to ask the questions, then the principle which applies is exactly the same as that applicable to confessions made to police officers. It is admissible provided it was not obtained

---

[93] *Imbrioscia v. Switzerland* (1993) 17 E.H.R.R. 441.
[94] *Hamilton v. H.M. Advocate*, 1980 J.C. 66.
[95] n. 34 above. The admissibility of taped interviews is now embodied in s.277 of the Criminal Procedure (Scotland) Act 1995.
[96] *e.g.* in which the accused refers to previous convictions.

"unfairly". If an official acts outwith their powers then any resulting confession will almost certainly be inadmissible.

In *Morrison v. Burrell*,[97] a sub-postmaster suspected of having abused his position to post off fraudulent bets was interviewed by Post Office officials, and in the course of that interview admitted certain transgressions. In ruling that his confessions were admissible, the High Court was particularly influenced by "the circumstances under which the investigation was conducted and the absence of any hint or trace of impropriety, unfairness or misuse by the investigators of their position—a factor of vital importance in all cases of this kind".[98]

In *H.M. Advocate v. Friel*,[99] the "fairness" test, that subsequently became the main test for all confessions *per Lord Advocate's Reference (No. 1 of 1983)*,[1] was applied to questions and answers during an investigation by customs officers. In such investigations the absence of a caution is one factor to be considered in the wider context of fairness. In *Pennycuick v. Lees*[2] incriminating answers given by a person being interviewed by DSS officers were admissible despite the lack of a caution, as the questions were fair and proper and there was no suggestion of unfairness or deception on the part of the interviewers. In contrast, in *Oghonoghor v. Secretary of State for the Home Department*[3] the statements of a suspected illegal immigrant were held inadmissible when given in the absence of a caution as to the consequences of the answers. This seems largely to have been due to the assumption in *Oghonoghor* on the part of the interviewer, that the accused was an intentional illegal immigrant, although ostensibly the questions were being asked only to establish whether or not she had out-stayed her visa.

Even when a statement is made to a private person such as a friend, the court will wish to ensure that it was "fairly" made and is therefore voluntary. As Lord Cameron observed[4]:

> "confessions to a private party will be admissible unless the circumstances in which [it] has been made or extracted are such as to raise doubt as to whether it has been falsely made in order to escape from further pressures or in response to inducements offered, and ... this is an issue which is essentially for the jury to determine upon the evidence laid before them. A case could also be figured when, by arrangement with police officers, a private person could be used to

---

[97] 1947 J.C. 43.
[98] Lord Justice-General Cooper at p. 49.
[99] 1978 S.L.T. (Notes) 21.
[1] n. 34 above.
[2] 1992 S.L.T. 763.
[3] 1995 S.L.T. (Notes) 733.
[4] "Scottish Practice in relation to Admissions and Confessions by Persons Suspected or Accused of Crime", 1975 S.L.T. (News) 265 at 268.

exercise upon a suspect pressures which would be fatal to the admissibility in evidence of a confession extracted by them by the use of such pressures: in such a case it cannot be doubted that any confession so obtained would be inadmissible."

STATEMENTS BY ACCUSED PERSONS IN RELATION TO OTHER CHARGES

Where an accused faces more than one charge, and the facts that **14.18** give rise to both charges are the same, can an incriminating statement in respect of one charge be used against the accused as a confession regarding a different charge? The cases are reviewed in Renton and Brown,[5] and the conclusion reached is that such a process may be used when the first charge is more serious than the second, but that the position remains uncertain when the reverse is true.

In *Willis v. H.M. Advocate*[6] the court admitted, on a charge of culpable homicide, an incriminating statement made in respect of a murder charge. However, in *James Stewart*[7] the trial court in a murder trial refused to admit evidence of S's declaration given earlier when the charge was assault to the danger of life. But, in the later case of *H.M. Advocate v. Cunningham*[8] the court saw nothing wrong in allowing in such a statement in similar circumstances. It seems that *Cunningham* has now become the leading authority, since in *McAdam v. H.M. Advocate*[9] the court allowed in evidence statements made by M on what was originally a charge of assault to severe injury, even though by the date of the trial the Crown had raised the charge to one of attempted murder. Lord Justice-General Clyde[10] ruled that the important test in such cases was that:

> "each of the charges must substantially cover the same *species facti*. I say 'substantially' because all the articles which have been stolen may not have been ascertained, when the earlier charge is made, or the full extent of the injuries to the victim may not be known. None the less, justice demands that the jury be informed of the reply given, after caution, to the limited charge originally made."

---

[5] *Criminal Procedure*, para. 24–63.
[6] 1941 J.C. 1.
[7] (1866) 5 Irv. 310.
[8] 1939 J.C. 61, in which *Stewart* was not cited.
[9] 1960 J.C. 1, in which both *Stewart* and *Cunningham* were cited.
[10] at p. 4.

McAdam was followed in *H.M. Advocate v. McTavish*[11] in which M, a nursing sister, had made certain incriminating statements concerning her administration of an injection to a patient at a time when she was charged only with assault. The patient died, and the court held that her statement was admissible on a charge of murder because the *species facti* were substantially the same on the assault charge as they were on the murder charge. The principle laid down in *McAdam* was also approved by the Scottish Law Commission,[12] which added only that the two charges must fall into the same general category (dishonesty, personal violence, etc.).

---

[11] 1975 S.L.T. (Notes) 27. Note that M's conviction was quashed on other grounds.
[12] Memo No. 46, para. T.40.

CHAPTER 15

ILLEGALLY OBTAINED EVIDENCE

INTRODUCTION

As we saw in the previous chapter, the principles governing the **15.01** admissibility of evidence that is relevant to a case, but which is obtained without lawful authority, go to the heart of civil libertarian values. Evidence that is unlawfully obtained, such as recovery without a search warrant, or where the terms of a warrant are exceeded, is not automatically inadmissible. It is always a question of balancing two distinct interests: the rights of the accused and the interests of the state. In seeking to achieve this balance, the Scottish courts have developed a number of guiding principles against which to evaluate admissibility.[1] As each case is determined according to its own specific facts and circumstances, judicial discretion plays an extremely important role in this area. This creates some difficulties in defining the boundaries of the circumstances in which evidence is obtained unlawfully but which, nevertheless is deemed admissible. The approach taken in England to the status of unlawfully obtained evidence is expressed by Crompton J in *R. v. Leatham*: "It matters not how you get it; if you steal it even, it would be admissible in evidence."[2] Although a case of some vintage, recent English cases have affirmed that evidence obtained through entrapment, invasion of privacy or unlawful searches may still be admissible.[3] However, in England, in terms of section 78(1) of the Police and Criminal Evidence Act 1984, a judge can exclude evidence recovered by unlawful means if it would be unfair to the defendant to include it.

The position in Scots law is more muted. There is no equivalent statutory provision to section 78(1), and instead, guiding principles

---

[1] For a discussion of comparative approaches to the question of admissibility in this area see S. Kines, "Why Suppress the Truth? U.S., Canadian and English Approaches to the Exclusion of Illegally Obtained Real Evidence in Criminal Cases" (1996) *Res Publica* II (2) 147–162.

[2] (1861) 8 Cox C.C. 498 at 501.

[3] *R. v. Khan (Sultan)* [1997] A.C. 558, H.L.

of admissibility have emerged from a very extensive body of case law. Some of the decisions appear inconsistent and are not always easy to reconcile, but this is predictable when courts are required to interpret a general rule that itself embraces two competing interests.

Issues of admissibility of improperly recovered evidence arise in both civil and in criminal cases, and different criteria apply. The latter is considered first.

CRIMINAL CASES

15.02 One of the earliest influential cases in this area was *H.M. Advocate v. McGuigan*,[4] in which Lord Justice-Clerk Aitchison observed that: "an irregularity in the obtaining of evidence does not necessarily make that evidence inadmissible". This observation was perhaps *obiter*, since the police had acted in accordance with their common law powers when, after arresting McGuigan on charges of murder, rape and theft they searched the tent in which he had been living, for evidence.[5]

However, in the *locus classicus* of the modern rule, *Lawrie v. Muir*,[6] Lord Justice-General Cooper adopted the *McGuigan* approach, and cast it in a broader principle which has been applied ever since. The facts of the case concerned the inspection of dairy premises occupied by Mrs Lawrie in order to locate stolen milk bottles. Two inspectors under contract to the Scottish Milk Marketing Board, searched the premises of the accused with her permission, but outwith the terms of the search warrant, since the accused was not a S.M.M.B. milk distributor. The accused had believed that the warrants covered the search, as did the inspectors, but it was argued that the evidence of the discovery of stolen bottles could not be led because of the false representation of authority.

In holding that the evidence was indeed inadmissible, Lord Cooper highlighted the two conflicting interests which every court must weigh together in every such case, namely:

> "(a) the interests of the citizen to be protected from illegal or irregular invasions of his liberties by the authorities, and (b) the interest of the State to secure that evidence bearing upon the commission of crime and necessary to enable justice to be done shall not be withheld from Courts of law on any mere formal or technical ground."[7]

---

[4] 1936 J.C. 16 at 18
[5] For details of this common law power of search, see Renton and Brown, *Criminal Procedure*, Chap. 7.
[6] 1950 J.C. 19.
[7] at p. 26.

In referring to Lord Justice-Clerk Aitchison's opinion in *McGuigan* that an irregularity in recovery of evidence does not necessarily render that evidence inadmissible, Lord Justice Cooper said:

> "Lord Aitchison seems to me to have indicated that there was in his view, no absolute rule and that the question was one of circumstances. I respectfully agree. It would greatly facilitate the task of Judges were it possible to imprison this principle within the framework of a simple and unqualified maxim, but I do not think that it is feasible to do so."[8]

The principles articulated in *Lawrie v. Muir* have been applied ever since, but have attracted some criticism.[9] In undertaking this role of balancing the competing interests of the citizen and the state, the underlying principle of "fairness", so dominant in determining the admissibility of confession evidence, also plays an important part. As we saw in the previous chapter it is a principle that will remain highly significant given the incorporation into U.K. law of the European Convention on Human Rights, particularly Articles 6 and 8. One of the leading cases in this area is *Teixeira de Castro v. Portugal*[10] where two men who had been arrested for their suspected involvement in drug trafficking, complained of entrapment on the part of undercover police officers resulting in a of Article 6(1).

The European Court recognised that admissibility of evidence was largely a matter for regulation in domestic law, and also acknowledged the need for particular measures to combat the fight against organised crime. Nonetheless, the court stated that the activities of undercover agents must be controlled and the general requirements of fairness demanded by Article 6 must be observed. In this case the court held that the police officers had stepped over the bounds of acceptable conduct and had induced the applicant to commit an offence in circumstances where there was no evidence he would otherwise have done so.

Lawrie v. Muir has often been applied in cases involving irregularities in the granting of the search warrant. In *Bulloch v. H.M. Advocate*,[11] a warrant granted to the Inland Revenue under the Finance Act 1972 was held to have been unlawfully used because it was undated. In *H.M. Advocate v. Bell*[12] items recovered under a

---

[8] at p. 27.
[9] Macphail, *Evidence*, Chap. 21.06 who observed that "it seems inconsistent to exclude a confession obtained by illegal means but to countenance the admission of real evidence obtained by illegal means".
[10] (1999) 28 EHRR 101.
[11] 1980 S.L.T. (Notes) 5.
[12] 1985 S.L.T. 349.

warrant were rejected on the ground of irregularity as it was unsigned. In *H.M. Advocate v. Cumming*[13] the warrant granted under the Misuse of Drugs Act 1971, and the evidence obtained under it, was successfully objected to on the ground that it failed to specify the premises to be searched or the officers authorised to search. In *McAvoy v. Jessop*[14] the search of a bedsit in a multi-occupied building was held unlawful as the warrant specified a different bedsit.

15.03   Separate from the granting of the warrant, issues of admissibility may arise if, in the course of the search, the police exceed their powers. This can arise in a number of situations, and under the test laid down in *Lawrie v. Muir* such evidence may well be ruled inadmissible. However, the courts are also willing to recognise that it is sometimes expedient for the police to seize items of evidence that might otherwise be lost, or items that are stumbled across accidentally.[15] As Lord Justice-General Cooper acknowledged in *Lawrie v. Muir*, there are situations in which the police do not have the luxury of time in which to follow some contorted statutory procedure, but may have to act in an emergency in order to preserve vital evidence. As *McGuigan* shows, such urgent actions may be authorised at common law anyway, but in other similar cases the courts have shown a willingness to exercise leniency in the admission of evidence obtained in an "urgent" situation.[16]

In *McHugh v. H.M. Advocate*,[17] M was charged with robbing a shop. After his arrest the police searched both his person and his house. On his person were found certain numbered banknotes that connected him to the robbery, but the accused maintained that the search had taken place before he was charged and without his consent. Although the appeal court was persuaded on the evidence that the search had been lawful, it went on to find that even if it had not been, the evidence would have been admissible because it had been obtained as a matter of urgency.

It appears that common law powers of the police to act without a search warrant in an emergency are not overridden by statutory powers unless the statute in question expressly provides for this.[18] In *Cairns v. Keane*,[19] C objected to the admission of all evidence relating to the taking of a breath and blood sample from him. His objection was based on the grounds that when the breath sample had been taken, the police had been trespassers in his house,

---

[13] 1983 S.C.C.R. 15.
[14] 1998 S.L.T. 621.
[15] *Tierney v. Allan*, 1990 SLT 178.
[16] See, *e.g. Allan v. Milne*, 1974 S.L.T. (Notes) 76.
[17] 1978 J.C. 12.
[18] *MacNeill v. H.M. Advocate*, 1984 S.L.T. 420.
[19] 1983 S.C.C.R. 277.

having chased him up the drive to his house and in effect made a forced entry to the house behind him. The sheriff, observed that[20]:

> "the 'rule of law in Scotland concerning the right of a constable to enter any premises for any purpose' was that, except when investigating serious crime, police officers are no more entitled than any other member of the public to enter upon private property without a warrant and without the consent of the owner; and that if they do so they must be prepared to justify their conduct by reason of special circumstances before any evidence so obtained can be rendered admissible . . ."

The sheriff went on to find that such special circumstances existed. In reaching his finding, the sheriff refused to accept that the common law power given to police officers to act in an urgent situation was affected by the statutory provisions relating to the taking of breath and blood samples. The High Court rejected C's appeal against conviction without even delivering any opinions.

The presence or absence of urgency can lead to some fine distinctions on the facts, resulting in decisions that are hard to reconcile. Thus, in *H.M. Advocate v. Turnbull*,[21] T's premises were searched under a warrant alleging tax frauds, and a large consignment of papers was removed and passed on to the Inland Revenue without being examined by the police. The Revenue examined them, and found evidence of further offences not covered by the original warrant, and further charges were brought against T as a result. In rejecting the evidence relating to the further offences obtained during the search, the court was primarily influenced by the fact that the search had not been carried out as a matter of urgency, and that this was not a case of evidence accidentally coming to light, but simply a general "fishing expedition".

By contrast, in *H.M. Advocate v. Hepper*,[22] the accused had consented to a search of his house in respect of one charge, and in the course of that search a briefcase was found which was taken away in the belief that it related to that charge. It turned out to contain evidence relating to another offence entirely, but the court held that the evidence was admissible on the new charge because the original search had been lawful, the discovery of the briefcase had been incidental, and the consideration of urgency justified its removal.

15.04 Subsequent cases involving unlawful searches, or lawful searches which exceed their remit, tend to be grouped behind one or other of *Turnbull* and *Hepper*, with the determining criterion being either

---

[20] at p. 281.
[21] 1951 J.C. 96.
[22] 1958 J.C. 39.

whether the evidence was recovered as a matter of urgency or accidentally.

In *Leckie v. Milne*,[23] L was arrested on petition in respect of a charge of theft from a doctor's surgery, and the sheriff granted the usual search warrant *quoad* articles connected with that offence. Armed with that warrant, police persuaded D, who lived with L, to allow them to search the house, and in the course of that search they discovered evidence which led to L's conviction on new charges of theft from a school and an office. In quashing the convictions, the High Court followed *Turnbull* in holding that the search had been unlawful, being authorised by neither the warrant nor any implied consent from D (who was assumed to have consented only to the extent authorised by the warrant). Noting that the officers who conducted the search were not made aware of the contents of the petition, did not have the warrant with them, and appeared simply to have been instructed to search for evidence of theft, the court held that the search was random, and the fruits of it were therefore inadmissible.

In *McNeill v. H.M. Advocate*,[24] on the other hand, the court followed *Hepper* and used the "urgency" principle to justify admitting in evidence the fruits of a search of a house in Liverpool under an Excise warrant to search for drugs obtained following the discovery of drugs on a yacht moored in the Clyde. The court was not convinced that the search and seizure of drugs was unlawful but held that even if it was, it was justified by the urgency of the situation coupled with the very serious charges involved.

Another example of improperly recovered evidence being admitted under the "urgency" principle is the case of *Burke v. Wilson*,[25] where a number of pornographic videos were recovered during a lawful police search of shop premises for "pirate" videos. The court held that the pornographic videos were admissible evidence as if they had not been seized as a matter of urgency they could easily have been disposed of.

Examples of "accidental" recovery of evidence (otherwise improperly obtained) include *Drummond v. H.M. Advocate*[26] and *Baxter v. Scott*.[27] In the latter case, police officers discovered stolen items while checking the boot of a car belonging to a driver they had arrested. The Crown successfully argued that the police had a general duty to check the contents of vehicles in their temporary custody for dangerous or perishable goods, and that stolen goods recovered from such a search were legitimately recovered. In

[23] 1981 S.C.C.R. 261.
[24] 1986 S.C.C.R. 288.
[25] 1988 S.L.T. 749.
[26] 1993 S.L.T. 476.
[27] 1992 S.C.C.R. 342.

contrast, in *Graham v. Orr*,[28] some cannabis that was recovered from the parcel shelf of a car following the arrest of the driver for failing a roadside breath test, was held inadmissible evidence, as the police had no common law powers to conduct such a search. The case law indicates that a fine line divides evidence recovered properly from that recovered improperly. It is very much a matter of the specific circumstances of the case.

If the court is not satisfied that there are urgent or accidental circumstances surrounding the recovery of evidence then the evidence will be inadmissible. In *McGovern v. H.M. Advocate*,[29] the court rejected evidence obtained from fingernail scrapings taken from an accused who was under suspicion of safe-blowing, but had not been charged. The necessary evidence could have been obtained quite lawfully, either by applying for lawful warrant or by charging the suspect, but in the absence or either of those procedures, the evidence was deemed inadmissible.

The impact of the human rights legislation will be to ensure that where there is a suggestion that evidence has been improperly obtained, any assessment of its propriety will have to take into consideration whether there has been a breach of Article 8 of the European Convention on Human Rights. Article 8 provides for a right to respect for private and family life, home and correspondence and declares that:

> "there shall be no interference by a public authority with the exercise of this right except such as is in accordance with the law and is necessary in a democratic society in the interests of national security, public safety or the economic well-being of the country, for the prevention of disorder or crime, for the protection of health or morals, or for the protection of the rights and freedoms of others".

In short the courts will have to perform precisely the same kind of balancing act of competing interests as that which they have been accustomed to doing, albeit now with the benefit of a new body of human rights jurisprudence.

THE FRUITS OF THE POISONED TREE

Where further evidence is discovered as a result of statements **15.05** made by an accused person that are later deemed inadmissible because of the way in which they were obtained, the question arises

---

[28] 1995 S.L.T. 30.
[29] 1950 J.C. 33.

Evidence

as to the status of that further evidence. Even although the statements, or information, which led to that discovery are themselves inadmissible, can the additional facts unearthed be admitted? Or, to adopt the terminology of the American courts,[30] may the court consume the fruits of the poisoned tree?

In Scots law the question has only been partly answered, and that in the context of evidence revealed by inadmissible confessions. The answer in such cases is in the negative. Thus, in *Chalmers v. H.M. Advocate*,[31] C made a full confession to murder which the court later deemed to be inadmissible. During the course of that confession he offered to take the police to the place where he had hidden the victim's purse, and evidence was led to the effect that he had done so. On appeal, it was held that the evidence of the visit to the *locus* (a cornfield) was inadmissible because it was "part and parcel of the same transaction as the interrogation and if the interrogation and the 'statement' which emerged from it are inadmissible as 'unfair', the same criticism must attach to the conducted visit to the cornfield".[32]

The strategic difficulty for the Crown, is that of how to bring to the attention of the court an incriminating fact (*e.g.* that the accused knew where the victim's purse was buried) a fact which only someone involved in the crime might be expected to know, without relating it to the inadmissible statement which led to it. The court in *Chalmers* seemed to be suggesting that the fact that the accused was able to take the police to the *locus* could not be revealed to the jury because he had first offered to do so during an inadmissible confession. As Gordon comments[33]: "The situation may be different where the whereabouts of the property themselves incriminate the accused."

Macphail,[34] the Thomson Committee[35] and the Scottish Law Commission[36] all favour a more flexible test which would allow the court to make use of the fruit of the poisoned tree provided that it was not of itself obtained by unfair means, and the Crown do not disclose the origin of the information.[37] The Scottish Law Commission[38] were of the opinion that this might already be the law.

---

[30] See, *e.g. Olmstead v. U.S.* (1928) 277 U.S. 438.
[31] 1954 J.C. 66.
[32] at p. 76. N.B. that the Thomson Committee (Cmnd. 6218), para. 7.26, agreed with this ruling.
[33] In Renton and Brown, n. 5, para. 24–45. And see *Leckie v. Milne,* n. 23.
[34] n. 9 at Chap. 21.04.
[35] Cmnd. 6218, para. 7.27.
[36] Memo No. 46, para. U.02.
[37] *Quaere* whether the origin of the information could be said to be the accused himself, or the inadmissible statement, or both.
[38] Memo No. 46, para. U.02.

CIVIL ACTIONS

The sole test of the admissibility of illegally obtained evidence in **15.06** civil cases has traditionally been simply that of whether or not it is relevant. The leading case is *Rattray v. Rattray*,[39] in which a letter, sent by the defender to the co-defender in a divorce action based on adultery, was stolen from the Post Office by the pursuer, and used by him in evidence. Theft of a letter from the Post Office was a criminal offence and the pursuer was in fact successfully prosecuted. On appeal in the civil case, although it was held that there was insufficient evidence of adultery, the majority court ruled that the letter had been rightly admitted in evidence. The justification of admissibility despite the fact of the theft was stated by Lord Trayner thus: "the policy of the law in later years (and I think a good policy) has been to admit almost all evidence which will throw light on disputed facts and enable justice to be done".[40]

This observation was essentially *obiter*, and there was dissenting opinion, notably from Lord Young, but the case has set an uncomfortable precedent for later courts to follow.[41] Any application of this principle to criminal cases was eliminated by *Lawrie v. Muir*,[42] and it is only in civil cases that it is still possible to cite *Rattray* as authority for the alarming suggestion that even evidence obtained by criminal means is admissible.

Later courts have, however, felt obliged to follow *Rattray* because it was a ruling by a full court of the Second Division, and no other opportunity to reverse or reconsider the full implications of it has occurred before that court since. In some cases the courts have expressed discomfort but have been unable to extricate themselves from the rules of precedent and *stare decisis*. Thus, in *McColl v. McColl*,[43] Lord Moncrieff was clearly unhappy at having to follow the authority of *Rattray* to admit in evidence a letter from the defender to the paramour which had been intercepted by criminal means. Similarly, in *Duke of Argyll v. Duchess of Argyll*,[44] Lord Wheatley admitted that: "I must confess that I find the reasoning of Lord Trayner [in *Rattray*] . . . difficult to follow . . . but . . . I feel bound by the decision if unconvinced by the reasoning in that case."

Certainly, in so far as evidence has been obtained by underhand means which fall short of being criminal, the courts appear to admit it routinely without objection being taken. In *MacNeill v.*

---

[39] (1897) 25 R. 315.
[40] at pp. 318–319.
[41] The precise grounds for doubting the binding nature of the case as a later authority are well laid out by Macphail, n. 9, Chap. 21.08.
[42] n. 6 above.
[43] 1946 S.L.T. 312.
[44] 1962 S.C. 140, at 141–142.

MacNeill[45] and *Turner v. Turner*,[46] for example, no objection was raised to the use in evidence of letters passing between defenders and paramours which had been intercepted by both pursuers. And in *Watson v. Watson*[47] it was held that the pursuer might found upon a torn-up draft letter by the defender to the paramour which he found.

In the notorious case, *Duke of Argyll v. Duchess of Argyll* certain diaries were admitted in evidence which belonged to the Duchess and which were acquired by the Duke by theft. Because adultery was historically treated as a quasi-criminal offence,[48] Lord Wheatley felt himself entitled to treat *Lawrie v. Muir* as applicable to a modern divorce case, and he added that:

> "There is no absolute rule, it being a question of the particular circumstances of each case determining whether a particular piece of evidence should be admitted or not. Among the circumstances which may have to be taken into account are the nature of the evidence concerned, the purpose for which it is used in evidence, the manner in which it was obtained, whether its introduction is fair to the party from whom it has been illegally obtained and whether its admission will in fairness throw light on disputed facts and enable justice to be done."[49]

The principle of subjecting illegally obtained evidence in civil cases to the same tests as that in criminal cases has found favour with other commentators.[50] It is largely the principle that now governs the position in England, where the court has discretion to exclude evidence that has been obtained improperly, subject to the overriding objective of the interests of justice.

---

[45] 1929 S.L.T. 251.
[46] 1930 S.L.T. 393.
[47] 1934 S.C. 374.
[48] And at the time the standards of proof of crime and adultery were the same, namely beyond reasonable doubt.
[49] 1963 S.L.T. (Notes) 42 at 43.
[50] See, *e.g.* Macphail, n. 9, Chap. 21.14; J. D. Heydon, *Cases and Materials on Evidence*, p. 409; Wilkinson, *Scottish Law of Evidence*, p. 118; Scot. Law Com., Memo No. 46, para. U.06.

CHAPTER 16

OPINION EVIDENCE

INTRODUCTION

As a general rule, when a witness is called to give evidence, the **16.01** court is interested in hearing only of those facts of which he or she has personal knowledge or experience of and which are relevant to the case. The court is not interested in the witness's opinion of what might have happened, or suggestions from the witness as to how the facts being given in testimony should be interpreted. This is because such conclusions as may be drawn from the facts should be drawn by those who have been charged with the duty of adjudicating on the facts—the judge or jury. It is not for the witness to pre-empt that function by, in effect, giving the court an opinion on how it should assess what it has heard:

> "The general rule is that it would be quite wrong, and inadmissible, to put a witness into the witness box to tell the jury what the evidence they have been listening to ought to convey to them".[1]

It is sometimes stated that "opinion evidence" is not admissible in a court of law, and that the only opinion that is relevant at the end of the day is that of the court. However, there are many circumstances in which a court will, consciously and willingly, hear opinion evidence. These circumstances may be classified into two main categories. The first category, increasingly common, involves matters so technical or otherwise beyond everyday human experience that the tribunal of fact requires guidance before it may reach an informed conclusion on the facts as a whole. Obvious examples are the evidence of cause of death in a murder trial, and evidence of the condition of a vehicle's brakes in a reparation action. This guidance normally comes from a person called as an "expert"

---

[1] Lord Sorn in *Hopes and Lavery v. H.M. Advocate*, 1960 J.C. 104 at 113.

witness.[2] An expert witness is entitled to give an opinion based on facts which have either been personally observed (*e.g.* the condition of the deceased at the time of the post mortem, or the condition of the brakes when the vehicle was examined in the workshop) or, more rarely, facts which are put to the expert in the form of an hypothesis, and proved by other witnesses.

In the second category of cases, the person giving an opinion is not an expert at all. Rather it is a witness testifying to the circumstances of something personally experienced and which necessarily includes some element of personal opinion. For example, the witness who identifies the accused as the person who assaulted him is in effect telling the court that in his *opinion* the person who assaulted him and the person now sitting in the dock are one and the same. It is an opinion based on his powers of observation (which may well be challenged by the defence), and since he was uniquely placed to make the comparison between the two, his opinion is acceptable as an item of evidence.

In both categories of case, the court will be prepared to receive the opinion, but only under important safeguards, considered in the remainder of this chapter.

THE ROLE OF THE EXPERT WITNESS

16.02 The precise role of the expert witness in any case, whether civil or criminal, and the limitations placed by law on that role, were summarised by Lord President Cooper in *Davie v. Magistrates of Edinburgh*.[3] He said of expert witnesses:

> "Their duty is to furnish the Judge or jury with the necessary scientific criteria for testing the accuracy of their conclusions, so as to enable the Judge or jury to form their own independent judgment by the application of these criteria to the facts proved in evidence."

The expert witness is only required in order that certain facts may be assessed and understood in their specialist (usually scientific) context. The standard of proof to which an expert gives evidence on an essential fact is on a balance of probability.[4] The facts themselves must still be established by evidence, usually from the expert, may be challenged, and may even be discarded, as indeed may the opinion itself if the court is not satisfied with it for some reason.

---

[2] For a detailed examination of this topic see C. Jones, *Expert Evidence*, 1994 and Kenny, "The Expert in Court", 99 L.Q.R. 197.

[3] 1953 S.C. 34 at 40.

[4] *Hendry v. H.M. Advocate*, 1988 S.L.T. 25.

On occasions a case is overturned on appeal when expert evidence should have been led but was not.[5] Alternatively, a court will refuse to make a finding on a particular point where expert evidence is required but is not made available. In *Columbia Steam Navigation Co. Ltd. v. Burns*,[6] a collision occurred between two vessels during a thick fog on the River Clyde. The trial court refused to draw inferences concerning the speed of one of the vessels at the time of the collision from the nature and extent of the damage to the other, because no expert evidence was led on the point. Although the court was sitting with a nautical assessor, it was held to be incompetent simply to invite his opinion.

With scientific advances, there is increasing emphasis on reducing uncertainty and establishing, by technical processes, the truth or otherwise of certain allegations. This forces the courts to rely on expert testimony especially when the advances made are not yet "generally accepted" in the scientific community or involve complex technological issues. Courts have traditionally been reluctant to give too much prominence to expert witnesses and the role of the expert in Scottish courts is very different from the expert in the American system. There is an anxiety that the traditional judicial process should not simply be replaced by a system of trial by experts. As Lord President Cooper put it, in *Davie*, above: "The parties have invoked the decision of a judicial tribunal, and not an oracular pronouncement by an expert."[7]

Although as medical science and technology develop new complexities there is a commensurate growth of expert opinion, both the Scottish and English courts have kept comparatively strict controls on the use of expert evidence.[8] For example, the use of DNA profiling has required specialist forensic experts to give evidence in this field, as well as experts on statistical probabilities. Similarly, the defence of battered women's syndrome as a basis for a plea of diminished responsibility for battered women who kill their partners, has required expert testimony from psychiatrists and psychologists.

ESTABLISHING THE EXPERTISE OF THE EXPERT WITNESS

The credentials of an expert must be established before any **16.03** opinion is given in evidence. This is to safeguard against a party to a case improperly seeking to influence the tribunal of fact by

---

[5] See, *e.g. U.S. Shipping Board v. The St Albans* [1931] A.C. 632.
[6] (1895) 22 R. 237. See also *Muir v. Stewart*, 1938 S.C. 590, where a reparation action against a pharmacist failed for lack of evidence of the relevant professional standards of care.
[7] See also *Hendry v. H.M. Advocate*, n. 4 above.
[8] Unlike, for example, the United States, where there is a proliferation of expert testimony on every conceivable subject, resulting in what some commentators have described as the introduction of "junk science" into the courtroom.

evidence from a person who claims to be an expert, but is not. In the normal course of things, the expert witness will belong to a profession or a branch of the sciences. In such cases, it is normally only necessary for the party calling the expert to establish the witness's identity and then enumerate the degrees, diplomas and professional membership and reputation held by the witness. On occasions, however, as in *Davie*, above, it is necessary to prove a particular specialist knowledge claimed by an expert.[9]

In *Hewart v. Edinburgh Corporation*,[10] for example, the Court of Session held that it would be competent to ask a police officer and three council employees whether they believed a particular hole in the road to be dangerous because it was their duty to report such dangers. In *Hopes and Lavery v. H.M. Advocate*[11] Lord Sorn held that a typist might have become an expert on the authenticity of a transcript from a tape recording on which she had worked. This was on the basis that there was "no rigid rule that only witnesses possessing some technical qualification can be allowed to expound their understanding of any particular item of evidence".

What matters is not so much the academic qualification or the formal recognition as the expertise. It does not matter where this comes from, provided that the court is satisfied that it exists, and that the person called as an expert witness is fit to guide the court in an area beyond its experience. In an early English case,[12] for example, a solicitor was allowed to give expert evidence on handwriting, a matter in which he had acquired expertise as a skilled amateur.

It also follows from this general principle that although a person may be an expert for one purpose, opinions must not be offered on matters outwith that person's expertise, even if those matters are closely related to the matter on which the expert is testifying.[13] However it may be permissible for an expert to refer to literature in a related field provided the literature has a bearing upon the subject in which the witness has expertise.[14] An expert witness may also seek to support the evidence being given by referring to documents such as books and learned treatises. In doing so the passages which are thus "adopted" become part of the expert's evidence, and part of the general body of evidence available to the tribunal of fact. But the remainder of such a book or treatise is not evidence, and may not be relied upon, even to challenge that

---

[9] 1953 S.C. 34.
[10] 1944 S.C. 30.
[11] 1960 J .C. 104 at 114. See also *Haq v. H.M. Advocate*, 1987 S.C.C.R. 433.
[12] *R. v. Silverlock* [1894] 2 Q.B. 766.
[13] As for example in *U.S. Shipping Board v. The St Albans* [1931] A.C. 632. in which it was held that land surveyors could not testify to a diagram constructed from a photograph.
[14] *Main v. McAndrew Wormald Ltd.*, 1988 S.L.T. 141.

expert witness's opinion.[15] Published academic literature may be put to an expert in chief or cross-examination without such literature being previously lodged as a production.[16]

A witness may not testify as to matters that are well within the knowledge and experience of the court. This was rule laid down in *R. v. Turner*,[17] where T was charged with the murder of his girlfriend apparently carried out while he was in a blind rage induced by her sexual taunts and admissions of infidelity. His defence was that of provocation,[18] and psychiatric evidence was led to the effect that while the accused was perfectly normal mentally, the sort of experience to which he had been subjected might provide intense provocation even to a normal person. The appeal court firmly rejected the notion that an expert's opinion was any substitute for that of the jury:

> "The fact that an expert witness has impressive scientific qualifications does not by that fact alone make his opinion on matters of human nature and behaviour within the limits of normality any more helpful than that of the jurors themselves; but there is a danger that they may think it does."[19]

The appeal court stated that once the psychiatrist had advised the jury that the accused was mentally normal, there was no further role for expert evidence, because:

> "Jurors do not need psychiatrists to tell them how ordinary folk who are not suffering from any mental illness are likely to react to the stresses and strains of life."[20]

This view of the role of some forms of expertise in the courtroom has been criticised for revealing a rather narrow and uninformed view of the behavioural sciences and for creating a hierarchy of science.[21]

---

[15] *Davie v. Magistrates of Edinburgh*, n. 3 above.

[16] *Roberts v. British Railways Board*, 1998 S.L.C.R. 577.

[17] [1975] Q.B. 834.

[18] Which has the same function under English law as under Scots, in that it reduces a murder charge to the lesser charge of "manslaughter", the equivalent of culpable homicide.

[19] *R. v. Turner* [1975] Q.B. 834 at 841.

[20] *loc cit.*

[21] See, for example, R. D. Mackay and A. M. Colman, "Excluding Expert Evidence: a tale of ordinary folk and common experience" (1991) Crim. L.R. 800; and P. Alldridge, "Forensic Evidence and Expert Evidence" (1994) 21(1) Brit. J.L.S. 136.

PRESERVING THE MAIN ISSUE FOR THE COURT

16.04 The function of the expert witness is to assist the tribunal of fact to come to a decision on the main issue presented to it, and not to make that decision him or herself. However closely associated the evidence of the expert may be with the ultimate outcome of the case, a clear distinction must be maintained between the expert's role as a guide through a specialist area, and the role of the tribunal as the ultimate arbiter of fact. This latter function is jealously preserved by the courts, even at the expense of discounting the expert evidence altogether.

In *Gellatly v. Laird*[22] a magistrate was held to have correctly refused to hear expert evidence on whether or not books were indecent or obscene, since that was "the very matter remitted to the opinion of the magistrate".[23] Similarly, in *Meehan v. H.M. Advocate*[24] the High Court refused to arrange for an accused to be examined under a "truth drug", because in respect of any resulting statement, "the medical man would take the place of the jury as a judge of credibility".

There appears to be no clear statement under modern civil law to the effect that an expert witness may not give an opinion on the main issue, or ultimate issue, before the court. The nearest to it is a statement by Lord Justice-Clerk Inglis in *Morrison v. Maclean's Trs*,[25] a case in which it was alleged that a testator had been in a state of "facility" at the time when he signed his will. The medical witnesses in the case had been asked to comment on his mental state, and no objection had been taken to this line of questioning by counsel for the executors. Nevertheless, the jury were carefully directed by the trial judge that the issue of capacity to sign was a matter for them, and not the medical witnesses.

A similar consideration lies behind the rule of interpretation found in the law of contract that the terms of that contract are to be interpreted by the court, using the normal everyday meaning given to each word used by the parties, and without the aid of experts.[26] Only if a contract uses technical words which create a need for specialist interpretation is it competent to refer to such experts.

---

[22] 1953 J.C. 16. This case was followed in *Ingram v. Macari*, 1983 S.L.T. 61, but see *H.M. Advocate v. McGinlay*, 1983 S.L.T. 562. In *Hendry v. H.M. Advocate*, n. 4, it was held that the jury in a murder trial must decide for itself whether or not the causal link between assault and death is proved beyond reasonable doubt, and that it is improper to invite an expert witness to usurp the function of the jury by expressing his opinion on this question.

[23] at p. 27.

[24] 1970 J.C. 11 at 14.

[25] (1862) 24 D. 625 at 631.

[26] See *Tancred, Arrol & Co. v. Steel Co. of Scotland* (1887) 15 R. 215; affd. (1890) 17 R. (H.L.) 31.

CHALLENGING THE EXPERT WITNESS

An expert witness, although giving a professional opinion that **16.05** might be expected to command attention and respect, is at the end of the day only one witness in a court action. Like all witnesses the expert is open to challenge, both as to the validity of his or her opinion and the accuracy of the facts or assumptions on which it is based. It is not unusual for experts to be ranged on both sides, and to be called for both parties in such a way that their expert opinions conflict with each other. This is particularly true when the specialism which they represent is one which admits of diversity of assessment. Nor is it by any means unheard of for expert witnesses called by the same party to contradict each other.[27] The function of the expert witness is to assist the court in coming to a conclusion, and not to proclaim some set of universal truths.[28] There is often a fine line between drawing appropriate inferences and speculation based on assumed facts.[29] Even if the expert gives evidence that is not contradicted and appears credible and reliable, the court is not bound to accept it.[30]

The most significant grounds upon which expert opinion may be challenged by non-experts are twofold. First, a failure to lay a suitable basis of fact for the opinion and second, the reliability of the scientific technique or conclusions being put forward. These are dealt with in turn.

Laying a basis of fact

The opinion of an expert must be based upon facts proved to the **16.06** satisfaction of the tribunal of fact, and to the appropriate standard of proof. In the great majority of modern cases, expert testimony is a mixture of fact and professional opinion. The expert is called in to make an examination, or conduct a series of tests, and the court is receiving the expert evidence not just as a pure opinion, but also as evidence of the physical condition of something or someone. Obvious examples are the evidence of pathologists describing post-mortem examinations on the deceased, police surgeons describing the results of examinations of rape victims and psychiatrists giving evidence of the mental state of patients in their care.

In civil cases, experts are frequently called in to describe the state of some object or other, and regularly appear in court in reparation actions arising from road accidents, describing the scene of the accident and/or the state of the vehicle.

---

[27] See, *e.g. Davie v. Magistrates of Edinburgh*, n. 3 above.
[28] *Dempster v. Motherwell Bridge and Engineering Co.*, 1964 S.L.T. 353.
[29] For two examples of the rejection of evidence on this latter ground, see *S.S. Rowan v. S.S. Malcolm*, 1923 S.C. 316 and *Gardiner v. Motherwell Machinery and Scrap Co.*, 1961 S.C. (H.L.) 1.
[30] *Beaton v. H.M. Advocate*, 1994 S.L.T. 309.

It is for the party leading an expert witness to ensure that a relevant basis of fact has been laid for the opinion evidence of the expert. The expert evidence may otherwise be excluded. In *Blagojevic v. H.M. Advocate*[31] an accused on trial for murder did not give evidence but, unsuccessfully, tried to lead evidence from a clinical psychologist that he would have been suggestible under pressure at the police interview. The court ruled the expert's testimony inadmissible as no foundation in fact had first been laid for it.

In *Stewart v. Glasgow Corporation*,[32] the tenant of a council house sought compensation from the local authority for the death of her child as the result of an accident allegedly caused by the corroded state of a clothes pole in the back green of the tenement in which she lived. The accident had occurred in October 1953, and the pole was examined by an expert witness for the pursuer in January 1954. The expert stated in evidence that in his opinion, based upon his examination of the pole, it must have been in a manifestly dangerous state for at least the previous six months, and was not cross-examined on this point. The pursuer had sought to have the pole examined by a second expert witness, but the defenders had failed to produce it for this purpose. The second expert therefore simply gave his opinion, which agreed with that of the first expert, on the assumption that the pole was in the state described by the first expert at the date of his examination of it. It was held that there was insufficient evidence in law upon this factual point to form a basis for any expert opinion. There was no corroboration of the evidence of the first expert, either from the second expert or from the lack of cross-examination of the first expert. The corroboration required was the actual state of the pole in January 1954.

Similarly, in *Forrester v. H.M. Advocate*,[33] the accused was acquitted on appeal of charges of safe-blowing because the Crown had not satisfactorily established that material found in the accused's pocket corresponded with material from a bedspread used in the crime. Although microscopic fibres had produced potentially incriminating results, no evidence had been led of the source of these fibres and thus there was no connection proven between the bedspread and the material in F's pocket.

This important rule—that the opinion of expert witnesses must be grounded in proven fact—was applied in the case of *McGowan v. Belling & Co.*,[34] which involved the best evidence rule.

---

[31] 1995 S.L.T. 1189.
[32] 1958 S.C. 28.
[33] 1952 J.C. 28. See also *Ritchie v. Pirie*, 1972 J.C. 7 and *Russell v. H.M. Advocate*, 1946 J.C. 37.
[34] 1983 S.L.T. 77.

Various people who had been injured in a house fire sued *inter alia* the manufacturers of an electric fire which, it was alleged, suffered from certain defects in design and manufacture which had caused it to catch fire. The heater in question was not available either at the proof or at any time after the fire. Expert evidence was, however, given by two witnesses who had examined another fire of this type on earlier occasions (three years and one year previously) and who testified that the design of this type of heater made it susceptible to cable overheating. The heater which the two experts had examined was not proved to be identical to the heater in question, although it was still available at the university where they had both examined it, and could have been lodged in production. It was held that since it was vital to know if the heater that had been examined was identical to the one in issue in the action (particularly in the matter of the cable connectors), the "best evidence rule" required its production, and without it the expert evidence was useless. As Lord Cowie put it: "An oral description of its condition in its absence was inadmissible, and any expert evidence based on its alleged condition was also inadmissible."[35]

In seeking to lay a factual basis for their opinions, experts occasionally find themselves caught up in "collateral" issues, and with the principle that a court should not pursue every remote issue that might conceivably have a bearing on the case in hand. However, the courts seem to allow considerable latitude where it can be shown that the apparent departure from the main issue will allow a more accurate, or more informed, expert assessment to be made. Thus, in *Swan v. Bowie*,[36] in an action of damages for slander the defender was alleged to have written around nine anonymous letters of a "scurrilous and abusive nature", only two of which were sent to the pursuer and his wife. The pursuer wanted to have the remaining seven letters produced as evidence. The court acknowledged that ordinarily these seven letters might be regarded as collateral to the main issue but was not willing to exclude them from proof on the ground that they could provide a valuable comparison for handwriting experts.

The reliability of the scientific technique or conclusions

In criminal cases the evidence is seldom clear-cut, principally **16.07** because the main item of evidence against an accused is frequently scientific. The witnesses who give evidence as experts are at the same time providing the crucial facts leading to conviction and

---

[35] at p. 78.
[36] 1948 S.C. 46. See too *Houston v. Aitken*, 1912 S.C. 1037.

although the opinion of the expert does not require corroboration,[37] the facts upon which that opinion is based may well do.[38] Additionally, while expert testimony does not necessarily require to be corroborated, if it is not, there is more scope to query its reliability.

For this reason, it is a rule of practice that in any criminal case where expert evidence is to be led, there will be two experts available, the second normally corroborating the first on a joint report that bears their signatures.[39] The statutory provisions contained in sections 280—284 of the Criminal Procedure (Scotland) Act 1995 relating to the use made of expert evidence of this nature, have already been mentioned in Chapter 7. The effect of these sections (gathered together under the heading "Routine Evidence") is that reports become documents spoken to by only one witness unless the defence give prior intimation that they require both witnesses to be called. These provisions reflect the fact that in reality, formal forensic reports are not often challenged as to their accuracy, and that if the defence can disprove or cast doubt upon a conclusion contained within such a report by cross-examining the main witness, this will suffice for them. The heading employed in the statute of "Routine Evidence" clearly implies that the process prescribed by those sections will only apply where the evidence in question is non-contentious.

Section 280(4) states that *any* report "purporting to be signed by two authorised forensic scientists shall . . . be sufficient evidence of any fact (or conclusion as to fact) contained in the report and of the authority of the signatories". In such a case, it will not be necessary to call witnesses to speak to the report, but the prosecution have the same duty to notify the defence of their intentions, and the defence have a right to object within a specified time limit. The emphasis is once again on the efficient disposal of items of expert evidence which are non-contentious, while at the same time preserving the defence right of challenge when there is something concerning the report with which they disagree.

16.08   Apart from the 1995 Act, there are other statutes that allow expert evidence to be taken in certificate form, the certificate being probative in effect if it is unchallenged. One of the most commonly used is now found in section 16 of the Road Traffic Offenders Act 1988. This provision allows the court to regard as probative the certificate issued following an analysis of the blood or urine of a

---

[37] See, for example *M v. Kennedy*, 1992 S.C.C.R. 69.

[38] As in, *e.g. Stewart v. Glasgow Corpn*, n. 32, and *Forrester v. H.M. Advocate*, n. 33 above.

[39] Following the general requirement for corroboration in criminal cases explained in *Morton v. H.M. Advocate*, 1938 J.C. 50 at 55, and dealt with more fully in Chap. 7.

person accused of a drink/driving offence, showing the level of alcohol or drug found in that person's blood or urine, and the certificate of the police doctor that he took a blood sample from that person with his consent. In both cases, the qualifications of the expert signing the certificate will also be taken as established by the very certificate itself. In all cases the prosecution is required to serve a copy of the certificate on the accused. The accused may challenge it and require the attendance as witnesses of the forensic scientist or police doctor, and the defence must, at the time of the taking of the sample, be provided with one-half of it for their own analysis.[40]

Separate from any procedural irregularity that might be challenged in expert evidence, it is apparent there is an increasing willingness to challenge even established science. As we have seen in Chapter 7, it is now well established that an accused may be convicted solely on evidence relating to fingerprints,[41] palm prints,[42] handwriting[43] and DNA profiling.[44]

Since *Hamilton v. H.M. Advocate*[45] it has been accepted in Scots law that an accused may be identified by fingerprint evidence, and that there need be no other evidence in order to secure a conviction. In that case, there were two police officers giving evidence as to the identity of the accused via his fingerprints, and they corroborated each other. In *H.M. Advocate v. Rolley*,[46] four police forensic officers gave evidence that no two palm prints were ever the same. The only evidence against R was a palm print lifted from the *locus* of a housebreaking which matched his, and the defence conceded that this would be sufficient evidence in law if the jury accepted it, which they did. The correct procedure in all cases involving finger or palm print evidence is to produce two witnesses to testify to where the print was found, two witnesses to testify to the taking of comparison prints from the accused, and two expert witnesses to testify to the fact that the two sets of prints are the same. If necessary or more convenient, these may be the same two witnesses in each case.

The apparent conclusiveness of fingerprint evidence has, **16.09** however, been severely shaken by the case of Shirley McKie, a former detective police constable with Strathclyde police. McKie was involved in the murder investigation of Marion Ross in Kilmarnock in January 1997. Fingerprint officers, backed up by expert witnesses from the Scottish Criminal Records Office Fingerprint Bureau, alleged that McKie's fingerprints were on a door

---

[40] Road Traffic Offenders Act 1988, s.10(3) and (5).

[41] *Hamilton v. H.M. Advocate*, 1934 J.C. 1.

[42] *H.M. Advocate v. Rolley*, 1945 J.C. 155.

[43] *Richardson v. Clarke*, 1957 J.C. 7; *Campbell v. Mackenzie*, 1974 S.L.T. (Notes) 46.

[44] *Welsh v. H.M. Advocate*, 1992 S.L.T. 193.

[45] 1934 J.C. 1.

[46] 1945 J.C. 155. See also *H.M. Advocate v. Dennison*, 1978 S.L.T. (Notes) 79.

frame in the murder victim's house, and in a sealed off area. McKie denied she had ever been to that area of the house. She gave evidence to that effect at the trial of David Asbury who was accused of the murder of Marion Ross. Asbury was convicted and sentenced to life imprisonment. Part of the evidence against him was the victim's fingerprint supposedly found on a biscuit tin in his house. McKie was subsequently prosecuted for perjury. At her trial in May 1999 two expert fingerprint witnesses from the United States were called on her behalf and successfully discredited the evidence from the SCRO Fingerprint Bureau. She was acquitted. It was apparently the first time in the history of the SCRO that there had ever been a challenge to the expertise of its staff and McKie's acquittal has had far-reaching ramifications.

The first consequence of her acquittal was an announcement by the Lord Advocate, Colin Boyd, that a system of independent checks would be instituted in all present and future cases involving fingerprint evidence. The Lord Advocate's statement was in response to the interim findings of a report by the Chief Inspector of Constabulary, Sir William Taylor. The report exonerated Shirley McKie and concluded that the SCRO Fingerprint Bureau was "not fully effective and efficient". A further consequence has been Asbury's successful application for release on bail pending an appeal against his conviction for murder.

A review is underway into the processes of fingerprint identification. One recommendation of the Taylor report was that the current reliance on a 16-point match in similarity between sets of fingerprints was an inadequate form of identification. Although some reassurance can be drawn from the fact that there are few cases where fingerprint evidence alone results in a conviction, the McKie case is an important reminder of the dangers in over-dependence on scientific testimony. Even where the scientific method is dependable, it is always subject to interpretation by individuals and that invariably carries risks of human error.[47]

16.10　Other scientific processes have been employed and accepted in the provision of evidence of identification. In *Hay v. H.M. Advocate*[48] the accused in a murder trial was convicted partly on the evidence of a dental impression left on the body of the victim which matched his own. While the bulk of the appeal case rested on the legality of the taking of the dental impression from him (on which point the appeal was refused), there was no suggestion that the evidence thus obtained could not otherwise be used to identify him. Handwriting has also for many years been an acceptable means of identifying an accused, without the need for further

---

[47] See reports of the McKie case in *The Herald*, June 23, 2000, August 23, 2000 and September 15, 2000; and *The Scotsman*, May 15, 1999.
[48] 1968 J.C. 40.

corroborating evidence of identification.[49] In *Campbell v. Mackenzie*,[50] C was charged with having written letters under a false signature in which unfounded allegations were made to the police about another person. The only real evidence against Campbell was that of two handwriting experts who testified that the letters were written by him. It was held that it was for the court to assess the evidential value of such testimony, and to convict on the strength of it if they wished, and since there had been no contrary evidence the conviction was allowed to stand.

Identification of an accused by means of a video film is competent following *Bowie v. Tudhope*.[51] In that case, B was charged with assault and robbery in a shop. The incident was recorded on a video camera, and at the trial it was not suggested that the film was anything other than a genuine record of the incident. The shop staff were unable to identify B, either on the video or in court, but at a date prior to the trial two police officers viewed the video separately, and were both able to identify him from it. At the trial the film was shown again, and again the two police officers identified B as the person in it. In rejecting B's appeal, the High Court ruled[52] that:

> "we are of opinion that there is no reason in a situation such as arose in the present case why two police officers, who were familiar with the accused, should not have been able to view the video recording and then to give evidence to the effect that one of the individuals appearing in the recording was the appellant".

Accepting video evidence as competent is distinct from any endorsement of the merits of such a form of evidence in providing reliable identification. Advances in technology and the growth of CCTV to monitor crime in public places have given rise to concerns that the increase in the use of such technology will compound the "inherently unreliable" nature of eyewitness testimony. Professor Vicki Bruce,[53] one of the leading researchers in this field has noted that:

> "CCTV images are very variable in quality, and camera and lighting angles may conspire to produce no more than a

---

[49] Since at least *Richardson v. Clark*, 1957 J.C. 7.
[50] 1974 S.L.T. (Notes) 46.
[51] 1986 S.C.C.R. 205.
[52] *ibid.*, p. 209. Presumably there is no reason why the court itself may not view such a video and form its own opinion of the identity of an accused from it.
[53] "Fleeting images of shade: Identifying people caught on video", The Psychologist, 1998 11(7) 331 at 332. See too, Bruce and Hall, *In the Eye of the Beholder: The Science of Face Perception*, 1998, Oxford University Press, Oxford.

poorly lit messy image of the top or back of a person's head. Recent research findings suggest, however, that the process of matching identities across different images may be remarkably error-prone even when image quality is reasonably high."

The unreliability of eyewitness identification is well settled within the research literature. In 1976 the Devlin Commission[54] reported, in regard to English law, numerous weaknesses with this type of evidence, encouraging extensive applied research in the area.[55] While it is probably a more significant issue in jurisdictions like England that do not have a requirement for corroboration, Scots law also regards it as a matter that must be given primacy.

16.11 In the last decade DNA profiling or genetic fingerprinting has featured regularly in criminal cases, though few are reported.[56] The technique seems attractive for the degree of certainty that it appears to produce. Much debate has been generated about the reliability of DNA profiling. Undoubtedly it has huge potential to provide incriminating—and exonerating—evidence of an accused to a high level, but some critics have questioned the methodology of the testing procedures.[57] In broad terms DNA evidence is presented to court as a "match probability", *i.e.* statistical scientific evidence of the probability of finding the DNA profile of an accused (or party in a civil case) in a person randomly selected from the population. However, the presentation of this evidence can easily mislead, resulting in a situation that has become known as "the prosecutor's fallacy". This was explained in the English case of *R v. Deen*[58]:

"The prosecution case had confused the DNA match probability with the likelihood ratio. It was necessary to ask what the probability was that a defendant's sample could match the crime sample given that he was innocent (match probability), and what the probability was of a defendant being innocent although his sample matched the crime sample (likelihood ratio). Giving the answer to the first question as the answer to

---

[54] *Report to the Secretary of State for the Home Department of the Departmental Committee on Evidence of identification in criminal cases*, London, HMSO.

[55] For details see P. Ainsworth, *Psychology, law and eyewitness testimony*, 1998.

[56] But see *Welsh v. H.M. Advocate*, 1992 S.L.T. 193.

[57] Reference is made only to a selection of the extensive literature: P. Alldridge, "Recognising Novel Scientific Techniques: DNA as a test case", 1992 Crim. L.R. 687; M. Redmayne, "Doubts and Burdens: DNA Evidence, Probability and the Courts," 1995 Crim. L.R. 464; M. Redmayne, Presenting Probabilities in Court: The DNA Experience", 1997 1 E & P 187; I. Evett, A. Foreman, G. Jackson and J. Lambert, "DNA Profiling: A discussion of issues relating to the reporting of very small match probabilities", 2000, Crim. L.R. 341.

[58] *The Times*, January, 10, 1994.

the second is "the prosecutor's fallacy". In the instant case, the fallacy in the expert evidence led the judge to sum up on the basis that probability was near to certainty, when on a proper assessment of the evidence the unexplained discrepancy was fatal to the prosecution's case."

In *Welsh v. H.M. Advocate*,[59] it was suggested by experts in relation to the match probability of blood samples, that the DNA profile of a sample of fresh blood found on the deceased's clothing was identical to that of W. Moreover, the experts contended that W's profile was common to only one person in every 88–99 million. The appeal court refused to lay down any particular standard of statistical probability that had to be reached before a jury would be entitled to rely on DNA profiling. The court preferred instead to rest on the usual principle that if there was sufficient evidence a jury could convict.

Another controversial aspect of the debate on DNA profiling is the admissibility of expert evidence based on Bayes theorem, a statistical method of analysis. Although dependence on Bayes theorem has been decisively rejected in England on the ground that it is apt to confuse and mislead a jury,[60] expert evidence based on statistical analysis has been admitted in Scotland in *Welsh*, above.

Perhaps the most fundamental challenge that may be made against opinion evidence is to question the expert's competence or integrity. This may be done diplomatically, for example by suggesting that the expert does not have sufficient experience to form an opinion in the particular case. This type of challenge arose in a series of appeals in the 1970s and 1980s involving the evidence given by a leading Home Office forensic scientist. It was suggested that his evidence was tainted by bias, and did not display the level of objectivity required of a person in his position. The process began with a Scottish appeal, *Preece v. H.M. Advocate*,[61] in which a man who had already served seven years of a life sentence for murder had his conviction quashed on the ground that the Crown forensic evidence had been deeply flawed. It was acknowledged that evidence of blood samples and seminal stains had played a significant part in his conviction, but it was claimed that the tests had been conducted and the results had been interpreted in such a way that the Crown's chief forensic expert had presented unwarrantable conclusions. Significant information had been omitted from the written expert report and unsustainable claims had been made. These flaws in the expert evidence were fatal to the

---

[59] n. 56 above.

[60] *R. v. Adams* (Denis Johns) (No. 2) [1997] 1 Cr.App.R. 369.

[61] [1981] Crim.L.R. 783.

conviction since the testimony fell short of the standards of accuracy and objectivity required of an expert witness.

THE OPINION EVIDENCE OF NON-EXPERTS

16.12 At the start of this chapter, the point was made that sometimes the court is hearing opinion evidence from a witness who is not an expert. This is because:

> "Unless opinions, estimates and inferences which men in their daily lives reach ... as a result of what they have perceived with their physical senses were treated in the law of evidence as if they were mere statements of fact, witnesses would find themselves unable to communicate to the judge an accurate impression of the events they were seeking to describe."[62]

The most obvious example of this process arises in the context of identification. Every witness who is asked to identify a person or an object is in fact being required to assert his or her opinion that the person or object which is now being identified is the same as the person or object seen before. Even if there exists a special means by which a witness is able to identify an object (*e.g.* because of a signature on a document or label, or because of initials scratched on the back of an object), what is actually being offered is an opinion that the signature, etc., is that of the witness, by means of observation and familiarity.

Similarly, the best evidence of handwriting comes from the person who actually wrote it, confirming that it is their handwriting. The second best is the evidence of someone well acquainted with the writing of the alleged author, or someone who actually saw the author perform the writing in question. In the latter case, the court is receiving what in effect is the opinion of the witness.

Apart from questions of identification, there are occasions upon which the opinion of a non-expert constitutes an important item of evidence. For example, police officers in a drink/driving case are asked as a matter of routine whether or not they formed the impression that the accused had been drinking in order to show the "reasonable cause" necessary before they may ask a suspect to take a breath test. Similarly, witnesses to a road accident are regularly asked questions such as: "Would you say that the car was travelling fast?" Only rarely will exception be taken to that sort of question, whereas the question, "Do you think that X was exceeding the speed limit?" should lead to an objection from the other party.

---

[62] 17th Report of the Law Reform Committee, Cmnd. 4489 (1970), para. 3.

In *Wilson v. Wilson*,[63] a divorce action for adultery, evidence was given by a lamplighter that he passed the defender lying on a common stair with a lady, in circumstances which he took to indicate immorality, although he did not actually see anything immoral taking place. His evidence was accepted as leading to the conclusion that they were there for an immoral purpose, although as it transpired there was insufficient corroboration for a finding of adultery.

The relevance and admissibility of non-expert opinion is almost entirely a question of circumstance and degree, and there are situations when it is accepted, largely for practical reasons that outweigh any strict rule of law.

---

[63] (1898) 25 R. 788.

BIBLIOGRAPHY

Ainsworth, *Psychology, Law and Eyewitness Testimony* (1998) (Chichester: Wiley)

Alison, *Principles of the Criminal Law of Scotland* (1989) (Edinburgh: Law Society of Scotland, Butterworths)

Anton with Beaumont, *Private International Law* (2nd ed., 1990) (Edinburgh: W. Green)

Brown, *see* Renton and Brown

Brown, Burman and Jamieson, *Sex Crimes on Trial* (1992) (Edinburgh: Edinburgh University Press)

Bruce and Hall, *In the Eye of the Beholder: The Science of Face Perception* (1998) (Oxford: Oxford University Press)

Clive, *The Law of Husband and Wife* (4th ed., 1997) (Edinburgh: W. Green)

Cross and Tapper, *Evidence* (9th ed., 1999) (London: Butterworths)

Cusine, *see* Rennie and Cusine

Dent and Flin (eds.) *Children as Witnesses* (1992) (Chichester: John Wiley & Sons)

Dickson, *Evidence* (3rd ed., 1887) (Edinburgh: T. & T. Clark)

Dobie, *Sheriff Court Practice* (1986) (Collieston: Caledonian Books — reprint of 1948 edition, Glasgow: Hodge)

Field, *Annotation to the Civil Evidence (Scotland) Act 1988* (1988) (contained in Scottish Current Law Statutes, volume 2, 1989, Edinburgh: W. Green)

Gloag, *Contract* (2nd ed., 1985) (Collieston: Caledonian Books — reprint of 1929 edition, Edinburgh: W. Green)

Gloag and Henderson, *Introduction to the Law of Scotland* (10th ed., 1995) (Edinburgh: W. Green)

Gordon, *Criminal Law* (3rd ed., 2000) Vol. 1, (Christie ed.) (Edinburgh: W. Green)

Griffiths, *Confessions* (1994) (Edinburgh: Butterworths)

Gudjonsson, *The Psychology of Interrogations, Confessions and Testimony* (1992) (Chichester: John Wiley & Sons)

Hajducki, *Civil Jury Trials* (1998) (Edinburgh: W. Green)

Halsbury's Laws of England, (Hailsham ed.) (4th ed.) (London: Butterworths)

Harper and McWhinnie, *The Glasgow Rape Case* (1983) (London: Hutchinson)

Henderson, *see* Gloag and Henderson

Heydon and Ockleton, *Evidence — Cases and Materials* (1996) (London: Butterworths)

Jones, *Expert Witnesses* (1994) (Oxford: Clarendon Press)

Keane, *The Modern Law of Evidence* (5th ed., 2000) (London: Butterworths)

Lees, *Carnal Knowledge — Rape on Trial* (1996) (London: Hamish Hamilton)

McBryde, *The Law of Contract in Scotland* (1987) (Edinburgh: W. Green)

McBryde, *Bankruptcy* (2nd ed., 1995) (Edinburgh: W. Green)

MacDonald, *Criminal Law of Scotland* (5th ed., 1948) (Edinburgh: W. Green)

MacLaren, *Court of Session Practice* (1916) (Edinburgh: W. Green)

Macphail, *Evidence* (1987) (Edinburgh: Law Society of Scotland)

Macphail, *Sheriff Court Practice* (1988) (Edinburgh: W. Green)

McWhinnie, see Harper and McWhinnie

Maxwell, *The Practice of the Court of Session* (1980) (Edinburgh: Scottish Courts Administration)

Norrie, *see* Wilkinson and Norrie

Ockelton, *see* Heydon and Ockelton

Rennie and Cusine, *The Requirements of Writing (Scotland) Act 1995* (1995) (Edinburgh: Law Society of Scotland, Butterworths)

Renton and Brown, *Criminal Procedure* (6th ed., (with Gane) 1996) (Edinburgh: W. Green)

Robinson, *The Law of Interdict* (2nd ed., 1994) (Edinburgh: Law Society of Scotland, Butterworths)

Stair Memorial Encyclopedia, *The Laws of Scotland* (1989) (Edinburgh: The Law Society of Scotland, Butterworths)

Tapper, *see* Cross and Tapper

Temkin, *Rape and the Legal Process* (1987) (London: Sweet & Maxwell)

Twining, *Rethinking Evidence: Exploratory Essays* (1990) (Oxford: Blackwell)

Walker, *Delict* (2nd ed., 1981) (Edinburgh: W. Green)

Walker and Walker, *Law of Evidence in Scotland* (Ross with Chalmers ed.) (2nd ed., 2000) (Edinburgh: Butterworths)

Walker and Walker, *Law of Evidence in Scotland* (1st ed., 1964) (Glasgow: Hodge)

Wigmore, *Evidence* (1935) (Brooklyn Foundation Press)

Wilkinson, *The Scottish Law of Evidence* (1986) (Edinburgh: Law Society of Scotland, Butterworths)

Wilkinson and Norrie, *The Law Relating to Parent and Child in Scotland* (2nd ed., 1999) (Edinburgh: W. Green)

INDEX

357